The Bureaucracy of Beauty

The Bureaucracy of Beauty

DESIGN IN THE AGE OF ITS GLOBAL REPRODUCIBILITY

Arindam Dutta

Routledge
Taylor & Francis Group
New York   London

Routledge is an imprint of the
Taylor & Francis Group, an informa business

Routledge
Taylor & Francis Group
270 Madison Avenue
New York, NY 10016

Routledge
Taylor & Francis Group
2 Park Square
Milton Park, Abingdon
Oxon OX14 4RN

Printed in the United States of America on acid-free paper
10 9 8 7 6 5 4 3 2 1

International Standard Book Number-10: 0-415-97920-X (Softcover) 0-415-97919-6 (Hardcover)
International Standard Book Number-13: 978-0-415-97920-7 (Softcover) 978-0-415-97919-1 (Hardcover)

Library of Congress Cataloging-in-Publication Data

Dutta, Arindam.
    The bureaucracy of beauty : design in the age of its global reproducibility / Arindam Dutta.
        p. cm.
    Includes bibliographical references and index.
    ISBN 0-415-97919-6 (hb) -- ISBN 0-415-97920-X (pb)
    1. India--Cultural policy--History. 2. Architectural design--India--History. 3. Great Britain--Colonies--Economic policy. 4. Great Britain. Dept. of Science and Art--History. 5. Nationalism--India--History. 6. India--Colonial influence. I. Title.

DS428.D85 2006
720.1'03--dc22   2006028336

Visit the Taylor & Francis Web site at
http://www.taylorandfrancis.com

and the Routledge Web site at
http://www.routledge-ny.com

The way they taught us, you know… Do one's bit, that's the thing. Can't do more. All part of a pattern. Design.

John le Carré, *Tinker, Tailor, Soldier, Spy*

Contents

List of Abbreviations

AMP: Asiatic Mode of Production
BoT: The Board of Trade
DPA: Department of Practical Art
DSA: Department of Science and Arts
DTFI: *Documents of the First International.* Vols. I-V. London: Lawrence & Wishart, 1974
e.a.: emphasis added
EINC: Zaidi, A. Moin and Zaidi, Shaheda: *The Encyclopaedia of Indian National Congress.* Vols. 1–18. New Delhi: S. Chand, 1976
HCC: Henry Cole Collection, SNAL
HCD: Henry Cole Collection, Cole's personal diaries, organized by year, SNAL
HCL: Henry Cole Collection, Files marked "Correspondence", SNAL
HCM: Henry Cole Collection, Files marked "Miscellanies", SNAL
HMSO: Her Majesty's Stationery Office
Home: Home Department Proceedings, India
i.o.: italics in original
IOL: The Oriental and India Office Collections at the British Library
ISAD: Indian and South-East Asian Department, V&A
JD: Journal of Design
KP: Kipling Papers, Special Collections, University of Sussex Library
MECW: Karl Marx, Frederick Engels: Collected Works. London: Lawrence & Wishart, 1975-
NAI: The National Archives of India, New Delhi
NAL: The National Art Library, Victoria & Albert Museum, London
PP: Parliamentary Papers

PP-*x, a-b,* p.c: Parliamentary Papers, followed by year of publication *x*, followed by serial order number of report *ab,* and *c* – page number

PRO: Public Records Office

q.: quoted by...

SKM: South Kensington Museum

SNAL: Special Collections at The National Art Library, Victoria & Albert Museum, London

SoA: Society of Arts

V&A: Victoria & Albert Museum, South Kensington, London

VAA: V & A Archive, Blythe Road, London

Acknowledgments

The ambitions of this book would have been unlikely to come to fruition, were it not for the influence of some protean teachers: Gayatri Chakravorty Spivak, Mark Wigley, Alan Colquhoun, and Georges Teyssot. Truly rare camaraderie and support from my colleagues at MIT, Mark Jarzombek, David Friedman, Caroline Jones, Nasser Rabbat, Stanford Anderson and Erika Naginski, were critical in nurturing this project beyond its rather wooden dissertation phase. The timbre of thought in this book would have been very different were it not for colleagues and friends whom I have had the fortune to have met and learnt from in a number of contexts, with the caveat that the book's failings are of course mine: Vikramaditya Prakash, Reinhold Martin, Felicity Scott, Wendy Hui Kyong Chun, Chris Czikszentmihalyi, Tapati Guha Thakurta, Geeta Kapur, Vivan Sundaram, Tuli Bannerjee , Abhijit Bannerjee, Rupinder Singh, Ijlal Muzaffar. Reinhold and Felicity gave generous comments on chapter 4 for an eventually aborted attempt to publish it as an article; their labor has not gone in vain. The postscript was a response to the events and aftermath of September 11, 2002—it benefited significantly from a series of conversations with Kryzstof Wodiczko. At Routledge, William Germano took an early interest in the project, facilitating in its seeing the light of day. Graduate students at MIT, Katharine Wheeler, Zeynep Celik, Winnie Wong, Michael Osman and Pamela Zahra Karimi, read and gave very useful comments on different chapters of the book. Lucia Allais looked over the cover design and offered helpful tips.

Superlative administrative support from a number of people allowed the daunting logistics of this book—travel, shipping, correspondence, photocopying, printing, library borrowing—the *real* stuff of research, frivol into effortlessness: at Princeton, Benita Williams, Patricia Ponzoli, and the irreplaceable Frances Chen; and at MIT, the equally indefatigable Anne Deveau, Melissa Bachman, Eylem Basaldi. Special gratitude is due to Deans David N. Redman and F. Joy Montero at Princeton.

The following people directly or indirectly influenced the thought processes that led to the making of this book: Robert Gutman, Stanley N. Katz, J. Meejin Yoon, Mark Goulthorpe, Bish Sanyal, Diane Davis, Alessandra Ponte, M. Christine Boyer, Som Majumdar, Dipak Malik, Nita Kumar, Yaduendra Sahai, Parul Dave Mukherjee, and Partha Mitter.

The project has benefited substantially from a number of patrons: the Getty Grant Program; at MIT, the Blackall daughters who funded a chair in Architectural History in honor of their father, Clarence H. Blackall, of which I am a beneficiary, the Cabot Fund, the HASS fund; and at Princeton University, the Woodrow Wilson Society, the Graduate School, the Centre for Arts and Cultural Policy Studies, the Dean's Fund for Scholarly Travel, the Council for Regional Studies, the Centre of International Studies and the Compton Fund, and the Cramer Travelling Prize.

Officials at the following institutions where I conducted research were very helpful to this work:

In the United Kingdom, in London: the National Art Library, V&A; Oriental and India Office Collections at the British Library; the Indian and South-East Asian Department, V&A; V&A Archive (Blythe Road); the V&A Repository (Battersea); Patent Office Library (Chancery Lane); RIBA Library; Kipling Archives, University of Sussex Library.

In India, in Jaipur: Government Central Museum, Albert Hall; City Palace Museum; Shri Raj Rajeshwari Research Library and the Dr. Durga Sahai Foundation; in Calcutta: the National Library and the Government College of Arts and Crafts Library; in Lahore, National College of Arts; in Madras: the Tamil Nadu State Archives and the School of Fine Arts Library; in Mumbai: the Maharashtra State Archives and the J. J. School of Art Library; in Delhi: the National Archives of India and the Nehru Memorial Library and Museum.

In the United States, the Smithsonian Institution Archives (Washington, D.C.); the Ronald Reagan Presidential Library (Simi Valley, CA).

Portions of the book were published in *The Journal of Arts & Ideas, Grey Room, Rendezvous*, and the *Journal of Contemporary Theory*. I am grateful to their publishers for allowing me to reuse some of this material.

The memory of two remarkable young men, Dipankar Dutta and Tanveer Mohammed, both snuffed out in the prime of life, haunts this book. Others were crucial to maintaining the lingering, thrumming, emotional upkeep of life itself: my parents Subir Kumar Dutta and Manju Dutta; comrades in India, Rajendra Prasad, Ram Rahman, Ashok Kumari, Shabnam Hashmi, Megha Kumar; not to forget Hongkyung Anna Suh, Ipek Yosmaoglu, Prateeti Ballal, Shanta Dutta, Fr. J. J. Morondo, Bhargav Adhvaryu, Ashish Dave, Bhaskar Narula, Jonathan Massey, Jorge Otero-Pailos, Maulik Parikh, Paul Moorcroft, Fozia Mohammed.

And Annie Reinhardt, *tera ġum hai to ġum-e-dahar kya jhagda kya hai*, you the man.

The Department of Science and Art: The Aesthetic in the Age of Its Global Reproducibility

This book notates a theory of change.

Mechanization will replace the work of the body; this master-*topos* has acquired an air of inevitability in modernizing narratives. This supposed axiom has had a host of corollaries that remain our deepest bequest from the nineteenth century: industry will subsume craft, the city will overwhelm the country, rationality will circumscribe culture. This *horoscope* of the industrial revolution has been a touchstone of rant or rave, boost or bust, no matter whether one is a proponent or opponent, zealot or skeptic. The proponents are legion—Andrew Ure, Karl Marx, Frederick Taylor, and the architectural polemicist Siegfried Giedion—as are the opponents—John Ruskin, William Morris, and Mohandas Karamchand Gandhi. At every turn, these *topoi* have stood as pennants in the unceasing tempests of debate, now blowing to the East, then West, now right, North, left, South, about the conflagrations of capital, of industry, of technology, material, labor, society, and nation.

To Henry Cole, one of the commissioners of the Great Exhibition of 1851, these billows of debate parsed themselves into a barrage of questions:

> It might be asked, What part does the artizan [*sic*] act in the production of manufactures? and answered, Simply to perform, almost as a machine, what his employer directs him. Does his employer— the manufacturer—want the artizan's greater education in art? Are the manufacturers's commercial transactions hindered for want of the

1

better art? Is he sensible of the want? Is he a competent judge of the better art if it were placed before him? As better art involves labour of a higher grade, and therefore increased cost, is he willing to embark increased capital in its production? Before we answer these questions, even others seem to claim precedence. Why are manufactures produced? Why are more Cotton fabrics woven than Silk ones? Why are Woollens manufactured at one season and Cottons at another? Why does the manufacturer decorate fabrics for the South American market in one way, and the metropolis in another, making a difference even here between the West and East Ends?[1]

As in almost all prefatory remarks that posit these sorts of portentous questions, this author was hardly likely to let such ambivalences stand. The questions represent an *aporia*, a rhetorical figure in which (the feigned or truthful nature of) the speaker's intent in the deliberation of an issue cannot be determined, a factor that further defers the resolution of the question being asked—for Cole had had an answer long before the questions were framed.

The previous paragraph appears among a series of "addresses" made by prominent officials and aesthetes in their effort to establish comprehensive institutions to carry forward the lessons of the Great Exhibition of 1851. These efforts culminated in the founding of a seminal bureaucracy, the Department of Science and Art (DSA), established soon after the exhibition under Britain's Board of Trade (BoT). In its narrowest compass, the DSA's mandate was to introduce superior design and artisanal sensibilities in industrial workers. If workers were inculcated into better taste, it was argued, their involvement in industrial processes would be less dispensable and alienable, thus making them more essential to production, therefore raising wages, and mitigating their widespread misery. For the DSA's liberal founders, in addition to enhancing the agency of the workers via their aesthetic sensibilities, this approach would have the added virtue of both adding value to industrial commodities and creating better standards for public taste. Once the long chain of reasoning between industrial alienation, the degradation of the public realm, the impoverishment of mass-commodity culture and taste had been made, the thrust of the argument could be reversed. Taste, and taste alone, would be the lever through which the entire concatenation would be reformed. The mandate was an emblem of its time, in a way that may today appear disingenuous. And yet, as we shall see, this disingenuousness, this invocation of the *aporia,* was precisely its ideological masterstroke.

The history of the DSA is a prologue to that of the Arts and Crafts movement, the Vienna Secession, the *Werkbunds,* and the Bauhaus. Its curricular structure would be replicated, significantly in practice and substantially in spirit, in each of these later movements and institutions. Quite in contrast to its later bantlings, though, the DSA had much more *direct* influence, given that its pedagogical systems were adopted by educational institutions throughout the British Empire, including Britain's prime colony, India. The dichotomy of the machine and the hand thus acquires an analogue in the uneven capitalization of the Empire, which straddled the areas of both maximum industrialization in Britain and maximum underdevelopment and deindustrialization in its colonies. This book uses the archive of the DSA and its strategies of educating both (metropolitan) worker and (colonial) artisan to map the asymmetrical contours of this uneven modernity.

The DSA was founded by the intellectuals and apparatchiks who had organized the Great Exhibition. The headquarters built for this gargantuan enterprise are today well-known as the Victoria & Albert Museum (V&A) and the Royal College of Art, located in South Kensington, London. The DSA's career spanned more than fifty years, from its inception in 1857 to its protracted collapse in the prelude to the First World War. By the end of the century, the DSA supervised no less than 180 schools of design in Britain alone, in addition to providing the prototype for scores of regional and international museums. The DSA was also responsible for hosting all the world exhibitions in London in the last half of the nineteenth century.

To perceive the DSA as a simple case study in design pedagogy would belie the force of the tremendous administrative engine assembled by its creators, the circle of aesthetes gathered around the bureaucrat Henry Cole. The founding ideals of the DSA were liberal, or "radical," to adopt mid-nineteenth-century terminology. Cole and his compatriots belonged to the reformist circle around Jeremy Bentham and the India Office bureaucrats James and John Stuart Mill. The abiding preoccupation of this caucus was to devise the "means" by which public institutions could be restructured to benefit the average citizen and worker. Particularly relevant here to the DSA's development were the theories of political economy of the younger Mill as a response to the perceived depredations of industrial capitalism. This liberal coterie of aesthetes and pedagogues is therefore significant not only for artistic discourse but as seminal experimentalists in the "modes of production" debates of the nineteenth century. The principal faculty of the DSA included, at different times, stalwarts such as Owen Jones, Gottfried Semper, Richard Redgrave, Christopher Dresser, William Morris, and, in India, John Lockwood Kipling and Ernest Binfield Havell.

Britain's imperial preponderance at this time meant that the DSA's influence would be global in scope. From the Museum of Fine Art in Boston to a provincial museum in Kabul, Afghanistan, museums using the DSA template were set up in every nook of the world, using even the exact cabinet dimensions and frame sections of the South Kensington originals. The keeper of art collections at the South Kensington Museum in the late nineteenth century, Caspar Purdon Clarke, would become the second director of the Metropolitan Museum of Art in New York. In India, DSA acolytes would occupy preeminent positions in all the art schools, where they indirectly influenced or directly supervised the functioning of myriad "vocational" schools aimed at refashioning traditional or artisanal labor. The DSA's program of exhibitions percolated into the rural and agricultural fairs routinely staged by the British administration to reorganize the traditional economies of India. There, the liberalism of the DSA enterprise cast itself as savior of the decaying native industries and Indian artisanry under the onslaught of cheap, mass-produced imports from the metropole. At first sight, therefore, this "preservative," localizing and decentralizing modus operandi of the DSA apparatus in colonial India, might appear to be an isomorphic extension of metropolitan "reform." This apparent symmetry notwithstanding, the book argues that liberal practice does not *play out in the same way* between metropole and colony. The DSA's preservative impulse, however isomorphic, served as a perfect foil for the hallmark strategies of late imperialism: "indirect rule" and "decentralized despotism." The Indian artisan, administratively attributed to and constrained by the localizing frames of caste and native authority, divorced from the rubric of the modern employment contract, became that much more susceptible to direct superexploitation by the metropolitan center.

In Britain or India, the DSA juggernaut saw itself as nothing less than a full-blooded enterprise of economic restratification through *aesthetic* means. In using the word *aesthetic,* the book takes up the cluster of pedagogical theories emanating from Europe's self-described "Enlightenment" of the eighteenth century. ("Enlightenment" was, in this sense, a terminological foil to cover over the political–economic transition away from mercantilism and late feudalism, reinscribing it as an intellectual current.) In John Stuart Mill's well-known apothegm, "Morality not a science, but an *art*," we can see the trace of an already century-old modernism: the amalgamation of ethical, civic practice with aesthetic, speculative thought. In Henry Cole, Mill's astute acolyte, and the DSA's founding spirit, we therefore see the personification of a significant strain of deliberation, from Burke and Kant onward, on the norms of what Schiller described as an "aesthetic education" for the masses. Kant's explicit interdiction that the systematic impetuses of truth and morality could be related to the aesthetic *by analogy alone*, that their founts were heterogeneous, only led to an obsession with conflating the aesthetic with ever elaborate schemas of systemic thought. In the aftermath of Kant, beauty, the pinnacle of imaginative power, becomes a superlative rule-giving apparatus. Beauty, as untrammeled element of thought, invites a bureaucracy, not to constrain its unruly appearance, but to perpetuate its moment, to prolong its sublimation. In tying the aesthetic to the logistics of the commodity, the DSA curriculum melded German idealist philosophy with an equally mature English history of workshop-based pedagogy. For these patricians, there was much to gain from a craft-based pedagogical effort that piously claimed solidarity with a newly alienated working class. The DSA thus also embodied the institutional culmination of a century of industrial paternalism that began with the treatises of Chippendale and Sheraton.

In the face of the continuous dissent experienced against governments everywhere throughout the nineteenth century, the DSA's ability to pursue its stated aims with the kind of sincerity and ambition as it did can be explained only by the fact that many of its key ideological standpoints were in fact paradigms of Victorian sensibility, *topoi* often shared by elite and dispossessed alike. The principal argument underlying the DSA's particular mandate—a premise shared by all the world exhibitions—was the faith that the continued preponderance of British global trade hinged on the superior aesthetic attributes of its products. Rhetoric of reform aside, the incredible reach of the DSA's colossal corpus of practice, its pedagogical critiques, its theorizations of the aesthetic, its patronage by industrialists and manufacturers, its innovations of policy and financing, its strategies of display, its demographic understanding, and its proliferating schools can be pared down to one overwhelming conundrum that underlay its entire enterprise: *how do economic markets move?* The force of this conundrum can be said to be felt as urgently then as now, because it addressed the fundamental inscrutability of the basic impetuses underlying changes within capitalism. The DSA's particular response was to entangle this inscrutability within the filigree of another avowedly indeterminate discourse on transient forms, that of "taste." Therein lay the core of its vanguardism. Because economic entrepreneurs were as much at odds to fathom the vicissitudes of taste and mercurial "fashion" in commodities, it appeared tenable that an aesthetic education for the workers could conform the dual objectives of capitalist profit and social justice.

Design was the new key word that emerged to capture this desired conformity, indicated in its many key uses, as in the Schools of Design, Cole's *Journal of Design*, and Richard Redgrave's *Manual of Design*. Design's ambit, as articulated within the DSA, was breathtaking in its ambition: both to transform the very basis of industrial capitalism and to confer on its mercurial behavior a predicative systematicity. The speculative strengths of aesthetic philosophy would be crucial to imagining this predicative power. The term *design*, in this sense, oscillates between its various lexical connotations: as a comprehensive, rationalizing, future-oriented intention on one hand and, on the other, the quite prosaic description of the (received) pattern or motif on your clothes. This book is a study of those oscillating connotations—between critique and object, between abstract and concrete— of the term *design* as a mark of modernity.

The book is not organized chronologically; rather, it charts a thematic course from the influence of eighteenth-century idealist and romantic philosophy on design pedagogy to the emergence of Indian nationalism as a response to the aesthetic or industrial policies of the colonial economy. The chapters illuminate the multifarious ambitions and ramifications of the DSA as a bureaucracy whose leitmotif, it seems, was a *programmed overreach,* the dream of a never-ending, ever-expanding civilizing monitor that might serve as a proxy for empire itself.

The book begins with the DSA's adoption of a policy of administrative decentralization as a better device to manage change and transience, linchpins of both taste and economic behavior. Chapter 1, "Empire '… in a Fit of Absence of Mind,' " examines the DSA's pioneering emphasis on decentralization as particularly equipped to address the shifting conditions of an ever-changing and indeterminate "present." The DSA's preference for an informal hierarchy of design education epitomizes a peculiar duplex of tying together universal policy and local initiative as a hallmark of oligarchic laissez-faire. The arrival of this attitude in India, the chapter argues, resulted in a full-blooded compensatory thrust toward "culture" as the rubric for appropriating agency from the native. The temporality of the present thus worked in two separate, albeit not unrelated, ways: toward undermining the excessive weight of history in the metropole and toward formalizing the ahistoricity of the colony.

As a caveat to this emphasis on temporality, chapter 2, "Architecture Upside Down," sets up *aesthetics* as the other major axis on which the story of the DSA and its influence is constructed in this book. The chapter examines the philosophical and ideological forebears of the DSA curriculum in post-Kantian organicism and its fondness for Oriental ornament: a theory that sought to project the growth of the organism as marked by a continuity, one that was deemed applicable to the commodity as well. If decentralization offered a managerial device to sew together administrative consistency with situational diversity, then the organicist pattern (think of Oriental carpets and paisley) offers as if the very image of this dis/continuity of wholes and parts. The organicist pattern was ubiquitously manifested in both the DSA's pedagogy and its understanding of taste in the industrial, mass-produced commodity. The third chapter, " 'Tardy Imaginations, Torpid Capacities, Tottering Thought,' " looks at the manner in which the aesthetic philosophy and design agendas laid out in the previous chapter actually manifested themselves in the pedagogical techniques of the DSA.

Through the influence of the DSA, a single pedagogy bridged a significant unevenness between industrial worker in the metropole and traditional artisan in the colony. This bridge was effected by the DSA's emphasis on *drawing* rather than on craft skills. This, ironically in a pedagogy aimed at artisans rather than at fine artists. Drawing afforded the DSA a conceptual apparatus that could grasp the commodity across different cultural contexts rather than emphasize the local idiosyncrasies of material and technology. There are two ironies here: in the mechanized metropole, the drawing curriculum emphasized the preindustrial, Oriental pattern as the paradigmatic motif of *industrial* education; by contrast, in India, artisans were being reintroduced to what was deemed as their *own* inheritance. The chapter concentrates on this exceptional construction of the pattern in the nineteenth century as a motif bearing the potential for economic and anthropological transformation in the context of uneven development.

This peculiar double status of the pattern, bearing the imprint of both craft and mechanization, is pursued further by implication in the next chapter, "Of AbOriginal and CopyRight," through an examination of a new legal regime of *multilateral*, that is, international, intellectual property rights introduced by the Cole circle. The chapter looks at the particular anthropological assumptions that undergirded the legal framework of intellectual property law. These assumptions created, I argue, a portcullis through which the conceptions of certain subjects could be assigned the status of "original," others "copies," and still others "unoriginal." These distinctions were not innocuous. By century end, the difference between original and copy had been irrevocably transposed as one between legitimacy and fraud. Through this new framework of criminality, the chapter bears witness to the birth of the designer, a new form of authorship in the industrial revolution, whose profile was shaped precisely by the legal stipulations on originality.

Chapter 5, "Cyborg/Artisan," examines the vicissitudes of a key piece of machinery through the past two centuries: the Jacquard apparatus. Appended to Charles Babbage's Analytical Engine of 1832, the Jacquard offered a model for human intelligence. Attached to looms of poor silk workers in France and India, it appeared to abstract the essence of the work of the hand. The chapter thus once again turns on the sort of duality played out in the earlier chapters between industrial worker and preindustrial artisan, this time turning to the examination of the character of work itself and the different models of spatial socialization that accompanied different conceptions of machines.

To be sure, these models of socialization were not devoid of political ramifications. This is the subject of the next chapter, "Congress: Gandhi at the World Exhibitions," which examines the Indian nationalists' response to the long colonial indoctrination of craft as the essential ethos of Indian civilization. Gandhi's self-staging as a spinner, an artisan presents a critical turn in this aesthetico-political response and, as such, was a crucial element in a series of counterexhibitions staged by the Indian National Congress and funded by native capitalists prior to independence. The chapter compares this nationalist turn with the Indian state-sponsored Festivals of India held in key investor countries—the United States, Britain, France, Japan—in the shift to neoliberal economic regimes in the 1980s. The festivals, with participation from designers such as Hugh Casson, Milton Glaser, I.M. Pei, Hans Hollein, Ettore Sottsass, and Frei Otto, in many ways harked back to the DSA's culturalist framing of the artisan.

The memory of nationalism is also at the core of chapter 7, "Unmaking Beauty: Aesthetics in the Shadow of History." Here, we encounter an installation by the contemporary Indian artist Vivan Sundaram in Calcutta's Victoria Memorial, a building conceived by the viceroy Curzon in the early twentieth century. Curzon is generally credited with the official sanctification of archaeological preservation in India. Given the DSA's interdictions against the historical organization of museum displays and preference for "material" categories, Sundaram's installation forces us to think again about the continuing and significant influence of the DSA on museums in India. The chapter brings to a denouement the book's discussions on history, colonialism, audiences, display, and nationalism by returning to a consideration of temporality and aesthetics.

The postscript, "Infinite Justice: An Architectural Coda," hints at the potency of a history that remains outside considerations of such as the DSA, and indeed of this book as well. It therefore points to a history that historiography such as this book can structurally *not do*. The postscript highlights one instance of dissent: the assassination of the Earl of Mayo, Benjamin Disraeli's appointee as viceroy of India, by an Afghan tribal Sher Ali, in the penal colony of the Andamans. The ethnic and geographical origins of the assassin suggest the fraught management of these concepts by colonial power. Mayo's assassination became the impetus for the establishment of the Mayo School of Art and Museum in Lahore, Punjab, the swan song of the DSA model in India. The story of its founder, John Lockwood Kipling, ex-professor of architectural ornament from the Bombay school of art, student of Cole and Owen Jones from South Kensington, found eloquent testimony in the opening scene of *Kim,* that much-hyped novel of the imperialist "great game" written by his son Rudyard. The novel was written with an eye to the crisis produced by Sher Ali's domicile, Afghanistan; in this crisis we can perhaps see a glimpse of the far distances traveled by, and the failures of, the intellectual complex that undergirded enterprises such as colonialism and the DSA in the nineteenth century, and perhaps some recent ones in our own.

Methodological Note: Can the Imperialist Speak?

> What, then, shall we say of ourselves?
>
> **—William Whewell, "The General Bearing of the Exhibition on the Progress of Art and Science"**

In recent years, a number of studies have emerged describing the colonialist representation of non-Western peoples within the world exhibitions. For scholars such as Timothy Mitchell, Zeynep Celik, and Paul Greenhalgh, the well-known images of live dioramas of tribesmen and artisans from non-Western countries in these venues have offered an ideal target of attack, replete as they are with resonances of the panopticist architectonic framed by Michel Foucault: "To colonise ... to construct a modern kind of power, it would be necessary to 'determine the plan.' "[2] For aficionados of the Saidian critique of Orientalism and various nationalist academies, this display of so-called less civilized peoples as objects of epistemic capture has offered a rich archive abounding with ever-blossoming examples of the discriminatory categorization practiced by post-Enlightenment power and knowledge.

By now, the ramifications of the Saidian critique have become fairly predictable: Western knowledge makes out the non-Western subject into a unidimensional "other," without access to difference. Behind it all, we are led to believe, is the equally unidimensional and repressive face of the Western subject, assumed as codified by the Enlightenment as the unproblematic bearer of reason. The question of causality in imperialism is answered by this framework with the presentation of a game plan. This move having been made, the historiography of the exhibition proceeds along more or less familiar lines, trotting out the panoply of critical terms developed through the recent rubric of "cultural studies." The terms include the critique of Orientalism, technological developmentalism, the society of the spectacle, psychoanalytic specularity, ideological state apparatuses, or the hegemonic formation of power-knowledge—so many ways to document the many propensities of the ontologically singular Western subject. The procrustean effort here is to imbue imperialism with a telos. Its historiography, to quote Sumit Sarkar, constitutes the singular objective of the "virtual folding back of all history into the single problematic of Western colonial cultural domination."[3] The history of imperialism, if sufficiently historicized in this way, can now read like a roster of civilizational right and wrong. If we understand what they (as imperialists) did wrong, we (*philosophe-citoyens*) can perhaps resolve our conundrums of historiographic authority and get along with a more self-assured modernity.

The Saidian focus on Orientalism and post-Enlightenment power and knowledge as the principal vector of colonialism can be glimpsed in the work of Gyan Prakash, who sees the phenomena of museums and exhibitions as instances of colonial "governmentality." A late entrant into the Subaltern Studies collective of historians, Prakash professes to follow the objectives of that group in attempting to recover subaltern murmurings within these categorizing discourses of dominance. Prakash's contention is that exhibitions and museums as repositories of power and knowledge fail to record the "subterfuges, paradoxes, distortions, and *failures*" that interpellate these institutions.[4] In looking at the archive of the colonial museum, Prakash attempts to read the muttering and responses of nonelite spectators in museums as the failed speech-acts of subalternity. In Prakash's view, museum officials, upholders of rational and "scientific" knowledge systems, inevitably misread these responses in their own cognitive frame. The administrative reaction to the prosaic laughs and giggles of nonliterate audiences was to weave them within a premodern, nativist ethos of "curiosity and wonder"; having created this equation, Prakash's attitude here is to simply reverse it, imbuing these responses of the colonized with some sort of "second sight," *in itself* therefore posing a critique of post-Enlightenment power and knowledge. The post-Enlightenment intellect's failure to fully appropriate this second sight is advanced as a symptomatic failure of European "reason." It is as if *the imperialist* cannot speak.

The late Foucault's astute linkage of the construction of the ethical "self" as the possibly intractable excess within the dispersal of power is crudely paraphrased within the above formulation as the consolidation of a Western "self" against a non-Western "other." This latter now becomes an idealized and pristine subaltern "consciousness," no longer only a historio-*graphic* figure but essentialized now into an "otherness" as such. Oblivious to what might otherwise seem as patent failures "on the ground," colonial authorities apparently had no compunctions in compounding their errors. Transposing the epistemological apparatuses described by Said into the critique of imperialism, the new object of opprobrium for cultural studies-type scholarship is the colonial bureaucracy, whose complex history is now seen only to epitomize the singular vectors of Western rationality and scientism. This phenomenological attempt to recover the "others" of colonial-modern speech can conveniently forget the strong oppositions of British administrative practice to Continental rationalism and positivism as well as the actual imperial penchant toward "thin" bureaucracies in both Africa and India. In the process, the specific complexities of *indirect,* partial governance, the dominant mode of political control in colonial contexts, can conveniently be ignored. The critique of "power" is assimilated, perhaps even against its Foucauldian grain, to a metaphysical urge to see representation itself as repression per se, even as phenomena brought to light under older, Marxist critiques of imperialism—including non-Foucauldian frameworks of physical and legal violence as well as economic depredation—languish as terra incognita within this unruffled tableau of phenomenologically opposed subjects.

Rather than see in these murmurs and cognitive failures some kind of psycho-biographical thumbprint from which to limn an organically evolved anthropological effigy of the subaltern, this book is based on the claim that the *promulgation* of such failure is critical to the enterprise of empire. As we shall see in various chapters, subaltern giggles and expostulations did not arrest some all-too-adamantine project of "reason" but were rather crucial to the sense of an extrarational perception of "wonder" that the British administration *wanted* to invoke in its subjects. The concept of "wonder" is not an *anti*rational sentiment in either Western philosophy or the colonial archive; rather, it invokes the invitation to knowledge and rediscovery of the alien object. As we shall examine more closely in chapter 3 in a discussion of Edmund Husserl, colonial administrators approximated a phenomenology that sought to instill in native subjects the critical ability to interrogate anew their own alienation with the colonial marketplace and public sphere, if only to become better subjects of colonialism. In its best sense, therefore, the colonial invocation of wonder can be situated close to Heidegger:

> What seems natural to us is probably just something familiar in a long tradition that that has forgotten the unfamiliar source from which it arose. And yet this unfamiliar source once struck man as strange and caused him to think and to wonder. ... Perhaps however what we call feeling or mood, here and in similar instances, is more reasonable—that is, more intelligently perceptive—because more open to Being than all that reason which, having meanwhile become *ratio,* was misinterpreted as being rational. The hankering after the irrational, as abortive offspring of the unthought rational, therewith performed a curious service. ... Is it only a curiosity or even merely the empty sophistry of a conceptual game, or is it—an abyss?[5]

Colonial functioning is in the order of performing such a curious service. Indeed, concepts of extrarational organicism might be seen as essential in imperialist valorization, whether this be the nonverbal gasps of exhibition voyeurs, the digital dexterity of artisanal skills, the all-too-reclusive knowledges from which fabric or lacquer were produced in intricate and arcane arabesques, the congealed relations of custom, and the transcendent cosmogony of religion that imbued the native with a preternatural quiescence.

In contrast to the late Subaltern Studies that seek to imbue colonialism with a unitary impulsion toward an exclusionist rationality, this book argues that colonial governance is marked precisely by a calculus of extreme sensitivity to situational circumstance. Rather than betray their own alienness, the codes of imperial power sought to be inextricably entwined with the native's own codes of cognition. It is this intertwined character that for the doyens of the early Subaltern Studies produced the *exceptional* moment of subaltern insurgency. In the words of Ranajit Guha,

> When a peasant rose in revolt at any time or place under the Raj, he did so necessarily and explicitly in violation of a series of codes which defined his very existence as a member of that colonial, and still largely semi-feudal society. For his subalternity was materialized by the structure of property, institutionalized by law, sanctified by religion and made tolerable—and even desirable—by tradition. To rebel was indeed to destroy many of those familiar signs which he had learned to read and manipulate in order to extract a meaning out of the harsh world around him and live with it. The risk "in turning things upside down" under these conditions was indeed so great that he could hardly afford to engage in such a project in a state of *absent-mindedness.*[6]

Rather than cast the colonial archive as the example of an overarching rationality, this book shares with the early Subaltern Studies group its scrupulous attention to the exceptionality of subaltern insurgency, its sensitivity toward the constitutive discontinuities of colonial governance. The methodological protocol adopted by the original group can be described as follows: whenever insurgency erupts in areas under the yoke of oppressive power, the discourses of power and knowledge that govern that situation undergo a mode of "crisis."[7] A disruptive phenomenon suddenly appears, disruptive because it appears to be an effect without a recognizable cause. This crisis is epistemological as much as it is logistical, in that *in addition to* unleashing the army, the wielders of power are pressed to confer a narrative of causality on the origins of that insurgency. Inevitably, the causative structure that is conferred as management of that crisis refers back more to the governing discourse's own frameworks of knowledge and ethics than to the cognitive domain of the insurgents. The governing power inevitably resorts to domesticate insurgency into an epistemological aberration through the use of euphemism, thus reverting the "crisis" into a mode of normative control using the rubrics of tradition, religion, or ethnicity. As such, this signals a "cognitive failure" to read the insurgency as already *outreaching* these rubrics. The "subaltern," defined as the figural agent of that insurgency, is not heard in that normativization or in Gayatri Spivak's well-known phrase "cannot speak."[8] As Paul de Man might have put it, the "tropological" violently recuperates the "performative."[9] The narratives of power and resistance to power, even as they are inexorably shaped by each other, are of different orders; they pass like ships in the night. Subaltern "studies" is therefore a mode of historiography that reads the historical archive with an ear open to the murmurings and whispers—the failed "speech-acts"—that are both muffled and linger as a palimpsest within the official record.

Warning against a constative, self-possessed, anthropological profile of the subaltern, Spivak has situated this historiographic strategy within the more general problematic of speech-acts and the receiver; we are persistently reminded here that *all* speech-acts must fail, not just that of subalterns.[10] Power is *constituted* by cognitive failure, not undone by it. To think otherwise would be, in Guha's memorable words, to create "a *theoretical pretext* for the fabrication of a literal absurdity—the absurdity of the idea of an uncoercive state."[11]

The concept of crisis is critical to this book's understanding of "imperialism" as well. Lenin's 1917 theory of imperialism represents an effort by a coruscating mind, suddenly faced with the responsibility of governing an empire, to explicate the abrupt dissolution—and potential reformation—of a centuries-old imperial arrangement.[12] Writing in the wake of Hobson and Hilferding, Lenin characterized the imperial system as an administrative hodge podge riven by constitutive discontinuities. Rather than attributing imperial ascendance to mere military or political dominance, Lenin described imperialism as undergirded by a productive and systemic disorganization of political arrangements superposed by the successive expansion and consolidation of *economic* territory. The superposition of these incompatible frames continually produces waves of generative crisis; propelling itself from (realization) crisis to (realization) crisis, capitalism enters a state of decay. "Decay" here does not mean economic stagnation. Rather it refers to a periodic series of interruptions, or moments, into which both economic and noneconomic elements enter as new elements of capital, such as new subject-constitutions or the further valorization of "dependent peoples." One has to be attentive to the peculiarly German philosophical origins of Marx's theorization of discontinuity to relate decay in this sense with generative power. One opens up the way for the other while being fundamentally unrelated to it. For this continual and crisis-borne entry of heterogeneous subject-constitutions or terms into the power structure, I have used the term *morphogenesis*. Imperialism *is* modernity—what needs to be unraveled here are not the terms *imperialism* and *modernity* but what equates these two heterogeneous terms linguistically in that sentence, the copula that is also a phenomenological mark: the *is*.

The Nature of Historical Transitions: Ruse, Function, Emergence

The DSA was one of the biggest bureaucracies to be created in Europe during the nineteenth century, ironically by a cadre for whom bureaucratic "jobbery" was something of a *bête noire*. Its principal collaborator in India, the Public Works Department (PWD) was the largest building organization in the world. Given this self-effacing mode of bureaucratic expansion, several chapters in this book look at the modalities that appear as a response to the unguarded moment when something unforeseen happens and interrupts the teleology of a discourse, occasioning a shift of protocol in power and reading. This book argues that such *crises,* or "emergences," do not necessarily mark an undoing of power as much as trigger its *morphogenetic* capacities.

As I have said before, the principal attempt of this book is to notate a theory of change, that is, to theorize the nature of historical transitions. It is the conventional business of historiography to unravel the causes underpinning historical transitions, or "shifts" or "breaks," such that the qualitative facets of an event are inexorably bound within a temporal scheme. The desire therein is to bring the relationship of cause and effect within a continuum or architectonic, to cover over, post hoc, what Jean-François Lyotard has phrased as the "unintelligibility of the phenomenon."[13] For our purposes, Siegfried Giedion, who saw in the DSA the unconscious presentiment of a later self-assured modernism, may well serve as example of this widespread historiographic desire:

> At this point I became concerned with the problem of continuity, with those elements that remained constant despite the advent of mechanization and the tragic nineteenth century rift between thinking and feeling [we will look at this presumed "rift" and feeling in chapter 8]. … The foremost question was the relation between constancy and change. Constancy does not imply mere continuation, but rather the ability of the human mind suddenly to bring to life things that have been left slumbering through long ages. In contemporary art we can perceive an inseparable interweave of past, present, and future.[14]

Structural inequality or unevenness between heterogeneous genres, of "thinking" and "feeling"—what Lyotard would term the terms of a "differend"—is transmogrified in the previous paragraph into epistemological equivalence through being posed as contrast, placed as the continuum of a "before" and "after." The particularity of a historical predicament is thereby removed to an existential or transcendental question of deciphering the "constancy" within phenomena. Depending on point of view, transition can then be safely either embraced as triumph or mourned as loss. We know that violence is being done here. The two poles of the "dialectic" cover over a hidden triumph, of the agency—imperialism—that pits this heterogeneity as putative contest, say between tradition and modernity, handicraft and machinery, feeling and thinking, in the first place.

The DSA's agenda presents an attempt at what might be called *planned* or *willed* transition in the face of an unprecedented macrocrisis: industrialism. A planned activity is a procedure wherein an "emergent" term is subsumed as a "functional" one. Functional terms are those that are in accordance with the predictability of any given scheme, historiographic, bureaucratic, or otherwise. Emergence, on the other hand, refers to the unruly elements that erupt into a discourse, "neither a dialectical movement or any kind of continuum,"[15] where "the results were neither predictable nor controllable … a multiplicity of seemingly random transactions gradually coalesce into [an apparently] self-organized pattern, generating results that could not have been planned at the outset."[16] In chapter 1, we will see the DSA strategy of squaring off emergent, unpredictable situations on the ground through the adoption of an ostensibly open-ended bureaucratic apparatus; the procedural protocol was touted as morphotropically calibrating itself in response to situational exigencies, a *systemic* corollary of the fabled "men on the spot" of Empire.

The "gaze" of power operates here through a binocular vision: one eye sees to clarify and classify (the Foucauldian architectonic), whereas the other eye is blind, abocular; it feels around, gropes around with the persistent intuition that vision plays tricks with the mind. The left hand of strategy will not know the right hand of tactics; this bihanded enterprise might therefore be construed as epitomizing the imperial *modus* in its very firmament. It also begins to explain why the self-professedly most liberal government in the world could create and assemble under it a variety of neofeudal administrative arrangements to better secure its hold over colonial territories. In the event, the tactics employed on the ground—whether in relationship to subaltern insurgency or artisanal production—might therefore be said to be liberal in (asserted) cause but not liberal in (practiced) effect. Unmodern agency—whether subaltern or artisan—found its transition to modernity percolated by a permeable prophylaxis of empire that formally consigned it to an abocular "tradition": simultaneously precapitalist and self-organizing, and the emblem of an unmitigated and originary unruliness.

The effect of this binocular vision was most palpable on the deemed agent of production at the imperial periphery: the artisan emerges as a figure precisely at the point where imperial capital finds itself thwarted by nonmodern forms of labor. As such, the artisan constitutes an interruptive, unruly figure, both the form of resistance to and a morphogenetic trigger for flexible accumulation and liberal despotism. Marx's principal fallacy lay in his understanding of the global spread of capital as reliant on the stipulatory structure of the factory-form as the ineluctable telos of industrial capitalism; the artisan was for him largely an atavism. As is well-known, Marx considered mechanized industrialization as historically necessary for any mature political forms of opposition to emerge. Against that "modernizing" grain, this book makes the claim that "tradition" is an essential element, the name for the emergent, unguarded figure through which industrial capital expands at its peripheries. In India, for instance, in contrast to the mechanistic armature with which the European laborer was sought to be cast, the artisan was understood as intrinsically part and parcel of larger administrative units, be it anthropological concepts of "village communities," caste, or tribe.

Unburdened by the weight of this modernizing ethos, the DSA's atavistic formulations and influence in the colony afforded it an empirical understanding of a world that Marx had dismissed completely in his theorization of abstract labor. To understand better this felicity between the liberal premises of the DSA in the metropole and the unmodern dispensation of imperial administration, a sketch of the DSA's institutional history is necessary.

The Department of Science and Art

After the unprecedented success of the Great Exhibition of 1851 held at Hyde Park, London, the conveners set themselves to work on carrying forth into the long term what they construed as the "lessons" of the exhibition. These lessons, it is not surprising, were the same as the preconceptions that had inspired it in the first place. One could briefly compound them as follows. Universal industrial progress can be best goaded by the open display of the works of industry. By comparing materials, products, tools, machinery, and artifacts from different countries and regions, visitors to the exhibition, workers and capitalists alike, could gauge the relative advances of industry in different parts of the globe. Most important, the alienation of workers within industrial capital could be alleviated by their encounter with the best commodities from home and abroad. Armed with this new sensibility of a universal aesthetic, they would more actively engage in industrial production, thus positively informing the different stages of production from below. These contributions would create in turn a new compact between capitalist and laborer.

The DSA was accordingly placed under the same institution that had backed the exhibition: the BoT. In the latter half of the nineteenth century, the DSA was the primary bureaucratic body responsible for technical education in Britain, and its duties included devising the national curriculum for not only the key elements of drawing and design but also their (apparently) kin subjects of biology and mathematics. The teaching of these subjects, imparted mostly at the tertiary level, was carried out through the several provincial Schools of Art, whose graduates were subsequently employed in teaching at the elementary level, in grammar schools, and in officially recognized local art classes. The DSA also prescribed and supervised the drawing curriculum at the basic school levels. In 1883 there were as many as 767,194 students imbibing its curriculum at elementary day schools (in addition to 6,891 in evening classes), while no less than 3,476 drawing teachers were being trained to teach in these schools. In that same year, 26,424 students were receiving the DSA's art education in semiformal "art classes," while the Schools of Art had an enrollment of 35,909 students,[17] whose subsequent careers in artistic fields, it was hoped, would lead them into industry or teaching, thus exponentially augmenting the doyens of aesthetic taste among Britain's variegated social strata.

"King Cole"

Much of the DSA's manner of functioning and inordinate institutional influence was the direct legacy of Henry Cole, the DSA's founding spirit and supreme official in its first two decades. Cole was born in 1808, the son of a Dragoon officer. Having won a silver medal for writing in school, he obtained employment at a very early age under Francis Palgrave at the Record Commission in 1823. Around 1826, Cole came to the attention of Thomas Love Peacock, the well-known man of letters, who, noting the young man's promise, introduced Cole to the circle of young radicals who met regularly and talked of fomenting reform in the Britain of the 1820s and 1830s. These included John Stuart Mill, Horace Grant, Edwin Chadwick, Charles Buller, and others who became household names in Britain in the following decade. Most of these men were passionate admirers and often protégés of another radical generation before them, the circle around the Utilitarian philosopher Jeremy Bentham and Mill's father, James Mill. Cole participated regularly in the various debates and energetic campaigns undertaken by the group, including the movement for universal suffrage and a secret ballot, with the younger Mill acting as Cole's mentor during this formative period of his life.[18]

At the Record Commission, Cole's ambitiousness and obstreperousness nettled Palgrave, leading to his summary dismissal. In response and with the support of Mill's circle, Cole undertook a public campaign to expose the corruption and fiscal waste at the commission. The group orchestrated a strategy of writing pamphlets and letters to various newspapers and magazines, with Cole often responding to his own letters under a variety of assumed names, in a multiplication of authorship that we will examine in more detail in chapter 4. As a result of this concerted campaign, in 1836, a Select Committee was appointed to probe the affairs of the Record Commission. Cole was reinstated as an assistant-keeper. Cole's subsequent career there saw him flower into something of a minor historian, as he disinterred and reorganized archival materials and wrote a series of popular guides, many of them on medieval topics. These included a survey of documents from thirteenth- and fourteenth-century England, a treatise on Henry VIII's scheme of apportioning church property and powers, and a detailed study of the architecture and art works of Westminster Abbey.

At the same time, his children were growing up in the 1840s. Cole wrote and published more than twenty children's picture books under the pseudonym of Felix Summerly, collectively called *The Home Treasury*. Two recent biographers have even credited him with the invention of the Christmas card.[19] In addition, Cole was also involved in the public effort to reform mail and postage rates. As the "great railway mania" got underway in the middle of that decade, he published a series of "railway charts," informing novice rail travelers of the various views of prominent buildings and scenes to be had out of the windows. Cole also had a spotty journalistic career, writing for periodicals such as the *London and Westminster Review* and *The Railway Chronicle*.

During the same period, Cole embarked on an aesthetic career with a publication on the works of Albrecht Dürer. In 1846, he won a prize from the Society of Arts[20] (SoA) for a tea service that he had designed and turned himself at his friend Herbert Minton's factory at Stoke-on-Trent. Minton's firm subsequently reproduced hundreds of thousands of Cole's tea sets, which remained in production at least until the late 1870s. Simultaneously, Cole was increasingly becoming involved with the affairs of the SoA. With his friend John Scott Russell as secretary, they soon packed the committee with their own supporters, and Cole eventually turned it into an executive appendage to promote his own interests and campaigns.

Through the SoA, Cole came to the notice of Albert, Victoria's German consort. As one of the SoA's delegates to the French National Exhibition of 1849, along with Minton and the architect Matthew Digby Wyatt, Cole became Albert's confidante on the latter's proposal to the SoA to host a similar exhibition in London. As a member of the committee subsequently formed for this purpose, Cole distinguished himself by being at the forefront of deliberations, with an energy, enthusiasm, and abrasiveness that put others in the pale. It was largely at Cole's urging that the scope of the Great Exhibition was extended to cover the industry of "all" nations, and it was because of his support in the face of more conservative opposition that a design by a gardener named Joseph Paxton was chosen over other alternatives. In large part, the Great Exhibition owed its spectacular success to Cole's special ability to convince various factions—manufacturers, financiers, domestic and foreign governments, local advocatory bodies, railway companies, working-class organizations, trading firms—that the exhibition would be beneficial to each of their otherwise divergent interests.

The Birth of a Bureaucracy

During the deliberations for the establishment of a permanent department of industrial art after the Great Exhibition, Cole appeared as an automatic choice for heading this initiative, given not only his involvement with the exhibition but also his earlier report on the Schools of Design. In 1848 Cole's career as the designer of "Summerly's Art Manufacturers" (objects for household decoration) and his association with the SoA had marked him as a prime candidate for the BoT's project of reforming the schools, which were under its jurisdiction. The schools had been founded in 1837 by a Parliamentary Committee set up two years previously to develop a state system of education for artisans and workers in industry. The objective was to respond to the perceived threat from continental imports. The first "Normal" (or teacher-training) School of Design was established in Somerset House in London in 1837, with twenty-one schools added by 1852. The schools had a clear mandate, because of the BoT's premium on utility and trade, to avoid fine art and devise means to disseminate the techniques and skills of industrial design instead. As we shall see in chapters 2 and 3, the demands of this brief led to a unique pedagogical formulation. By the late 1840s, however, the schools' functioning was in disarray, owing to internecine agendas and personal animosities within the board, in addition to conflict between the Normal Schools and local administrative bodies and patrons of the many branch schools.[21]

It was against the background of this petty tumult that Cole was appointed in 1849 as member of a Parliamentary Committee to investigate and reform the running of the schools. The chairman, Milner Gibson, was a close ally, and the two of them schemed to turn matters to their advantage. To press home his own agendas on the public relations front, Cole started a new magazine, the *Journal of Design*. Cole's strongest ally in this conflict was the manufacturers' lobby within the BoT, and together they campaigned to rid the schools of the influence of fine artists, hoping to transform the institutions to service the needs of industry. From behind the scenes, Cole worked indefatigably to discredit the current running of the schools. Perhaps at the cost of revealing his own ambitions, Cole compared the administration of the schools to the functioning of the Records office, his own berth. In addition to castigating the lack of accountability and the inefficient devolution of responsibility within the schools, Cole painstakingly assembled large amounts of data on their operation. The evidence he brought to the fore is remarkable in terms of its detail and managerial acuity. He compared the employment and salary schemes within the government-managed schools to precedents in industry, arguing that the mode of remuneration verged on the assumption of unpaid volunteerism on the part of teachers, vitiating both authority and accountability.

In the aftermath of the exhibition, with the SoA behind him, Cole was now in a commanding position with regard to the direction of the Schools of Design. After a three-year campaign, Cole was appointed as the full-time official head of a new department within the BoT, the Department of Practical Art (DPA), and given powers that more or less matched his own recommendations. According to these arrangements, Cole was to have one artist as his assistant and adviser on academic matters. This position went to a person who was to prove himself as Cole's deputy in the years to come: Richard Redgrave. Two other significant names became essential components of the Cole circle in the running of the new department: Mathew Digby Wyatt, an architect, and Owen Jones, the talented, seminal theorist of ornament and designer of the color scheme for the Crystal Palace.

Together, the Cole, Redgrave, Digby Wyatt, and Jones caucus set about reforming the administrative structure by which the branch schools were governed, making them relatively autonomous with regard to everyday operational responsibilities. At the same time, they made the curricular structure of these branch schools more dependent on the London school by devising a fiscal system of outlays that came to be (notoriously) named as "payment upon results." By making the operation of the schools *economically* reliant on what was termed as a coupling of "self-help" and "Government aid" rather than a *political* hierarchy involving fiats and commands, Cole could effectively dissemble what was an increased level of centralization in the running of the schools with an appearance of decentralization.

The "contrastive" fracas that was Victorian society—Raymond Williams's well-known appropriation of Pugin's term is useful here[22]—makes the sheer scale of the DSA's profile almost inexplicable. Rafael Cardoso Denis has described the DSA's growth in terms of a "bureaucracy by stealth," and it is critical that this clandestine character be understood precisely as an index of the bihanded sensibility of Victorian "reform": that of maximal vehemence in public discourse and of minimal fiscal investment into actual institutional support. What is significant about the DSA is not its size per se but the tremendous range of fiscal headings—most of them mere lip service to this or that reformative agenda—that came to came to be sheltered under its omnibus marquee.

At different times, the DSA's motley charges would contain the Geological Survey, the Government School of Mines, the Museum of Practical Geology, the Museum of Irish Industry, the Royal Dublin Society, a patent museum, the Registrar of Designs, and the National School of Cookery. This list is indiscriminate enough to remind readers of Foucault's invocation of Borges's apocryphal Chinese encyclopedia in the *Order of Things*. Quite in contrast to Foucault's concept of the *epistémé*, however, the DSA's particular menagerie was assembled under one roof with no such buried assumption of association. Rather, it reflected a new managerial doctrine of reduced fiscal headings and maximized hierarchical efficiency. A master bureaucracy precluded the replication of duties across separate bureaucratic organizations, or so the theory went. Grasping this modus operandi is critical if one looks at the DSA's primary bailiwick: art and design education. Upon its founding in 1856, the DSA inherited all the existing Schools of Design. Soon enough, the Cole cohort moved to whittle down staff; the rationale adopted will strike a chord of familiarity with observers of current-day industrial downsizing. From this pared-down managerial strategy, an empire—with a real Empire as its archetype—could be built with very few invested resources. This is an example of centralization not in the interests of a singular dictatorship (although Cole's persona did much to attract precisely those aspersions) but in the service of budgetary stringency. The Benthamite double entendre of administrative "accountability" and fiscal accountancy thus devolved into a potent organizational broth: as long as the basic formulas of downsizing, reduced duplication of tasks and physical plant, and reduced salary benefits could be applied, *any* department could be subsumed into this one.

One of the Cole clique's first challenges was to recalibrate the conflicting interests that had reared their heads in the operation of the schools. Although the schools had been established to serve the needs of industry, these institutions were hardly able to satisfy their presumed constituencies, workers, or manufacturers. As Adrian Rifkin has succinctly put it, workers could hardly spare the time to devote themselves to art after the rigors of a hard day's work, and manufacturers were conveniently willing to forego the costs of hiring designers by simply copying fashionable imported designs by the season.[23] It was often the case that the schools' most enthusiastic pupils were middle-class women pursuing art for leisure or upwardly mobile women who could use the cheap artistic education to obtain positions as governesses in upper-class households. Besides, different industries had different needs in relationship to design: clearly carpentry could not use the same kind of input in training and education as pottery. Consequently, the schools were hard put to bridge divergences of trade within its pupils.

Instead of doing away with these eccentricities in the schools' functioning, Cole attempted to integrate the diverse populations served by the schools by devising different schedules and fee structures for different kinds of students. One of the key problems faced by the Schools of Design was the relative paucity of students who had received drawing education at the basic level. To address this, Cole reenvisioned the department as facilitating the introduction of drawing into the regular curricula of primary schools. Approaching the Committee of the Privy Council on Education (Britain did not yet have a ministry of education), Cole moved to have the department recognized as the official training body for drawing teachers at the primary and secondary level. The schools therefore abandoned their aim of exclusively training specialized artisans, opting instead for the goal of incorporating drawing education into the mainstream. The rationale advanced was that with a more widespread inculcation of the norms of "taste"[24] in not only artisans but potential consumers as well, manufacturers would be even more enjoined to elevate their standards. In one fell swoop, the new department had become an essential part of Britain's burgeoning state educational infrastructure, a development all the more propitious given developments in the 1860s and the eventual passage of the 1870 Education Act and the ensuing establishment of school boards.

In addition, the Cole caucus designated the London school as the teacher-training school for instructors in the branch of Schools of Art and Design. One of the Cole circle's initiatives at this point was to establish a museum of objects of design as an essential element of design pedagogy. Stationed at Marlborough House and christened the Museum of Ornamental Art, this institution received all the instructional plaster casts from the former collections of the school in Somerset House. In addition to this, a portion of the profits from the Great Exhibition was dedicated to acquiring new collections. Cole used almost all this money to purchase objects displayed in the Crystal Palace. In addition, manufacturers donated their products as examples of contemporary design, seeing the museum as the ideal advertising venue. With continued support from Parliament and Cole's perseverance, the museum soon grew into a substantial collection, forming the seeds of today's V&A.

Mandated, in Cole's words, to collect "objects wherein fine art is applied to some purpose of utility," Cole, Redgrave, Jones, and A.W.N. Pugin were designated as the selection committee. Under their direction, the new museum acquired extensive collections in all manner of commodity: Renaissance bronzes, ladies' underwear, photographs, tapestries, furniture, silks, shoes, silver, jewelry, glass and crystal objects, metalware, and even a section called "Animal Products," part of which was to germinate into the V&A's sister institution, the Natural History Museum. Within a year of its founding, in 1853, the museum boasted the most extensive and finest collection of ceramics in Europe.[25] Eventually, the DPA's paired format of a museum attached to a school would be replicated across the British Empire.

The DSA in Action

In 1856, when the DPA also took on the task of overseeing science education under the aegis of the Privy Council of Education, it was renamed the Department of Science and Art, a title that it would retain until its dissolution. Around that time, with the proceeds from the Great Exhibition, the exhibition commissioners purchased a large parcel of land in the southwestern London suburb of Brompton to build a permanent establishment for its headquarters. Cole was less than impressed with the plebeian name, and he rechristened it with reference to the elite London suburb to the north, Kensington. The eighty-seven acres that the commissioners purchased in newly named "South Kensington" left no doubt as to the department's expansive ambitions for the future.

The new decentralized system of operation brought into being by the DSA operated in the following manner. First of all, regional and local committees had to petition the DSA for funds to establish a school in their area. Prior to this, the committees had to gain the support of three public schools in the vicinity that would commit all of their students to receive one drawing lesson per week, and pay the teacher's wages, half the cost of models, and other teaching equipment dispatched from South Kensington. In addition to this, the local committee would also have to commit to offering midday classes at a given fee rate and evening classes (for workers) at a lower rate and to pay the drawing master from these fees.

If all of these conditions were fulfilled, the DPA and BoT would dispatch a trained master for the area, guaranteeing his salary at a certain level, and supply officially prescribed pedagogical materials at half cost. With the formation of the DSA, South Kensington ceased even appointing or providing for masters, concentrating only on the delivery of the instructional material. Local committees were given absolute liberty in terms of running the schools; grants would now be dispensed based on a system of examinations and evaluations conducted by the department. With these incentives, provincial schools and regional museums sprouted by the score. The South Kensington system would also have global followers—driven as much by its fiscal model as its formula of judging pedagogical efficiency by dictating the terms of its own success or failure—with aficionados and acolytes of the Cole circle fanning out in countries such as France, Russia, Spain, the United States, Australia, New Zealand, and India.

Designing the Modern

The DSA's history is a prolegomenon to the modern movement. The relationship of the modern movement to ornament and craft is complex. Recent scholarship has argued that the professed eschewal of ornament by twentieth-century modernism was nothing else but an argument for a new kind of ornament.[26] If modernist taste at the turn of the century found its apotheosis in the rejection of ornament, theoretically pitting its generative basis in mechanized industry rather than in art, it is not because ornament becomes a part of the irrecoverable past. Rather, with the bringing of the entire diversity of production under the centralized circuitry of capital, with the inexorable commoditization of life itself, *everything* becomes ornament. The construction of ornament as the appearance of value is examined in greater detail in chapter 3 through a comparison of the writing of Marx and the DSA's Christopher Dresser.

The twentieth-century avant-garde's professed eschewal of ornament also drew from a phantasmatic obsession with mechanization as the privileged motor of production. This eschewal has had the effect of producing a permanent myopia about architecture's continued reliance on hand-based production to the present day. One can argue that this myopia had less to do with transformed modes of production than with the desire of a new class of professionals to distance itself from the oppressive association with labor and poorly rewarded artisanry. In the DSA's and the Arts and Crafts movement's efforts to reverse this "alienation," by comparison, the historian is faced with a tremendous archive of observations of labor. The singular "modern" subject forwarded by the 1920s architectural avant-garde would hardly exhibit the anthropological sophistication, empirical documentation, and global comparativist polemic thrown up by the DSA. Certainly, part of the DSA's sophistication might also be attributed to the great institutional preponderance that Cole's coterie enjoyed within the far-reaching infrastructure of the British Empire. For the DSA, ornament was not only the apprehensible appearance of the industrial object but the imprimatur of globalized labor as well.

The DSA's attention toward the anthropological underpinnings of globalized production was foretold right at the time of the Great Exhibition. Many leading personalities who visited the exhibition remarked on the perceived superiority of Oriental, handcrafted wares over their Occidental, industrially produced counterparts. For most British and many Continental aesthetes, the exhibition represented an anthropological watershed.[27] Prominent aesthetes and intellectuals as diverse as Gustave Flaubert and Gottfried Semper, as well as a host of British public figures, decried what they deemed the execrable taste of the objects produced by mechanized industry in Europe. Comparing these to the handmade textiles, metalwork, and ivory work from the East (most notably India, which had a bigger display than any non-Western country and most Western countries in the Continent), aesthetes and officials alike commented on what they deemed the superior patterns, the harmony of color, the richness of material, and the "subtlety" of application. (Ruskin was the notable exception.[28])

The irony was not lost on these Victorian intellectuals. For a midcentury progressivist mind-set whose principal precepts had been built on the thought of James Mill and Macaulay, this paradox of civilizational "backwardness" juxtaposed against the high quality of commodities presented its own conceptual challenges. What the Orient presented, in its alternative structures of production, was the possibility to rethink the relationship between "industry" in its nineteenth-century sense and "society." Indeed, as this book argues, the increased documentation of the anthropological situations of the Orient, deemed by liberals to be entirely imbricated within custom, effectively defined the very framework through which industry in the metropole was understood by way of difference.

South Kensington and India

Because of the spectacular appreciation elicited by Indian goods in the Great Exhibition, when the DPA apportioned monies from its founding budget to purchase goods from the Crystal Palace, *more than one-third* of the goods purchased were of Indian origin. Because the price structure of a colonial market such as India can be assumed to be only notional at this point, the goods obtained were exponentially higher in number than those purchased from the Continent for a comparable amount of money. In subsequent years, the DSA continued to make substantial purchases of ornamental objects from India. It sent deputations, some led by Cole's own son, Henry Hardy Cole, to obtain plaster casts of architectural monuments and other wares. Today, the V&A remains the biggest repository of South Asian wares outside of the subcontinent. Even within South Asia, the V&A's principal competitors in this respect today were all either established or significantly influenced by the South Kensington axis.

The effects of this policy were manifold. Even as the DSA started a campaign to acquire Indian wares, the unique status of India as the only area in Asia where Britain had direct control over administrative polity led to the DSA's substantial influence in determining its cultural affairs. DSA officials precociously realized that the untrammeled influx of mechanized products was devastating the artisanal industry of the subcontinent. South Kensington thus advocated a preservationist stance for the "traditional" modes of production and the artifacts of India.

Figure 1 Plaster cast of South Asian architectural ornaments, collected by the Indian section of the South Kensington Museum. These casts were subsequently destroyed in 1955. In the spirit of "modernist" frenzy, copies of ornamental detail were deemed of little value. Nonetheless, each destroyed fragment was scrupulously photographed and archived. Courtesy: V & A Images.

At the time of the DSA's establishment in London, a number of colonial institutions in India already ministered to the pedagogy of vocational skills. Many of these were evangelist outfits, although they overtly espoused objectives of commercial improvement and industrial training. The School of Industry in Madras established in 1850 by Alex Hunter is an example.

However, as news arrived of the Great Exhibition and the formation of the DPA, several bodies in India, including native financiers and industrialists, were inspired to create similar institutions to support local industries. The new schools of art in Bombay and Calcutta in the mid-1850s were a result of these campaigns. Because there had been no pedagogical expertise developed in the vocational fields, the South Kensington curriculum was borrowed and adapted for Indian schools. Very soon, all three schools, Madras, Bombay, and Calcutta (the three major colonial trading centers), were obtaining textbooks, models, plaster casts, drawing materials, and other equipment from the South Kensington repository.

By the mid-1860s, schools of art in India were recruiting DSA graduates for their teaching positions. The first batch was composed of John Lockwood Kipling, John Griffiths, and Henry Hoover Locke, all of whom were to become superintendents of the various schools, the last two of the Bombay and Calcutta institutions, respectively. Kipling, whose son Rudyard was born on the campus of the J.J. School of Art in Bombay, eventually found a new school and museum in Lahore in the following decade. At the turn of the century, South Kensington's influence acquired a permanent afterlife in India through the arrival of another of its graduates, Ernest Binfield Havell, head of the Calcutta school, whose contribution was critical in the imagining of a nationalist art in India. Almost all the significant advocates of artisanal production in India had substantial links with the DSA apparatus, including influential officials and pedagogues such as George Birdwood, Swinton Jacob, Thomas Holbein Hendley, Ram Singh, Caspar Purdon Clarke, and J.H. Rivett-Carnac.

Because of the South Kensington connection, the dyad of museum and school of industrial art became the prevalent format of artistic pedagogy in India, and, as in the British schools, fine art was pushed to the margins. With the four schools in Madras, Bombay, Calcutta, and Lahore as models, a number of princely states, Baroda, Hyderabad, Jaipur, Alvar, and others, set up similarly coupled institutions. Along with the museums, the DSA faction also instigated a series of exhibitions within India, their schedule performing a well-choreographed tango with their lavish metropolitan counterparts. This network in turn facilitated the magnificence and generous size of Indian galleries at almost every international exhibition. The swan song of the DSA's career in India was South Kensington's *Colonial and Indian Exhibition* of 1886, by far the biggest world exhibition held in Britain until that point. A direct result of the 1886 exhibition was the sumptuously produced *Journal of Indian Art,* whose publishing run of twenty-five years made it the principal and exhaustive archival source for research on Indian artisanal manufactures in this period. It is in this state-supported journal that we find perhaps the first technical treatise, in 1888, written by

Figure 2 Disseminating Design—Shadows of South Kensington. South Kensington style display cases, Lahore Museum, Lahore. Photo: Author.

Figure 3 Nineteenth-century casts kept at the J.J. School of Art, Bombay. Companies like Messrs. Brucciani, located in Great Russell Street, London, supplied the pedagogical needs of the global DSA network. Photo: Author.

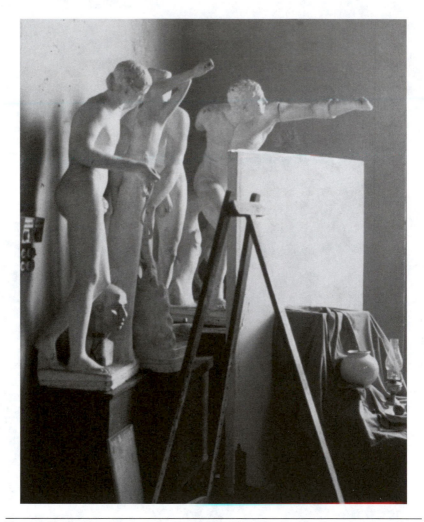

Figure 4 Nineteenth-century casts kept at the J.J. School of Art, Bombay. Photo: Author.

Chobe Raghu Das, assistant superintendent of revenue in Kutch, on "tie and dye" work in that province. The DSA can thus be justly credited with introducing to the Western world an important sartorial element of the antiestablishment, do-it-yourself counterculture of the hippie era.[29]

The pedagogical efforts in India were complemented by the South Kensington Museum's own efforts to collect, document, and analyze the varieties of material phenomena from India. Ray Desmond has written about the India Museum, a shadowy and amorphous institution, which in the 1870s, under the guidance of its director John Forbes Watson, brought out a series of encyclopedic studies on the flora, fauna, economic products, processes of production, and anthropological variety of India. In 1880 the collections of the India Museum, integrated the year before with the South Kensington Museum's own extensive collections of Indian objects, were opened to the public as a distinct and brand-new "Indian section." The section subsequently acquired its own separate building within the South Kensington campus at the turn of the century, the only "nonmaterial," *nationally* defined section of the V&A until the 1970s.

With the increased power of trade unions as representatives of labor, the DSA's paternalism would gradually become irrelevant, even as its derived ideology moved on to regions experiencing new industrialization in the twentieth century. The respective Werkbunds in Germany are an example. In India, on the other hand, as a colonial territory experiencing mass-scale deindustrialization and underdevelopment in its indigenous economy at this high tide of imperialism, the DSA discourse became all the more entrenched within the general terms of administrative policy. This book contends that, as British India moved toward an early version of what Mahmood Mamdani has described in the African context as "decentralized despotism"—an administrative polity advocating customary self-governance and therefore reduced responsibilities at the ground level—the DSA's invocation of the "artisan" would become a key alibi for tradition-based superexploitation. All the chapters in this book address this thesis of the relationship between "indirect" governance and exploitation in varying yet comparable ways.

The colonial artisan epitomized the anthropological armature on which notions of British imperial responsibility turned. As a figure of difference, the artisan does not disappear with the advent of industrialism. Rather, it appears within it. The imago of the Oriental artisan is born and bred in the anthropological chrysalis of industrial capitalism. If for Marx the artisan had to be violently alienated from custom before she came into an understanding of herself as the agent of capital, for the DSA, industry could succeed only if the disjunction between artisan and industrial worker was properly reintegrated as an unruffled continuity. In this book, I argue that the artisan is essentially a futuristic figure—a cyborg structure—posed *otherwise*, "abconstructed", within the narratives of modernization.

South Kensington's pedagogic interest in India, encompassing as it did dozens of art, industrial, and vocational schools, museums, and exhibitions, was shot through with this very contradictory concern: how to restore the (Indian) artisan to her former state of preindustrial excellence and yet harness her productivity more efficiently within the imperial economy. By bolstering customary modes of production, or so South Kensington acolytes in India argued, the unspoiled attributes of Indian artisanry could nevertheless effect an undisturbed transition into wage production sans the dehumanizing telos of the factory floor. Given that India was well into an extended period of "deindustrialization," this nostrum was predisposed towards failure. In empirical terms, this failure can be gauged differently across the different regional schools, comprising as they did different populations and different kinds of vocational or customary provenance. Norma Evenson has written in detail about the various schools' respective difficulties in drawing on local artisanal pools for their student body, which came to be populated instead mostly by aspirants to government employment as drawing teachers or draftsmen.[30]

The very different trajectories of the respective art schools in India (or, for that matter, in Britain) demonstrate the fact that the DSA's "artisan" was an elusive figure to come by in actuality, just as workers played truant from British art schools. In general, the Calcutta school, even as it absorbed substantial elements of the DSA curriculum, was furthest from the spectrum of the "artisan." This was owing to its location in a city where the cultural elite had already identified themselves with elements of romantic individualist art tied to a protonationalist movement. The Madras school, on the other hand, with its roots in a vocational and reform school, quickly adapted to the modifications of the DSA curriculum. Bombay's J.J. School maintained a mix of emphasis on both fine art and artisanal work. Only Lahore's Mayo School of Art catered substantially in practice to the anthropological clientele idealized by the DSA faction in South Asia. John Lockwood Kipling routinely scouted the surrounding territories, bringing artisans to the school, and established direct links with various "craft" centers to facilitate the collection and distribution of their products in both commercial and pedagogical arenas. The pedagogical primacy of the Lahore school was reinforced at the Art Conference held in Lahore in 1894, when most of the other school superintendents pointed to Kipling's creation as the model to be emulated.[31] As we shall see in chapter 1, however, this model was a direct reflection of the difference of manner in which the Punjab, among the last territories annexed by the British, was administered in legal and political terms. Within a few years, the rise of nationalism in the Bengal school would take the debate over indigenism to an entirely other place, privileging the fine artist over the artisan, thus reversing the DSA's own hard-fought victories in Britain from six decades ago.

Officials or graduates of the four principal schools of art were often directly or indirectly responsible for the supervision of scores of vocational schools run by the colonial government in mofussil or rural areas. Schools of carpentry, weaving, masonry, and so on dotted the map. Some of the vocational school graduates serviced the needs of the colonial machinery in local areas, whereas others either started new occupational pursuits using their education or continued in the line of their forefathers. With the exception of the Punjab, most art school students wound up as drawing tutors or teachers, PWD draftsmen, and the like rather than in customary trades. The demographic disparity of the student body in relation to the professed programmatic aims of the vocational schools and the schools of art make an interesting analysis in itself. Unfortunately, we will have to leave such an analysis for another occasion. Generally speaking, the story of the DSA in India can be considered to be an overwhelming failure in terms of its stated intentions, commensurate with its record in the metropole.

This failure would sometimes manifest itself in counterintuitive ways. In their desire to shore up native production against the depredations of colonial exploitation, later DSA acolytes such as Ernest Binfield Havell could even identify with the anticolonial nationalism of the Indian National Congress, hoping that it would act as the restorative agency of native tradition. However, as we shall see in chapter 6, the Congress, on the other hand, was well on its way to being co-opted by emergent peripheral capitalism managed by native entrepreneurs, the interests of which *competed* with colonial capital rather than providing an *alternative* to it. Perhaps taking a cue from the DSA, perhaps even seeing through its contradictions, the Congress would stage industrial exhibitions in every one of its annual conventions from 1901 onward. The massive scale of the DSA operation to manipulate the present is matched only by its cognitive failure in gauging some of the larger portents of its moment.

The Schools of Art in Britain displayed the same lack of fit between their pedagogy and their constituencies throughout their history. The DSA had to reconcile itself to the realization that in many instances art classes earmarked for male artisans engaged in industry were mostly populated by women seeking upward mobility through inculcation of elite taste. On the other hand, the same DSA remained practically blind to the fact that far from being constrained within the regressive spheres of secondary or domestic labor, women made up the bulk of principal labor in many key economic sectors, including textiles. However, the Victorian elite's promulgation of separate gendered spheres forestalled their ability to address this patent contradiction.

If the colonial lack of fit created the opening for the emergence of an elite art posed as a national art, in the metropole the effort to wed concepts of individual creativity to that of the citizen and laborer translated instead into an alibi for the emergence of the modern avant-garde. In the twentieth century, the emergent figure of "design," relating to the orchestration of taste, in all of its academic, industrial, and artistic connotations, would reside far from the context in which the Cole circle had originally conceived it: as a way of enhancing average social entitlement and the quality of life of the productive citizen. In the metropole or colony, both approaches were deeply flawed, steeped in a tradition of misreading irreconcilable distinctions between ethics and aesthetics. This book does not seek to simply critique, by mere hindsight, these misreadings to advocate a program of modernity more acceptable to contemporary political-economic or culturalist concerns. The DSA is, to date, historically the biggest-ever bureaucratic body able to wangle authority on issues of design and material culture directly pertaining to crucial political and economic policy. The unprecedented ambit of the DSA's curriculum vitae therefore necessarily found itself having to redraw the boundaries between any pat oppositions formulated by idealist thinking in its own period or ours.

This book will examine these misreadings and failures as nonetheless immensely productive in the articulation of pedagogical programs, individual praxis, and administrative policy. If anything, this charge of a flawed premise belies the fastidious accountability with which DSA officials in both Britain and India beheld themselves to the populations whose interests they claimed to represent. The DSA would make a separate report to British Parliament every year, running into hundreds of pages. It served as a platform for vigorous debates that developed between industrialists, bureaucrats, and aesthetes on devising standards for procedurality and policy, financial accounting, and administrative management. It commissioned detailed reports and research into the nature of artistic production in industrialized and nonindustrialized regions across the globe, thereby undergirding the then newly emerging terms of political and cultural internationalism. Both the data and the terminology framed by the DSA were crucial in framing treaties and covenants that are intrinsic to the global economic system even today. The 1886 Berne convention on international copyright, applicable to this very book, is an example.

The book therefore seeks to use the significant armature of the South Kensington apparatus and its institutions as a way of examining the asymmetrical relationship between metropolitan and colonial subjects within the strategies of imperial governance. Thus, if the aesthetic was perceived as the attribute of an undifferentiated "universal" subject, then the DSA could hardly ignore the asymmetries produced by new forms of anthropological determination in the nineteenth century. The difference between what the DSA coterie construed as the industrialized worker and the tradition-based colonial artisan would occasion complex policy formulations that offer a singular case study in the divagating fates of the "aesthetic" and its routinely misread categories in the service of "practice." In this sense, the DSA's pet conceit—that capitalist production could be transformed through aesthetic means—presents yet another routinely ignored instance of the hiatus between an *elective modernity* and *enforced modernization*. The book uses the meticulous self-documentation of the DSA as its principal archive. On the other hand, it also uses more recent critical terms and experiences to examine continuities between the DSA's frame of reference within the British Empire and late twentieth-century neocolonial globalization. Today, borders once again are perceived to be redrawn, throwing up new series of contrasts that seem to animate, once again, a (post)modernity without stable compass.

This book attempts to get beyond the framework of "postcolonial" studies, to the extent that the field tends toward an inordinately *culturalist* understanding of the colonial encounter. In bringing attention to the DSA, an institution whose power relied as much on the visible brunt of policy as on the less discernible strands of ideological influence and dispute, the effort here is to map out the interplay between state and society in their negotiations with globality. Rather than point out the inevitable cognitive failures within this interplay as indicative of some epistemic insufficiency, this book focuses on these points of crisis as essential in the formation of what one might term a modern sensibility of power; of the aesthetic as being rent by fragmentary intuitions of parts and wholes, superposed by phantasms of past tradition and fervent schemas for the future.

The culturalist dismissal of bureaucracies as all-too mechanical, alternatively overbearing, or perfunctory apparatuses has likewise influenced fields of aesthetic study such as art and architectural history. There, the procrustean reliance on the avant-garde as the primary archive of shifting aesthetic sensibilities has reduced the state and government to a monolith, where these institutional vectors are portrayed primarily as interference in the aesthetic rather than as foundational to it. Quite in contrast to its eighteenth-century origins, for contemporary criticism, the play of ideas of the aesthetic remains strangely immured in the heads of exceptional individuals and networks rather than defining a governmentality *as such*. From Siegfried Giedion onward, this caricature of the state has resulted in a peculiar tokenism toward the DSA within historical "surveys" of modern art and architecture. Every modern survey has had to acknowledge the critical role of the Cole circle and the DSA in the establishment of a modernist aesthetic. By the same token, no survey has devoted more than a page or two on the topic. Indeed, the elucidation of explanatory models to understand the interplay between formal and informal spheres of influence—the DSA's hallmark—remains quite foreign to these surveys. To give an instance, the many histories of the Bauhaus typically describe the school as an aggregation of personalities. Where government does enter into the picture, it is as interloper, as *deus ex machina* censoring the drama of erratic geniuses at the institution's demise. The *founding* role of government in establishing the Bauhaus is generally underplayed in these accounts.

I argue that this embarrassment of the state plays out in quite different ways in the contemporary coverage of the South. With the ongoing shifts of transnational investment and the changed clientele of American universities, curricula have borne an increased emphasis on "non-Western" or "global" content. Produced as this demand is by the features of contemporary globalization, with its marked bias against the (welfare) state, studies and curricula pertaining to "non-Western" peoples have tended to ignore the infrastructural supports of the aesthetic. The extreme codeterminacy between the establishment of the state and the emergency of the "aesthetic" as defined above and elsewhere in this book is generally glossed over as a global given, thereby surreptitiously inserting art's function as a civilization standard. This association having been made, the tables can quickly be turned to locate aesthetic attitudes as a barometer for modernity or lack thereof. The demolition of the Bamiyan Buddhas can therefore be portrayed as a symptom of universally condemnable savagery rather than a specific response to a particularly fraught institutional history. The dogged legacy of the Enlightenment in its characterization of art as an incubator for the *natural* imagination continues to produce an equivalence between aesthetic attitude and cultural disposition. Artistic description therefore continues to appear in the garb of an anthropological account rather than the tenuous thumbprint of fraught institutional responses to these very cultural predispositions. In the proliferating world of today's biennale culture, this all-too opportunistic shorthand—given that it has the convenience of inveighing against the state—is carried further. Here the primary effort is directed instead towards conjuring up two alternate paths of art in the erstwhile Third World: producing the image of a counter-avant-gardes as if *ex nihilo* (as individual numens holding forth *despite* their supposedly restrictive environs) or the study of extrastatal networks (public-sphere collectives posited *against* the state). At the core of multiculturalism, the aesthetic is restored to a "universal" intuition. To be sure, institutional encounters continue to be the subject of advanced research, but these as such are inevitably relegated to "area"-bound casuistry, of no import for the generalist understanding or the "survey."

The DSA's transnational and hybrid trajectory, as it reached out to the global scene of production in quite unexpected ways, poses some impenetrable problems for these sorts of critical bulwark. In my view, this blind spot, the inability to read institutional inputs in terms other than a barrier repressing the flowering of a truly "individual" genius, accounts for the simultaneously central and marginal role accorded to the DSA's influence on modern aesthetic theory. I argue that this strange paradoxical locus is less a relegation than an actual methodological failure at the core of aesthetic theory, an ineptitude towards reading aggregate behaviour in the development of aesthetic thought, even as aesthetic thought consistently invokes the aggregate entity of "culture" to establish its juridical power. The historiography of aesthetic modernity, even as postmodern capital willingly accommodates different critiques of the Eurocentric "universal," is devoid of a theory of the global. By following the DSA's trajectory along its many vicissitudes in the pursuit of proper "design," this book is also an attempt to craft the rudimentary outlines of such a theory.

"There is time," the time of imperial maps painted red and pink … in "the taking of a toast and tea." Vivan Sundaram, "Journey towards Freedom: Modern Bengal," Victoria Memorial, Calcutta, 1998. Photo and courtesy: Vivan Sundaram.

CHAPTER 1

Empire "... in a Fit of Absence of Mind": Toward a Vulgar Theory of Imperialism

... the British rulers of India are like men bound to make their watches keep true time in two longitudes at once.

—Henry Sumner Maine, *Village-Communities in East and West*

And as in the game wherein the Japanese amuse themselves by filling a porcelain bowl with water and steeping in it little pieces of paper which until then are without character or form, but, the moment they become wet, stretch and twist and take on colour and distinctive shape, become flowers or houses or people, solid and recognizable, so in that moment all the flowers in our garden ... sprang into being, town and gardens alike, from my cup of tea.

—Marcel Proust, *Swann's Way, Remembrance of Things Past*

Economists may bristle, but empire is about taste: gold, silver, spices, silk, tea, textiles, the view, furniture, opium, coffee, bananas, paisley, arabesques, gasoline-driven "ways of life."

Drinking tea is no less a cog *of* the imperial wheel than is a quelling of anticolonial insurgency. A curator at the Indian and South-East Asian Department at the Victoria & Albert Museum (V&A) tells me that although its Indian collection is the largest outside of South Asia, this quantitative superiority should be qualified by the fact that it also contains certain "inconsequential" items such as samples of Tibetan tea. This anomaly may appear a curatorial mistake, because the museum was always primarily devoted to visual, rather than gastronomic, taste. Even so, how did a specimen of tea come to be lodged in the eye of an aesthetic maelstrom such as the South Kensington Museum (SKM) in the nineteenth century? Its inclusion was certainly not accidental at the onset; the SKM's administrators were one of the most meticulous, if idiosyncratic, in their curatorial procedures.

The sample of Tibetan tea is a ruined and obscure fragment, a tenuous *folie*, of evidence that perhaps tells us even more about the global battlegrounds of the museum's history, more so than the carpets or tiles that have been so proudly hung on the walls. Caught between the museum's own absorption in classifying objects by genres of material (tea), qualified by regional anthropologies (Tibet), its place belongs to a cartographic imaginary that the contemporary museum is perhaps hard put to explain. To enter such an imaginary, one would have to bring into reckoning the amazing covert operations of the Survey of India in Tibet[1] or the economic rewriting of colonial landscapes by the introduction of cash crops such as tea and opium in the nineteenth century. Emblematic of this global map, Indian tearooms were a prominent feature of the world exhibitions from

Figure 1.1 Indian tearoom, 1889. *Exposition Universelles,* Paris. From *Journal of Indian Art,* III, no. 28 (October 1889).

Melbourne to London. If one keeps in mind Henry Cole and John Stuart Mill's frequent meetings over morning tea at the India Office throughout the 1840s and 1850s, then one can imagine that the wafting aroma of tea, even as it dissipates into London's smog-laden ether, bears within it the weight of the ineffable archive of the relationship between metropole and colony. Drinking tea may well have brought about the Department of Science and Arts (DSA) itself, if Henry Cole's self-serving paean to the tea service designed by him in 1846 for Herbert Minton is taken seriously:

> I venture to think that this Tea Service may be regarded as a link in the chain of circumstances leading to that great Exhibition which sowed the seed for the beginning of the South Kensington Museum.[2]

There is a rupture between the living of the everyday "effect" as a normative phenomenon and the trajectory of its cause. Drinking tea, wearing clothes, eating food, even if one does these every day, does not belong to the everyday. The daily crave for the astringency of caffeine, even as its pleasure stimulates greater productivity and sociality, is inseparable from a global rapacity that marks the very pores of its production. The everyday is the name of a "great game" that renders inseparable the quiver of the nostril that takes in an aroma of taste and the debilitated, impoverished hand that plucks the leaf from the swaying branch. "There is time," Prufrock may have added to his observations, the time of imperial maps painted red and pink, the time of famished millions, time for smoking gunboats, time for the great migrations of labor, in "the taking of toast and tea," time not just for the growth and movement of the plant, which follows its own funereal and enticing story from the starvation of China—and its reciprocal relationship with the opium trade—to the indentured labor on the foothills of the Indian Himalayas but also for the taste for the teacup and the tea service, the pattern on the teapot, the table and the tablecloth, the new forms of sociality and the rearranged furniture of modern rooms, mobile chairs that secede from the reassuring support of the wall, the new emptiness of the wall, the transformed configuration of the surfaces of the room, indeed, all the rooms of the household. Time seems to have come undone, urging its dwellers to stitch together again its split seams, patch together the unraveled threads of this domestic tableau in the operational theater of the museum.

The Time of Imperialism

> Must we not at least hold … that the Empire is ephemeral, and that the time is not far off when we must withdraw from the country? …

The end of our Indian Empire is perhaps almost as much beyond calculation as the beginning of it. There is *no analogy* in history either
for one or the other.

—J.R. Seeley, *The Expansion of England*

Can imperialism change the experience of time? In other words, can
concrete experience challenge the primacy of the abstract? The Victorian
historian J.R. Seeley thought it could and did. It was he who, diagnosing a
pathological amnesia among Britain's metropolitan population, coined the
famous expression that epitomized the tremendous ambiguity regarding the
causes and uses of empire: "We seemed, as it were, to have conquered and
peopled half the world *in a fit of absence of mind.*" In his book *The Expansion of England,* he chastises both the English population and its scholars
for not expanding the boundaries of their imagination in consonance with
the unanticipated breadth of their imperial domains. "They do not perceive
that … the history of England is not in England but in America and Asia."[3]
Seeley's primary intention here was not to exhort his readers to become
expansionist hawks. The book's addressees are not just English settlers,
expatriates, the "Tommy Atkinses," or colonial officers residing at the far
corners of the map painted pink, and the book is not particularly directed
toward officials in the Foreign and India offices, for whom an education in
imperial history could be expected as *de rigueur.* Neither is the exhortation
to understand this geographic breadth directed toward some pragmatic
end, say, the better control of policy decisions in the future. The mind-set
Seeley wants to transform is that of the average British citizen within the
borders of Britain; the large majority of which had no direct relationship
with and mostly avowed disinterest in imperialist decision making.

Seeley's most insistent assertion is that the interests and destiny of the
English nation could no longer be equated with merely that of the population ensconced within the Isles. Unable to apprehend their territorial
demesne, Englishmen could not gauge their proper temporal and historical moment. Their experience of the present was *inauthentic,* if one may
borrow an expression from Heidegger. A preternatural and permanent
state of expansion, Seeley contends, characterizes the history of England
as opposed to any European state; English history has become in crucial
ways coterminous with global history. Without the English interests in
India—he devotes half his book to this particular relationship—the history
of the world would have been significantly different. Some of the wars with
France might have taken a different turn; England may even not have taken
the interest she did in the recent war between the Turks and the Russians.
In all likelihood, even the Crimean War may not have happened.

British citizens must magnify their imagination, extend their horizon to a fully global compass that takes in the vast corners of its empire. The cognitive domain of English consciousness needs to readjust its focal point from a national to a transnational scope. Only if they learn this suppressed geographical expanse of their own history can the English finally begin to gauge their present successfully; only then can they gain an authentic experience of the time to which they belong and that belongs to them; only then can they restore to their experience of the present a *present mindedness*. Seeley's counsel has this one unintended effect. It seeks to think of the metropolitan subject as buffered by the vicissitudes of its global domains. The traditional, outward-bound view of the empire is displaced by a view of the imperialist that looks in on itself from the outside. The global is not, to put it in the contemporary official jargon of the day, simply a matter of "foreign" or "colonial" policy, an item of interest in the newspaper. It is rather the very optic through which the subject construes its present; in the fabled tranquility of the English teacup there brews many a tempest of the global. Other than its exhortatory intent, Seeley's narration here also reveals a formal, disciplinary ploy of the historian. A temporal problem—understanding the present—is transmogrified into the understanding of a spatial map. Once the historical question has been reverted to a geographical one of deciphering the pink areas of the globe, the complex experiences of temporality and temporization can be reduced to a narrative of succession, a series of events, each event the effect of a former one. The Englishman's authentic experience of his time is that of an accumulation of historical sediments rather than a temporal rupture.

If Seeley asks us to spatialize the unconscious continuity of time, keep present the memory of the global traffic of material and personnel that undergirds the everyday, Michel de Certeau takes something of the opposite attitude. *The Practice of Everyday Life* begins with a colonial example. When the Spanish colonialists imposed their power on their Indian subjects in the Americas, the Indians' noncomprehension of the rationale behind these new regimens granted them a certain autonomy from complete subjugation to that power. Even as they followed the new norms in form, in spirit, they remained "*other* within the very colonization that outwardly assimilated them," thereby deflecting the dominant discourse of power.[4] Their failure to come to full consciousness of their condition gave them a measure of protection against the abjectness of that condition. This absentminded temporization, this curious obliviousness of the material and physical degradation that might be coterminous with that colonization, is carried over to de Certeau's invocation of the "reverie" in train travel. The train is a symptomatic materialization of our modernity: a "box of space" that differentiates us into ranks and hierarchies, "classes" of travel, "puts us in our place," so to speak. In the midst of this confinement, the reverie is like the Indians' "other" language, transporting our temporal being elsewhere even as the body is held in place on a path guided by rails.

Between Seeley and de Certeau, between the imperial desire for a unified discourse of power and its description as an overwhelming architectonic, we can gauge some of the temporal indeterminacy that we will try to examine in this chapter. In 1848, at the height of the so-called Railway Mania, Henry Cole, under the pseudonym of Felix Summerly, wrote the railway *Travelling Charts: Or, Iron Road Books*. The *Books* acquainted the travelers of this novel transport with the historical, natural, and cultural landmarks they were likely to see out of their left and right windows. Summerly describes himself as an industrial-day cicerone, virtually accompanying rail travelers on their power-driven journey. The books are

> for perusal on the journey. In which are noted the Towns, Villages, Churches, Mansions, Parks, Stations, Bridges, Viaducts, Tunnels, Gradients &c. the Scenery and its Natural History, the Antiquities and their Historical Associations, &c. passed by the Railway, with numerous Illustrations, constituting a novel and complete Companion for the Railway Carriage.[5]

The reverie is hardly the locus of undetermined power; it is no less programmed than the trajectory of the train. The *Iron Road Books* organize the reverie, reining in its temporal externality, like a *camera obscura,* into a discursive frame. Nonetheless, de Certeau's premise provides us with one critical insight: that the experience of time is a primal ontological axis through which the subject of power construes its practice. These differentiated temporalities are quintessential to the manner in which different subject populations recognize themselves as each other, "emerge" into modernity so to speak, apprehend the frame of their unfreedom. The subject of power is not just the crepuscular effigy in some portrait but a temporally indeterminate figure. And in its interest in orchestrating the reverie, power reveals itself as open ended, not restrictive; empiricizing as much as universalizing; morphogenetic and productive of discourse and commodities, not submitted to an emasculating teleology. Imperialist expansion is not just differentiated but differentiating.

Analyzing the Present

We shall start out from a *present-day* economic fact.

—Karl Marx, *Economic and Philosophical Manuscripts*

What was once functional and transitory, however, begins today, at an altered tempo, to seem formal and stable.

—**Walter Benjamin,** *The Arcades Project*

I'm glad that the Exhibition chaps have so far left you in peace. I'm already being plagued by them.

—**Engels to Marx, letter on May 9, 1851**

With the overbearing hold of the Frankfurt School on postmodern thought, a certain correspondence between the world exhibitions and Marx's theorization of the commodity (usually focusing on its "fetish" character) has started to gain a veneer of plausibility. In most cases, this hindsight is significantly reliant on Walter Benjamin's particular, certainly not untendentious, recapitulation of the nineteenth century. This is surprising, because what is curious, despite Marx's presence in London both on May 1, 1851, the date of the opening of the Great Exhibition *and* the opening of the 1862 exhibition, given the latter's much-touted influence on the First International, is his *lack* of commentary on the topic. For all their putatively stupendous presence on the world-historical stage, Marx, resident of London and theorist of the global, seems to have largely ignored the world exhibitions.[6] In his prepared tracts, the only mention we can find of the Great Exhibition is in "The Eighteenth Brumaire," when, in passing, he refers to its role in exacerbating the overproduction leading to the "general trade crisis" of 1851. Marx perceived the exhibition more or less as symptomatic of the English "commercial-crisis"-driven competition with the French domination of the luxury goods market.[7]

As is well-known, Marx was making his living as a journalist during this time, and his prolific writings of the period document the minutiae of historical developments in that period. His telegraphic dispatches during the 1850s, here to the *Neue Rheinische Zeitung,* there to the *New York Tribune,* here to Engels in Manchester, there to one of the revolutionary councils in Europe, epitomize the journalist's vocation to translate the everyday into history. His studies of mobilizational patterns, both revolutionary and capitalist, intentional and unintentional, temporizing the daily drifts of political and economic turpitude across continents, render his indifference to the Great Exhibition a mobilizational venture par excellence, even more vexing. He never attended in any significant detail to London itself, his home from 1848 until his death. It was the industrial North—cities such as Manchester and Liverpool and their physical terrain of factory production—that held his attention. Buried in the British Museum, browsing through the Blue Books, Marx remained barely cognizant of the immense changes being undergone in London's urban physiognomy.

Marx is on the track of capital's role as cause; the empirical and normative aspects manifested within capitalism are of significance to him only as evidence of capital's preponderant causative power. The geography of the imperial city more or less escaped his notice. His theoretical interests in London in 1851, other than the goings-on in Parliament, were mostly directed toward its newspapers. In addition to the Blue Books and official dispatches from diplomatic or colonial offices abroad, newspapers served as Marx's primary archive. Journalistic opinion represented, for Marx, the epitome of ideology, in that it institutionalizes "rumor"; that is, it transforms extrahistorical evidence into reportage. In the newspaper, the cognitive failures of gossip are instituted as historical record (a point we will keep in mind for chapter 7). By monitoring the fluctuating news and opinions in the *Times,* Marx attempts to sift out a historiography of the present.[8]

Marx sees the newspaper as the unstable, *incomplete* archive of a present that is *indeterminate.* In the journalistic archive, the verifiability (Husserl would call this "ontic validity")[9] of the present is permanently deferred, rendered inseparable from the mutability of gossip and rumor. Marx's description of the import of European political affairs in 1851 linked rumor with the metaphor of photography:

> At the same time the shadow took on colour, like a variegated daguerrotype. If one looks up the European daily newspapers for the month of September and October one finds, word for word, suggestions like the following: "Paris is full of rumours of a coup d'état. ..." The news reports which brought this information always closed with the fateful word "*postponed,*" ... The shadow of the coup had become so familiar to the Parisians as a spectre that they were unwilling to believe in it when it finally appeared as flesh and blood.[10]

The present oscillates between its unwitting postponement and its unexpected arrival; this is like the varied temporal exposure of light on a daguerrotype.[11] Marx reads the photograph at its surface, as a chemical patina divesting the historical mise-en-scène of its depth. The photograph captures the ephemerality of the everyday, not as representation but as mechanism, as a technology that captures the temporal variegations of light in a given frame. We must remember here that the temporal analogues of photography in the mid-nineteenth century are very different from those in the twentieth century. Although the jurors of the photography section in the Great Exhibition could foresee its development to a "new era in pictorial representation ... [to capture] the scenes daily passing around us," it would take the "half a century" of Benjamin before photographic technology could advance to the point where everyday events could be documented in exposures under several tenths of a second.[12]

William Whewell, historian and philosopher of the "inductive" method, lecturing in 1852 on the future import of the Great Exhibition, used the temporality of light in photographic technology as a model for the variegations of history. For Whewell, the Great Exhibition captures in a simultaneous instant the different evolutionary stages reached by different nations around the world. To dramatize his point, he painted a portrait of a sixteenth-century traveler attempting to gain comprehensive knowledge of all the cultures of the world, so as to "have ... in his mind a representation of the whole progress of human art and industry up to the last moment, and a picture of the place which each nation occupied in the line of that progress." This endeavor would probably require the better part of his lifetime to carry out his survey:

But what time, what labour, what perseverance, what hardships, what access to great and powerful men in every land, what happiness of opportunity, would be implied in the completion of such a survey! A life would scarcely suffice for it; a man could scarcely be found who would achieve it, with all appliances and means which wealth and power could give. He must, like the philosophers of ancient days, spend all his years of vigour in travelling; must roam in the varied regions of India; watch the artisan in the streets of the towns of China; dive into the mines of Norway and of Mexico; live a life in the workshops of England, France, and Germany; and trace the western tide of industry and art as it spreads over the valley of the Mississippi. And when he had done all this, and however carefully he had done it, yet how defective must it be at least in one point! How far must it be from a *simultaneous* view of the condition of the whole globe as to material arts! During the time that he has been moving from place to place, the face of the world has been rapidly changing. When he saw Tunis it was a barbarous state; now that he has to make up his account, it is the first which asks for a leading place among the civilized communities of the industrial world. When he visited the plains of Iowa and Wisconsin, they were wild prairie; they are now the fields from which the cereal harvest is swept by the latest improved reaping machine. When he was at the antipodes, the naked savage offered the only specimen of art in his rude club and frail canoe; now there is a port whose lofty ships carry regularly to European market multiplied forms of native produce and manufacturers. Even if his picture be complete as to surface, what anachronisms must there be in it!

How much that expresses not the general view of the earth, but the accidental peculiarities of the traveller's personal narrative![13]

The Great Exhibition simultaneously captures the anachronism of everyday global history. "By annihilating the space which separates different nations, we produce a spectacle in which is also annihilated the time which separates one stage of a nation's progress from another."[14] Historical temporality can thus be drawn out as spatial distances measured along the vector of light. Traveling faster than light—Whewell betrays himself to be a tad in the dark about optics here—it would be possible to pick a point at the other end of the solar system, a photonic Archimedean point, where one could still view the image of the first inhabitant of England setting foot on its coast. On the way, the traveler would also view English history in reverse order, as he moved farther and farther away, with the successive advents of the "English, Norman, Saxon, Roman and British" peoples.

The photograph can capture only one single instant. Even if it were to capture all the contemporaneous developments of the globe in a single, instantaneous frame, exhibiting them side by side, it would be the view of only a single moment of human history. The Great Exhibition, on the other hand, "annihilate[s] space *and* time." It is like a photographic plate that travels faster than light; it captures not only the present but also the entire diachronic unfolding of human events. For other visitors to world exhibitions as well, this was the key distinction between the exhibition and the conventional museum. "And when, *tired of the present,* we wished to dive into the past, we have been able to scan at one glance, the accumulated treasures of the public and private museums of all the world."[15] The exhibition is a snapshot of the sedimented present; the museum or the photograph is merely a selective repository of the past.

Temporizing South Kensington

This department of the Board of Trade, which, in within a few short months has twice changed its designation, seems to be permanently subject to periodic crises.

—*The Art Journal,* 1854

The lag in exposure time renders the photograph *anachronistic* with respect to the pace of history. It is too slow to capture the celerity of the ephemeral, too fast to note its principal moments of transition. The image of the photograph transposed onto the Great Exhibition would be transferred to South Kensington as well. In his book on the English decorative arts titled *Travels in South Kensington,* the American writer and fervent abolitionist Moncure Daniel Conway posed himself as a tourist in London approaching a photograph vendor specializing in views of London's principal buildings. When asked for pictures of the SKM, the man responds that he has none:

> "What, no photograph of the South Kensington Museum!" I exclaimed, with some impatience. "Why, sir," replied the man mildly, "you see, the museum doesn't stand still long enough to be photographed." And so, indeed, it seems; and this constant addition of new buildings, ... is the physiognomical expression of the rapid growth and expansion of the intellectual and aesthetic epoch which called the institution into existence, and is through it gradually climbing to results which no man can see."[16]

The SKM was a museum dedicated to changing the state of contemporary design, toward transforming the present. Throughout the museum's career, this programmatic indeterminacy haunted its physical form. For its first forty years, the museum underwent scores of modifications and transformations that reflect the museum's embrace of shifting programs and content. It is as if the museum, in taking forward the lessons of the Great Exhibition into the future decades, is unable to get rid of the primary attribute of the exhibition, its ephemerality. Throughout its history, because of the incessant construction on site, the building appeared as if perennially in motion. "Permanent is ... a poor description of the SKM as a physical building," its state of permanent incompletion prevented it from attaining the sedentary silhouette of the "state museum."[17]

For this continual construction, Cole succeeded in seconding an entire detachment of sappers from the Royal Engineer Corps, ostensibly for their own training, a testimony to the experimental and exhibitional mood in which each building was realized. Both Cole and Francis Fowke, member of the Royal Engineer Corps and the SKM's first designer, perceived the museum as a demonstration of contemporary technological and aesthetic mores. The situational versatility of the military, personified in Fowke, was seen as perfect counterpart to the abilities of decorative artists. In its early stages, the building operated as a life-size exhibit of the Construction and Building Materials section of the museum. Ornamental tile, fireproof flooring, enameled iron plates, terracotta, and a plethora of building materials were on display both under glass cases and on the surfaces of the building. Military engineers proved themselves adept at producing buildings under loosely articulated programs without any of the budgetary fuss or aesthetic scruples attributed to the architect. It was almost as if the indeterminate expansions had no singular authorial will whatsoever; as a contemporary wag had it, it was the department's policy "to shift these designers from one subject to another, lest they should hereafter claim the originality of any one design."[18]

The building, as it progressed, was thus an agglomeration of buildings. In the minds of the Cole circle, the institution would wax and wane with its periodic variations of program; the indeterminacy is spelled out in his vision of the museum as a *"temporary* refuge for destitute collections."[19] [e.a.] The building became an exhibit of its various temporal moments in the very mode of its making. This machinic quality was seen as a direct critique of academic architectural discourses that stressed finality of composition over programmatic imperatives: the parts, defined by the building's various contents, took precedence over any overarching conceptual schema. "It is no longer a matter of opinion or of discussion how a building shall be constructed for the purpose of exhibiting pictures and other articles. The laws of it are as fixed as the multiplication table."[20]

This sensitivity to the variegations of the indeterminate moment manifested itself in the programmatic functioning of the institution as well. In its early phase, the SKM included a section where manufacturers could display their wares for limited periods of time. The curatorial vocation thus became procedural and automatic, devolving itself into contemporary commodity trends as decided by the manufacturer:

> [In order to undermine] the prejudice, which undoubtedly did exist against the admission of modern works into museums strictly so called ... the scheme therefore was to aim at founding, as a comprehensive and complete unity, a collection which, whilst gradually accumulating and effectually preserving the treasures of past ages, *should every day receive fresh acquisitions in the current productions of the period, thus illustrating and keeping pace with the progress of the age.*[21]

South Kensington's operational strategy is thus procedurally defined rather than canonically prescribed. Consciously constructed as process without end, the museum's programmed incompletion was epitomized by the very laying out of the site, its administrators preferring a policy of everincreasing aggregation of parts rather than a unified vision of the whole. In a memo from 1859, Cole characterized the building plan in the following way:

> The ground has been laid out that any works which may be undertaken by the Commissioners at the present time will not prejudge any future operations, and will not be likely to be rendered useless by any future works not at present determined upon. ... To whatever extent any works may now be undertaken they may be rendered complete in themselves. ... By leaving space for future buildings *outside* the

Corridor, such buildings may be executed by degrees without disturbing the laying out of the Grounds *within* the Corridor.[22]

The building of the SKM thus reflected a transformation in the aesthetic implications first served up by the technological fait accompli of Paxton's Crystal Palace. As an open-ended assemblage of building materials rather than *a* building in its sense of a bounded entity, the key determinants of the Crystal Palace were in its details of connection, "its combination of pane, sash bar, louvre, gutter, beam, truss, and column" into modular and extendable frames that could in principle be extended across the globe.[23] Thus, engineers and manufacturers could begin the production of the building parts *before* the plan was finalized. The length of the building was capped at an arbitrary 1,851 feet, commemorating the year of the exhibition. The spatial boundaries thus referred to an entirely unconnected temporal reference. Its primary impact was industrial as much as aesthetic. The glass used in the palace was equal to 40 percent of Britain's total glass production at the time. The coloring scheme was realized through the use of small painting machines that moved along the trusses. The Crystal Palace was the crystallization of a *system,* not the realization of an "architecture"; the SKM was explicitly conceived of as continuing in this tradition.[24]

The Systemic City

The Crystal Palace and the SKM can be said to offer an allegory of London's own urban profile, which also epitomized such a fragmentary logic. At midcentury, *London* was simply a floating signifier for an undefined urban agglomeration, the likes of which had never before been seen in the world. Twice the size of Paris, London's population grew from 2.5 million in 1851 to 6.5 million at the turn of the century. In 1900, Britain accounted for 75 percent of all global capital movements, much of it routed through the City of London (the financial "square mile" in the city's southeast).[25] Not only was the city the political and economic epicenter of an immense empire, it also contained within it a tremendous variety of trade and manufacturing skills. The 1841 census recorded no less than 840 distinct occupations within the capital.[26]

The City of London, the financial hub of the metropolis and the only defined and independent corporate entity, presented a phenomenon only tangentially related to the manufacturing hive that surrounded it. As British finance became the fuel for the metropolitan surge in industrialization and the global extraction of resources, the power of the City transcended the parochial concerns of municipal administration of the undefined urban agglomeration around it. The City's financial clout and Britain's imperial preponderance underpinned much of the financial "stability" of the world system. As the lesser imperial powers such as France and the United States experienced rapid industrial growth in this period, they ran up a heavy joint deficit owing to the significant increase of their raw material imports from underdeveloped regions. To meet this deficit, these countries increased their exports to Britain, thus fueling their own industrialization and contributing to Britain's financial power. Britain's significant investment income and "invisible income" made her into a capital exporter, while her colonies were made to absorb large magnitudes of British manufactures "to keep the multilateral payments system intact."[27]

This unprecedented macroeconomic profile, however, failed to provide the wherewithal for any legal, bureaucratic, or political body to define either the geographical or administrative jurisdiction for London. The City's nose was turned toward India, far in the East, more than to its own East End; the prevailing dogma of free trade left the City with very little responsibility for its immediate urban surrounding. Outside of the City (which had its own ancient form of government), the only geographical definitions that impinged upon it were the Act of 1829, identifying a seven-hundred-square-mile area as a single police district, and the Registrar General's 1833 extension of the Bills of Mortality, monitoring an eight-mile radius around St. Paul's for epidemic outbreak.[28] Public needs and infrastructure were dealt with through a fragmented system of county magistrates and parish vestries, sometimes even through public meetings of local inhabitants. "No authority existed capable of taking a strategic view of London's needs."[29]

London's mid-nineteenth-century being is oracular: an entity without body, it inhabits the future of others without being able to announce its own present. Its immense political and economic significance in global terms was belied by its own humdrum physiognomy. Its institutional anomalies were reflected in the relative absence of the traits of the imperial city. At midcentury, the place-name *London* had neither boundary nor axis, it did not have a Schinkel-designed center as in Berlin or the magnificent palaces of Vienna.[30] This lacuna drove a massive midcentury mandate to make over the face of the city, occasioning a burst of institutional projects. Much of London's urban image today derives from this mandate: landmark buildings conceived in this period include the Houses of Parliament; the Admiralty Office; the British Museum; Burlington House; the new Colonial, Foreign, and India offices; the National Gallery; the Royal Courts of Justice; the New Public Offices; the University of London; the War Office; the Natural History Museum; and the SKM. The programmatic content of these buildings reflected a comprehensive shift in imperial governmentality.

Only in 1855 was the first adequate, multifunctional agency, the Metropolitan Board of Works, founded to address London's burgeoning infrastructural needs. Owing to the previously mentioned projects and those initiated by the board and the railways, as John Summerson put it, "in the seventh decade of the nineteenth century, London was more excavated, more cut about, more rebuilt and more extended than at any time in its previous history."[31] Aided by the expansion in transport networks, London witnessed an unprecedented building boom that radiated out of the city on the side of its ever-extending highways and railway lines. It was this last aspect, its transport network, that finally conferred on the city its only plausible unifying system. As an urban entity, London acquired cohesion only as a matrix.

Temporizing South Kensington, Part II

The "eternal way," as the English have baptized the railway, is not immortal by any means. It is subject to constant metabolism. The iron, which is continually being lost by wear, oxidation, and new manufacture, has constantly to be replaced.

—Karl Marx, "Statistical Observations on the Railway System"

At the height of the railway mania, Cole was offered several commissions relating to Britain's transport system. Between 1845 and 1848, Cole worked to advocate the integration of Britain's haphazard systems of railways and dockyards into a less fragmented and privatized network.[32] The imperial implications of these improved networks were never far from his mind. In the following excerpt from an essay found among Cole's effects, relating to the campaign for Grimsby docks, the words of the author could well be his own:

Time—the most valuable commodity of modern commerce—is lost by every mile of unnecessary inland navigation. [With the linkage of rail and dockyard] ... the delays and risks of the inland [waterbound] voyage will be spared. A ship will enter the basin in deep water direct from the sea. She will deliver her cargo into the railway waggons alongside the quays; they will be transported without delay to the manufacturing districts inland. In a week the raw materials she may have imported may be spun, woven, dyed, finished and again placed on board as manufactures for export: thus, by the combined wonders of modern railways and modern machinery, a ship may have delivered her cargo, got it manufactured, reloaded and sent out to sea in less time that [sic] in an inland harbour she would have been kept waiting for a tide to enter the docks, or a fair wind to take her out of the river. Thus it will be found that railways have materially altered the question of selection of a harbour, and turned the scale against the old system of inland navigation. The *shortest possible sea voyage and the longest extent of railway communication* are the two circumstances which will now combine all the interests of the ship-owner, the merchant, the manufacturer and the consumer.[33]

The sensitivity to travel time that Cole acquired during this research was crucial to the manner in which the Great Exhibition was conceived. Arrangements were made with the London and North Western lines, with whom Cole had close contacts, to bring up spectators to London for the cheap round-trip fare of five shillings. These two lines alone accounted for over three-quarters of a million visitors to the exhibition. Maps of London were published on the eve of the exhibition prominently highlighting its railway stations and the routes to the exhibition. The relationship between the exhibition and the railway did not end there. While the exhibition committee was wrangling over the plan of the exhibition, the extremely short time frame (eleven months) necessitated that construction begin *before* the finalization of the scheme. The railway engineer Charles Fox was pressed into service to design its connections and joints and was ultimately responsible for the supervision of its prefabricated modular assembly.[34]

Early on in the process of the acquisition of the first tracts of land in the newly named "South Kensington," with active support from Albert, Cole actively campaigned to locate the proposed railway station at the South Kensington location.[35] Cole was prescient enough to link the site's development with a parallel proposal to construct a railway station that would act as an interchange between the trains from southern England and the metropolitan network. In the initial layout for South Kensington, Cole and Redgrave had marked the southwest corner of the plot as the site for a "Railway station." In 1864 the construction of the South Kensington station was authorized at the desired spot with the passage of the Metropolitan and Metropolitan Districts Railway's Act. Eventually, an underground passage was constructed from the railway station to the corner of the museum buildings, further strengthening the perception of the SKM as an organic element in Britain's imploding transport network. Note, how, in the following extract, dated March 1865, from notes prepared for the DSA's annual report, Cole distinguishes the transport network's capacity to displace geographical notions of center and periphery with regard to the museum's siting:

The inner circle of the metropolitan railways will bring the Museum into connection not only with all parts of the metropolis but with all parts of England. An exchange station will be within 200 yards of the Museum and probably a passage of communication will be made between it and the station. A map has been prepared which shows the proposed railway communication with this museum and other similar public institutions. *By means of this railway the South Kensington Museum will be practically as accessible as the very center of London, Smithfield, is theoretically.*[36] [e.a.]

For Cole, the SKM's relationship with the railway epitomized the DSA's own construction as a decentralized network; a feature that he was often fond of contrasting with the purported aloofness of the British Museum.[37]

The railway was instrumental not only in providing Britain's provincial audiences with a link to metropolitan taste but also in disseminating the SKM's own collections around the kingdom. From 1852 onward, the Department of Practical Art had its own "Circulation Department" for the loan of art objects from the Marlborough House collections to all the provincial schools. The department had its own specially designed railway truck, grandiosely titled the "Circulating Museum," which in the first four years of its existence was seen by as many as 307,000 people.

Figure 1.2 Artwork being unloaded for South Kensington Museum from rail wagon. Courtesy: V & A Images.

A significant portion of the displays carried in the truck was actually from the Great Exhibition, thus bringing the exhibition to provincial doorsteps in its aftermath. The DSA's extreme scruples regarding proper modes of arrangement and display resulted in the design of special, portable "South Kensington-type" glass cases, which could be dismantled and reassembled in provincial locations. Cole was emphatic that his linkage of circulation, transport, and museum would undo the hierarchy of city and country:

> But it is not only as a metropolitan institution that this Museum is to be looked at. Its destiny is rather to become the central storehouse or treasury of Science and Art for the use of the whole kingdom. As soon as arrangements are made, it is proposed that any object that can properly be circulated to localities, should be sent upon a demand being made by the local authorities. The principle is already fully at work. ... It may be hoped by this principle of circulation to stimulate localities to establish museums and libraries for themselves, or at least to provide proper accommodation to receive specimens lent for exhibition. ... Of course, any other spot, at Birmingham or Derby would serve equally well as a center for radiation. But the present site has in addition the public advantages of having a larger resident population than any provincial town, and it may be born in mind that half the population of the metropolis is made up of natives of the provinces.[38]

It is not just that the development at South Kensington appears to be in constant motion, a process-bound "state of permanent incompletion," refusing to "stand still long enough to be photographed," but that its very organization portends an unfixed location, no proper site as such where architecture can acquire the stability of its facade. The railway network provides the DSA with both the metaphor and the matériel for decentralization, for a virtual deterritorialization of the hierarchical relationship between metropolis and province, for the disintegration of center and periphery. The SKM is not a building so much as a node where several networks—technological, spatial, and pedagogical—tentatively coincide. It is not an incomplete building *but the incomplete, as system, that is built.*

The rhetoric of decentralization borne by the railway also pervaded the framing of the regional exhibitions held in India during the nineteenth century. During the Punjab Exhibition of 1864, the Agra Exhibition of 1867, and the Bharuch Exhibition of 1868–69, special trains were commissioned to bring mofussil and intercity audiences to the exhibitions. In most of the Indian exhibitions, the state's central role in the financing of both railway expansion and regional exhibitions led to an extraordinary level of collaboration between these two sectors. Not only were railways used to ferry regional exhibition-goers to the exhibition site but prefabricated building materials from the railways came very handy in the construction of the temporary buildings for these ephemeral events. Also no other building sector in India had quite the same level of expertise in ironwork, the preferred technology for large exhibition buildings. Cole's son, Henry Hardy Cole, was the designer and engineer of the Agra Exhibition of 1867, and his report is a testimony to this intimate relationship.[39] In the Bharuch Exhibition, not only was the exhibition site located on both sides of the railway station but, because the state fiscally guaranteed both railways and exhibitions in India, the Bombay, Baroda, and Central India Railways undertook to retransport all unsold goods from the exhibition to their points of origin.[40]

The principal function of the exhibitions in India was to tie together the diversity of different regional administrative entities and economies to the mainstream imperial economy. Exhibitions were therefore venues for introducing new kinds of technology in areas where no such modes of production existed, to harness and more strongly direct rural production. Unlike metropolitan exhibitions in Europe that paid much lip service to their pedagogical purpose, the Indian exhibitions until the mid-1870s were avowedly efforts to market British goods in the regional hinterlands. Local Indian goods from the surrounding or other regions were also displayed at these venues, but their primary message was to foster a sense of native commercial prosperity under British governance. The Indian exhibitions were spawned as full-blooded attempts at economic penetration, but political gains were another leitmotif. A particular example was the Punjab Exhibition of 1864, where recently quelled potentates from this newly expropriated province were given a particularly spectacular dose of imperial fanfare.

Perhaps the most striking example of the interreliance between exhibition, railway, and economic penetration was the Nagpur Exhibition of 1865. Nagpur, situated on the proposed route between the two administrative capitals of Bombay and Calcutta, also lay at the eastern end of the partially built Great Indian Peninsular Railway. The line was available for public travel until before Badnera only, short of the Wardha River and seventy miles west of Nagpur. The railway contractors took responsibility on themselves for conveying the goods for the exhibition—comprising in part heavy agricultural machinery—from Bombay to the river (forty miles from Badnera). Anticipating difficulties, several important pieces of machinery, including steam ploughs and cultivators, had been left behind. At the river the rails ended abruptly on a high embankment, and from this bluff the goods had to be lowered to the riverbed, where a temporary road had to be constructed across the riverbed and up the opposite bank. The goods that were carried across in this laborious manner included several pieces of ironwork weighing between one and three tons, including a five-horsepower steam engine. Subsequently, with the assistance of engineers from the railway, the goods were loaded onto bullock carts and hauled up the "common country cart track" for the remaining fifty miles, with several valleys and rivers impeding the journey. Throughout, the soft rural mud tracks could not support the bulky loads, and so the road had to be made literally "yard by yard" in advance of the caravans carrying the exhibits. On arrival in Nagpur, the goods were displayed in the semiconstructed and unoccupied buildings of the railway terminus, which served as the venue of the exhibition.[41]

Theorizing the Differential: Toward a Vulgar Conception

To be ontological does not yet mean to develop ontology.

—**Martin Heidegger**, *Being and Time*

Don't it always seem to go / That you don't know what you've got / Till it's gone.

—**Joni Mitchell**, *Big Yellow Taxi*

Kya tum history *ho, jo padhkar bhool jaaon*? (Are you a history book, that I can read and forget?)

—**Character from Hrishikesh Mukherjee film** *Golmaal*

The exhibition arrives *before* the railway, and in a manner of speaking, the train arrives, laden on bullock carts, before the rails are laid. There is no preordained temporal order of succession for a system—a mode of operation characterized precisely by discontinuities—to be put into place. The economic expansion of empire does not hinge on any particular progression that leads to a pregiven telos. The exhibition is an infrastructural element that is not reliant on any other particular mode of infrastructure; it can build its own foundations from the surrounding terrain. It builds its own inroads into the interior. What is activated here rather, is "culture"—definable here as the key word for differentia *as such*—and manifested here by the interaction of high technology with the earthen track and the bullock cart. In this sense, "culture" is always already an analogue of the machine, the efficient putting to work of the discretely empirical. (This will be studied in greater detail in the chapter on the cyborg.) Culture thus becomes the conduit through which economic penetration is delinked from any insfrastructural a priori. Bullock carts can take the place of railways, and the metropolitan exhibition can dissemble itself as a cattle fair. This infrastructural bricolage signals a basic indeterminacy in the very praxis of imperialism and capitalism. The exhibition/museum is not an a posteriori manifestation of some a priori epistemic dominant.

Imperialism expands *only* in the "absence of mind." It is not driven by any philosophical prolegomena or ontological authenticity. Its temporality is what Heidegger called vulgar: "irresolute" and "inauthentic" in its present. Its subjects can inhabit time without a predetermining horizon in mind;[42] it cannot be ascribed with a causality. The "grand narratives" of race, gender, class, and culture are the *effects* and *conduits* of imperialism rather than its primary determinants, explanations resorted to by those at advantage and disadvantage within it—the triumphalists and the victims, the Seeleys and the Saidians—to explain the inexplicability of the phenomenon.

Robinson and Gallagher's coinage of "informality" in their landmark 1953 essay "The Imperialism of Free Trade" can be said to attempt precisely such a "vulgar" theory. The authors aver that expansion was a steady facet, the most palpable and primary phenomenon, of the British Empire *irrespective* of policies at home, of whether public and political opinion ebbed or peaked in relationship to the acquisition and administration of new territory.[43] If, at the time of Columbus, there was a maximum of 24 acres of land to support each European, then in the short space of four centuries, this had been augmented by a fivefold increase in their "ghost acreage." By 1900 every European was the indirect beneficiary of production from 120 acres of global land.[44] This phenomenon did not have any direct relationship to conscious policies at the center. Compared with the modest acquisition of 5,700 square miles per year to British territory under the hawkish Disraeli, the Liberal governments under the anti-imperialist Gladstone expropriated territory at no less than the whopping amount of 87,000 square miles a year.[45] Robinson and Gallagher's strongest contention is that although imperialist expansion was thus a constant and persistent feature of the nineteenth century, the tactics by which this was achieved in every instance were *an exception* to their antecedents.

Robinson and Gallagher argued that empire is characterized more by its "informal" modes of persuasion and coercion than by the formal conquest of territory. Capital expands through the indirect exercise of power as much as through direct subjugation, as an exercise in differentiation rather than unification. Imperialism is not simply a variegated experience whose vicissitudes can be confined within the critical matrix of disciplinarity *but rather the very opening into variegation itself.* It is here that William Whewell's image of the exhibitions as *temporal* rather than spatial condenser is appurtenant. The colonized native is not cast into the immobilized freeze-frame of an unchanging antiquity. Human history, however differentiated, is everywhere on the move. The Great Exhibition is unique because it offers a dynamic cross section of this temporal difference.

Theorizing the Differential, Part II

Let us return now to the imagined domestic tableau of 1857: Cole and John Stuart Mill are having tea at the India Office. One may point out here that it was through Mill's intervention that the Company actively procured objects for the Great Exhibition, which also became the mainstay of the early SKM. In 1857, Cole, archbureaucrat with a professed dislike of bureaucratic interference in the private realm, is conceptualizing the biggest bureaucracy to be created in Britain in the nineteenth century. Mill, East India Company mandarin and philosopher of government, is unwittingly writing the epitaph of another bureaucracy. Jarring the idyll of this metropolitan setting are the distant, muffled echoes of the Indian Mutiny. The fortnightly dispatches bring in news of battles in place-names as yet unfamiliar to the British ear: Berhampur, Barrackpur, Meerut, Lucknow, Delhi, Jhansi, Gwalior. Even as it struggles to wrest control over a distant insurrection, the Company is reaching the end of its ideological tether in London. Parliament is moving in to curb its untrammeled power; when the Mutiny has been smothered, it will take away the company's monopoly over India and administer it directly. Mill is writing "A Constitutional View of the India Question" to thwart this move, in which he is laying out a retroactive manifesto of the East India Company at the end of its career.[46] Given the circumstances, this document is also the ratiocination of an ongoing genocide.

The journalist Marx all too quickly encapsulated the unraveled moment of the Mutiny as an indication of India's supersession of its precapital past into a globalized economic framework. For him, the staccato tone of the dispatches predicts the eventual rise of bourgeois nationalism in India. Marx is as unable to read the script of subaltern insurgency as his brutal colonial counterparts. Instead, he theorizes the Mutiny as manifested by a generalized crisis of capital as it encounters non-European modes of production.

Marx's understanding of temporal difference can be sketched out from his brief comments on competition from the notes in the *Grundrisse*. For Marx, the definition of competition, as the differentiation between various modes of production, becomes critical to a theory of capital that builds on discrepancies between different societal arrangements of production. Under examination here are the anthropological profiles that serve as the a priori for conventional political economy, the basis for the unilinear theories on the origins of capital. Marx points out that this anthropological singularity is in fact a metalepsis: what is deemed as the causal origin of economic development is in fact its "effect"; bourgeois relations are anachronistically substituted as the reason for capitalist accumulation when in fact they are its outcome. His critique is directed specifically at Mill:

> It is the fashion to preface a work of economics with a general part—and precisely this part figures under the title "production" (see for example J. St. Mill)—treating of the *general preconditions* of all production. … While this is of value as an insight, to elevate it to scientific significance would require investigations into periodization of *degrees of productivity* in the development of individual peoples, an investigation which lies outside the proper boundaries of the theme, but, in so far as it does belong there, must be brought in as part of the development of *competition* [e.a.], accumulation, etc. … The aim is, rather, to present production—see e.g. Mill—as distinct from distribution etc., as encased in eternal natural laws independent of history, at which opportunity *bourgeois* relations are then quietly smuggled in as the inviolable natural laws on which society in the abstract is founded. … In distribution, by contrast, humanity has allegedly permitted itself to be considerably more arbitrary.[47]

The "arbitrariness" and indeterminable causality that Marx attributes to human history is not a chance comment. In an illuminating passage in his "Economic and Philosophical Manuscripts," the early Marx had pointed out the aporia between the "open book" of the empirically irrecoverable minutiae of history and the "closed book" of disciplinary historiography. Historiography can "never become a real science with a genuine content. What indeed should we think of a science which *primly* abstracts from this large area of human labour, and fails to sense its own inadequacy?"[48] Marx is gesturing toward the discipline of political economy as well.

Marx, like Whewell, also sees the "human" subject everywhere on the move. The "present" for him is constituted as an assemblage of variegated temporal states. One such temporal state is what Marx names (only once in his corpus) the *Asiatic Mode of Production* (AMP). Marx uses the term AMP to signal not so much as a geographic category as a differentiation within the existing, that is, historically derived, production apparatus of capital.[49] Encompassing not only "India" and "China" but also the early Celts and Slavs within its rubric, "Asia" is an instance that enters capitalist production as a wholesale system of *communal access to* rather than *individual property in* land. It therefore appears as a *second* historical axis of the precapitalist–capitalist succession, other than the feudal–bourgeois transition in Europe.[50] Precapitalist India, the AMP, and the like cannot be equated with the European feudal relations of serf and landlord.

Marx is perspicuous enough to notice that this heterogeneity does not create an actual prophylaxis between extant production systems. Capital perforates the prophylaxis; "competition" is the mode through which capital forces different systems—Europe and Asia—in *direct* relation with each other. Competition is the suture through which different temporalities and histories now suddenly confront, in practice, their (theoretical) difference. Two heterogeneous entities are placed in a necessary unity. They are not opposed, and they do not constitute among themselves the negated poles of a dialectic. For Marx, world history is economically asymmetrical:

> Thus, for instance, if in England a machine is invented which deprives countless workers of bread in India and China, and overturns the whole form of existence of these empires, this invention becomes a world historical fact.[51]

This asymmetry within the world of historical fact can be established either by coercion (as in colonization) or by contract (as in trade). Both colonization and competition assist in the expansion of capital as global axiomatic, which brings these different histories, now metaleptically fused as successive "stages of production," into asymptotic relations with each other.[52] Marx reads imperialism like he reads the photograph: at its surface. If the photograph is comprehended in its capacity to capture the variegations of light, capital in its imperialist *Erscheinungsform* captures the variegations of the local. As universal "cause," capital behaves like the temporal equivalent of the snapshot.

For Marx, the genesis of the Mutiny comes from Britain's failure to read the text of Indian property relations correctly.[53] Marx's archives here are the official dispatches from the Indian administration; his insight on this score is entirely guided by the viewpoints of revenue officers in the Indian interior. His approach is to read these telegraphic missives as ideological fragments of what he presumes to be the unified cohesiveness of bourgeois political economy at the economic periphery. In attempting to demonstrate this cohesion, Marx cannot comprehend the tactical modifications of colonial administration as it adapts to different regional conditions and authorities. Perceiving colonialism only as conquest, he reduces the colonial venture to *direct* economic relations: administration is only taxation, political annexation is only confiscation of land. The actual incorporation of customary relations and the intricacies of *indirect* rule by the British legal–administrative apparatus remain beyond his reach.

Intermediacy and Indeterminacy

If you want a thing done do it as well as you can but at any rate if you can't do all you wish do as much as you can.

—Henry Cole

Once again to the tempest brewing in the teacup under Mill's angular nose: "It is now proposed to abolish this *intermediate* body," Mill writes in his "Constitutional View," opposing the parliamentary threat to dissolve the East India Company's monopoly in the affairs of India.[54] The ethical defense therein devolves from the principle of decentralization. Because Parliament is located in and (putatively) answerable only to the population of the Isles, its direct control of Indian administration risks subsuming the particularities of local Indian interests to metropolitan debates and concerns. For Marx, as we have seen, the cognitive failure of British administration in India stemmed from Anglocentrism. Unable to acknowledge this, Mill locates the pitfall in the devolution of state power. Faction-ridden Parliament lacks the requisite field exposure to varied regional conditions that is available only to Company officers in the interior. "Public opinion of England, unacquainted with Indian affairs, can only follow the promptings of those who take most pains to influence it, and these will generally be such as have some private interest to serve."[55] Far from providing it with the sage circumspection supposedly gained by distance (Mill is here going against the grain of his father's claims in his *History*),[56] parliamentary alienation from the ground situation in India will make the direct control of *everyday* Indian affairs victim to the domestic wrangles of London rather than Lucknow. "The public opinion of one country is scarcely any security for the good government of another."[57] On the other hand, when asking himself if the time is ripe to accord direct political representation to the people of India, such that Indians participate and bring their own concerns to Parliament like any other British constituency, this most "radical" of British muses responds "*not yet*." "I do not think that India has *yet* attained such a degree of civilization and improvement as to be ripe for anything like a representative system."[58] Marx is acute in his judgment of Mill in this respect. The average Indian subject cannot be accorded political representation because customary relations in India do not offer the linchpin prerequisite of representative rights as inherited in British custom: the (bourgeois) individual right to property.[59] The time of imperialism is out of synch.

The question is not whether Parliament has the *ultimate* authority to "superintend" the affairs of the company but whether it has the *intermediate* wherewithal to manage everyday events on the distant subcontinent.

Parliament can decide from the *hindsight* of knowledge only, thus allowing the moment to slide by in indecision. Company officers on the ground, on the other hand, are guaranteed adroitness and immediate efficacy, because their decisiveness stems from *experience*. Mill's name for this formalization of informal experience is "administration." Administration reveals the inadequacy of mere epistemology in managing the affairs of a people.

The legacy here is Edmund Burke's. "The rights of men are in a sort of *middle, incapable of definition,* but not impossible to be discerned."[60] [e.a.] If Mill uses the name "administration" to configure the yin of a governmental agency that mediates the indefinable and intermediary field of the local from above, Burke's term for the yang that moulds this discriminating exercise of power from below is "tradition."[61] Political acuity in Burke's view is the exercise of an organicist circumspection that does not violate the morphology of extant customary institutions. This is a felicity, "the providence of a vulgar prudence," that he finds lacking in the radical absolutism practiced by the Jacobins.[62] Burke's notion of tradition in its "indefinability" is not very different from Marx's "open book" of history, the infinite minutiae of human activity and relations that are lost in the coarse-grained sieve, the "closed book," of the abstractions of revolutionary constitutionalism.

Burke's emphasis on a mediated exercise of power finds its echo in the following statement by Mill: "A government must be composed out of the elements already existing in society, and the distribution of power in the constitution cannot vary much or long from the distribution of it in society itself."[63] For Mill, it is here that the East India Company has its calling—as supplement to remote parliamentary diktats—in its exercise of a "vulgar prudence." "It is the *administration,* not the *government* of India, which is carried on by the East India Company. ... The proposal is, that the superintendence should cease to be 'superintendence' and should become direct administration."[64] And elsewhere,

> Next to a national representation, the most important of all political principles is, that the only affairs directly administered by the Imperial Government should be the general affairs of the nation; and that all local affairs, whether they be those of any particular part of the United Kingdom or any foreign dependency, should, if possible, be administered by some intermediate body, constituted expressly for the purpose. ... [Parliamentary ministers] cannot possibly make themselves properly acquainted with the affairs of every separate locality or dependency of the empire.[65]

Burke's emphasis on tradition thus undergoes an exact reversal in Mill's thought in the articulation of Indian agency. India cannot have parliamentary ("national") representation because there is *as yet* no tradition of people's representational government in India. It is Britain's long-term vocation to advance that tradition in India. *In the meantime,* for the Mill defending his job—the question of political representation excepted—there is no other modal difference between the current *administration* of England and of India. In two successive essays, both written in 1858 in defense of the Company's continued tenure in India, he brings up an entire roster of examples to demonstrate the bifaceted character of British government in Britain.[66]

In Britain, the management of the poor is distributed between a centralized government board and the various local boards: "double government, divided responsibility," superintendence by a cabinet minister, "administration" by the local boards. Ditto for the sanitary administration of towns, where responsibility is shared between a parliamentary board and the various corporations: double government, divided responsibility. Education, railway, even the management of lighthouses are all governed by this principle, superintendence by the center, administration by the local. The examples proliferate until Mill has us end up with the colonies. The Company is therefore only doing in India what is already being done in Britain. The administration of the colony should also be an instance of divided responsibility. Unlike Burke, who cites "Mahomedan law" as universally regulative in Asia and refers colonial officials to its literal text,[67] Mill views "India" only as an aggregation of the local. It cannot have access to the generality—the abstract constitutionality—of the universal.

The Copula of Bureaucracy

"Administration" occupies the intermediary ground between the (irreducible yet unattainable) abstractions of constitutionalism and the (lived yet indeterminate) dispositions of culture. It behaves as a copula, a connective element of identification between the state and culture, between governance and tradition. And because *direct* political representation in the case of the colony is infinitely deferred owing to customary differences in the right to property, what devolves to it is sheer bureaucracy. Bureaucracy in the context of the nineteenth century is thus radically redone. It emerges in the precise area where the state encounters the factor of culture in the expansion of its demographic polity. Liberal bureaucracy is the epitome of "vulgar prudence," a state apparatus "in the middle," an entity coterminous with yet not entirely assimilable to the singular expansion of the state apparatus into a representative system.

In the Indian context, one needs to distinguish the different phases of according "native agency" in indirect rule, from the early Orientalism of the eighteenth century to the differentiated formalization of customary legal codes in the mid-nineteenth century. There are significant distinctions between the imitative Nabob culture of the early days of the Company, an era where officials would dissemble themselves as natives, and this later bifaceted character of administration through traditional authority. The persistent makeover of imperial in the latter phase through the appropriation of local and customary law is demonstrated by a whole range of examples: the recoding of Hindu and Islamic personal law, the doubling of political and economic offices between the bureaucratic and the village network (e.g., the *patwari cess*), the transition from the so-called "Regulation" provinces (e.g., Bengal) to the "non-Regulation" provinces (e.g., Punjab).

When the Punjab was taken over by the British after the last of the Sikh wars in 1849, its designation as one of the new non-Regulatory provinces meant that its administrative structure was thinned to the bare minimum to shore up the native apparatus to manage the traditional aspects of the polity. Now that a certain hierarchy had been formalized for the dissemination of authority in which the native had a clearly articulated place, the Punjabi could, it was hoped, govern himself, insofar as the immediate exigencies of local self-government were concerned. This system of "double government, divided responsibility" had clear advantages: to establish a full-fledged direct governing apparatus that would penetrate into the everyday affairs of the indigene required more infrastructural involvement than any profit-motivated colonial government could afford. This is the principal characteristic of the colony: as a joint stock company only barely covered over by the sheen of a governing polity, it cannot accrue large amounts of public debt. The indigene is thus culturally framed through the invocation to traditional autonomy precisely at the moment that it confronts the economic equation of increased budgetary outlays. In the Punjab, somewhat elaborate systems were established to ascertain the nuances of local custom, whether these pertained to matters of marriage, inheritance, adoption, disposition of property (testamentary or other), contracts, sale, mortgage, debt, commercial usury, or the creation of intermediate juridical and administrative strata from within the population. Because external interference in native personal affairs risked antagonizing the population, the nonregulatory framework ensured that customary matters remained outside in the particular *yet on the whole within* the administrative apparatus. John Lawrence, chief commissioner of the Punjab from 1853 onward, described this arrangement in the following terms:

> Our civil system may appear rough and ready; whether it would be suited to other provinces, in a different stage of civilization and with a different machinery at command, may be a question; but in the

Punjab it attains the broad and plain object aimed at, and without doubt gives satisfaction to the people.[68]

This "rough and ready" approach to administration underlines a mode of political bricolage that defines all aspects of colonial functioning. The experimentation undergone in India would develop into a full-blown bifurcation in Africa at the turn of the century, which Mahmood Mamdani has described as the tendency toward thin administration on the ground manifested as a system of divided control throughout the continent.[69] Imperialism insinuates itself at the ground level by dissembling itself as the continuum of what looks like "tradition": the structure of property, the institution of law, the sanctification of religion. The subject of imperialism, in center or periphery, construes the rough conditions of its present in terms of what appears as the "normal."

The term "gone native" is a tautology. *All* imperialism is imperialism gone native. At the ground level, imperialism functions without a game plan: it can act resolutely on the ground without reconstructing its determining cause. Heidegger had averred that there is no ontological necessity to comprehend ontology. Imperialism is also able to operate without a developed theory of imperialism. The normative agent of imperialism, the Indian, the African, the colonial bureaucrat in the interior, can act in the interest of imperial expansion without a sufficient grasp of their historical "moment" or without an "authentic" experience of their time. Imperialism covers over its determining cause, that is, the crisis-prone expansion of capital, to establish its primacy in an even more pervasive manner. It needs no "ontic validity"[70] in its agents for them to be able to perform their teleological functions. The colonized can (and does) always act "as if [colonization] made no difference."[71] The metropole need imbibe no history books; one *can do* with reading the news, even if it arrives a couple of weeks late from Lucknow.

Temporizing South Kensington, Part III: The Recourse to System

> To offer any very decided opinion upon the results of the Exhibition would probably be premature. Those results, whatever they may be, must develop themselves indirectly and in the course of time, and we only infer what they may be.
>
> —**Theodore Hope,** *Report of the Broach Exhibition, 1868–69*

The bifaceted character of administration laid out previously needs to be kept in mind when trying to understand the development of vanguard liberal bureaucracies of the mid-nineteenth century such as the DSA.

As we saw in the introduction, Rafael Cardoso Denis has characterized the emergence of the DSA as a "bureaucracy by stealth." Far from loud assertions of liberal dogma or strident statements about Victorian "values," South Kensington strategy can be essentially described in terms of a "double think" that was intrinsic to liberal reformulations of the state in the 1840s and 1850s. A regulative institution such as the DSA could be formed only by the likes of Cole and Mill using the ideology of individualism to weaken the formal structures of state power precisely to make these structures amenable to the play of laissez-faire, *informal* interests without the constraints of institutional regulation.

Denis offers an analogy here between mid-Victorian mores and the neo-liberalism practiced by global financial agencies and superbureaucracies such as the International Monetary Fund, the World Bank, and the World Trade Organization in the 1980s and 1990s. South Kensington can be seen, comparably, as an official *ruse* to facilitate the play of private, commercial interests in determining state policy and the orchestration of "reform." This double movement, the ability to sequester tremendous power within a relatively small administrative structure, Denis contends, is premised less on actual institutional precepts than on the ability of its officers, "particularly Henry Cole … to muddle along," overcoming the obstacles that stood in the way of their expansion.

No single constitutional document guided the development of a liberal bureaucracy such as the DSA. Its success was fundamentally premised on an ability to gradually encroach upon new institutional boundaries through constant reorientations and negotiations. Note the affinity with colonial strategy in Denis's observation about the DSA: "What could not be won by force was won by diplomacy, and vice versa. The end result was an administrative empire vaster than any that had preceded it, and twice as slow to come apart."[72] One need not wait for a Vladimir Illych Lenin to make the detection that a decentralized network is precisely a foil for increased centralization. DSA officials such as David Lindsay Crawford were proudly asserting the same a half-century before:

> In England we centralize a great deal in matters of art; but then we have devised a system by which we can decentralize our centralization most advantageously.[73]

In the nineteenth century, the bureaucracy is saddled with the task of negotiating the gap between constitutional minimalism and the heterogeneous demands of custom, that is, culture. The bureaucratic "exigency," so to speak, stems from the prosaic understanding that abstract constitutions are fundamentally inadequate in articulating the concrete powers and functions of government. For Burke, therefore, it was just as well that England does not have a written constitution. England should be governed by institution rather than by constitution. In other words, there is no "contradiction" in the fact that liberal bureaucracy says one thing and does another. Constitutive contradiction, "muddling along," describes both its functioning and its very function. Its *indeterminacy* is predicated by its *intermediacy*.

In 1854 Cole was approached by the Board of Trade to produce a report on the establishment of a permanent civil service. Much of his response reflects the mood of his time to streamline hierarchies so as to endow each function with transparent forms of accountability.[74] The radical credentials of Cole's formulation of the bureaucracy should not be underestimated, given the fact that civil service in Britain until the 1830s hardly merited the terms *civil* or *service*. Traditionally, bureaucratic appointments incorporated several norms appropriated from custom: inheritance, apprenticeship, and local influence. In many cases, government positions did not carry a salary; appointees extracted their livelihood instead by deducting a percentage from collected revenue.[75] The authority of these officials was also customary, devolving from the Crown. With the increased influence of commercial and middle classes in Parliament, it was inevitable that this archaic structure was seen as the repository of "jobbery" and sinecureship in public life. As a result, we have "the century of Northcote–Trevelyan," named after two India hands and members of the Board of Trade, Charles Trevelyan and Stafford Northcote, who were commissioned by Parliament in 1854 to report on the reorganization of the permanent civil service.[76]

Cole's recommendations, produced in the same year as the Trevelyan–Northcote report and with more than a nod to the latter's points of emphasis, placed their thrust on instituting a system of civil service examinations and basing appointments and promotions on merit. Predictably, Cole offered the Schools of Design under his superintendence as the paradigmatic example on which to model change in other bureaucracies. On one hand, there was the need to establish uniformity and probity in public affairs, to undo the practice of appointing sinecures; on the other hand, this could be achieved only if localized agencies were properly induced into the business of preparing candidates for public service, be they at the level of messengers or the prestigious India writers. Cole could almost have been talking about the DSA when he suggested that this induction be achieved through the institution of standard examinations and certifications at the national level, the responsibility for administering that would devolve to local bodies. Cole pays copious lip service to liberal principles of safeguarding local autonomy. Because local institutions would be the best judges of their needs, this principle would also have the serendipitous effect—Mill's political economy is pivotal in this conception—of causing an immaculate match between supply and demand. However, local agencies could not be entirely entrusted with the work of determining general policy. Cole makes a direct appeal to Mill's theory of education when, "remembering the infant stumbles before it walks upright," he emphasizes that aspects of the national good such as education are a state prerogative.

The DSA is the felicitous example that is designed to flounder through these two conflicting imperatives before a more sure-footed polity comes along, "*meanwhile, we have to administer the mixed principles adopted in this department.*"[77]

> I may say that the Department maintains two principles of administration which are essential to all sound management, and both of nearly equal importance. All administration carried on either by central governments, or parish vestries, or joint stock companies, to be good, must insure, first, responsibility as direct, clear, and as defined and individual as possible, and second, full publicity. ... Publicity is indeed the keystone of this Department; and it can only prosper in proportion as the public is made acquainted with its proceedings and values them. ... It may be asserted that *there is not a single detail in the action* of this Department—in its schools, examinations, award of prizes, museums, and libraries—which does not invite the fullest publicity. Every purchase in the Museum and Library is publicly exposed, and may be criticised. Even the prices of the articles are published.[78]

Note the direct affinity here with John Stuart Mill's famous exposition on the role of "writing" as the primary mode of ensuring accountability in colonial government:

> I conceive that there are several causes as to why I think the Government of India is being carried out satisfactorily; probably the most important is, that the whole Government of India is carried on in writing. All the orders given, and all the acts of the executive officers, are reported in writing, and the whole of the original correspondence is sent to the Home Government; so that *there is no single act done in India,* the whole of the reasons for which are not placed on record. This appears to me a greater security for good government than exists in almost any other government in the world, because no other probably has a system of recordation so complete.[79]

The colony is in the vanguard of the metropole in managerial experimentation. "There is not a single detail in the action," "there is no single act done" without the sanction of writing. Indeed, writing is the very sanction on which the act is based. Writing intervenes in the space of constitutionality; the recorded archive becomes the open-ended instrument of a future retrospective justice *that also sets out its justification in advance.* The claim to the comprehensive post hoc retrospection ("no single act … not placed on record") of bureaucratic behavior within the official record is pivotal for the possibility of ad hoc action.[80] It is easier to beg forgiveness than to seek permission, to kick the representational can of worms down the road. The written archive renders bureaucratic practice into a procedural, provisional, "actionable" exigency.

Bureaucratic writing sequesters bureaucracy from the responsibilities of either origins or ends. In being set to prose, bureaucracy becomes a format for research into the indigene that constantly modifies its assumptions based on the apprehension of new experience. The circumspection of the committee report, the urgency of the telegrammatic dispatch, and the normativity of the rotational circular become critical instruments to move government into different modes of temporal behavior. Writing enters colonialism into the discontinuous structure of a system.[81] There is no propaedeutic field in bureaucratic functioning; in Seeley's words the empire has "no analogy." One can therefore enter the colonial archive at any point of its assembly. Writing is thus an instance of how bureaucracy appears as the copula of governmentality, the connective element that identifies power with, and therefore *as, the local.*

Race, Sect, and Caste—Englishman

> With reference to your letter No. 1048, dated 12th April 1893, and telegram dated 24th *idem,* regarding the verification of Mr. J.L. Kipling's service … I enclose a copy of a letter, No. 4859 … which was communicated to this office by [the] Financial Department, endorsement No. 89.[82]

The impetus to create schools of industry in India was triggered by news of the Great Exhibition and the establishment of the Department of Practical Art. Charles Trevelyan urged as much to a parliamentary committee on India in 1852:

> I would make the institution at Marlborough House the model for a College of Art. Art is taught there systematically. I would establish an institution at Calcutta on that model … for it is our duty to give our Indian fellow-subjects every possible aid in cultivating those branches of art that still remain to them.[83]

Before this intervention, only one comparable school existed: the School of Industry in Madras, founded in 1850 by Alexander Hunter, a medical surgeon. The school was, however, more of a "civilizing" station for "vagrant" children (e.g., Eurasians and orphans), with the intent of educating them in remunerative vocations. Trevelyan's call was answered in 1854 by the establishment in Calcutta of a School of Art. This example was followed shortly in Bombay by a Parsi businessman Jamsetjee Jejeebhoy, who had made his money as a trader and financier of the British opium-running operations in China and had been awarded a knighthood for his collaboration.[84] Jejeebhoy's appeal to the governor general to allow him to endow a school in Bombay made a direct appeal to the precedent set by the Great Exhibition, sketching out a vision for improving the extant artisanal industries of India.[85] The confraternity between the Board of Trade and the India Office offered a ready-made nexus by which the Indian government could draw on DSA expertise and modules to provide personnel and materials for institutions of technical learning in India. On their part, DSA officials contrived in various ways to gain an indirect handle over artisanal production in India. This was in the interest of the "preservationist" attitude toward native political economy and obtained large numbers of specimens for display in the DSA schools, museums, and exhibitions in Britain. The Royal Engineer Corps was another nexus through which this collaboration expressed itself, because its officers' knowledge of drawing made them ideal seconds to both the DSA and the newly established Archaeological Survey of India. In 1867 Henry Hardy Cole, son of our Cole and a lieutenant in the corps, was appointed to the survey in the North-West Provinces, where he was given responsibility for organizing the Agra Exhibition and obtaining art wares for the Paris Exposition, both held in that year. As we have seen before, Cole Jr. also designed the buildings for the Agra Exhibition. He would later become the superintendent of the Archaeological Survey in the North-West, an institutional involvement the ramifications of which we will look at in greater detail in the postscript.

The links between the DSA and the Indian administration did not end there. In 1880 Caspar Purdon Clarke, a DSA-trained architect and director of the Indian section at the SKM, was sent to India to purchase contemporary artisanal wares that would make the museum's collection comprehensive. Clarke spent two years in India, where he bought no less than 3,421 items for the museum's collections. In addition he performed a host of other surveying and consulting assignments, under the guise of a so-called second secretary in the diplomatic service.

The DSA's early resolve to base art education in India on Indian sources of art is therefore as much a consequence of the bihanded bureaucratic sensibility mentioned earlier as a reflection of the praise showered on Indian artisanal wares by prominent aesthetes at the Great Exhibition. In the next few chapters, we will examine the manner in which this aesthetic appreciation expressed certain theories of intentionality, productivity and agency rather than any historicist judgments about Indian art. In any case, the emphasis on an Indian curriculum was less national in character than differentiated into the regional genius attributed to the surrounding of each school. John Griffiths, principal of the J.J. School, retrospectively noted as much at a conference in 1892:

> I can see no good whatever to be gained by associating by Committees in England, for they cannot possibly know anything practically of the diversified conditions of the art industries in the several provinces of India. From the reports of the Proceedings of these Committees, it will be found that many of the members talk of Indian Art as if it were a concrete art, and not as diversified and marked by as many styles as the art of Europe. Mr. Kipling at Lahore, Mr. Jobbins at Calcutta, Dr. Hendley at Jeypore, and Mr. Havell at Madras, are far more likely to know practically what are the local requirements necessary for the encouragement of art than any Committee in England.[86]

In the provinces directly under British governance, the character of technical and art institutions reflected the regional political structure. The creation of the Mayo School of Art in Lahore, for instance, was clearly seen as a reflection of the province's non-Regulatory status. Its mission, headed by John Lockwood Kipling, transferred from the Bombay school, was to reinvigorate the existing artisanal groups of the Punjab and North-West Frontier Province rather than training students into new vocations.[87]

When Kipling retired in 1892 from his position in Lahore, the list of responsibilities that was advertised for his replacement gives us an insight into the expansive breadth of the DSA's influence on bureaucratic vision in India. In addition to being principal of the Mayo School, Kipling was also the curator of the Lahore Museum. His post required him to make routine sorties into the interior parts of the surrounding region, both to ascertain the pools of rural skill and craft and to supervise the existing vocational schools and jail manufactories inside the entire province. Kipling also frequently scoured the province for specimens to be displayed in the various regional museums and exhibitions, in addition to fulfilling procurement requests from the DSA museums and exhibitions in Britain. As an official of the Revenue and Agriculture Department (which oversaw the "Museums and Exhibitions" heading), he was required to run regular workshops with provincial artisans. These were reciprocal exercises wherein the artisans were seen as availing opportunities to modernize their techniques, while Kipling documented their extant skills, and their potentials for further commercial development, for the government records. Moreover, he was called upon to write articles and edit the *Journal of Indian Art,* a publication of the Revenue and Agriculture Department strongly patronized by the DSA, in addition to having his students prepare drawings for publication.[88] Kipling also oversaw the engagement of Mayo School students in the ornamentation of several public works projects and elite residences. This included a room in the "Indian" style for Victoria's palace at Osborne, delegated to and executed by Kipling's trusted assistant and successor, Bhai Ram Singh.

Although Kipling was innovative in his own right, much of the outline of his duties was systemic rather than an outcome of personal initiative. The dissonance between the left-hand categories and the right-hand entries in Kipling's application for pension demonstrates this bihanded sensibility and nativized sheen of British administration on the ground:

Application for Pension

1. *Name of applicant*—John Lockwood Kipling, C.I.E.
2. *Father's name*—Joseph Kipling
3. *Race, sect and caste*—Englishman
4. *Residence, showing Village and Pergunnah*—London.[89]

It is from this bifaceted and hybridized periphery of empire that Kipling's son Rudyard would use his father's museum as the launching pad for the story of an Irish orphan, a subject uncoupled from patronymic moorings, who not only dissembles himself as Indian but in fact can think as one.

An AbConstructed *Cogito*

Only point a camera at a native, and notwithstanding his natural grace, suppleness of limb, and easy carriage and bearing when taken unawares, from fear of being shot, or converted into some uncouth animal by means of necromancy, he becomes on seeing you as *rigid* as the camera-stand, or moves away altogether or neither moves nor stays. All the posturing and explaining and reasoning and coaxing or offers of money you can bestow upon him in the course of an hour or two will not induce him to *unbend*.[90]

Colonialism must bend to make the native unbend. It will not do to have the native freeze into an immobile, lifeless stance, reduced to epistemic certainty. The political philosopher Uday Mehta has argued that liberal philosophy of the British Empire drew on an anthropological minimalism that derived more from British custom than from a critique fashioned on universalism.[91] Although mostly untheorized by philosophers or political thinkers during its era, the British Empire's reliance on liberalism as its principal ethical mechanism stemmed from liberalism's marked deflection *away* from the universal. This distance, or rather this *ablation,* is foundational for an imperialism that casts the indigene into a temporality of perpetual deferral: the native can "not yet" represent itself as subject. In Mill's "not yet," we see a hint of the great bitemporal imaginaries of empire, from the orphan Kim dressed as a native, the Englishman "gone native," or Macaulay's dream of an administrative class "Indian in blood, English in taste" to the prejudices against Irish speech as suffused with irony and pretense.

It is this immense bihanded machine that needs to be kept in mind when one reviews the colonial interest in reviving the traditional bases of native arts and crafts. Throughout the nineteenth century (and certainly until the present time) the lack of clear differentiation between "modern" labor and craft meant that the aesthetic appreciation for nonmodern craft could become the foil for expropriating labor outside of bilateral contractual arrangements. For instance in India the wholesale shoring up of customary authority in the rural interior allowed the administration and companies to sequester large labor pools for work on building India's substantial railway network with relatively little outlay. Through modest payments made to village chiefs or clan patriarchs, large numbers of men, women, and children were employed in railway work with little or no compensation. This relationship could easily be reversed into an aesthetic frame: in Kipling's *Journal of Indian Art,* Indian carpenters building a wood model of the Howrah railway station in Calcutta are depicted almost as if they were traditional artisans building the railway.

The network supplements the staging of tradition, which in turn itself appears as an elusory network whose nodes appear to be perpetually eluding the light of rational critique. The network is a grafting device that serves as a *ruse* to open up customary spheres of production into a manageable field. The organizers of the 1910 United Provinces Agricultural and Industrial Exhibition in Allahabad recognized as much when they located the exhibition at this important railway confluence at the time of the Kumbh Mela, the highest-attended Hindu religious festival in northern India:

> It must not be assumed that the influence of the Exhibition will be limited to the United Provinces. Allahabad is centrally situated for the whole of the Northern and Central India: it is served by six lines of railway, and has few rivals as a resort of pilgrims. The date of the Exhibition has been fixed so as to coincide with the chief pilgrimage of the year; it is estimated that during its course Allahabad will be visited by about half-a-million pilgrims from all parts of India, altogether apart from the visitors attracted by the Exhibition itself. In India these pilgrimages are recognised to be most efficient dis-

Figure 1.3 Craftsmen building the model of the Howrah Station, the terminus for the East Indian and Bengal Nagpur Railway. From *Journal of Indian Art*, XIV, no. 117 (January 1912).

seminators of information, a machine that is favourably noticed at the Exhibition will be discussed in many hundreds of villages scattered over the country.[92]

We repeat: imperialist expansion is not just differentiated but differentiat*ing*; the calculation of "difference" is part and parcel of the strategies of imperial expansion. Rather than introduce a global sensibility of standardized time, it introduces the global subject into a kind of temporal indeterminacy.

It has been noted that the unplanned and ad hoc demolitions and rebuilding of nineteenth-century London caused a greater displacement of population than Baron Haussman's "surgical" incisions into the urban fabric of Paris.[93] The radical visibility of change in the French capital, along with the shifts of political power that accompanied it, has appeared as an attractive foil for historiographies of transition. Although the latter occupies a significant place in the history of modernity through *national* or statal determinations, the localized character of and relatively tempered resistance to London's urban transformations offer perhaps a better template of the *global* frame of imperial expansion.

If imperialism were to have a motto, Kant's formulation of purposiveness from the Third Critique would not be inappropriate: "Die Zweckmässigkeit kann also ohne Zweck sein" ("Purposiveness can exist outside of purpose"). Imperialism does not cast the history of the world into a linear teleology. Its vectors are not constricted and repressive but open ended, liberal, and empiricist. This very empiricism leads to the invention of "tradition" as a rubric for systemically appropriating anthropological variegations on the ground. In this sense, "tradition" is not the "hidebound [and] cramped" enclosure of dead habit, as John Stuart Mill described it, but the opening onto differentiated spheres of production. The precepts of imperial administration neither liberate the indigene into becoming a free agent nor freeze their agency into photographic immobility. Had colonial officials found no artisanry in the vast territories under imperial control, it would have become necessary *to invent some*. The "artisan" is the conceptual rubric used within modernity to produce differentiated arenas of informal labor.

Tradition is the precise imprint of imperial modernization on the colony; as such this segues well into the great nationalist imaginaries of the early twentieth century. One response that would reverse the tradition–modernity dialectic and forge the artisan into a figure of resistance is Mohandas Karamchand Gandhi. Like imperialism, nationalism too would radically dissemble itself into the image of a lowly spinner. But we will leave this for another chapter.

CHAPTER 2

Architecture Upside Down:
The Morphotropy of Value

I paint on the floor and this isn't unusual—the Orientals did that.

—Jackson Pollock, in interview with William Wright

With [Hegel, the dialectic] is standing on its head. It must be turned right side up again, if you would discover the rational kernel within the mystical shell.

—Karl Marx, *Capital*

This "turning right side up again" is merely gestural, even metaphorical, and it raises as many questions as it answers. How should we really understand its use in this quotation? It is no longer a matter of a general "*inversion*" of Hegel, that is, the inversion of speculative philosophy as such. ... Anyone who claims purely and simply to have inverted speculative philosophy (to derive, for example, materialism) can never be more than philosophy's ... unconscious prisoner.

—Louis Althusser, *For Marx*

There is a yarn about contemporary art that we all know, one that reveals all its stereotypes. A group of people is standing in a gallery, admiring a canvas on a wall. The canvas is square and white; centered exactly in its middle is a large red circle. As the visitors discuss the painting, a frowsy person enters the gallery, takes one look at the painting, and throws a fit. This is the artist. Screaming, he demands to see the curator. The curator arrives and asks him what the problem is. "Ze painting," the artist exclaims, "it is ze … 'ow you say, *upside down*!!"

There is also the inevitable moment, in any art or architectural lecture when the slide drops, wrong side up, into the slot. Hesitating for an instant, the lecturer decides to go with it, with a quip that the inadvertent inversion does not affect the brunt of her argument. Certainly, in the case of a painting by Jackson Pollock, this affirmation of the unintentional would have some critical weight. There, nonintention is performed by placing the canvas on the floor and pouring paint from all sides, depriving the canvas of its transferred epithet, its "upright" posture. There are other, distinctly modern, examples. The surrealist interest in suspension of the temporal moment—embodied best in Philippe Halsman's *Dali Atomicus* or Duchamp's upturned urinal—presages the late-modernist linkage of artistic subversion and vertical orientation.

There is an isomorphism that cannot be ignored between this kind of vanguardist aesthetic that persistently inverts "conventional" relationships of form as the unraveling of intent and the early Marx's poetic pronouncement that the "money-form" was turning relationships "upside down."[1] The isomorphism stems from the status quo being attributed with a compositional composure that is weighed down, tied to the ground, by a putative gravity. The composure is broken, the gravity is up*ended* when an unexpected term comes into the equation. This compositional form that speaks of "ends" and orientations—of tops and bottoms, of foundations and structural rectitude—we will call, later in this chapter, *morphotropy*. But first a historical road map of this trope will be necessary, for this is indeed a tropology in the literal sense of the word. The road travels through the Department of Science and Art (DSA):

> Fact, fact, fact. … You are to be in all things regulated and governed by fact. We hope to have, before long, a board of fact, composed of commissioners of fact, who will force the people to be a people of fact, and nothing but fact. You must discard the word Fancy altogether. You have nothing to do with it. You are not to have, in any object of use or ornament, what would be a contradiction in fact. You don't walk upon flowers in fact; you cannot be allowed to walk upon flowers in carpets. You don't find that foreign birds and butterflies come and perch upon your crockery. You never meet with quadrapeds going up and down walls; you must not have quadrupeds represented upon walls. You must use for all these purposes, combinations and modifications (in primary colours) of mathematical figures which

are susceptible of proof and demonstration. This is the new discovery. This is fact. This is taste.[2]

An unnamed gentleman fulminates with these words when visiting M'Choakumchild's classroom with Thomas Gradgrind, the inspector of schools in Coketown, the setting for Charles Dickens's novel *Hard Times*. Sissy Jupe, "Girl number twenty," has had the temerity to opine, in response to the gentleman's question, that she would carpet her room, or her husband's, with representations of flowers. We will come shortly to Kant's differentiation between flowers as "free natural," therefore *pure,* as opposed to *adherent* beauty. The previous passage is significant for quite another reason. In Dickens's notes for the chapter from which the previous extract is taken, we find the words "Marlborough House Doctrine." As we remember, Marlborough House was a domicile of the DSA in its earlier incarnations. Sure enough, in the margin next to the unnamed apoplectic gentleman of this passage, there is the telltale scrawl "Cole."[3]

The previous chapter looked at the manner in which the mobilization of discontinuity was felicitous for a global theory of decentralized administration. In this chapter, we will see the manner in which natural and aesthetic philosophy of the eighteenth century became "regulative" for the industrial conundrums of the nineteenth century. Central to this superimposition was a theory of change, within both nature and the commodity, that sought to bring perceived discontinuities within a theoretical unity. As we shall see, the particular aesthetic rubric that emerges in the nineteenth century to capture these dissonances of part and whole, aesthetic and production, is the "pattern."

The first part of the chapter concentrates on developments in natural philosophy in the wake of Kant. It looks at the manner in which Kantian and post-Kantian thought framed nature as both absolute—categorically invariable—in its universality *and* changeable in its parts, thus occasioning a need to develop an analytical complex that would encompass these two not-quite-opposed categories. In the later part of the chapter, we will see how this analytical complex insinuates itself into a discourse of design through its aesthetic corollaries. This "applied" field is both quite against the grain of Kantian thought—which strictly interdicted any applied potentials of the aesthetic—and yet ironically produced by it. The satirical paragraph that we have already cited from Dickens could serve as a symptomatic entry point to precisely this sort of structured paradox in mid-nineteenth-century aesthetics.

There is much in Dickens's caricature of Henry Cole that consigns it to just that. Dickens, as we shall see in chapter 4, had collaborated with

Cole since the mid-1840s. As co-member of the committee for the Great Exhibition as well as others, Dickens had many opportunities to observe Cole from close quarters. The distorted portrait of Cole has as much to do with Dickens's sententious style of depicting class and power relations as with the misplaced ascription of an overtly Utilitarian ethos ("Fact, fact, fact…") to Marlborough House doctrine. Notwithstanding this misconception, however, the paragraph cited previously is remarkably astute in capturing an entire complex of notions that exercised mid-nineteenth-century aesthetic thought, and certainly that of the DSA. Some of the components of this complex are recognizable. The aesthetic of the carpet, languishing beneath one's boots, cannot draw on the classical verticality of the picture plane, which is the conventional frame to address flowers and nature. The objects of the interior, subject to the regular inversions—the toppling and tipping over, the folds and wrinkles—of everyday use undo the inexorable verticality of the picture plane.

For mid-nineteenth-century aesthetes, a new set of rules of the aesthetic, "which are susceptible of proof and verification," become necessary to assimilate this wobbly morphotropy of the everyday object. The DSA complex constitutes one attempt to frame the rules; there will be many others. This complex, a discursive response to a particular historical predicament posed by industrial capitalism, is epistemological inasmuch as it is aesthetic; it is in fact expressive of a desired association between the two—more than just these two, because the complex ties together quite diverse fields of interest. In the nineteenth century, these can be concatenated as the following: the creation of principles for the design of everyday objects to construct the grounds of public taste; the reliance on epistemological frameworks of verifiability or "fact" as the template for such principles; the elevation of nature within aesthetic discourse as a preexisting critical format rather than as a mere object for pictorial imitation; and, last, the recourse to geometry—"mathematical figur[ation]"—as both the model and the object of this desired set of rules.

It is to this last conceit that we will first turn our attention. Kant addresses geometry in his First Critique, or the *Critique of Pure Reason*, and flowers in the Third Critique, or the *Critique of Judgement*.

"… A Kind of Vertigo"

Geometry is a kind of harmony.

—**Victor Hugo,** *The Hunchback of Notre-Dame*

In the second preface (1781) to the *Critique of Pure Reason* (the First Critique) Kant modeled his exposition of the faculty of reason on the example of geometry: "left groping about for a long time (chiefly among the Egyptians)," geometry found its true course when put into the hands of "that admirable people the Greeks," who developed it along the "secure path of a science."[4]

Geometry is critical in Kant's schema of the critiques. "Nature," as repository of objective plenitude par excellence, triggers, by means of representation, a plenitude ("manifold") of intuitions within the subject. Without organizing ("synthesizing") this plenitude into the unity of a concept, understanding cannot create the framework for judging its own "knowledge." The name for this framework of judgment, or verifiability, is "reason." As such, reason cannot rely on the empirical chance insights of externally determining objective stimuli. It must create its own *internally* consistent set of principles without any objective reference whatsoever, residing entirely within the subject. The paradigm for such an internally consistent set of principles without objective reference is geometry.

Geometry can be used to describe the entire diversity of objective phenomena, from macroscopic to microscopic infinity, without relying in the least on external, objective conditions. If the critical elucidation of reason will now require a lengthy exegesis, it is because the originary historical deduction of geometry is mired in myth or, rather, is mysterious. That this move, from empirical observation to transcendental abstraction, was indeed a deduction relies on the ascription to this move of an agency, through the provisional exigency of the inventor's proper name:

> A new light broke upon the first person who demonstrated the isosceles triangle (whether he was called "Thales" or had some other name).[5]

In the next chapter, this nominalism, this "Thales," will be brought to the dock by Edmund Husserl in his phenomenological critique of Kant's transcendental deduction.[6] The proper name is the conduit through which the Greeks could develop geometry toward a paradigmatic critical system. This exigency being established as such (notwithstanding its actual lack of veracity), the *chronological* progression of human history could now be measured by the yardstick of the *logical* advances in geometrical principle. Pythagoras is not just a proper noun but a nomenclature for a coterminus advance of geometry and history. The Greeks are afforded historical agency, because their story can be written according to the deductive norms of a historiographic method modeled on the advances of geometric principle.

This method-derived agency reassured Eugène-Emmanuel Viollet-le-Duc, architectural ideologue, restorer, and author of the *Dictionnaire Raisonné,* at a vulnerable moment when his intellect seemed to give way when faced with the intricate patterns of ornamental geometry from Islamic Egypt:

> Those of us who have tried to draw some of these Arab ornamentations we refer to as interlace will know that one is initially seized by a kind of vertigo in face of the tangle of straight and curved lines which combine to form a harmonious, concrete whole, but in which the combination of elements seem to defy analysis. These drawings bring to mind the kind of network of tracery produced when sections of vegetal or animal organs are placed under the microscope. But if we proceed by the analytical method, if we first trace certain lines which appear to be controlling the system, we realize that the principle of these complex compositions is one of perfect simplicity.[7]

Arab ornamentation challenges the upright orientation of the spectator. For a while, syllogistic science appears to be nudged off its moorings, vision seems to play tricks with the known. In the end, knowledge eventually reasserts its "secure path" under the force of the analytic.

This reassertion has more than one relationship with a certain Cartesian understanding of vision. Descartes saw the bodily eye as a potentially misrepresentational device in its reception of objective phenomena. In the natural eye, perspective distorts circles into ovals, rectangles into rhombuses, when received on the surface of the retina. Ocular perspective is *literally anamorphic;* it distorts spatial depth; it is as if the surface of the retina reduces all volumes to surface. It is the "soul," or mind, that synthesizes this attenuated, disconnected image into the unified perception of depth, such that three rhombuses with interconnecting sides are restored as a cube, as is the oval as the top of a cylinder.[8] The mind's faculty in the Cartesian schema is comparable to Kant's depiction of the subject's synthetic capacity.

Arab art thus appears as an example for what eidesthetic thought constructs as its presynthesized propaedeutic: Arab art cannot see perspective. Its depthless vision, attributed to religious interdictions against naturalistic imitation, appears as an anthropological instantiation of a prior stage of the synthetic *cogito.* Viollet-le-Duc's observations are taken from his preface for a volume on Arabic ornamentation in Egypt published by the architect Jules Bourgoin in 1873. Bourgoin's introduction reiterates Viollet-le-Duc's, and also Kant's, civilizational account of historical origin: in the Orient, geometry is arrived at from a route other than reason. Arabic geometry, entirely entangled within the pattern form, offers a structural map of psychological meandering rather than a historical progression recuperable through logic. Its domain is not the "secure path of a science" but rather the nonpurposive variations of a noncogitative "*art*":

The application of these principles essentially constitutes what we mean by the "line" in Arabic art. Now this application is entirely subordinate to the skill of the artisan and in no way supposes reasoned, scientific knowledge of geometry. In fact, we should not imagine that the Orientals, in the period when they constructed the buildings, had a well-defined theory on which to base their richly varied intention. The Arabs made use of geometry without any understanding of the science of geometry and when they invented stalactite vaulting and interlace this was not the deduction of a hitherto unknown theory—and this is particular to their art—the simultaneous perception of pure form and of the work to be accomplished. Art, unlike science, does not require a rigorous enumeration and definition of its component parts. Art sets in motion the creation of a spectacle for the eyes; whether the basic elements are great or small in number is unimportant, everything depends on decisions made by the architect concerning the means at his disposal.[9]

This framing of Oriental pattern as nonanalyzed geometry characterizes the modalities of the DSA's own embrace of Oriental ornament as well, often in unintended and unexpected ways. In 1880 Caspar Purdon Clarke, director of the Indian section at the South Kensington Museum (SKM), was deputed to India to collect specimens for the museum. Among the innumerable objects that Clarke gathered during his two years in India were drawing portfolios, made under his guidance, of the ornamental surfaces of Fatehpur Sikri, built by the Mughal emperor Akbar in the 1570s. The plates in Clarke's portfolios are composed almost entirely of the intricate geometric patterns of screens and friezes from the complex, setting aside any other forms of architectural representation such as plans or perspectives. This bias reflected the DSA's own interest in nonimitative and geometrical art as its principal inspiration for industrial design. Clarke's preoccupations derived strongly from guidelines set out by works such as those of Owen Jones, whose landmark portfolio on the Alhambra and the *Grammar of Ornament* were significantly instrumental in increasing the currency of Oriental patterns in European design. Although Clarke's South Kensington training had prepared him to appreciate these patterns, their geometric construction appears, at times, to have eluded his analytic abilities. All the final versions of the plates were made from rubbings. Nonetheless, in the case of at least one plate, Clarke's superlative drawing skills seem to have been confounded. Very few of the squares, unlike in the original building, are *true*.[10] The "vertigo" Viollet-le-Duc spoke of manifested itself in the very construction of the drawing.

In the case of Clarke, however, this impressionistic misapprehension signals the limits of the analytical attitude rather than a simple failure

Figure 2.1 Caspar Purdon Clarke, drawings from rubbings, Ahmedabad, 1882. Courtesy: V & A Images.

of verisimilitude. In addition to the Sikri drawings, Clarke also acquired on his return journey a portfolio from the posthumous collections of "Ustad" Mirza Akber, the architect to the Persian court, obtained from the latter's pupils Khodadad and Akber. The drawings are of hybrid character, composed mostly of elevational fragments. Some of the more orthogonal drawings are on graph paper, whereas others reveal the use of compasses and setsquares. However, these latter drawings do not appear set onto a parallel rule, as in the formal conventions of engineering and architectural drawings in Europe. In describing three-dimensional objects, the drawings affect a pseudo-geometrical pictoriality, relying on freehand representation rather than on stereometric construction. This is particularly evident in the case of the Ustad's drawings of *muqarnas,* the stalactite-like pendentives characteristic of Islamic architecture. Attempting a partially naturalistic depiction rather than the systematic conveyance of three-dimensional information, these drawings present a marked contrast from Renaissance-era "traits" used to specify the shapes of irregularly cut stone components of buildings. The partially naturalistic depiction suggests that the drawing is indexical rather than stereometric or stereotomic in character; the folds

Figure 2.2 Drawings by Mirza Akber, architect to the Persian court in mid-nineteenth century. Collected by Caspar Purdon Clarke, superintendent, Indian section, South Kensington Museum. Courtesy: V & A Images.

are relational rather than dimensional, suggesting that the users of this knowledge relied on well-honed canons of hand-based skill rather than on the rule-bound projections of geometric space. This skill-based canon suggested a finite palette of forms as opposed to the potentially infinite number of forms possible within stereometric construction. In an address made to the Royal Institute of British Architects (RIBA) after his trip, Clarke may well have been talking about the Mirza Akber drawings in his description of architectural drawing in Asia:

> In India, as in Persia, the architect and builder are [*sic*] the same individual. Their social position is not a high one, and as far as I can

ascertain the builder-architect is regarded as inferior to the ordinary shopkeeper. He has no special education as an architect; but, on the other hand, has received a thorough training as a builder and as a master craftsman in one of the arts he employs. Three separate build-ers I employed in Persia [to make displays for the SKM] had each been workmen, could design, carve and paint. ... *It would be unwise to hamper such a man with large detailed drawings, and indeed, a drawing of a façade strictly to scale would greatly puzzle him;* the length and height, the position of the door or doors, and the number of windows, would be quite sufficient. Such proportions are not guess-work with Orientals, but are laid down strictly by their "can-ons." The number of curves in a foliated arch, and its shape, whether bulbous or pointed, depend entirely upon the proportion of height to width; *the exact curves so difficult for us to draw are laid down in a table* which I saw in use in Persia, and ... at Jeypoor. This I can briefly describe. They first select from a stock of patterns a foliated arch drawn on paper ruled with small squares. The outline of the full-size arch is obtained by dividing the space in to the same num-ber of squares, and drawing the arch through it in the same manner as scene-painters enlarge from sketches. Every *part* of the ornamen-tal detail of a building *has a name and a reason.*[11]

"It would be unwise to hamper such a man with large detailed drawings" of facades that are "so difficult for us to draw," even as the man knows how to construct these complex shapes from encoded tables and graphs. This difficulty, manifested in the misapprehended rubbings from Fatehpur Sikri, signals not so much a failure of the analytic as a deviation from its ends. Oriental geometry, art rather than science, meanders in a morass of details, of endlessness. Its tropes do not lack "a name and a reason," only they are attrib-utable to the multiplication of parts rather than to the whole. Schematization in the "large" eludes it entirely. This is why the architect in Asia is no differ-ent from the (lowly) builder. He cannot access the propriety of the authorial name (we will examine this aspect in greater detail in chapter 4); this con-demns him only to repeat the pattern without infusing it with an analyti-cal originality. The names of Mirza Akber, and the myriad others of his ilk, figure only as *informant* in a civilizational narrative of analytical vicissitude, quite in contrast the perturbation over proper names such as Thales.

An Idiot Science

Clarke's unintentional misrepresentation of a "difficult" art and the Ustad's imprecision in conveying scientific intentionality are therefore not classifiable in the same way, but they signal an anamorphosis within the figuration of the analytic, indeed of reason itself. This anamorphosis stems from an inherent ambiguity that rives the archaic association of geometry with intentionality in Western thought. In the introduction to his sixth book of architecture, Vitruvius attributed the incidence of geometry with anthropological significance. He gives the story of the Socratic philosopher Aristippus who, after being shipwrecked, was reassured of civilized human habitation upon finding geometrical figures on the coastal sands of Rhodes. In its Renaissance retelling, Aristippus' recognition of the imprint of human intention underwent further qualification by Daniel Barbaro, associate of Palladio, who averred that the regularity of the patterns constituted the nonerrant signifier of human presence, "not (the tracks) of wild animals."[12] Indeed, cogitative geometry and random pattern perennially run the risk of being mistaken for one another. One is never certain whether the pattern already exists in the object, already caused, or is a post hoc ascription, an effect, by the subject. Such is the disquiet in the mind of the unnamed Magistrate as he chances on the artefacts of the Barbarians in Coetzee's novel:

> [I am yet …] another grey-haired servant of Empire who fell in the arena of his authority, face to face at last with the barbarian. How will I ever know? By burrowing like a rabbit? Will the characters on the slips one day tell me? There were two hundred and fifty-six slips in the bag. Is it by chance that the number is perfect? After I had first counted them and made this discovery I cleared the floor of my office and laid them out, first in one great square, then in sixteen smaller squares, then in other combinations, thinking that what I had hitherto taken to be characters in a syllabary might in fact be elements of a picture whose outline would leap at me if I struck on the right arrangement: a map of the land of the barbarians in olden times, or a representation of a lost pantheon.[13]

Symmetrical pattern appears as the signature of both barbarian and civilized, as imprint of either autism or dexterity. Straddling the different cognitive domains of idiot, artist, infant, and automaton, geometry is rent by an inherent duality. As in the spirograph, or tessellations (and Henry Cole would write a series of children's books called *Tessellated Pastimes*), one cannot decide if it is the province of the savant, involving complex trigonometric equations, or the plaything of a child. (There are other examples of this doubling of intuition and rationalization: the fruit seller who *knows* how to stack his fruit more efficiently than the geometrician who, until very recently, could not *prove* this to be so.) It is not clear whether geometry is an inherent facet of the world, or some kind of primary psychic rubric through which one apprehends, or yet again a speculative structure that is imposed on object-phenomena.

This deductive indeterminacy is crucial to the conceptualization of nineteenth-century aesthetic pedagogy and "design," in that the latter word connotes in itself a sort of intentionality. As we shall see, this indeterminacy will allow geometrical patterning to be framed as both the posed problematic of, and the response to, the conundrums of the aesthetic in the industrial era. William Dyce, author of the original curriculum for the Schools of Design, introduced his drawing textbook with a similar statement of indeterminacy:

> It may be very true, that were a student made aware (so far as verbal explanation can suffice to show), what qualities in natural objects he ought to imitate, he might, by dint of trial and perseverance, hit at length on the very methods of execution, which experience has long since shown to be the best; but this only amounts to saying, that were the arts to begin again *de novo,* they would, in respect to their manner of working, come at length to the very condition in which they now are. *It is also quite true that, in the history of the arts of design, the discovery of right methods of execution is, in order of time, posterior to the effort of imitation to which the methods are subservient; and that they have arisen in a great degree out of the necessities of the means of imitation employed: but it does not follow, that in teaching the art of design this order can be pursued with advantage.*[14] [e.a.]

The formal stages of education, through which art is pared down to its essentials, are not assimilable to the actual stages of its historical progress. Method, or the analytic, is posterior to the originary deductions of imitative practice. Pedagogy, on the other hand, cannot pursue the same progression: method has to be taught before imitation.

In the DSA's conception, geometry is the model for "method". Dyce's curriculum borrowed heavily from a cluster of pedagogical ideas that he had had the opportunity to study in Bavaria while on deputation from the Select Committee on the Arts and Their Connections with Manufacture in 1837. His mission had been to devise a model for the Schools of Design based on comparable institutions on the Continent. In the event, his curriculum had as much to do with ideas formed within German pedagogies for infants as about artisanal training in the *Gewerbeschule.* Dyce's method directly addressed the task of designing industrial objects rather than the norms of fine art. To this end, it moved away from a paradigm of imitation to one of geometric and pattern *construction* as its principal aesthetic device.

190   SCIENCE AND ART GEOMETRY.

GEOMETRICAL PATTERNS.

The Octagon.—Mosaics, floor cloths, wall patterns, etc.

Figure 2.3 Illustrations from drawing textbooks published by private printers in conformity with the South Kensington curriculum. From T.W. Good, *The Science and Art Geometry. Section I: Geometrical Drawing. For Students Preparing for the Elementary School Teacher's Certificate "D"; the Second Grade Drawing Certificate; the Art Class Teacher's Certificate.* London: George Gill and Sons, 1888.

Dyce's curriculum constitutes part of an immense corpus of deliberations in the early nineteenth century on pedagogy directed at first-time entrants into humanistic schooling, adult or infant. Earlier in the century, the Swiss pedagogue Johann Heinrich Pestalozzi had devised a series of exercises for kindergarten, breaking down the components of knowledge into systematic fragments, with concrete lessons to be drawn at the end of each exercise. In the case of drawing, Pestalozzi criticized a pedagogy that relied entirely on the wherewithal of individual artists. Even the most well-trained artist cannot reconstruct the basic steps that lead to skill:

Each [artist] has his own peculiar mode of proceeding, which, however, none of them is able to explain. Hence it is, that if he comes to teach others, he leaves his pupils to grope in the dark, even as he did himself, and to acquire, by immense exertion and great perseverance, the same sort of instinctive feeling of proportions. This is the reason why art has remained exclusively in the hands of a few privileged individuals, who had talent and leisure sufficient to pursue that circuitous road. And yet the art of drawing ought to be a universal acquirement, for the simple reason that the faculty for it is universally inherent in the constitution of the human mind ... let it be remembered, that a taste for measuring and drawing is invariably manifesting itself in the child, without any assistant for art, by a spontaneous impulse of nature.[15]

Just as historical retracing of aesthetic traditions will confuse method, mere imitation will confound the (formative) natural impulse. Pedagogy must create autonomous, structural techniques to nurture the latter. The pupil is to be led through a series of steps that begin with acquaintance with the straight line, positioning it along different inclinations. Subsequent exercises in Pestalozzi's curriculum introduced the students to parallel lines, perpendiculars, intersecting lines, angles, triangles, *the* circle, *the* square, "the horizontal, and perpendicular rectangle; the curve, the semicircle, the quadrant, first oval, second oval, third oval," and so on. The child would then be inculcated in relations between these forms, using them for measuring and subdividing more complex spatial forms. Pestalozzi speaks of an "alphabet of forms," into which the mother would cut up cardboard shapes. Eventually, the child would learn to recognize all natural forms as complex figurations of this basic alphabet: "Every child is thus enabled, by the simplest means that can be imagined, to form a correct idea of the outline, and position of any object in nature, and to express his view of it in precise terms."[16]

Dyce's continental travels coincided with the establishment of the Home and Colonial Society, the purpose of which was training kindergarten teachers in Pestalozzian principles, and thus with the official migration of Pestalozzi's ideas to Britain.[17] On its part, Dyce's curriculum prescribed exercises for young students that began with parallel lines, progressing through increasingly complex geometrical arrangements into intricate patterns. The next significant stage appears with the introduction of "botanical" shapes or patterns, with an emphasis on the bilateral symmetry of curvilinear elements. The final exercises depict the application, through repetition and symmetry, of these patterns onto geometrically basic objects such as circular dinner plates or architectural cornices.

If Pestalozzi saw fine artists as unable to transmit a critical corpus of knowledge for the infant to grasp, Dyce saw academic high-art punctiliousness as irrelevant to a pedagogy that sought to inculcate artisans and workers in the processes of industrial production. Perspective was therefore abolished in the Schools of Design, and the traditional exercises of still life and the human body were discouraged. Although freehand drawing was reinforced, interpretative or gestural lines were proscribed; exercises emphasized instead the regularity of line and shade. Shades were worked in by increasing the density of lines, evenly pressured, across a field. Within any given field, clearly demarcated by boundary lines into basic geometrical shapes, colors were avoided as texturing tools, indicating the predisposition toward industrial usage. Colors, selected on the basis of formulaic chromatic relations, were filled in flat, thus reflecting contemporary mechanistic processes of dyeing and printing rather than painterly effects.

> In all the French schools … the human figure is the first object of study. In the German, the pupils commence with the elements of ornament, and proceed to the figure as the terminating point. … To the system of the majority of the French schools I have already stated my object, which is, that in many cases a loss of time is occasioned by the obligation it lays the pupils under of applying themselves to a study, which can be of no direct service to them. … On the whole, therefore, the German arrangement appears to be the best considered. By making the previous study of ornament the condition of admission to the classes of the human figure, a school is made to retain its proper place, and to operate as it is intended, in the capacity of a *nursery* for industrial design, rather than as an elementary academy for artists, to which in the absence of proper restrictions, it may be perverted. … The neglect of the accurate and intelligent study of ornament among our professors of fine art, has absolutely expelled from this country the practice of one of its most charming branches, or left it in the hands of house painters, whose education has been too imperfect, or whose acquaintance with the productions of the ancient masters in that kind too limited to supply deficiencies of artists of the higher class. I mean arabesque painting.[18] [e.a.]

Dyce's choice of basing an adult, vocational curriculum on the principles of kindergarten ("nursery") is significant. Many scholars have portrayed this seeming relegation as the infantilization of working classes in nineteenth-century industrial reform, in many ways affirming the views of the DSA's contemporary critics, which included luminaries such as Benjamin Haydon and John Ruskin. The roots of this reductionist approach, however, lie in a profound transformation in aesthetic thought, evincible in the extract from Pestalozzi cited previously. Artistic sensibility cannot construct a "method" that leads to itself as a replicable apparatus. In the Pestalozzian system, it is not the aesthetic that is being infantilized but the growth of the infant (and the non-Western indigene) that is being structured along a discourse of method.

Horace Grant's (a member of Cole's group of early mentors) statement that "artisans and other partially educated persons are, in this respect, only 'children of a larger growth,' " refers less to an infantilization of the working class than to what might be termed a "minimalist anthropology", to borrow a phrase from Uday Mehta, of the (aesthetic) subject in the nineteenth century.[19] This minimal subject was the precise hinge through which a claim to the universality of the aesthetic could be made. In quintessential ways, however, this minimalism is significantly dependent on the particular combination of critical aesthetics and taste, theories of natural life and form engendered during the Enlightenment.

The Sublime: Reason in the Articulation of the Aesthetic

The apoplectic gentleman in Dickens's novel offers us a clue. Sissy Jupe has made the capital mistake of suggesting that she would have flower patterns on her carpet. You do not walk over flowers, the man rants. Flowers cannot be abused by use.[20]

> Flowers are free natural beauties. Hardly anyone other than the botanist knows what sort of thing a flower is supposed to be; and even the botanist, who recognizes in it the reproductive organ of the plant, pays no attention to this natural end if he judges the flower by means of taste. Thus this judgment is not grounded on any kind of perfection, any internal purposiveness to which the composition of the manifold is related. … Thus designs *à la grecque,* foliage for borders or on wallpaper, etc., signify nothing by themselves: they do not represent anything, no object under a determinate concept, and are free beauties.[21]

The words are Kant's, from the *Critique* on aesthetics (the Third Critique). This paragraph is important because it encapsulates, with several objective examples, the peculiar Kantian relationship between the natural and the artificial worlds, between efflorescence and flowery wallpaper. Kant thus inaugurates a specifically modern mode of analogy between the biological and the manmade, whose heirs will include Goethe, Hegel, and the Romantics, a discursive mode, which in many ways the DSA would adopt almost as received wisdom. To return to Kant, again elsewhere from the Critique,

> In order to find something good, I must always know what sort of thing the object is supposed to be, i.e., I must have a concept of it. I do not need that in order to find beauty in something. Flowers, free designs, *lines aimlessly intertwined in each other under the name of foliage,* signify nothing, do not depend on any determinate concept, and yet please. The satisfaction in the beautiful must depend upon reflection on an object that leads to some sort of concept (*it is*

indeterminate which), and is thereby also distinguished from the agreeable, which rests entirely on sensation.[22] [e.a.]

Beauty is an entirely subjective instant, defined by lack of use for or "interest" in the object. Cautious about sensations that are contingent on the vagaries of the individual mind, Kant speaks of the subjective satisfaction in the beautiful as seeking in this satisfaction a *universal* voice. This universalized (*as if* universal, not actually universal) sensation, unlike reason, does not have the determination of concepts and is therefore without interest or purposiveness, which, one may recount, are critical in elucidating the topics of the first two Critiques, that is, reason and morality, respectively. A danger appears here: the disinterestedness inherent in the perception of beauty threatens to delink itself entirely from either reason or morality, from the regulative frameworks arrived at the first two Critiques. The lapse into sensation without adequate bridles is after all the hallmark of the voluptuary.

The danger, however, is only apparent, a red herring that signals some greater game afoot. Kant soon reveals his hand. Although beauty cannot seek a purpose in its object of satisfaction, its universality, and therefore its power as the "judgment" of taste, derives from being subjectively determined by a "purposiveness without purpose," intentionality without intention, pendency without end. If beauty cannot seek causality, "it has a causality in itself, namely that of *maintaining* the state of the representation of the mind and the occupation of the cognitive powers without a further aim."[23] Beauty puts the automobile of the mind on a treadmill, keeps its motors running for use at more opportune times, namely, the exercise of reason and morality. Beauty maintains indeterminacy as the engine that drives determination.

Flowers are the fuel of such a treadmill-like operation. We can sense that they have a purpose, indeed biologists *know* they have one—as the sexual organs of the plant—but for us they may just as well be the fruit of an active yet fruitless contemplation. Nature, both in its biological form such as flowers and in *analogon* as design—"lines aimlessly intertwined in each other under the name of foliage"—pleases in its indeterminate hint at a determination that is elsewhere. This indeterminacy cuts off, for all intents and purposes, the way to art as a *practice of realizing beauty*. One cannot make beauty, because to do so would be to declare an interest in it. One can only linger in its nonanticipatable moment.

The Romantics will see in this proscription an ulterior motive: to place philosophy above art, ideality over action. As outlined in the so-called Oldest System-Programme of German Idealism, they will attempt to give to sensuousness a predicative value, a value with direct reference to a fleshly construct of the "people" rather than to the idealist philosophical subject. The body will orient the mind. The move to situate art over philosophy, however, cannot be undergone by a correspondingly simple reversal of situating beauty over ethics and reason. The Romantics were aware of the danger of delinking the third Critique from the first two. The analogon set up by Kant between aesthetics and morality cannot be dismantled so easily, for the aesthete cannot do away with the sanction of the aesthetic as setting stage for knowledge production, that is, the field of reason. The formulaic post-Kantian response to this danger will be to place the idealist constructs of the subject in the formative principles of the object, thereby explicitly violating Kant's interdiction on confusing subject and object. To this end, at least one German aesthete, Goethe, will head off into the forest to research the formative elements of natural phenomena.

The elision must be well-articulated here. For Kant, "nature" is the principle of phenomenality *as such,* the name for that which resides outside the tripartite critical system and the archetype for all the three faculties of reason, morality, and the aesthetic. Nature is the extratheoretical paradigm on which theory is modeled. Less interested in formulating the internal principles of critique, Goethe uses a logic that is perhaps more intuitive: nature inheres in both subject and object.[24] Or rather, both subject and object are *of* nature. Nonetheless, Goethe seems unwilling to let go of the Kantian elucidation of the analytic. The analytical procedure, therefore, that "mediates" between object and subject is "experiment."[25] The particular experimental science that interests Goethe is organicism, defined as the study of inner, biological change—"metamorphosis"—through the study of outer, representable form.

If Kant resolutely divorces beauty from any empirical apprehension of the object, Goethe's reconciliation of organicist science and the critical system attempts to locate a resonance, even a conflation, between unity in (objective) nature and the unifying characteristic of the (subjective) aesthetic. "Nothing happens in living nature that does not bear some relation to the whole."[26] To do biological research is therefore to find the continuity between the fragmentary, empirical finding and the unifying generality of natural law. Methodologically therefore, experimental science must model itself on the example of mathematics, a deductive structure that makes sure to establish continuity with the entirety of its past at every stage of its advancement: "From the mathematician we must learn the meticulous care required to connect things in unbroken succession, or rather, to derive things step by step ... we must always work as though we had to satisfy the strictest of geometricians."[27]

And if the very structure of mathematics as a critical system allows one to project backward to its origins—Kant's attribution of the isosceles triangle to a (possibly apocryphal) "Thales" returns to mind—nature can also be similarly deduced back to an originary organism: the "archetypal" organism or the *Urpflanze*. The *Urpflanze* is not *of* nature but *from* nature, even as nature itself is from the *Urpflanze*. But there is a difference in the two procedures, between the two "froms". The former process, of distilling a singular archetype from a plenitude of specimens, also signals a corresponding move into the subjective, abstract sphere: "the particular can never serve as a measure for the whole. ... The (subjective) *idea* must govern the whole, it must abstract the general picture in a genetic way."[28] On the other hand, in the second procedure, the proliferation from the archetype, the *Urpflanze*, to the manifold or empirical is therefore a progression from the subject to the object as well. In this double procedure, we find a causative structure par excellence.

A return to Kant is again essential to elucidate this causative structure. For Kant, beauty is a pawn in the larger game of the three Critiques; in addition to rehearsing the faculties necessary for the proper exercise of reason and morality, its immediate function is to create the terms for his theory of the "sublime." I contend that for Kant the sublime is an attempt to elucidate *a theory of change*: a "contrapurposiveness" that confronts the "purposiveness without purpose" of beauty. It must be noted that the Third Critique also proceeds by way of a certain mimicry, a formal analogy, with the first two Critiques; the sublime also points to a crucial lack in the other two. The first two Critiques, of reason/knowledge and morality/freedom, respectively, concentrate on jerry-rigging the internal consistency of thought and will in accordance with concepts. Minus the sublime, this conceptual province of critical system is both atemporal and nonphenomenal; one is not given a road map as to how critique is able to produce *new* concepts from itself. The sublime is the pivot for such advancement, the mark of knowledge frayed at its limits as it contemplates the infinite.

This formulation of change rests on the particular relationships between the constitutive elements of the sublime. Kant cleaves the critical framework of the sublime into two distinctly heterogeneous faculties: apprehension, which refers to reason, and comprehension, which refers to the imagination. Apprehension, like reason, is described in the terms of a mathematical model. By adopting a basic, immediately intuitive, measure, one can potentially apprehend the infinite extent of nature, however miniscule or great its scale. Through apprehension the absolute becomes intuitive. Like numbers whose progression reaches to infinity "through comparison with others of the same species," apprehension is the grasp of the absolute as synthetically measurable through an unbounded series. Comprehension, in contrast, grasps the infinite in one single intuition, at one fell swoop, through the exercise of the imagination. More important, it reveals the infinite as exceeding the ability of progressive apprehension to grasp its absolute magnitude.

The paradigmatic example for this exposition, the backdrop against which Kant develops the third aesthetic, is Nature. Kant uses the term *Nature* as the archetype for all the three faculties of reason, morality, and the aesthetic. Nature is rational, moral, and beautiful beyond compass, beyond measurement. Reason allows apprehension to travel to nature's minutest secrets, for instance through the use of the microscope, or to its farthest expanses, as with the use of the telescope. But even as it establishes this measure of the minimal and the maximal, "the proper unalterable *basic measure of nature is its absolute whole,* which, in the case of nature as appearance, is infinity comprehended."[29] [e.a.] But the "whole" as *basic* measure is a "self-contradiction," because the basic, by definition, does not allow any subsequent division into parts. In grasping the whole, comprehension therefore leads the sensation of the sublime to a counterintuitive, supersensible strata, which is "contrapurposive" to both faculties. The sublime does violence to the imagination even as it radically exceeds the syllogisms of reason. In doing so, it extends the powers of both. If beauty puts the motor of the mind on a treadmill, keeping cognition attuned to its potential use, through the sublime "the aesthetic judgment [therefore] becomes purposive for reason, as the *source* of ideas."[30] [e.a.]

Apprehension reveals knowledge/reason as unbounded. Comprehension reveals this unboundedness as inadequate to gauge the infinite. There is therefore more than a simple dialectic in these two faculties. There is no third term that raises this conflict above itself, because the two contestants are heterogeneous. They gush from two different wellsprings; the conflict within the sublime is therefore between two terms mutually *unopposed* to each other. At the same time, each appears to extend the other; Lyotard has called this unsolvable and perpetual dispute the "differend": "this synthesis involves the *incommensurability* of one power of thought with another."[31] [e.a.]

Kant speaks of two different kinds of sublime. The "mathematical sublime" refers to magnitude. The "dynamic sublime," on the other hand, relates nature as a whole to the conceptual powers. Nature is revealed both as being superior to and—through the conflictual exercise of reason and the imagination—as having "no dominion" over the cognitive subject. As the paradigmatic mise-en-scène that triggers the sublime, nature ironically lays the foundations for the subject's *separation* from nature. The subliminal "terror" aroused when the imagination grasps the absolute limitlessness of nature summons to its aid the exercise of reason to dispel it, thus paradoxically forming the rational subject's autonomy at the very site of its regression.[32]

But the dynamic sublime also reveals one more important attribute about the faculties of the mind. The relevant paragraph is complicated but well-known:

> The disposition of the mind to the feeling of the sublime requires its receptivity to ideas; for it is precisely in the inadequacy of nature to the latter, thus only under the presupposition of them, and of *the effort of the imagination to treat nature as a schema* for them, that what is repellent for the sensibility, but which is at the same time attractive for it, consists, because it is a dominion that reason exercises over sensibility only in order to enlarge it in a way suitable for its own proper domain (the practical) and to allow it to look out upon the infinite, which for sensibility is an abyss.[33] [e.a.]

The imagination perceives nature to present the primordial schema for ideas, but the infinity of nature fills it with fear, inhibits its receptivity to [new] ideas. Reason forcefully holds the hand of the imagination, takes it step-by-step to the precipice, gives it the courage to look out into the abyss of the absolute. Ideality is at the same scale of impossibility as the "absolute" of nature and yet utterly unlike it; reason puts the screws on the imagination to recognize the comparable compass of these incomparable entities. Once again, the paradox arrived at is distinctly Kantian, one that explicitly invokes the subject of the Second Critique—the exercise of freedom in accordance with morally determined will—as its analogue: imagination comes under the subjugation of reason precisely to be able to throw off its shackles.

Something needs to be pointed out lest one miss the implications: Kant is surreptitiously setting up a framework for culture. This framework becomes necessary because the place of the subject in Kant is empty. Not everyone can experience the terrific thrill of the sublime, because to do so would require that reason be developed to its utmost limits where one would acknowledge its unboundedness. Otherwise the sublime would be not a thrill, a "negative pleasure" from terror, but just good old incuriosity and fear of the unknown attributed to traditional viewpoints. "Thus the good and otherwise sensible Savoyard peasant had no hesitation in calling all devotees of the icy mountains fools."[34] The abyss of the sublime also reveals it as the principal aporia of the Enlightenment. To paraphrase Heidegger, "one either looks for the problem of [unshackling the imagination through the experience of the sublime], or one leaves the aporia alone."[35] The Eastern voluptuaries and the Savoyard peasant, subjugated by the mysteries of nature rather than reason, are not able to construct the terms of their subjective autonomy; they leave the moral-aesthetic aporia alone and forever wallow in the eddies of their irrationality. We will return to this aporia—one that the East (Egypt) or the barbarian cannot cross—toward the end of this chapter. This aporia would become central in the critical figuration of the artisan–subject and its relation to art and science.

The Aesthetic of Morphology

The same conclusion which the French architect [François Blondel] had reached after customary measurement and examination, we [Germans] came to intuitively. After all, there is no law requiring that one account for impressions which take one by surprise.

—Johann Wolfgang von Goethe, *On Gothic Architecture*

Kant speaks of the experience of the sublime in almost physiological terms: at different times he speaks of the "movement" and "vibrations" of the mind. The brain is after all a muscle; this muscle is rattled by the sublime. It is precisely this muscular movement that Hegel seizes on to establish a connection between the natural and the conceptual (ideal), which for Kant are heterogeneous entities. Citing Cuvier, Hegel positions these two as superimposed in the working of the same animal or organism. Cuvier's claim of reconstructing the whole animal from a single bone therefore indicates a unique coalescence between rational extrapolation and the wholistic workings of inner nature. The faculty through which these heterogeneous entities are bridged is "sense." Kant's strong exception to the incommensurability of objective and subjective is gotten around by a superb wordplay, which refers "sense" to a colloquial double entendre rather than to critical use:

"Sense" is this wonderful word which is used in two opposite meanings. On the one hand it means the organ of immediate apprehension, but on the other hand we mean by it the sense, the significance, the thought, the universal underlying the thing. ... Now a *sensuous* consideration does not cut the two sides apart at all; in one direction it contains the opposite one too, and in sensuous immediate perception it at the same time apprehends the essence and the Concept.[36]

Sense "in this sense" straddles the (bodily and) sensual and the conceptual, the phenomenological and the critical. Hegel's gesture here is toward Goethe, whom he attributes with a doctrine that establishes a connection between the sensuous, empirical examination of objects and their accordance with concepts. (This very methodology, Hegel asserts at the beginning of a treatise that will superpose an aesthetic critique with a historiography, characterizes history as well: empirical events and individuals acquire significance precisely because of their connection with historiographic concepts. We will return to this theme in chapter 7.) If Hegel persistently works around the (incommensurable) differend by rendering it as a(n oppositional) dialectic, Goethe's opposition to the Kantian schema does not quite dismiss it through the adoption of a third term that effectuates the *Aufhebung*. In the following account of his fortuitous meeting with Schiller, the disagreement with Kant is spelled out clearly. Nonetheless, connection between phenomenology and critique is expressed as the site of desire rather than of actuality. The conditional construction ("surely ... must") is crucial in this paragraph:

> I gave an enthusiastic description of the metamorphosis of plants, and with a few characteristic strokes of the pen I caused a symbolic [i.e., archetypal] plant to spring up before his eyes. He heard and saw all this with great interest, with unmistakable power of comprehension. But when I stopped, he shook his head and said, "That is not an observation from experience. That is an idea." Taken aback and somewhat annoyed, I paused; with this comment he had touched on the very point that divided us. ... [When I retorted] He answered as a cultivated Kantian, and when my stubborn realism touched off a lively rejoinder we embarked on a long struggle, then arrived at a truce. Neither of us could claim victory; each was convinced his position was impregnable. Statements like the following made me quite unhappy: "How can we ever have an experience which conforms with an idea? An experience can never be congruent with an idea—that is precisely what makes the idea unique." If he viewed what I called experience as an idea, *surely* some mediating element, some connecting element, *must* lie between the two![37]

Goethe, like the British colonial administrator in the Punjab, yearns for continuity between the ideal and the sensuous(ly empirical). This desire for a continuum thus became the foundational thesis for a distinctly *modern* subtext of organicism in biological science where "associating plant forms with creative mental activity ... played a decisive part in establishing not only a new view of artistic creativity but also a new conception of plant life and form."[38] The aesthetic perception of unity was seen as corresponding to the axiomatic wholeness attributed to nature: life in the organism cannot be sustained if cut up into its constituent parts. The critical turn here is therefore toward an aesthetic model and a scientific method that seeks unity as internal to the object as opposed to something that is imposed, as in a plan. The desire for conceptual unity underlines as well a theory of change in the organism, whether this is manifested as growth in the individual specimen or as evolution in the collective species.

The term that encapsulates this conceit for Goethe, of governing intent without governing end, is *morphology*. Goethe was among the first to use the term in a series of essays written during his lifetime, notably in his journal *On Morphology*, where he described it as an "independent science" distinct from the disciplinary constraints of other fields—natural history, anatomy, physics, chemistry, and physiology—dealing with similar subject matter.[40] For Goethe, morphology described the analysis of inner, life-giving principles through the study of outer, manifested form. Because mechanical dissection could only piece apart elements of dead matter, the principle of life could be gleaned only from the whole organism through the exercise of—and Goethe is once again in the debt of Kant—"intuitive perception":

> To be sure, what is alive can be dissected into its component parts, but from these parts it will be impossible to restore it and bring it back to life. This is true of many inorganic substances, to say nothing of things organic in nature. Thus scientific minds of every epoch have also exhibited an urge to understand living formations as such, to grasp their outward, visible, tangible parts in context, to see these parts as an indication of what lies within and thereby gain some understanding of the whole through an exercise of intuitive perception. It is no doubt necessary to describe in detail the close relationship between this scientific desire and our need for art and imitation. Thus the history of art, knowledge, and science has produced many attempts to establish and develop a theory which we will call "morphology."[41]

The study of morphology, according to Phillip C. Ritterbush, "seek[s] to elucidate the *processes* governing achieved structure rather than describe the structure itself."[39] *Process* therefore indicates a dynamic model where the progressive and incremental framework of reason is related, through the aesthetic, to growth in the organism.

The commonality between science and art is forged in their respective study of figure ("*Gestalt*") as it is transformed ("*Bildung*") from one changeable state to another. This principle of "metamorphosis" applies not only to natural phenomena but, by extension, to artistic expression as well: "When something has acquired a form it metamorphoses immediately to a new one."[42] In Goethe's terms, metamorphosis transcends the apparent randomness of natural phenomena to point the way to an underlying principle that orients change. The concept of a figuratively elusive but unifying motive, that maps transformations over time, as well as discontinuities within a comparative framework, will become a leitmotif of Romantic analysis. Subject and object, so rigorously kept apart in the Kantian sublime, have been transposed onto each other. As I have suggested before, a causative structure is also implied here.

The Indirect Imitation of Nature

> For the body is not one member, but many. ... And the eye cannot say unto the hand, I have no need of thee. ... That there should be no schism in the body; but that the members should have the same care one for another.

> **—Corinthians, chapter 12**

Barbara Whitney Keyser has offered a succinct genealogy of the intellectual relationships between anatomists, biologists, and aesthetic thinkers and the influence of this interaction on design theory in the mid-nineteenth century. If the *aesthetic provenance* of detecting signs of unity in nature went unacknowledged in the sciences, then in the arts the argument for synthetic unity was nonetheless received as a *scientifically* derived natural "order of things." The "intuited" character of these tenets of so-called natural law became an essential armament in the crusade against the "direct" imitation of nature. Keyser has termed the ascendancy of this aesthetic ideology—most visible in industrial design and the decorative arts—the "indirect imitation" of nature.[43]

Between 1830 and 1850, significant works of German natural philosophy were becoming available in Britain. As might be expected their impact was felt as strongly in theories of aesthetics and art education as in scientific circles. Within schools of art and design, an interdisciplinary space was opened up by regular lectures given by anatomists and biologists. In the Schools of Design, the immediate effect was to sideline the teaching of the human body as primary artistic exemplar, while geometric schemas (such as the "golden section") deemed inherent in nature gained ground. Organicist ornamentation appeared as the aesthetic framework whose implications encompassed not just the territories of art and science but also the division of "industry" into its component arenas of labor, value, technology, and design. The discussion over ornament emerged as a common ground and unifying terrain at the exact moment that manufacturing and trade groups were experiencing ever-increasing degrees of diversification in organization.

The discontinuities inherent in Goethe's morphology are crucial to understanding the derived analogies offered between industrial design and biology in the nineteenth century. With the DSA, the post-Kantian complex became critical in the conceptualization and design of the industrial object, more so than the so-called fine arts. In the following introduction from a reprint of Dyce's curriculum, now officially prescribed for Cole's new department, the distinction made between design ("ornamentation") and fine art indicates as much the transformed status of nature as art:

> The artist, it has been observed, has for his art the representation of beauty as it appears in its natural subject; the ornamentist, the application of beauty to a new subject. To the former, therefore, artistical [*sic*] imitation is an essential requisite. ... To the latter it is not an essential, but only a useful acquirement. The reason of this is obvious: in few words, the ornamentist refers to nature for the purpose of learning the contrivances by which she has adorned her works, that he may be enabled to apply the same forms and modes of beauty to man's handi-craft; and this purpose necessarily leads him, as it were, to anatomise her works and resolve them into elements, rather than to view them in the aggregate with the eye of an artist; and to deal with minute particulars of form and colour more as they really are than as they appear modified by visual laws. As he does not aim at that fictitious resemblance of nature which it is the purpose of fine art to effect, but, so far as he goes, at the identical repetition of natural forms and colours in some new material and for some new purpose, it is obvious that the power of representing objects in the form of diagrams is to him far more necessary and valuable than that of imitating them with all their effects of light and shade, of surface or of material, as an artist does.[44]

The artist and designer "labour in common ground ... in regard to the *beautiful* in the works of nature."[45] Their purpose, however, is different. We remember here Kant's admonition against purpose in beauty or interest in the object. Design, on the other hand, not only *assumes purpose as inherent* in the object but is also defined as the interest in producing "new" objects. The proper province of Kantian beauty is nature, while the modern designer is faced with the task of replicating it in a nonnatural object. However, like Kantian critique, the task is to reflect back from the beautiful in nature to "learn [her] contrivances" so that they can be "applied" to the realm of the commodity-object. The reflection implicitly calls on the critique of reason as its model.

Geometry ("the form of diagrams") is the rubric that appears to inhere in both these fields: as paradigm of ideality for reflective reason and as *found pattern* in nature. Geometry is therefore both subjective and objective. The paragraph cited previously is immediately followed by a discussion that divides the form of natural objects into two "species": one characterized by straight lines, as found in crystalline forms, and the second characterized by curved lines of varying degrees of regularity, as found in life-forms. According to the *Introduction,* geometry as rational practice only partially assists in the construction of the latter, because their regularity derives less from geometric axiomatics than from the inner processes of natural growth. As opposed to the purely mental province of rectilinear geometry, the curvilinear forms of natural life can be replicated only through (artisanal) *skill,* that is, through a trained tactility rather than formulaic indoctrination into geometric formulas.

The distinction between straight and curved geometries is also significant because crystalline forms—snowflakes and rocks—were typically seen as "dead" phenomena in nature: as mechanically aggregative rather than organic in principle. In the crystal, the sum of the parts was exactly equal to the whole; breaking it down did not deprive it of the irreducible unity conferred by life. This distinction also separates the mechanical from the biological. For Coleridge, Romanticism's exponent in Britain, therefore, the difference between crystalline and curvilinear forms also described the difference between man-made and natural forms. In the following passage, he is paraphrasing Schlegel:

> The form is mechanic when on any given material we impress a predetermined form, not necessarily arising out of the properties of the material, as when to a mass of wet clay we give whatever shape we wish it to retain when hardened. The organic form, on the other hand, is innate; it shapes as it develops itself from within, and the fullness of its development is one and the same with the perfection of its outward form. Such is the life, such the form. Nature, the prime genial artist, inexhaustible in diverse powers, is equally inexhaustible in forms. Each exterior is the physiognomy of the being within, its true image reflected and thrown out from the concave mirror.[46]

The machine is a bachelor, it cannot (re)generate itself; it can only be built upon a plan. For writers at the turn of the nineteenth century, the metaphor of autogeneration was gleaned from external differences in form. The curvilinear surfaces of generative plant parts thus offered a new image of the creative imagination that exceeded the mathematical models of nature forwarded by the materialist psychologists.

Note the similarity in this respect to the DSA's attitude: "The method of the ornamentist sometimes inclines to that of the artist, sometimes to that of the mechanic."[47] The designer realizes the inner impulse of beauty in nature, thus going beyond a realist depiction of it. On the other hand, he brings this realization to coincide with the rational processes of the machine. It is this potential of elucidating morphology that places the lowly artisan and the designer at a cut above the mimetic picture plane and the anthropocentrism practiced by the fine artist:

> We did not want artists who were eminent draughtsmen and anatomists; we had only logs of wood to hew, and for this we did not want razors, but hatchets. ... The objects on which, in a School of Design, artistic imitation is to be exercised, extend over the *whole domain of the works of nature. Whatever may be employed as material of ornament, whatever may be applied to ornamental uses, whether it belongs to the animal, the vegetable, the mineral, or the fossil world, is the proper object of artistic imitation in the elementary studies of the School of Design.*[48] [e.a.]

In the DSA, the parallelism drawn between the art and the science of nature resulted in a significant research apparatus, involving collaborations between designers and scientists in addition to the museum acquiring organic and geological specimens for the purposes of artistic study. This focus would make the South Kensington site ideal for the relocation of the British Museum's Natural History Museum in the second half of the century. More important, the universalist scope of biological research within Britain drew upon significant imperial institutions such as the Royal Botanic Gardens at Kew, with its new Department of Economic Botany, which spearheaded biological research in the far corners of empire.[49] The post-Kantian complex of aesthetics and nature was persistently entangled in the British Empire with the phenomena of commodity production.

Perhaps the stellar proponent of the professional interrelationship between botanical science and design was Christopher Dresser, vanguard Victorian designer and student of Owen Jones. A student of the London School of Design, Dresser also studied botany at Kew Gardens. His work at the latter institution attempted to link Goethe's theories of metamorphosis to ornamental design, for which he received an honorary doctorate from the University of Jena, bastion of the German romantics, Froebel's alma mater, and sometime berth for Hegel. Dresser joined the faculty of the London school in 1859, where he taught classes in regular botany and botanical drawing.[50]

In the same year of 1859, Dresser published two books, called *The Rudiments of Botany* and *Unity in Variety, as Deduced from the Vegetable Kingdom,* written to be read in sequence in the botany classes at the DSA. Ostensibly based on his research at Kew Gardens, both books rehearse rather well-worn programs of natural philosophy set out by the Jena circle two generations earlier. The title of the second book betrays not only its genealogy but also its one-point thesis, even as he establishes the scholarly basis of the book by wading through a surfeit of Latin generic and specie names of plants to "deduce" principles well in place from the turn of the century:

There are certain ornamental and geometric forms which may be found amidst all creation; thus, we may take an hexagon, with radii proceeding from the centre to its angles: we have it in the top view of the flower buds of most Endogens, we have it in many crystals, and we have it in animals, as in the Spoonbill Sturgeon (*Polyodon spatula*), in its osseous dermo-skeleton. See also a transverse section of a tooth of *Orycteropus,* and section of the bark of the Ivory-nut (*Phytelephus macrocarpa*) ... there is a unity in the artistic effects of plants, for monotony is inimical to all, and variety makes all more beauteous. ... These facts [the illustrations given in the book] not only establish the existence of a unity between all the parts of a plant, but also the existence of a concord between the members of all plants, and between plants themselves.[51]

A Sublime Symmetry

In spite of the scientific tone, the principal novelty of Dresser's research lay in its understanding of ornament rather than of nature. For Dresser, the regulative principles—Redgrave's "ruling motives"—acting on an undulating nature principally manifest itself in a sophisticated theory of *symmetry*. Dresser distinguished his notion of symmetry from ordinary, bilateral symmetry, the latter characterized by the human ("*bimana*"). Dresser's studies concentrated rather on exploring the disjunction between two-dimensionality and three-dimensionality, demonstrating that apparent randomness in one picture plane can be revealed to have an inner order if

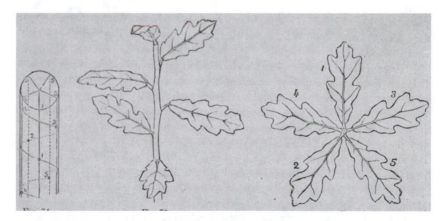

Figure 2.4 "Art Botany"; Dresser's drawings depicting principles of symmetry in nature. From Christopher Dresser, *Truth, Beauty, Power: Principles of Decorative Design.* London: Cassell, Petter & Galpin, [1859?].

viewed from another. We will call this demand for a shift of viewpoint, in the disjunctive elucidation of unifying principle in nature and ornament, "organicist symmetry." An instance of this sort of symmetry is offered by a group of illustrations in *Truth, Beauty, Power* (1859), where Dresser places two views, one bird's eye plan and one elevation, of a twig with leaves next to a schematic diagram.[52] At first glance, the elevation reveals very little about the underlying regularity of its growth pattern. It is the plan drawing and the accompanying diagrammatic clarification that drive home the point: the stalks and tips of the leaves are dispersed along the radial lines marking five congruent angles of a circle, thus creating a perfect spiral in three-dimension. One can arrive at this resolution, however, only by *straightening* the parent stem so that it approximates a single, linear axis. A discontinuity is signaled between the inner, motivating impulses of nature and their outward appearance. The symmetrical disposition of leaves can therefore be the outcome only of a dual epistemic projection. The first, structural aspect, epitomized in the act of propping up the stem, perceives randomness (the limpness of a stalk) only in degrees of divergence from an idealized rectitude. The second projection, which is representational, comprises in aligning this rectitude with the perpendicular axis to the picture frame, the frame of ornament. Organicist symmetry thus not only attempts

Figure 2.5 These placards are very likely the ones that Dresser used to teach "art botany" in the South Kensington classroom. Diagrams would be complemented by caption placards describing the roots principles of the example in natural law. Courtesy: V & A Images.

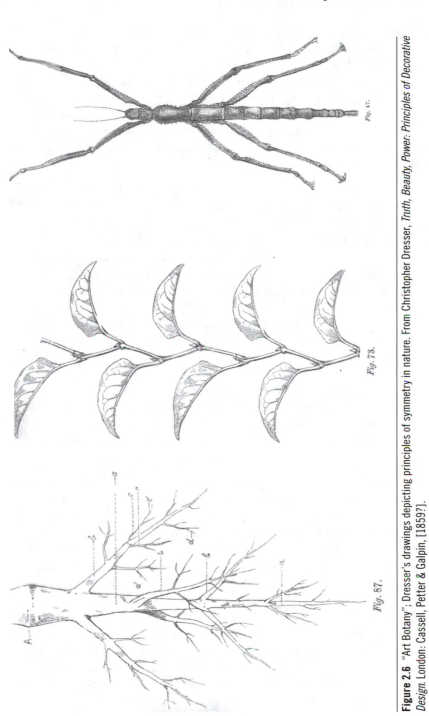

Figure 2.6 "Art Botany"; Dresser's drawings depicting principles of symmetry in nature. From Christopher Dresser, *Truth, Beauty, Power: Principles of Decorative Design*. London: Cassell, Petter & Galpin, [1859?].

to sift out the geometrical principles underlying natural phenomena but also construes nature as visually dissembling these principles with an apparent randomness.

Symmetry becomes a *miraculating* principle within nature, rather than being immediately perceptible in its external forms.[53] This principle can be brought to representation only through projection. In this sense, organicist symmetry connotes not only the concept of symmetry but, more important, *the symmetry of the concept.* Again Kant gives us a foretaste of this use of symmetry:

> In a thing that is possibly only through an intention, in a building, even in an animal, the regularity that consists in symmetry must express the unity of the intuition, which accompanies the concept of the end and belongs to the cognition. But where only a free play of the powers of representation (although under the cognition that the understanding does not thereby suffer any offense) is to be maintained, in pleasure gardens, in the decoration of rooms, in all sorts of tasteful utensils and the like, regularity that comes across as constraint is to be avoided as far as possible; hence the English taste in gardens or the baroque taste in furniture pushes the freedom of the imagination almost to the point of the grotesque, and makes this abstraction from all constraint by rules the very case in which the taste can demonstrate its greatest perfection in projects of the imagination. All stiff regularity (whatever approaches mathematical regularity) is of itself contrary to taste: the consideration of it affords no lasting entertainment, but rather, insofar as it does not expressly have cognition or a determinate practical end as its aim, it induces boredom.[54]

Organicist symmetry is symmetry without aim or "end," symmetry jogged by the changeability and metamorphosis implied within the sublime. It does not so much expose the fact of symmetry in nature as enact the perennial search for it. Space becomes dense, teeming with unseen correspondences and elusive consonances. Skirting just beyond the reach of tangibility and accessible only to intuition, organicist symmetry cannot be phenomenally resolved. It is rather a regulative principle, orienting evolution and metamorphosis, from which all heterogeneity, indeed difference, not only becomes imaginable but also finds its generative core. Organicist symmetry offers a bloodless dissection of epistemic formations, dangling elusive and ever-receding "patterns" to be pursued and unraveled. It is in this sense that the search for the pattern marks studies in a plethora of disciplines, whether that of natural behavior, human society, historical epochs, or decoration.

The residues of Dresser's teaching materials for his botany class demonstrate this paradigmatic role of symmetry.[55] Drawings would be made on pasteboard demonstrating the unifying geometric principles underlying different natural specimens. Following Dyce's (and ultimately Pestalozzi's) injunction to break down the elements of knowledge from general to particular, Dresser's boards were arranged as a successive series of "universal laws" of nature, cut up into digestible tidbits. Diagrams detailed and labeled different plant parts, indicating their accordance with different symmetrical orders. Drawing from direct observation of the specimens was prohibited because both Dresser and the DSA strongly held that the underlying principles could be intuited only by the supplemental process of formal indoctrination. Large plates would reinforce in text the lesson of the visual illustrations.

Things Upside Down: Morphology as Morphotropy

We may twist and turn a single commodity as we wish; it remains impossible to grasp it as a thing possessing value.

—Karl Marx, *Capital*

Dresser's unraveling of an imperceptible symmetry into a spiral structure effected a reversal of the natural principles set out in Goethe's essay "The Spiral Tendency in Vegetation." Goethe resolved plant growth or metamorphosis into two principal vectors. The first he construed as the "vertical tendency" of the plant, which is theorized as a "spiritual staff supporting the plant's existence and maintaining it over long periods of time."[56] The vertical tendency, deriving from biological *heliotropy*, acts as a structural vector, motivating the plant to extend itself from its last state. The spiral tendency supplements the vertical tendency, acting as the vector of autocultivation and "development," maturing the phenotypes at every vertical stage. The two tendencies are interreliant; the components wilt if one develops too far from the support of the other.

Art must also follow this model. For Goethe, the particular tribulation of the German, "modern," artist is the near-impossible task of making "the transition from shapeless mass to form, or if he succeeds, to *maintain* it."[57] Art must capture the formlessness of nature, move along with its ever-transforming and self-metamorphosizing vectors. It must keep pace with its relentless changes even as it persistently reestablishes the universal principles manifested in these changes. Morphology is always manifested in a turning movement that renders it incapable of stasis; the spiral, by way of heliotropy, represents its inevitable resolution into a *morphotropy*.

It is in this tropic character that nature acquires its strongest analogue with the commodity. For the DSA, the commodity—the object of design—also never stands still; it is constantly being moved, truncated, inverted by use. This fluidity of the commodity-object is thus inevitably at odds with the principal modus operandi of industrial production: mechanical repetition. Very much in the Coleridgean frame, the DSA saw the mechanistic attributes of the industrial commodity as the principal limitation in their articulation of taste. Richard Redgrave succinctly animates this problem in his discussion on the schism that opens up when a bolt of textile is cut and sown into garment, the former's field deriving from the logics of loom and printing and the latter by the cuts of tailoring and the sinuousness of the body:

> Let us take the application of art more peculiarly to manufacture by machinery; say that of calico-printing. In this instance, also, the precise imitation of natural objects is impossible, since relief is unattainable, although the appearance of relief may be given by light, shade, perspective and colour. ... [However] the garment it is intended to be made into is to hang full and in folds; thus the light, shade, and the very forms of the object which has been imitated, are confused and hidden, and that *imitation* which the manufacturer had been at such pains to produce is entirely lost and destroyed. [i.o.] *The garment moves with every motion of the wearer,* and any examination of this rare art, as we are enabled to examine the painter's work, is, in the use of this material, as impossible as it is desirable.[58] [e.a.]

Design must address the commodity in the condition of change, in metamorphosis. Even if design—realized in the proper use of symmetry—struggles to find its place in the industrial process through determining the surface of the commodity, the random disposition of commodity use in space threatens to disrupt this very symmetry and by extension the validity of the design-function. Thus, for Redgrave, "up and down" stripes and trails are to be preferred over lateral ones, because they both accentuate and are accentuated by the human body in motion. Also, smaller and busier patterns are therefore more preferable to large motifs, because folds and cuts make the disjunctions in the latter more noticeable.

It is a short step from textiles to architecture. It is here that the DSA's principal objection to painting and the classical picture plane manifests itself. The wall is the archetypal backdrop for painting. With the development of chromolithography, Redgrave argued, it had become possible to adorn the humble cottage walls of the indigent with the great works of the masters. Nonetheless, the picture frame of the painting required framing, repose, and viewing distance; great paintings cannot be repeated pell-mell next to each other as in wallpaper patterns. The most significant problem is posed by the corner, the wall's change of direction:

> It cannot be desirable to repeat even Turner's pictures, however beautifully rendered, over cottage-walls, fitting them into corners, and round chimney-pieces and windows, and cutting them to lengths and widths ... it is this suitable treatment of the surface of the wall which is sought to be obtained by the principles laid down for the ornamentation of paper-hangings—the product of machinery—leaving the question of the decoration of walls and buildings, by the hand of the artist, to his own genius and his own resources. ... Having shown, as I promised to do, that the conventional treatment, or ornamental display of plants, is consistent with those laws which Science teaches us govern their development, I would say a word or two on its agreement, in many respects, with that simple impression which flowers and foliage make on the casual and untaught observer in their natural state of growth.[59]

Symmetrical biomorphic patterns are therefore to be preferred over naturalist representation. As such, the pattern appeared as a unifying response to a widely perceived fragmentation that was deemed to be affecting the domestic interior, an effect also of the increased parcellization of labor.

The Morphotropy of the Orient

In his essay outlining the architectural implications of the Great Exhibition, Gottfried Semper, Marx's fellow émigré and exile in London and sometime professor in the London School of Design, offers us a portrait of the disaggregation wrought by industrial capitalism in the building of the domestic home.[60] The essay illustrates this through an inordinately long narration of the New York building industry by an unidentified German engineer. The basic width of the New York house, we are told, is determined by the modular length of standardized joists, which were in turn cut to conform to the standard width of the domestic plot. The division of labor is standardized with different tradesmen installing different prefabricated products, including ready-made doors and windows. Finally, a decorative wall is "pasted on" the front, with the client's particular affectation of taste accounting for the choice of materials, whether red sandstone, marble, granite, or decorative ironwork. The architect has very little role here except to furnish basic variations on a standardized plan. After the front facade is erected, "he troubles himself no more with the house and hands over the bare, empty rooms to the decorator and upholsterer for more extensive fittings."[61] The marketplace determines that the financial well-being of architects is reliant more on the quantity of buildings erected by them than on their quality. Architecture has been stood on its head.

The DSA's was the first official pedagogy to recognize design in architecture as a quantitative problem, as so much square footage involving folds and turns and corners that introduce the junction or connecting element as a specifically modern disjunction. The fold or the junction is the connecting link between heterogeneous fields; in the case of architecture, these heterogeneous fields, involving different materials and skills, also comprise increasing divisions of labor in the nineteenth century. The erect repose of painting's picture plane is at odds with the irregular morphotropy of the domestic wall. The indirect imitation of nature as design strategy negotiates the autonomous logics of the surface and the wall, signaling both the disjunction and the unification of two different scenarios of production into one field of value.

It is from this consideration of the surface and the corner or fold that architectural thought takes a turn, a turn that will lead it through the Wagnerian thematic of the *Gesamtkunstwerk,* in the Wiener Werkstätte and the German Werkbund, the "new unity" of the interior as envisioned in the Bauhaus, to the *Proun Spaces* of El Lissitzky, the architectural developed surfaces of Piet Mondrian, the De Stijl "environments,"[62] and of Le Corbusier's unfolded interior elevations. "This drawing can be reversed,"[63] says Le Corbusier in *The Modulor.* The desire to abolish the disjunction of the corner—a desire at the core of nineteenth-century decorative arts as well—will eventually lead to a search for a unified material aesthetic. In doing so, modern architecture only *appeared* to abolish the appliqué surface as a unifying field: ironically, the twentieth-century quest for honesty in revealing structural jointures is a direct legatee of ornamental theory in the nineteenth century.

For Semper, the house had increasingly become an assemblage of disparate logics of production, each with its own morphotropy. The use-value of a horizontal joist is transformed by the use of the same section as a vertical strut. Value is therefore both a disjunctive element that transcends merely "local" morphotropes of use and a conjunctive one, in that it puts the diverse morphotropes into relationship with each other: it actualizes a tropology. Design is the name for this transcending function. For Marx, the principal agency that is turning things upside down is capital. Capital renders the commodity into an abstract value, without regard to its orientation or use, opening it up to the play of association. Capital raises the commodity from the sensuous to the realm of the transcendent:

> [The] commodity … is a very strange thing, abounding in metaphysical subtleties and theological niceties. … The form of wood, for instance,

is altered if a table is made out of it. Nevertheless the table continues to be wood, an ordinary, sensuous thing. But as soon as it emerges as a commodity, it changes into a thing which transcends sensuousness. It not only stands on its feet on the ground, but, in relation to all other commodities, it stands on its head, and evolves out of its wooden brain grotesque ideas far more wonderful than if it were to begin dancing of its own free will.[64]

It is the table as conceptual artefact that becomes abstract rather than the undifferentiated mass of wood from which it is hewn. The upside-down table loses its use-value but not its exchange-value.

It is here that we see an affinity between Marx and a certain transcendent morphotropy that, for Semper, appears in the objects of the Orient. Semper's formulation is worth quoting here at length:

A marketable ware should allow the broadest possible use and elicit no associations other than what the object's purpose and material permit. The place for which it is designed is not determined; as little known are the qualities of the person whose property it will be. Thus it should possess no characteristics and local colour (in the broadest sense of the word), but should have the quality of harmoniously agreeing with every surrounding.

These conditions seem to correspond completely with the products of Oriental industry, and even more so when the latter are not intermingled with the splintered remains of annihilated, higher art phases, either their own or foreign ones. Oriental products are *most at home in a bazaar,* and there is nothing more characteristic of them, as we indicated before, than their convenient accommodation to every surrounding. The Persian carpets are suited to a church as well as a boudoir. The Indian ivory boxes with inlaid mosaic patterns can be incense holders, cigar containers, or work boxes, depending on the inclination of the owner.[65]

The exchange-value of the Oriental object was augmented by its ability to transcend singular morphotropes. Its provenance was in the *bazaar,* the capitalist fantasy of a precapitalist free market, thus the preindustrial Oriental ware presented itself as the epitome of industrial design.

The Occidental object, immured in the perspectival conundrums of the picture, was superfluous in its outlived semiosis. For Semper, the industrial commodity in Europe has not yet realized its transcendent morphotropy, its surface simply composed of unimaginative "copies" of Gothic and Renaissance modes of imitation. Modern gaslight was clad over with the patina of ancient candelabra or oil lamps. Marx might have muttered: the commodity was haunted by the "world-historical necromancy" of the past. Like the working class of 1848, it clothed itself in the garb of antiquarian symbols to ward off any cognizance of the present.[66] The estrangement of the Oriental pattern from its context of use becomes a foil for the estrangement of the industrial object from the normative anachronism of taste. Through the nonauthorial agency of the Orient, the commodity is restored to its own atemporality. The non-referentiality of the Oriental object exorcises this cultural sorcery over the capitalist commodity. Its semiotic rarefaction exactly mirrors the semiotic rarefaction desired for the industrial commodity. As Owen Jones put it in the catalog of Indian objects bought for the Marlborough House collection from the Great Exhibition,

> In the Indian Collection, we *find no struggle after an effect*; every ornament arises quietly and naturally from the object decorated, inspired by some true feeling, or embellishing some real want. That same guiding principle, the same evidence of thought and feeling in the artist, is everywhere present, in the embroidered and woven garment tissues, as in the humblest earthen vase. *There are here no carpets worked with flowers, whereon the feet would fear to tread, no furniture the hand would fear to grasp*, no superfluous and useless ornament, which a caprice has added and which an accident might remove.[67] [e.a.]

We have wound our way to a point exactly above Viollet-le-Duc's "vertigo" in the face of the Arab pattern, somewhere next to the unnamed gentleman in *Hard Times*.

The Oriental pattern signals a crisis of reason even as it satisfies the criteria of taste. It holds no "interest" in its object; this makes it ideally felicitous for design. Shorn of use-value, it invites reason to extend its free play with the imagination. The Oriental subject, on the other hand, wallows in the sinuousness of the pattern, unmindful of purpose. Although the rational European loses his balance in attempting to figure out the intricacy of the Oriental pattern, the Oriental remains unthreatened by the complexity he has himself produced. As perpetual producer of effects without cause—interdicted by an "irrational" religion to against imitating nature—the Oriental artisan is even better able to approximate a nature whose unifying causality remains irreducibly transcendent and insensible. At the same time, because he does not rely on reason to bring him to the limits of his imagination, he cannot despair at being made cognizant of its infinite scope. The Oriental artisan is therefore like one of Kant's Eastern voluptuaries who indulge in massages without being in the least curious about the internal working of bodily organs, who consume spices without being mindful of their unpleasant consequences. Unable to use reason to reflect back from the effect to the cause, the Oriental subject perennially construes its farts as the sign of some other agency. The origin of the (Oriental) pattern is mysterious; its causes cannot be traced.

To conclude, the nineteenth-century conundrum of unifying the increasing differentiation of materiality under industrialism resolved itself into an articulation of the surface as the bearer of the aesthetic. The surface not only is just a surface—in its sense of enveloping *over* the structure—but carries within it, as in Goethe's understanding of morphology, the "elucidation of the processes of achieved structure." The structure that is here *manifested* in the surface—whether in arabesque, white wall, or exposed brick—is that of an ulterior continuum among incommensurable discontinuities of material and function. I say manifested, and not "represented," because in its unifying role there is no depth behind this surface; the surface carries the unifying principle of substructuring and superstructuring phenomenality. The surface is therefore not just discontinuous with what is immediately behind it but *radically* discontinuous, that is, a categorical discontinuity rather than simply a material one. In other words, the surface bears the very essence of materiality within it, the precise imprint of the aesthetic imagination on the empirical and therefore the site of a turn, of a morphotropy. We remember here that a turn indicates a continuity encompassing a discontinuity. We will see very soon that this tropology epitomizes the discontinuities articulated by Marx in his theorization of "Value," that is, between use-value, exchange-value, and value in the abstract. It is hoped that this chapter has made clear that the differentiation produced between designer and preindustrial artisan in this morphotropy should alert us to corresponding asymmetries in the very production of agency within capital. To make this connection, it will be necessary to examine the divergences of the DSA curriculum between metropole and colony, even if they were seen as the sites of a privileged exchange. We will turn to this in the ensuing chapter.

CHAPTER **3**

"Tardy Imaginations, Torpid Capacities, Tottering Thought": Drawing at the Origin

… the thoughts of men are as if in a patterne …

—John Locke, *An Essay Concerning Human Understanding*

I have China, the largest country in the world, yet to conquer—and I don't mean "conquer" egomaniacally. I would love them to know about transferware [a type of decorated pottery] because, in fact, they developed it.

—Martha Stewart, in interview with Beatriz Colomina and Rem Koolhaas, *Wired* **(June 2003)**

Every true representation implies an adherence to the rules of perspective; but the artist in practice follows them as effects rather than causes. … Artistical [*sic*] imitation may be said to begin only where geometry leaves off.

—*Introduction to the Drawing Book of the School of Design*

The previous chapter surveyed some of the intellectual genealogies of the relationships between an organicist philosophy of nature and the pedagogy of industrial design. This chapter examines the manner in which these connections were deemed by the Department of Science and Art's widespread diaspora to resonate with both the particular entanglements of industrial society in Britain and colonial production in India. At issue are the specific pedagogical elements through which the DSA saw itself addressing production systems thrown up by industrial capitalism and the manner in which it justified its interventions in terms of anthropological constructs. The DSA's pedagogy of drawing was specifically meant to address the differentia produced by industrial and imperial capitalism in both metropole and colony. As we shall see, the anthropological figure of the "artisan" was crucial to this construction of drawing.

The chapters of Christopher Dresser's *Truth, Beauty, Power* of 1859 were first published as a series of essays for "workingmen" in the periodical *Technical Educator*. The critical force of Dresser's polemic lies in his conceptualization of design as a term encompassing the entire division of labor. In the following paragraph, Dresser's invocation to artisans of all kinds (We could almost hear Marx grunt, "Artisans of the world, unite!") reflects his own prolific output and the radically new function of the designer in bringing together a diverse array of skills and materials:

> We shall thus be led to consider furniture, earthenware, table and window glass, wall decorations, carpets, floor cloths, window-hangings, dress fabrics, works in silver and gold, hardware, and whatever is a combination of art and manufacture. I shall address myself, then, to the carpenter, the cabinet-maker, potter, glass-blower, paper-stainer, weaver and dyer, silversmith, blacksmith, gas-finisher, designer, and all those who are in any way engaged in the production of art objects.[1]

The formulation is remarkable if only for the fact that it isolates the heterogeneous textures of everyday use—the surface bearing the ornamental impress of mass manufacture—into a generalized aesthetic canvas. The function of the designer thus unites not only the heterogeneous skills of artisans but also their commodities as the multiform objects of the interior. For Dresser, this unifying agency is won through its ability to reorient the disparate morphotropies of different materials. Thus, the purposive quality of wood lies not only in its tactile and structural abilities but also in the visual attributes of its grain: a "natural" pattern equivalent to drawn pattern in terms of its value for the ornamentist. One cannot but point out a critical paradox in this advocacy of material honesty. The morphotropy of the material plays out not in the use of the grain as structural cue but rather in its composition as surface pattern. For Dresser, therefore, naturally occurring "accidents" such as knots were to be excluded from the surface, not because of the structural problems that this might create, but because to reveal the knot is to once again stumble into the pitfall of naturalist verisimilitude that makes the imitative painting defective for industrial replication. The call for "honesty" in material expression is thus inevitably a ruse for ignoring materiality altogether.[2]

Quite in contrast to this touted attention to material, the invocation of "design" and "pattern" reflects quite another transition in the history of making. Rather than signal a transformation in the commodity, we will soon see that it is the subjective agency of the artisan or worker that is principally being remade into a different model of work. The new language of design is also a signature of the radical transition from bespoke to industrialized work. For the DSA, the predicament and challenges of taste in the latter were radically different, because some kind of mass preference had to be articulated in advance for the product to be produced in bulk.

The adjudicatory role of design therefore both emerged and was seen as intervening at the precise point that the chaotic overabundance of products appeared to despoil all norms of taste. Sketching out the objectives of the department in 1853, Richard Redgrave echoed a vast spectrum of Victorian critics in assailing the fickle taste of the masses that easily capitulated to prevailing "fashion." He strongly berated the mind-set wherein "a pattern or design is known to be good, bad or indifferent, only after those who are supposed to be the best judges of such things, namely, the purchasers, have approved or condemned it. ... There are no legitimate standards of taste or design except the demands of the day."[3] (This metropolitan capriciousness was contrasted by another writer with the Orient, where "fashion, which here is as fickle as the wind, is in the East as steady as their monsoons, and has fortunately preserved some of the manufactures in their pristine excellence."[4])

Opining that the pendulum of taste had shifted from elite connoisseurship to the arbitrariness of the masses, he decried the irresolute crests and troughs of public taste as fundamentally *conservative* in character, because it relied on no guiding principle, relegating "truth and beauty [to] a price current."[5] Redgrave thus argued for the department's importance ("What ought the State to teach?"), opining that it was its "office to keep in the van of the public," stimulating "research" that would undermine the fickle vicissitudes of taste through a methodology that would unify the purposiveness of the commodity-object with that of the aesthetic. The principles of design therefore seek to reinstill an aesthetic rectitude in the worker and the consumer.

The reviling of this capricious taste has more than a passing relationship with the berating of the political timidity and "collective mediocrity" of the masses reviled in John Stuart Mill's essay "On Liberty." For Mill, the complacency of the average citizenry, unwilling to cultivate independence of spirit, made them all too happy to flow with the uncritical tides of public opinion. "There is no reason that all human existence should be constructed on some one or some small number of *patterns*."[6] For Mill, therefore, a degree of eccentricity is preferable to a conformist mediocrity. Of course, eccentricity cannot go untrammeled; radical freedom brings with it the responsibility of self-adjudication. The average citizen is, however, hardly cognizant of either the radical possibility of freedom or its responsibilities, and he or she does not possess the ability to reflect back to the "first principles" of ethical and political action. "Utilitarianism" is therefore precisely the philosophy that provides a handi-kit of "*secondary* principles," a series of "landmarks and direction-posts" that orient the traveler on the way.[7]

The principles of design, in the DSA's view, are a similar "approximative" handi-kit of secondary principles that abstract from the axioms of both imitative art and natural science:

> Now, though it might be possible to discover the rules for describing geometrically these authentic forms of ornament and their prototypes, the discovery would in practice be of little use, because there is less difficulty in drawing them with the hand accurately enough for all practicable purposes, than there would be in applying the rule if it were known. The outlines of Greek ornaments are only approximations to scientific forms; nor is more required in art. *The eye is satisfied with a degree of approximation attainable in practice,* and, were it possible to work with mathematical accuracy, would be unable to appreciate the difference between the truth and the approximation. But it is precisely because forms and lines of the kind alluded to must in practice be drawn empirically, that ornamentists *must undergo a study which can neither be ranked under the head of artistical imitation nor of practical geometry.*[8]

The artisan need not acquaint himself with the primary principles of either art or science. The formulation is extremely significant for a department that named itself on the hyphenated construct translated from the Aristotelian *techne*. Design *is neither art nor science;* it is only a rough approximation of both. The secondary principles are articulated in a clear discontinuity from what are deemed as primary ones.[9]

For Kant, the aesthetic is in the wild; nature as *found,* rather than intentionally sought, is its archetypal stimulus. One cannot regulate it or declare an interest in the object. Post-Kantian theories of art and design, on the other hand, defined themselves precisely by their interest in the object; the disinterested generality of the aesthetic therefore posed a crisis of intention for the mid-century aesthete. This crisis is the same as that described in the previous chapter, where the appearance of geometry produced uncertainty as to its provenance, whether of chance, natural order, or human making. By the same yardstick, machines too have the ability to produce pattern, without the discriminative intervention of the designer. As Dresser points out, sometimes beauty can be produced by this automatist repetition as well. The archetype of this is the kaleidoscope:

> The orderly repetition of parts frequently aids in the production of ornamental effects. The kaleidoscope affords a wonderful example of what repetition will do. The mere fragments of glass which we view in this instrument would altogether fail to please were they not repeated with regularity. Of themselves repetition and order can do much.[10] [i.o.]

Repetition sometimes can produce an autoaesthetic. Bearing within it an image of consonance, repetitive pattern can conform to a simple sense of the beautiful. Euclidean regularity thus has a predisposition toward beauty, as *The Science and Art Geometry,* one of the approved textbooks for the DSA, tells us:

> *Ornament may be purely geometrical.* On pages … , for instance, simple geometrical figures, such as the *square, equilateral triangle, hexagon, octagon,* pentagon, and rhombus are so arranged as to make very pleasing ornament. [i.o.] We have only given faint indications in the space at our command as to the mode of arrangement. The possible combinations in beautiful design by using these simple figures are infinite. Every student will be able to make new combinations for himself, and *anyone who can handle a pair of compasses and a straight edge* may elaborate ornament from these simple materials on ideas of his own.[11] [e.a.]

The basic elements of geometry already present a pattern: a grid is but a "checked" motif; a series of colored circles are polka dots; parallel lines are only but "stripes." "Anyone" or anything that can produce geometrical shapes can produce aesthetic pattern. Ornament can always be the product of automata, of accident, of the idiot. A crack on an ink roller can produce pattern in its repetition. Taste teeters on the precipice of fickleness and chance, on the naturalistic consonance of geometry and the mass-repetitive mechanisms of industrial capital. It is precisely to counter this tendency toward automatist taste that the DSA's advocacy of organicist symmetry located aesthetic judgment at the exact moment where the complexity of the pattern threatens to overwhelm the imagination. "Those proportions will be the most beautiful which it will be most difficult for the eye to detect," goes Proposition 9 of Owen Jones's "General Principles" in his *Grammar of Ornament.* The regular symmetry of a 4 to 8 ratio "will be less beautiful than the more subtle ratio of 5 to 8; 3 to 6, than 3 to 7," and so on. The aesthetic is determinability pushed to the precipice of chance. The ideology of design carves out a projective role for the intellect in the oscillation between intentionality and nonintentionality, between mechanical monotony and mass caprice.

To this effect, "at the very outset," Dresser's *Truth, Beauty, Power* assigns to design's projective role a conceptual term. The term straddles by implication the entire conceptual gamut of capital and specifically those elements of capital on which the design-function is deemed to have a direct bearing: labor, novelty, materiality, exchange, beauty, commerce, and society. The following is a paraphrase of Dresser's argument: the design-function is not reducible to skills or techniques, and its principal brief is not to produce objects, patterns, materiality, or even beauty in its paradigmatic sense. The designer's function produces an element that Marx would find familiar within his own framework of capital: "value." Here is Dresser:

> At the very outset we must recognize the fact that the beautiful has a commercial or *money value.* We may even say that art can lend to an object a *value* greater than that of the material of which it consists, even when the object be formed of precious *matter,* as of rare marbles, scarce woods, or silver or gold. This being the case, it follows that the workman who can endow his productions with those qualities or beauties which give *value* to these works, must be more useful to his employer than the man who produces objects devoid of such beauty, and his *time* must be of higher *value* than that of his less skilful companion. … Men of the lowest degree of intelligence can dig clay, iron, or copper, or quarry stone; but these materials, if bearing the *impress of mind,* are ennobled and rendered *valuable,* and the more strongly the material is marked with this ennobling impress the more valuable it becomes.[12] [e.a.]

Money, material, temporality, and intention ("impress of mind"): value is associated in four sentences with four distinct categories. "Value" maps these heterogeneous entities, supplements them, and links them into a semiotic chain. Value establishes continuities over inherent discontinuities of production. Although it can be realized through financial or commercial exchange, it is not entirely calculable in terms of the discrete quantum of the material used or labor-time expended alone. Design, Dresser avers, should steer clear of working with materials of "intrinsic value" such as gold and silver that would cloak its specific contribution; the "vicissitudes of war" and the greed of philistines can smelt them down into nuggets, thus undoing the artisan's "impress of mind." Instead, baser materials, clay, wood, iron, and stone, have the dual advantages of permanence, because breaking them down will make them worthless, and of availability for the poor artisan, because they are cheaper. "Workmen! It is fortunate for us that the best vehicles of art are the least costly materials."[13] The *single* worker can reproduce the entire mode of production in his own backyard. This vision of individual intentionality as the primary ingredient of value is more than a simple aesthetic corollary to the "Robinsonades" of liberal political economy: the man on the island who is able to reproduce the entire relationships of production within himself before entering into transactions with other, equally self-sufficient beings. Dresser theorizes the aesthetic as the very essence of economic activity, the principal element through which the worker is able to add value in the economic sphere.

Marx positioned value in a very different register. In contrast to liberalism's theoretical emphasis on the minimal anthropology of the individual, industrial capitalism for Marx could emerge only with the historical annihilation of "individualized and scattered means of production." Capital operates primarily as an abstract, *socializing* agency, employing normativizing instruments to assemble a vast workforce.[14] Far from being a significant interloper within the production process, Marx saw the individual as simply a philosophical abstraction created by society or, more to the point, by *some* societies. Critical of the founding fallacy of the "political economists" in cutting the suit of capital according to the cloth of metaphysics rather than material history, Marx theorized value as a direct reflection of the stage of production by which a society is organized. Value is a predicate of the historically produced social aggregate. Thus the different chronotopes inherent in the different modes of national production—Britain, France, Germany, the United States, India, Asia, Europe—produce different kinds of value (as we have seen, competition and colonialism put these different types into direct relations with each other).

Gayatri Spivak has suggested tracking Marx's use of the signifier *value* as a textual (i.e., discontinuous and open ended) trace animating abstract differentiations within the flow of capital. The different hyphenations of value—value *as such,* use-value, exchange-value, surplus value—each canceling the last stage, are a central thematic in Marx's unraveling of the production circuit.[15] Thus textualized—laid out in a semiotic chain—within the circuit of capital as a conceptual term that unifies both the division of labor and the diversity of commodity production, "value" is in the place of *symmetry,* the conceptual unity that produces a provisional congruence between each term and the next. We have noted Kant's understanding of this as the "symmetry [that] must express the unity of the intuition, which accompanies the concept of the end and belongs to the cognition." Symmetry is not so much a physical consonance but a principle of elusive correspondence, a cut through the episteme that makes discontinuity legible as a "pattern." In this sense, "value" is also a cut through the matrix of capital, the place of a perceived correspondence where heterogeneous and discontinuous elements can be entered into conceptually symmetrical, even if manifestly asymmetrical, morphologies:

> The formula capital-interest (profit), earth-rent, labour-wages presents a *uniform and symmetrical incongruity*. ... If we start by considering the disparity between the three sources, we find secondly that their products or derivatives, the revenues, all belong to the same sphere, that of value.[16]

Like the aesthetic, value is impossible to be defined in its totality. Value is epitomized by discontinuities, even as it establishes relationships between heterogeneous entities, like links in a chain:

> Firstly, the relative expression of value of the commodity is incomplete, because the series of its representations never comes to an end. The chain, of which each equation of value is a link, is liable at any moment to be lengthened by a newly created commodity, which will provide the material for a fresh expression of value. Secondly, it is a motley mosaic of disparate and unconnected expressions of value. And lastly, if, as must be the case, the relative value of each commodity is expressed in this expanded form, it follows that the relative form of value of each commodity is an endless series of expressions of value which are all different from the relative form of value of every other commodity.[17]

Dismissing intentionality as an ingredient of capital, Marx leaves use-value relatively untheorized; the resemblance here to a Kant who rules out "interest" in the three Critiques cannot be discounted.[18] For Marx, use-value, "whether [it] arise[s] ... from the stomach, or the imagination, makes no difference."[19] Note how, in the following passage, the DSA's liberal–utilitarian discourse might be seen to be overturning Marx's insight to project design as potentially mirroring the ubiquitous fields of value:

> Beauty of effect and decoration are no more a luxury in a civilized state of society than warmth or clothing are a luxury to any state: the mind, as the body, makes everything necessary that it is capable of permanently enjoying. Ornament is one of the mind's necessities, which it gratifies by means of the eye ... ornament is now as material an interest in a commercial community as the raw materials of manufacture themselves.[20]

Utility is indistinguishable from aesthetic. We therefore see developing between Marx and the DSA an unstated altercation regarding the agency of the artisan/worker, the commodity, and the role of intentionality in defining the boundaries of industrial capitalism.

As we saw earlier, this shared ethos does not obviate significant divergences in terms of their critical understanding of capital. The previous chapter examined the DSA's formulation of "method" as a post hoc recovery of the original impetus of imitative art, one that its theorists saw as structurally different from the historical development of pictorialism.[21] The methodology of the DSA curriculum therefore reconstructs aesthetic knowledge as retracing its steps in two very different directions: one, devolving "down" to the grasp of the illiterate worker and a minimalist anthropology; two, returning "back" to the phenomenological origins of art. Through this double recuperation, a sleight of hand—placing industry as the vanguard agency of the aesthetic—could be carried out. The ornamentist/designer is the felicitous intermediary that bears this dual burden: ornament thus "ranks midway between the fine arts and the arts purely mechanical, and partakes of the nature of both."[22] The ornamentist is the artist trapped within the regulative intricacy of method, chronologically posterior but logically anterior to imitation. This intermediary status also aligns ornament with architecture, "for the architect, so far as imitative art is concerned, is really an ornamentist."[23] In the conflict between production and taste, the commodity surface is the new canvas of the mass-produced object, the two-dimensional receptacle of morphotropy-as-value. In the nineteenth century there is an exponential boom in the mass-produced surfaces of architecture: wallpaper, tiles, terracotta, carpets, and glass. In 1883 one company could boast that it was annually producing six million rolls of wallpaper, each up to fifteen hundred yards long. Its output was by no means unique.[24]

The boom in the technologies of the surface brought with it a ravenous hunger for patterns. Patterns were the unifying element that could establish continuity among unlike objects. It could establish relationships of use and relationships between the object and its setting. Patterns indicated consanguinity between the teapot and the teacup, the saucer and the milk jug, identifying them as a "set" or "service" against the tablecloth. Through patterns, the nineteenth-century designer could organize the Babel of the commodity interior into one consonant morphotropy of taste. This functional relationship to industrial society and the designer distinguishes the nineteenth-century embrace of pattern from the eighteenth-century aesthete's *horror vaccui*. The surface was not so much a blank canvas as a value-producing one.

We may paraphrase Marx:

[With the patterned surface, use-value] ... is no longer a table, a house, a piece of yarn or any other useful thing. All its sensuous characteristics are extinguished. Nor is it any longer the product of the labour of the joiner, the mason or the spinner, or of any other particular kind of productive labour. With the disappearance of the useful character of the products of labour, the useful character of the kinds of labour embodied in them also disappears; this in turn entails the disappearance of the different concrete forms of labour. They can no longer be distinguished, but are together reduced to [surface]. … Since a commodity cannot be related to itself as equivalent, and therefore cannot make its own physical shape into the expression of its own value, it must be related to another commodity as equivalent, and therefore must make the physical [pattern] of another commodity into its own value-form.[25]

For the DSA, the unifying surface, the canvas of the designer, is as if the links in the chain of labor and value. The pedagogical project that placed the artisan at its center would therefore have to intervene at the scale of mass industry, the extent of which we will turn to in the next section.

A Pedagogy for the Worker

Most of the pioneers of the industrial revolution in Britain were uneducated. These were often people without formal training whose successes had been garnered mostly within their customary spheres of industry. Very few of the huge transformations wrought in industry owed anything to education or direct action from the state.[26] The inception of state involvement in education devolved, rather, from the need to create a politically homogenized, semiskilled, industrious, and pliant working population.

The DSA's program to generalize drawing education therefore constituted a chapter in a much larger enterprise involving the tremendous apparatuses of moral and vocational training and was set into motion by the culture of liberal reform during the nineteenth century. The first Select Committee on Arts and Manufactures convened in 1835, which marked the culmination and state recognition of a century of individual and private efforts to shore up the quality of industrial products through art education. Beginning with Christopher Wren's 1692 call to teach drawing to the orphans at Christ Hospital to employ them in "useful" trades, the eighteenth century had already witnessed a range of efforts by individuals and groups from the manufacturing trades to upgrade the manual skills of the working class. Although they ritually professed objectives of amelioration, the principal objective of these efforts was aimed at obtaining cheaper skilled labor for better commodity development. For instance, the foundation of the Royal Society of Arts in 1754 was explicitly posed as an institution aiding the economic competitiveness of British goods in the international market.[27]

The demand to inculcate higher aesthetic standards for industrial production acquired new urgency in the 1820s, when the resumption of trade
ties after nearly two decades of war in Europe brought home the old bogey
of competition based on the aesthetic attributes of commodities. The need
for an institutional redress to this perceived shortcoming was exacerbated
by the recognition that Britain's main trade and colonial rival, France, already
had a partially state-supported network of no less than eighty provincial
academies of art. Given that the French academies were mostly founded
in the eighteenth century, British manufacturers such as Thomas Chippendale, William Ince, John Mayhew, and Thomas Sheraton attributed the
ascendancy of French design in the luxury industries to these institutions.
When the Select Committee on Arts and Manufactures convened in 1835 to
address this issue, almost every invited tradesperson bemoaned his dependence on French designs for the sale of his wares. John Bowring—sometime
amanuensis of Jeremy Bentham and a member of an official committee
reporting on foreign trade with the Continent—pointed out that five-sixths
of France's silk industry was export-led, compared with the British figure of
one-eighth or one-tenth.

Despite their avowed beliefs in the organically self-governing eddies of
free trade, committee members were unanimous in urging more government intervention to improve the state of affairs. The free traders thus ironically found themselves having truck with social reformers such as Edward
Bulwer-Lytton, whose advocacy of increasing governmental intervention
toward universal education as a way of improving workers' lives came from
somewhat opposed tenets. The committee deliberations of 1835 and 1836
thus epitomize the larger public debates roiling Britain at the time: education, the status of free trade, and the increasing disaffection with the
elitism of the Royal Academy.

Typically, then, most of the pattern books that were published in the eighteenth century pertained to middle-end and luxury goods industries, such
as woolen and silk textiles, where British manufactures most dreaded being
swamped by foreign imports.[28] As a result, drawing became a new, gener-
alizable media for substantial exchange of aesthetic information between
disparate industries, such as textiles, cabinetmaking, upholstery, and pottery. New forms of publication such as pattern books were increasingly
able to claim an audience beyond the specific constituencies of individual
trades. As this new relevance of published drawings took hold, the institutional boundaries of art education also underwent a pedagogical shift from
classical, canonical paradigms to the more prosaic imperatives of vocational
industries. The emergence of drawing as the principal carrier of the aesthetic, epitomized in the DSA's curriculum, must therefore be related to the
general ascendance of the "visual" as a pervasive feature of liberal society.

This history also needs to be mapped within the increasing power of particular visual norms in economic, social, and political relationships: the emergence of what one may term a "specular" citizenry and the attribution of a certain set of visual conventions to different aspects of skill.

Barbara Maria Stafford's work on eighteenth-century norms of visuality has offered us a magisterial picture of the gradual subsumption of the mechanical, hand-based arts by the new equation between transparency and reason in visual demonstration.[29] The ubiquitous eclipse of the conjurer—practitioner of an arcane and "Oriental" art involving the dexterous use of hands in order to deceive—was fomented by the arrival in public arenas of the inventor or demonstrator and the scientific instrument. Even as they emerged from the very same theaters incorporating the visual duplicity of older performers—acrobats, tricksters, cheats; in other words, *artisans*—the experimentalists in the age of the *Encyclopédie* suffused the public sphere with the instruments and methods of the laboratory. A slew of new optical contraptions—microscopes, lenses, beakers, distillation vessels, bell jars—was used to reframe natural objects in a series of processes, emphasizing the role of labor and work in the determination of phenomena. The emergence of this new visual paradigm did not affect craftsmen alone. The knowledge sphere of the aristocratic dilettante, who came to his erudition in a spirit of play, also became increasingly suspect with the emergence of a new kind of expert: the civil bureaucrat. Even as manual knack was subsumed under a new visual regime of epistemic inquiry, knowledge became increasingly imbued as endless exertion: "The Enlightenment ideal of progress was pictorialized as tireless doing."[30]

As new visual paradigms overlapped manufacturing relations within a specular relationship, they edged out the intimate dexterity of the traditional virtuoso, the ubiquity of bespoke production, and their relationship to the object. At the same time, the emphasis on visibility in the processes of production endowed *cerebral* activity with an "aura" of individual creativity over the humdrum repetitions of manual work. Thus, Thomas Chippendale's appeal for increased clarity in client relations was underpinned by his emphasis on the use of drawing as a specificatory instrument in contractual documents.[31] In the nineteenth century, the spread of the pedagogical dyad of geometry and mathematics likewise impeccably paralleled the dyad of drawing and mensuration in contractual relationships pertaining to the commodity-object. The shift toward increased legal formalization and the stipulable also marked the transformative watershed of visuality in the modern era; the contractual drawing was increasingly introduced as "proof" of intent or its lapse during litigations. In the classical mind, visual conventions were often described in extensions of rhetoric (in terms of their ability to emotionally affect their audience). In the modern era, this rhetorical facet was explicitly sequestered as superfluous to law, whereas visual convention, nudged along by the widespread state-sponsored dissemination of drawing and geometry, slid handily into the arena of codification. As an appendage to a culture where transactions were being carried out more and more through new visual devices, the DSA curriculum epitomized an institutional prestidigitation in which visual norms were increasingly harnessed to draw the productive population within the legal field of the liberal state.

As Rafael Cardoso Denis has observed, British public life from the beginning of the nineteenth century was permeated by an extensive literature on the subject of observation and drawing.[32] Its scope extended from pamphlets, prescribing the norms of drawing as both an ethically and an aesthetically productive pastime for the leisure class (e.g., sketching or watercolors as a hobby), to a burgeoning number of tracts on geometrical drawing. In a speech at Manchester iterating the DSA's party line, Granville could describe the teaching of drawing as the cultivation of symmetry in normative behavior:

> I believe, after all, there is design in the cutting out of a frock; and a friend of mine went still further, and suggested that to lay a knife and fork parallel to one another required the sort of eye which was perfected by a drawing lesson or so.[33]

Drawing becomes essential in setting the table. In the combination of its descriptive ability and its perception as the projective capacity of the human, drawing bore the potential of prescribing the conflation of culture and nature. Drawing textbooks further sought to graduate their readers from aspects of culture toward a progressive mastery over regular and irregular shapes and forms. Within these textbooks, we see a distinct evolution from the early, casual exhortations for expanding aesthetic horizons to the more functional demands of newly organized professions. Books on geometry, likewise, demonstrated a progression from volumes on general principles to the more specific and technical conventions of discrete professions: mechanics, draftsmen, architects, builders, designers, carpenters, bricklayers, and so on. Correspondingly, by the 1850s, the prefaces of drawing treatises, replete with appeals to the patronage of professional bodies, also reflected the growing power of these bodies.[34]

The Dyce Curriculum

In 1837 the Board of Trade commissioned William Dyce to travel to Europe to prepare a report on the functioning of art and industrial schools in Germany and France and their relationship to domestic industry in those countries. Professionally untrained for the task at hand, Dyce's actions in preparation for his travel to Europe indicate British concerns about continental dominance over the luxury-goods trade. Within a few days, Dyce made a frenzied tour of various artisanal manufactories around London, including glass factories, porcelain warehouses and, most significant, the silk manufacturing district in the suburb of Spitalfields.[35] While in Europe, his most perceptive observations regarding industrial conditions were deduced from the French silk-manufacturing region of Lyons, which he described in greater depth than any other industry.[36]

Although Dyce praised highly the status accorded to industrial designers in France, in curricular terms he preferred the vocational training system in Germany, where he felt the training of artisans was more appropriate to British needs. His preference is curious given that the level of German mechanization was nowhere near Britain's. Neither comparable industrial standards nor pedagogical content can explain Dyce's predilection. It was rather the preponderance of the customary master–journeyman relationship undergirding the *Gewerbeschule* of Prussia and Bavaria that offered him an ideal social model that could address the tensions between industrial classes in Britain. Although Dyce saw the political difficulty of transposing the paternalism of taste inherent within the Prussian bureaucracy onto the British polity, he regarded highly what he deemed the particularly German distinction between industrial and high art. For British institutions, in his view, this distinction posed a political problem. Commenting on the subservience of artisanal guilds to state-appointed designers as in Schinkel's Altes Museum, Dyce noted that such a political arrangement would go against the grain of British liberalism. The role of the *Gewerbeschule*, as officially appointed client-suppliers of patterns and designs to manufacturers, only reinforced the hierarchy of labor between high art and industrial design, in that artists in the schools were highly paid, whereas underpaid designers copied the patterns they supplied to the factories. In Britain, manufacturers and free trade ideologues, of course, could hardly have tolerated such state paternalism or intervention:

> By the machinery of a liberal and extensive plan of instruction, it is proposed to cultivate, to as high a degree as possible, the national taste; and this is put (so to speak) into the hands of a few eminent artists, to be guided and moulded as their genius may direct. It is needless to remark, that in countries like France or England, a despotism of this kind would be utterly intolerable, or rather impossible. We gladly, with reverence, bow to the empire in art which the genius of a Raffaelle, a Cellini or a Dürer has achieved for themselves; but it appears to me a preposterous mistake in a Government, assuming from examples

such as these, that the influence of individuals on the cultivated taste of a country, is the readiest way of bring the arts to bear on manufactures, to create by enactments an authority of the same kind for certain artists of their own choosing.[37]

Aware of the disadvantages of transferring such a professional system wholesale, Dyce turned his attention instead to the curricular innovations then being undergone within the different principalities of Germany under the influence of pedagogues such as Pestalozzi, Froebel, and Stephani.[38]

Method as Ornament

Formally, Dyce's curriculum shares many of its characteristics with the Pestalozzian precepts of breaking down knowledge into its recognizably formal components. The key difference emerges with the relationship to so-called primary principles or concepts. Unlike Pestalozzi's precepts, where components were simply broken down from finite conceptual nuggets, the Dyce curriculum moved away from conceptual training to delineate an intermediary zone of interaction between industrial production and pedagogy in art. Pestalozzi's strategy, based on a critique of Socratic catechism, had sought to graduate the child into the realm of ideas through the newly recognized pedagogical function of the mother as adjunct for the state.[39] In contrast, Dyce emphasized the inculcation of corporeal *habits* rather than conscious, reflective thought—the legacy is that of John Locke[40]—as the vehicle to inculcate in each generation the accumulated knowledge of all its preceding generations. It is the fingers that must be trained in this congealed habit, not the mind.

At least part of Dyce's formulation came from the prosaic realization that the spatial frame of public art education required a shift from the unitary master–pupil (or mother–child) relationship to the *mass* pedagogy of the classroom. In the introduction to his 1842 drawing book for the Schools of Design, Dyce posed this transformation as the following contrast between "ordinary tuition in drawing" and the particular challenge faced by masters in the Schools of Design:

> There still remains the question, how we shall most rapidly and effectually impart to students of design the practical advantages afforded by the experience of their predecessors. Are we to place natural objects at once before them, explain the various modifications of form by visual laws, point out the effects of light and shade, lay down the rules given by artists for the execution of drawings, and so leave them to make their first effort? All these explanations must doubtless be given; but it is very obvious, that unless the explanations of the master,

in reference to the manipulation of the drawing proposed to be made, are accompanied by practical illustration, he must fail of [*sic*] conveying his meaning. If so, whence is he to derive this illustration? Either *he must himself execute part of the student's drawing, an expedient which, though in some instances it may be necessary, would never, as a general rule, answer in large schools, or he must refer to drawings already executed.*[41] [e.a.]

The imperative of mass pedagogy thus distinguished the DSA curriculum from both conventional art education and Pestalozzian child psychology. Although the DSA made some concessions to the importance of one-on-one teaching, especially with regard to its emphasis on the quality of line, the principal task for drawing teachers in the schools was described principally by imparting foundational habits rather than encouraging expressive exploration. This strategy was reflected by the schools' use of large blackboards and pasteboards set up in front of the classroom with exercises for the students to copy. Teachers, perceived as conduits for predetermined content rather than masters in their own right, would draw out the exercises in their entirety in advance, following the script laid out in the curriculum.

The very furniture used by the London school and recommended by the DSA further spatialized this strategy. Students used a vertical drawing

Figure 3.1 School being conducted in the South Kensington tradition at Birmingham, c. 1910. Courtesy V&A Images.

board supported on an upright desk to compare their drawings to that on the pasteboard in front of the classroom; the plane of the student's sheet and that of the board were therefore parallel. The relationship of teacher and pupil was further elaborated in the central position of the teacher's work in the student's visual "cone". In the DSA classroom, many such cones intended onto one object: the flat diagram in the front. Patterns were drawn on the board for students to copy exactly, emphasizing qualities of field and surface rather than interpretation of objects in the round. The pattern therefore not only cut out the volitional aspects of drawing but also carried the axiomatic lessons of indirect representation within itself. The pattern was not a representational framework but instead a schema of rules and principles whose consequences were explicitly tied to the modes of industrial production and the designer's role within it. In a hierarchy where teachers were hired for their ability to reproduce preestablished lessons rather than independence of taste, the pattern was also uniquely suited to being replicated down the line with the least degree of distortion. The curriculum, once set in London, could theoretically be copied exactly throughout the kingdom or elsewhere.

The desire for "flatness" therefore derived as much from ideas of aesthetic transference as from the organizational imperative to systematize the transmission of knowledge into an apparently decentralized hierarchy. The textbook–teacher–student relationship underpinned a mass pedagogy that would travel far and wide, including India as well. In 1854 the Madras School of Art and Industry described its conversion to the Dyce curriculum in the following terms:

> The course of instruction in the Artistic Department [has] been remodelled and the system of class teaching introduced. … [Quoting Redgrave] It has lately been found desirable to introduce into the schools of the Department, as extensive as possible, the plan of class teaching for all the more elementary stages of the course, the master going through the example on the black board before the assembled class, explaining the structure of the form, and the best means and most correct principles for thoroughly imitating it. Even in more advanced stages, all such matter as is necessary to communicate to every student is given in this manner. By this means a great saving is made of the time of the Master, heretofore too much given to individual correction, and instruction is more certainly and systematically conveyed to all.[42]

Pedagogical exigency was therefore as much a ruse for a theory of administrative hierarchy.

The Orient: The Function of the Antifunction

As we saw in the previous chapter, the recourse to the complex symmetries of Oriental pattern was a critical element in the strategy to wrest control over the intermingled attributes of surface, morphotropy, and value in the commodity. The surfaces of the European nineteenth century were suffused with mass-produced "Moorish," "Alhambra," "Turkish," and "Saracenic" styles and patterns.

As some of the aphorisms in Owen Jones's *Grammar of Ornament* declare,

> Construction should be decorated. Decoration should never be *purposely* [e.a.] constructed. ... Beauty of form is produced by lines growing out from the other in gradual undulations: there are no excrescences; nothing could be removed and leave the design equally good or better. ... In surface decoration all lines should flow out of a parent stem. Every ornament, however distant, should be traced to its branch and root. *Oriental practice.* ... All junctions of curved lines with curved or of curved lines with straight should be tangential to each other. *Natural law. Oriental practice in accordance with it.*[43]

Ornament is the aesthetic that *transcends* purpose in the commodity. The nonpurposiveness of the Oriental pattern trumps the empirical morphotropy of the individual commodity. Given this nonpurposiveness attributed to the Oriental artisan, how did the DSA curriculum fare when transplanted to the "Orient"? The question is significant, because unlike the metropole, the curriculum concerns a pedagogy that claims to instruct a population *that is already deemed to be a native* of the particular aesthetic formation that is being taught.

In many ways, the DSA's arguments about the urgency of art reform in India were comparable with its apprehensions regarding the future of British industry. Cheap, mass-produced commodities from Europe, DSA aficionados averred, were wiping out the sources of indigenous production in India. Although a narrow sliver of the crafts communities still survived owing to the export trade in particular luxury wares, Indian artisans must be prepared to compete with the deluge of industrial commodities from Europe *without* converting to machine-based production. At the same time, it was unconscionable to conceive of the colonial government as intervening in the "natural" and "self-regulating" eddies of "free trade." The state would not financially assist indigenous credit agencies or physical plants or create trade protections for the artisan. The state would instead offer pedagogy, leaving the primary onus on the artisan to extricate himself from his current impasse.[44] The DSA's decentralized framework would be critical in formulating this reserved benevolence.

Figure 3.2 Reay Art Workshop, held at the J.J. School of Art in Bombay in the early 1890s. Master artisans from the surrounding regions were brought in to teach students. From W.E. Gladstone Solomon, *The Bombay Revival of Indian Art*. Bombay: Times Press, [1923].

Because the traditional artisan was naturally adept at the aesthetic mores sought to be inculcated by DSA aficionados in India, he was not seen as lacking in conceptual grounding, even if this was deemed as immured in the regressive darkness of customary practices, realizing itself in instinct rather than in reflective knowledge. (And as we have seen above, in the metropole the effort was precisely to align the worker's instincts with the tropology of the machine.) The diagnosis made by Alexander Hunter, founder of the Madras school, to students of the Surat school of industrial art, is illuminating in this regard. The Indian artisan lacks a handle on the morphotropy of capitalist value:

> You must pay more attention to the geometry, and joinery of your work before ornamenting or carving it. This is the chief defect in many of our Indian manufactures. It can easily be remedied if you pay attention to the accurate drawing and fitting of the parts; remember, if these are neglected, your work will be rickety and easily broken. Many of the richly carved chairs and sofas of Bombay have this serious defect, and it is sometimes dangerous to sit down upon them. ... One of our best makers of cabinet work and furniture work in Madras, detected this fault, and set about remedying it in the proper way, namely, by insisting that the practical geometry and joinery should be sound, correct and strong before the carving is commenced.[45]

Thus totters the table of the Orient. The Oriental artisan produces patterns that destabilize the European mind, chairs that cause the body to lurch. Correct geometrical understanding, inculcated by the DSA-influenced curriculum in India, would rescue him from this gyring and gimbling, enable him to operate at par with European industries.

Hunter's analysis echoes opinions expressed elsewhere. Baden Henry Baden-Powell, artisanal reformer in India, brother of the Boy Scout movement founder, spoke of "the tendency of all Indian craftsmen to leave their work crooked in line and unfinished in joints, to spoil a carving by allowing an ugly knot in the wood right in the middle."[46] Amin Jaffer has attributed this perception to the mismatch between customary artisanal skills which emphasized fineness in carving, and the novel forms of European-style goods and furniture that were invading the colonial household. Although indigenous carpenters were renowned for their skill in copying any furniture, the structural aspects of Western furniture often eluded them.[47] The table was not only the processing house, the tableau for the composition of heterogeneity, but also the very imprint of colonialism:

> The demand for furniture of any kind is necessarily a thing of the present day. Furniture, excepting bed-legs, chests or presses, the *takht-posh* or low table, and the *píri* or stool, was hardly known to the forefathers of the present generation.[48]

Under the collaborative effort of DSA acolytes such as John Lockwood Kipling, John Griffiths, and Henry Hoover Locke, vocational and industrial schools in India underwent significant change from their former utilitarian ethos, composed of humdrum attempts to educate artisans "in their stations rather than above them, to make the son of a potter a better potter, the son of a mechanic a better mechanic, and so forth."[49] The DSA curriculum brought with it a global theory of value in relationship to the market. Rather than harp on the moral virtues of better work habits, DSA acolytes focused on the fact that crafts-based commodity production, even as it was being displaced by mass-manufactured goods in India, occupied a more lucrative sector of the market in Europe, in the same bracket as French products. Ernest Binfield Havell stressed that, in a survey commissioned by the Industrial Education Office of Bengal presidency, indoctrination into "expensive fine work" was preferable to "cheap common work," because it garnered better wages and profits for the "workman."[50] Interventions into the training of customary producers negotiated a dichotomy of use-value and exchange-value that was acutely perceived by art and technical instructors, on the lines of what Norma Evenson has termed "the long debate" between utilitarians and contextualists.[51]

On one hand, given the immense popularity of Indian wares in the world exhibitions, art pedagogues recognized the value-additive possibilities of the intricate ornamental skills practiced by indigenous artisans and their unique secrets handed down from generation to generation. On the other hand, this very strength also became for administrators the artisans' principal weakness: the artisans' dogged insularity in refusing to share their knowledge with colonial officials was inevitably cast as signs of a rigid and hidebound ethos rather than as a legitimate protection of trade interests. The fact that Indian artisans often, and quickly, *did* adapt to prevailing market conditions by copying European designs *in toto* was dismissed as simply confirming their penchant for mindless imitation. Copying the European, in the eyes of DSA-aligned officials, belittled Indian artisanry by divesting them of both their own native strengths and the ability to critically manipulate the shifting morphotropy of value. The theme of the degrading thralldom to Western industrial products was repeated over and over again in numerous industrial, exhibitive, and educational reports made by the various provincial governments. The following passage by Baden-Powell is an example:

> Another great trouble is the singular aptitude of even the best work-men and designers to get *poisoned*, if I may use the expression. The idea of doing something just like a real European article—"*asl wilayat ki muáfik*"—seizes upon them. Instead, for instance, of looking at the charming old architectural decorated forms, in doors, windows, balconies and mouldings, and gather suggestions from them for his cupboards and cabinets, the carpenter will exultingly take a wood-cut from an advertising English Furniture Warehouse catalogue, and make what he thinks is a copy. The cut being rough in itself and in some sort of perspective, the workman can very imperfectly understand it, and the result of his interpretation may be seen any day in the bazaars of our large stations. I can still recollect the pride with which—some years ago, it is true, but the spirit still remains—an accomplished carpet-weaver showed me a fender rug which he had ornamented with a blue sky and clouds, and a shaded scroll to represent *ormolu* moulding around the edge.[52]

Clearly, the response to this subjugation had to be orchestrated in such a way that the vital strengths of customary production could be preserved in conjunction with the task of making artisans aware of the axioms of "proper" taste in the imperial marketplace. Once again, drawing became the wedge that could pry open this anthropological fold. If metropolitan pedagogy taught drawing to make the industrial worker transcend the dull repetitions of the machine, in the colony drawing would empower the artisan to surmount his own automaton-like attributes. In 1854, on the eve of founding the school of industrial art in Calcutta, a Bengal engineer described the problem thus:

> In the make of every man and youth however rude or simple, whom we employ in manual labour, there are powers for better things. Some *tardy imaginations, torpid capacities, tottering thought;* yet it is our fault that they are torpid and tottering; and we should care for them in their feebleness or they can not be strengthened. We must get out to them the *thoughtful* part, whatever error or fault we may take with it. You can teach a man to draw a line and to cut one, to strike a curve and to carve it, with admirable precision, or to mould one of these elegant and tasteful forms, but if you ask him to think about the form, or consider if he can find any thing better in his own head, he hesitates and stops; he begins to think, and the chances are he thinks wrong, and makes a mistake in the first touch; but when you have once fairly aroused thought, and trained it as instrumental to design, you have converted the being from mere machine into a man![53] [i.o.]

The artisan's customary skills become a cultural analogue of the machine, conceptually blind but corporeally productive. The hand of the traditional artisan is like the glitch in the metallic roller that churns out design in spite of itself. For the DSA faction, the difference between a craft-based automatism and the machine marked out in abject terms something like the relative difference between industrial degeneration in "East" and "West." For the likes of Kipling, it was not so much that the Indian artisan was unable to inculcate the critical force of drawing as in his European counterpart but that he was *unwilling* to. This unwillingness was nothing less than a civilizational predisposition, an entirely other ethos of production:

> Their [the native craftsmen's] drawings are seldom to scale, perspectives are unknown, and the details are not carefully made out, for, as the mistry superintends the work himself, he does not think it necessary to elaborate on paper parts which will be better understood when they come to be worked *in situ*. The eye and the memory seem to have grown independent of the elaborate system of detail drawings common in Europe, and though such drawings are looked upon by the native workmen with more respect than they are always entitled to, he sees no need to emulate them.[54]

Drawing thus pulls metropolitan worker and colonial artisan into a discontinuous value-chain. In the metropole, aesthetic habit must be inculcated; in the colony, customary habit must be transcended for the two to confront themselves as heterogeneous equivalents. Drawing is the unifying analytical substrate that produces this asymmetrical parity. The analytical continuity between East and West offered by drawing needs to be also understood in the context of the larger initiatives in industrial education in India. By the end of the century, this asymmetrical equivalence posed by DSA aficionados between the metropolitan worker and the Indian artisan had developed into a full-fledged alternative consensus that nestled in the very core of the administrative apparatus.

Frederic Salmon Growse, maverick bureaucrat in the United Provinces and regular contributor to the DSA's *Journal of Indian Art,* described the transition from a Eurocentric to a nativist paradigm through an account of his own career. Growse writes, on arrival in 1864 as a neophyte into the principality of Karauli in the Mainpuri district, Agra division, of his immediate interest in the local *tár-kashi,* or wire-inlay work. Noting that the use of the decorative technique was limited to a few articles and restricted in variety of pattern, Growse regrets his own first response, which was to provide the artisans with Gothic patterns. By contrast, he was much more pleased with his other impulse, which he considered precocious for its time, which was to have the artisans apply their technique to different objects of European domestic utility: book rests, writing desks, and the like.

Growse recounts the ironic consequences these interventions had in the context of the regional Indian exhibitions. In the 1867 Agra Exhibition, for instance, the exhibitors refused to consider a writing desk made under Growse's direction, because the "wire-inlay" category did not include objects of European use. In contrast, some objects that Growse exhibited at the Simla Exhibition were categorized by Henry Hardy Cole and other officials as *antique* work. Decrying the apparent lack of "discernment" here, Growse, in reflecting on these cognitive errors, argued that the value of these experiments lay less in questions of antiquity or novelty, of authentic Eastern provenance or Western intervention, than in the potential for future innovation through this insinuative tutelage of tradition.

There is a discrepancy here that Growse seems anxious to both highlight and hide. After realizing his "error" with the Gothic patterns, Growse set to work culling patterns and designs from the architecture of the surrounding region, including an intricate one from the Buddhist stupa at Sanchi. Growse was keen to point out that this too was a foreign practice, because the customary habits of local artisans, in his view, would never be able to effect this transition themselves. Thus, inasmuch as he advocates the task of the local administrator was "to encourage native talent to develop itself on its own lines,"[55] an interventional role for European tutelage intercalates itself into this organic, seemingly self-propelled metamorphosis.

It is here that a certain contrast is posited between the English and Indian artisan regarding the respective need for tutelage on these two fronts. The formulation is worth going into in some detail, because Growse is one of those fabled "men on the spot" officials who sustained the ulterior objectives of colonialism in general even as much as they clashed against its bureaucratic routines in the particular. Critical of the DSA's efforts over the past three decades—the article is written in 1888—Growse attributed its failure to British tradesmen's marked preference for "a repeat" in matters of design. Adopting novel designs meant frequent hiring of designers and resetting the mechanical equipment to the new patterns, both financially onerous for the producer. In contrast, the Indian artisan, who used his hands, minimal tools, and largely produced bespoke piecework, was naturally predisposed to variation and change. Each handmade article, produced one at a time, could be made different from the last, admitting of infinite permutations.

The danger, however, and here Growse cites his long-term "experience," was that changes in each article occurred only in the direction of increased and aimless intricacy of pattern. This occasioned "over-minuteness of elaboration [and] ... protracted execution" of more complex patterns, but there was no palpable transformation in the general utility of the object. It was here that European supervision was necessary, "not in teaching novel designs, but in restraining the over-luxuriance of indigenous invention." European supervision would keep track of exchange-value and guard against superfluous morphotropy in the artisanal object, reorienting its grain toward imperial modes of utility. Through this transformation, a certain discontinuity between "outside" interloper and inside indigene is covered over. The biomorphism in Growse's formulation is conspicuous:

> So far as my experience leads me to believe, there is not a district in these Provinces where some indigenous manufacture may not be discovered. Inter-communication is now so easy that there is no reason why these industries should not continue to be strictly localized. Each can supply outsiders with its own speciality and take from them in return. It is a serious mistake—though one often committed—to attempt to force a new industry in an uncongenial environment, and to insist upon the universal adoption of a style simply because it has been found to answer under one particular set of conditions. ... I would rather advise [potential reformers] to seek some germ of indigenous growth, and on discovery, whatever it might be, to devote all their energies to its cultivation.[56]

Only then can "an industry take root in healthy soil." Growse's verdict—unsurprising given that he quotes Ruskin copiously—is against schools and institutional support for artisans, inveighing instead in favor of "personal" and individual patronage on the part of native and European elites.

Growse self-consciously characterized himself as an antibureaucratic gadfly, yet what is curious is that this anti-institutional ethos had become something like a full-fledged bureaucratic consensus by the turn of the twentieth century, pervading all aspects of the British administrative apparatus in India. As we have seen in the Cole circle at home, bemoaning officialese and officialdom was a permanent trait of official discourse in the nineteenth century. In India this lament was accompanied by the casting of the Indian artisan/indigene as the prime victim of bureaucratic functioning. Attempting to posit a view of the artisans as organic, genealogically motivated subjects, yet in need of official support, officials would routinely proclaim the undesirability of institutional intervention into native genius, while simultaneously calling for expanded institutional scope and European supervision to protect the artisans from increased vulnerability in the face of European competition.[57]

The antibureaucratic theme was a leitmotif of the observations made by the pedagogical bureaucrats in attendance at the art conference held at Lahore in early January of 1894. With the entire DSA faction in attendance— Thomas Holbein Hendley and Havell, among others—and convened in the immediate aftermath of Kipling's retirement, the conference was presented as an opportunity to take stock of the four decades of the DSA's influence in India. Different speakers cast the art schools as both the problem and the solution to the degradation of native craft. To some extent, this dilemma can be attributed to the divergent experiences of the respective art schools, whose regional surroundings determined their functioning to a large extent. Bengal was deemed as being the furthest and most undesirable in terms of the nativist aims stated by the conference: its artisanal bases had been wiped out by a century-long process of rapacious revenue extraction and mass-commodity inundation. The *bhadralok* and protonationalist affectations of its burgeoning bourgeoisie, compounded with widespread degradation of its artisanal base under the onslaught of early colonialism, rendered it infertile ground for the kind of intervention desired by the pedagogues at Lahore. "In Bengal there is but little indigeneous art work proper, and but few industrial art centers, as compared with other presidencies."[58] The Bombay school, under the successive direction of Henry Locke and John Griffiths, functioned on its part more as a Normal School, like its South Kensington parent, training drawing teachers for primary education. Only in the recent past, since 1891, had traditional artisanry become a significant focus of the school with the introduction of the Reay Art Workshops, which brought in master craftsmen from the region to train students in their respective crafts.[59] The industrial section of the Madras school, on the other hand, construed artisanal work as wage-earning trades with direct application to European domestic commodities. Classes—offered in jewelry, silversmithing, carpentry and cabinetmaking, carpet weaving, pottery and porcelain—taught skills that had little to do with local native expertise.

The overwhelming consensus regarding the model to be emulated pointed to Kipling's Mayo School in Lahore, now being run by his protégé Bhai Ram Singh.[60] Kipling's efforts to survey and establish strong paternal relationships with the artisans of the province were advanced as an incentive for further official initiative to penetrate modern industrial standards into rural interiors elsewhere. The infrastructural apparatus thus portrayed is that of an extremely localized and decentralized network, with the provincial art schools acting as Normal Schools, providing museums and schools at the district level with teachers, expertise, resources, and conduits to the imperial market through metropolitans, museums, exhibitions, and retailers. In this way, colonial administrators sought to project their intervention as facilitating a two-way traffic between the norms of morphotropy and utility created by the European market and the collation of the secret techniques and traditional skills of artisanal work. The sentiment is echoed in a raft of technical reports, questionnaires, surveys, and so on that were appended to the main of the 1894 report.

The consensus that emerged at the end of the conference was not unlike Growse's proposals six years earlier. Where the report differs is in its emphasis on the continuance of the art schools based on two principal functions. The first sought to play down an overbearing tutelary role, urging that the schools be viewed instead as administrative organs to oversee artisanal production in the field. If there was one area where the schools were envisaged to expand in terms of direct intervention, it was in the area of drawing, and this is the second point of emphasis:

[W.H. Jobbins, principal of the Government School of Art, Calcutta, stressed] the value of drawing as being an absolute necessity for every class of students, except, perhaps, those who would be satisfied with the very lowest standard of knowledge. It was in his opinion the foundation of knowledge, as by its means alone in many instances, an intelligent man could be able to express himself accurately. He said that some knowledge of drawing was necessary to enable a youth to understand even an ordinary map. He would have the subject made compulsory for all examinees, certainly for those who appeared at the University and even Middle Class examinations. The basis of all technical knowledge was drawing. Few people understood the value of drawing for *general* educational purposes. If the teaching of drawing were made compulsory, it followed of course that teachers would

Figure 3.3 Studies of architectural ornamentation by students of the Mayo School of Art under the tutelage of John Lockwood Kipling. Courtesy: V & A Images.

be required, and that, as these would not necessarily be of the stamp of the ordinary art masters trained in the schools, it might be desirable to educate men up to the standard of pupil teachers for the special purpose of teaching in district schools.[61] [e.a.]

What is critical here is the formulation of drawing as an element of a *general,* rather than a specialist, education. The engineer requires drawing as much as the artisan; the maid laying out silver on the English dinner table uses drawing as much as the Punjab villager trying to read a map. Drawing in this sense constitutes the basic visual education that produces the civil and laboring subject. Unlike the fields of engineering, where drawing teaching was directed toward mechanistic objectives, DSA policy in both Britain and India forcefully argued for a curriculum that was not hamstrung by the particular requirements of any individual trade. John Griffiths, principal of the J.J. School in Bombay, and another South Kensington product, expressed this clearly while elucidating his newly drafted educational policy for Bombay presidency in 1880:

This scheme [of teaching South Kensington-style drawing] has nothing to do with Indian art, or any other art, any more than that its object is simply to train the hand to express accurately and intelligibly what the eye sees and the mind conceives; and so important is this qualification thought necessary as a basis of technical education and the general training of youths in Europe, that the teaching of drawing is considered as important as the teaching of reading and writing, and is incorporated as a compulsory subject in the [European] system of education. ... I do not quite understand what is meant by [the idea of teaching different drawing skills tailored for different trades]. The drawing that is first begun in our elementary schools and then carried on to more advanced stages in the School of Art is that which is common to all trades and professions in which art is employed. ... What is required and what should be enforced is that all who are engaged in art industries should be trained to be good draftsmen. This is absolutely the basis of all good work, and this is one of the principal functions of a School of Art, viz., to teach good craftsmanship. To expect a man to turn out a piece of art-work before he can draw is very much like expecting a child to write before he has learnt his alphabet.[62]

Once again, the irony of artisans without a formal art training turning out specimens that were already objects of admiration for European consumers is happily elided in this argument. This presumed commonality between, and the *a priori* of trades, however, requires more qualification, when it is confronted by differentiations of cultural formation. Europe is in the vanguard of critical control in drawing even as the skills involved in drawing are globally identical:

The wood carver, the enameller, the embroiderer and the ornamental workers in metals all draw alike; they simply modify it to suit the requirements of their trade. Each craft does not use a special method of drawing. The drawing which Raphael used for expressing a hand or a foot is the same as that which he used in preparing his designs for the goldsmith, and is similar to what the silversmith of Kutch and the wood-carver of Surat use to-day—*the only difference being that the former expressed greater knowledge and refinement by his drawing than the latter.*[63] [e.a.]

The generality of drawing therefore has the character of a datum, in that its presumed universality actually underscores a surreptitiously inserted standard. It appears as intuitively readable and yet demands pedagogical intervention to decipher it. Thus, even as the DSA ideology located drawing as the *sub*strate of all craft, it also cast it as the epistemological, therefore *super*vening, determinant of craft. This bifaceted ascription also offered significant rhetorical advantages for a utilitarian administrative disposition that perennially invoked clarity of purpose as a subterfuge for its disinclination to increase budget costs. Even if this fiscal reluctance militated against significant transfer of technology from the metropole to the colony, the mid-nineteenth-century eschewal of technology (and industry) as restrictedly purposive nonetheless offered a felicitous metaphor of the administration's own ends in the colony. Art could act as a stand-in for the lack of science.

The teaching of drawing was thus doubly felicitous, because it straddled both the purposiveness of technology and the nonpurposiveness of art. Inasmuch as each of the provincial schools catered to particular regional trades, drawing appeared as corollary of the artisan as anthropological category: the name for a willed conflation between technology and art. More so, through drawing, art could appear to have the attributes and advantages of technology, as instrument for building productive subjects of the empire. The generality of drawing therefore bridges several dichotomies: between art and technology, between trained and untrained, between Orient and Occident, between craftsman and engineer. Each of these subjects can read drawing, but not in the same way.

For DSA acolytes in Britain or India, part of this perception drew from a willful disingenuity on their part in distinguishing between the distinctive functions of *technical* and *artistic* drawing, which by the midcentury period had separated into entirely different oeuvres with quite different institutional settings. Even as specialized drawing conventions were being honed as a reflection of increased division of labor in the metropolis, DSA pedagogues continued to proselytize drawing as an immediately transparent "universal language—intelligible to all the diverse races of mankind, needing no translation, but at once 'known and read of all men.'" Both Rafael Cardoso Denis and Molly Nesbit have written of the nineteenth-century identification of drawing with language, with clear metaphors in notions of "grammar," "idiom," "alphabet," and structured sign systems. With the DSA agenda, the generality of drawing could very quickly be translated into the universalist dream of an imperial Panglossolalia. Richard Redgrave described this universalism in the following way:

[Through drawing] ... we hereby obtain, so to speak, another language, another intelligible mode of communicating thoughts and explaining things; having, moreover, this advantage over other languages, spoken or written, that it is universal, that it is almost alike intelligible to all the diverse races of mankind, needing no translation, but at once "known and read of all men." But there is another and an equally great advantage, which is, that whereas words, spoken or written, even in our mother tongue, often convey but a confused and imperfect idea of things, dealing necessarily rather with generalities than with minute specialities, and requiring long and elaborate descriptions where accuracy is required, drawing supplies us with a power whereby long descriptions and pages of writing are at once superseded, and thus it is a condensed *short-hand* as well as a universal language; a short-hand, moreover, intelligible equally to him that writes and to him that would read it; useful not merely to the scientific man for his diagrams and illustrations, but in the every-day relations of life.[64]

Drawing facilitates the translation of knowledge into a universal cognitive datum. In this sense, it is not so much the local artisan who is enabled by the DSA agenda to read the morphotropy of the European commodity but rather the artisan who *is being read and translated* as a generalized counterpoint within industrial capital. The Oriental artisan does not produce the pattern; *it is the pattern that produces the artisan*, brings him within the matrices of a certain intricate, "contrapurposive", calculability. It is precisely through this reversal that Growse's warning against an "over-luxuriance" of the local acquires a realignment with the telos of colonial transformations of the native subject. It is because of this analytical function of drawing in decoding the artisanal that Thomas Holbein Hendley and Baden-Powell could advocate the supply of patterns collected from as far afield as Cairo and Budapest to Indian artisans as interchangeable motifs to prop up the market acceptability of native industrial techniques.[65]

Apprehending Drawing

Notwithstanding this appropriative mode of the imperium, the pedagogical question remains. What is being learned in this translation and transference of drawing? If drawing is always already readable, what is it that is being transmitted in the contract between the tutor and those being taught? This question is particularly critical where the pedagogical relationship is framed in response not just to the "unformed" persona of the child but rather to the fully formed anthropology, albeit abconstructed, of the artisan. We have noted here that the primary thrust of drawing teaching in the DSA curriculum was to inculcate geometrical concepts in the imagination of the artisan. How was geometry made available to the artisan and worker, characterized as being deprived of the original stimuli of either science or art and relegated instead to a phenomenal "approximation" of both?

The Raphael who has the everyday sense of geometry and operates at a cut above the Oriental artisan is not unlike the figure of a certain Galileo spelled out in Edmund Husserl's essay of 1936, "The Origin of Geometry." These proper names appear in Husserl's essay in the place where the historiographic status of the proper name seems most in question. There is an implicit swipe at Kant's invocation of a supposed Thales in the First Critique:

> In the first place, what sort of strange obstinacy is this, seeking to take the question of the origin of geometry back to some undiscoverable Thales of geometry, someone not even known to legend? Geometry is available to us in its propositions, its theories … we must and we can answer for this logical edifice to the last detail in, terms of self-evidence. … No one would think of tracing the epistemological problem back to such a supposed Thales. That is quite superfluous.[66]

Kant cites Thales as an ingredient of received wisdom. His motive is not unlike Husserl's: to get beyond the nominalism exemplified by Diogenes Laertius in his *Lives* to establish a conceptual principle of the kind of historical transition exemplified in the "demonstration" of the isosceles triangle and epitomized by the shift of civilizational primacy from the Egyptian to the Greek.[67] Husserl's dismissal of the proper name appears in the context of a comprehensive rejection of empiricism as a principle for elucidating historiography. The affixation of a proper name to the discovery of a new geometrical principle cannot constitute, by itself, an explanation for the change. By the same reckoning, the potentially endless recuperation and "naming" of the minutiae of everyday events in history, even if the present is the inheritor of the infinite, incommensurable, and "undetermined" matrix of the miniscule occurrences of the past, cannot in itself constitute the *disciplinary* basis for a historiography. This undetermined matrix of the legacy of an aggregate past, in Husserl's words, is "tradition," a variant of Marx's "open book" of history. Tradition is therefore the *passive* reception of what awaits *reactivation* through the delineation of historiographic method. (The relative aptitude for this reactivation, predictably, is the basis for the difference between the "primitive" and the civilizational primacy and horizon of Europe.)

Geometry presents an analogue for historiographic method, hence the query regarding its "origin." Like the experience of temporality, the transmission of geometry is also ramified into passive and active modes of reception. It is here that Galileo appears, at the beginning of the essay—in many ways setting the exemplar for it—as an indeterminate inheritor, a nodal point, for both geometry and historiography. Like the DSA's Raphael, then, Husserl's Galileo makes his mark by professing an investigation of geometry based on a critical understanding of its internal principles. Nonetheless, even as Galileo opened the way to active elucidation and enlightened reflection on its "meaning-origin," his grasp of geometry as a discipline was no less passive or ready-made than that of his unacknowledged and unnamed precursors.

An example of the passive transmission of geometrical knowledge is the school textbook:

> How the living tradition of the meaning-formation of elementary concepts is actually carried on can be seen in elementary geometrical instruction and its textbooks; what we actually learn there is how to deal with *ready-made* concepts and sentences in a rigorously methodical way. Rendering the concepts sensibly intuitable by means of drawn figures is substituted for the actual production of the primal idealities. And the rest is done by success—not the success of actual insight extending beyond the logical method's own self-evidence, but the practical successes of applied geometry, its immense, though not understood, practical usefulness.[68]

The textbook's *practical* success is its *critical* failure. The morphotropy of immediate use waylays the schoolboy recipient of geometrical instruction from proper reflection on its own principles. Like the DSA, for Husserl, the dyad of passive use and active reflection has its epitome in the operations of language. The linguistic analogy is important because it offers Husserl an opportunity to rehearse a response to what is deemed, from the phenomenological standpoint, a critical shortcoming in Kant. Husserl retains Kant's formulation of geometry as an ideal system. What is for Kant a speculative reflection back into ideality, however, becomes for Husserl a transcultural given affording no inroads for phenomenal apprehension. The question, for Husserl, is this: how is this ideality made communicable on an "intersubjective" level, especially down the generations, at a point where the original discoverer of a theorem is now absent? Crucial to this framing is Husserl's understanding of geometry as an aggregative science, where every new discovery, by definition, advances the cumulative entirety of principles discovered in the past.

The ramifications of geometric research are syllogistically and architectonically purposive; they build on the integral wholeness of the edifice, quite like buildings. This monolithic structuring is not without its internal differentiation; indeed, it is differentiation and fragmentation that most concerns Husserl when he creates the image of a geometer working in "his part of the building," oblivious of the foundations on which he stands.

The problem is averted by invoking a particular capacity of *writing* as a linguistic formation. Writing presages the eventual absence of its author. It transmits without ontological presence. Geometry could have come about only when cultures had already devised conceptual formulations that brought about something like writing, of recording linguistic

signs systematically so that they can be passed on through the generations. But language seems to have lost itself into a passive and associative matrix; it "falls victim to the seduction of language." As an idealist
system with clear articulation of principles, geometry thus offers, when
"fully" activated, an analogue for advancing communication without the
pitfalls of such associative seductions. It is here that we arrive at the kernel of Husserl's proposition. "The Origin of Geometry" is not a research
into the historical provenance of geometry but a philosophical inquiry
into language at its origin using geometry (and the sciences) as its model.
The phenomenological desire—or "attitude," as Derrida puts it—is quite
unlike Kant's in its schema. Kant positions a rigorous discontinuity
between the ideal and phenomenal worlds; in Husserl's phenomenology,
inasmuch as the latter is privileged, the phenomenon is comprehensible
only when *modeled* on the reflective processes of the former. Cultural
sense–intuition can be understood only to the extent that it follows the
contours of the sciences. Tradition can be understood only to the extent
that it is subject to the methodological rigors of disciplinary history. In
his "Introduction" to Husserl's "Origin," Derrida encapsulates this in the
following manner:

> The phenomenological attitude is first an availability of attention for
> the future of a truth which is always already announced. Instead of
> frantically investigating the options, we must strive towards the nec-
> essarily single root of every dilemma.[69]

This singular resolution approximates the idealist deduction, even as it
protests the primacy of the intellect. As to the question of geometry at its origin, this singular approximation is projected onto further regularizations
of shape—we note here that Hegel considered shape as the primary field
of beauty[70]—resolved through "practical" usage into surfaces and straight
lines. For Husserl, the inventor of geometry at this practical deduction is
therefore markedly *anonymous:*

> First to be singled out from the thing-shapes are surfaces—more or
> less "smooth," more or less perfect surfaces; edges, more or less rough
> or fairly "even"; in other words, more or less pure lines, angles, more or
> less perfect points; then, again, among the lines, for example, straight
> lines are especially preferred, and among the surfaces the even
> surfaces. … We can always presuppose some measuring technique,
> whether of a lower or higher type, in the essential forward develop-
> ment of [every] culture, (as well as) the growth of such a technique,
> thus also including the art of design for buildings, of surveying fields,
> pathways, etc., such a technique is always already there, already

abundantly developed and pregiven to the philosopher who did not yet know geometry but who should be conceivable as its inventor.[71]

For the DSA, it is precisely this pregeometrical apprehension that constitutes the aesthetic morphotropy of use. The morphotropy that defines the primary field of the ornamentist or designer, as we have seen before, is manifested in the surface. Here again is the introduction to the DSA's *Drawing Book*:

> In the great majority of cases, ornaments applied to surfaces by mechanical processes of reproduction, seldom go beyond outlines which are filled up with one or more colours, or with different tints of the same colour, and which in general make little pretence to truth of artistical [*sic*] imitation; bearing the same kind of relation to the actual appearance of the objects from which the idea of the ornament has been taken, as the *silhouette* does to the portrait; and, like the outline of the former, admitting of being filled up with any tin that suits the fancy or purpose of the draughtsman. Outline ornament, is, by itself, a species of ornamental art, the study of which is indispensable, whatever other exercises may be subsequently necessary to complete the education of a designer.[72]

For Husserl, the original arrival at geometry is a phenomenal approximation of its idealist deduction. Similarly the foundational impetuses of language can be recovered only by the peeling off of its sedimented "associations" accumulated by everyday usage. Linguistic research ought to restore to words their singular validity as a sort of naming function for things. By analogy, the long-lost sources of tradition can be approximated by the delineation of a historiographic methodology that restores to tradition its originary purposiveness.

I contend here that the DSA's pedagogical premises in India—to teach the artisan what he already knows—constituted an attempt to effect a similar methodical "reactivation" of what was deemed as the eviscerated passivity of tradition. As such, Husserl's linguistic analogy is paralleled in British India by the perceived necessity of incorporating vernacular tongues into official language and their role in mass pedagogy. In its desire to manage the local with greater efficiency, educational strategy in India was (and is) marked by fraught linguistic politics and the reorganization of myriad dialects and mother tongues into regional languages—a companion project to the work of documenting and catechizing patterns. Colonial governmentality in India thus represented a wholesale effort to reinscribe its "passive" traditions—epitomized in the new mother tongues and pattern languages of the nineteenth century—within a rule-bound grammatology.

Like artisanal pedagogy, the formalization of the mother tongue also presents a fundamental paradox. The mother tongue is *precisely that which is not learned* according to a set of rules; the immersion into the mother tongue, to use a Lacanian expression here, is presymbolic. Teaching the mother tongue—like teaching visual norms—is pedagogy in a language that the pupil already knows. Indeed here we are presented with the paradox of the pedagogical moment in general, because cognitive learning of new information can be imbibed only in the mode of already having known, in the mode of *recognition* rather than *cognition*. Kant's parable of the falling apple can be useful here. Humans *always knew* apples fell from trees; they did not have to wait for Isaac Newton to appear on the historical stage to apprise them of this fact. The mother tongue is in the place of the "always known." One cannot learn the mother tongue; *either one has a mother tongue or one cannot learn.*

Teaching the mother tongue—one might term this instituting the *vernacular,* a term pregnant with associations in both language and architecture—is therefore a way of instilling the boundaries of critique, of the necessity of rule-bound language rather than the rule itself. In this, it is coterminous with the Kantian conception of "Enlightenment".

The DSA's artisanal pedagogy is in the place of such a pedagogy of the mother tongue. Tradition is being methodized by a post hoc armature that bears the *analogical* force of rationality. Its purport has the appearance of adhering to supposedly new economic conditions. In the end, through this rationalized prosthetic, it is not the artisan who begins to read the hieroglyph of capital. It is rather the artisanal subject that is being submitted to a new mode of coding through its imprint in the pattern. Once again, Husserl's formulation of a latent validity is useful here. Geometry is paradigmatic because each advance within the field carries forward the entirety of the discipline, even if the original authors and proponents are absent from the scene, dead to posterity. Writing, recording—the DSA's primary activity in both metropole and colony—is the prosthetic through which this discontinuous carriage is achieved.

For the Oriental artisan, the geometrical pattern becomes the mnemotechnological supplement that operates in the place of writing in Husserl's linguistic analogy. Neither material technique nor mode of visualization, neither art nor science, the pattern is the script through which transition—emergent or willed—is effected in the discontinuity from precapitalist to colonial (neo-feudal) capitalism. If writing presages the death of the author, the pattern produces a temporal continuity at the exact moment that it foretells, indeed brings about, the eventual demise of the anonymous artisan. The pattern, as we shall see, remains like a genetic code to rebuild its replicant.

CHAPTER 4

Of AbOriginal and CopyRight

A humorous anecdote is related to the effect that an American baby gets out of its cradle, shuffles round it, hits on an improvement, and patents it before he is six months old. In this country [India] we are not so precocious.

—Messrs. Remfry and Remfry, patent agents, Calcutta, 1881

In 1998 two persons were sentenced to serve jail time in Bikaner, on the western periphery of the Indian state of Rajasthan. The charge: forgery. Recognizing this craftiness as also involving a *craft,* jail superintendents put them to work on copying designs onto the jail's century-old carpet industry.[1] This identification of craft as copy, as we have seen, inheres in the very rationale of drawing pedagogy in the context of nineteenth-century industrial education. The nineteenth-century pupil is asked to copy pattern again and again. Because neither metropolitan worker nor colonial artisan, however, can immediately locate himself as the empowered subject of reason, and therefore of taste, the "pattern" appears as the enigmatic figure through which the anthropology of both can be woven into the subjecthood of the laborer.

The nineteenth-century market in taste is an incessant circulation in patterns, loping dexterously between sites of tutelage and indenture. As a result of the huge demand in Oriental carpets after the Great Exhibition, prisons became key venues in which carpet weaving was introduced to both fuel and meet metropolitan demand. This penitent exertion had the dual benefits of subsidizing the costs of upkeep and of accordance with the

Victorian nostrum of reforming minds through the labor of the body. The carpet manufactory in the Bikaner prison dates back to the establishment of the prison in 1872, by its British-backed client-king Dungar Singh. The prison has its own legends, one of how Dungar Singh's descendant Ganga Singh showed to his courtiers some carpets he bought in Europe. After the king's sycophants had lavished much praise on his taste, a jailer politely pointed out that the carpets had been made in their own jail. In the circuitry of imperial trade, the signature of the artwork becomes unrecognizable at its (ab)origin.[2]

The possibly apocryphal tone of this tale nonetheless underscores the point that even as jail carpets were sold abroad as examples of native creativity, traditional production became the leitmotif for a global interchangeability forged on the functional anonymity of its aboriginal authors. In this chapter, we will examine the status of the Oriental pattern—moving between production sites as far afield as Stoke-on-Trent and Bikaner—as the metonymic substitute for aboriginal signature. Responding to international demands, jail superintendents traced patterns from Old Central and Persian collections in private repositories and circulated them through the prison network. By 1901 the South Kensington Museum (SKM), now named the Victoria & Albert Museum, was actively reintroducing patterns from its Indian and Persian carpet collection into production centers and industrial schools across India. Caspar Purdon Clarke, director of the Indian section, made the following offer to the Indian government, which it subsequently accepted:

> I am prepared to undertake, as a portion of my official duties in connection with the Indian Section of the Victoria and Albert Museum, to select, from our large store of Persian and Indian designs, patterns of the best periods and to send them to India with the necessary technical directions for their proper reproduction. Care will be taken to strictly keep within commercial bounds, and although a high standard of design and colouring will be tried for, no unnecessary fineness in the weaving counts will be used to increase the expense, which should not in any case exceed that of the ordinary commercial carpets of the Jail or Bazar factories.
>
> The Carpet industry is a subject with which I am well acquainted, having visited and studied the principal centres of manufacture in Turkey and Persia, besides a thorough investigation during two years spent in India and Kashmir, where … I revived many old patterns by causing copies to be made in the Jails of fine carpets, often but bundles of fragments, which were borrowed from the palaces of native Princes. In London I have been referred to as an *expert and arbitrator*

in legal cases concerning carpets. … [This would be particularly useful in the areas where] large numbers of hereditary carpet weavers would welcome any revival of their handicrafts, which owe much of their decadence to the bad patterns introduced from Europe.[3]

Note that for Purdon Clarke, the traffic in the copy manifests itself as an arena of *legal* expertise, "within commercial bounds". Indeed the promiscuity of the copy in the nineteenth century initiated a series of legal and legislative maneuvers that were critical to the commercial and pedagogical functioning of "design" as a profession. This chapter will frame design and architectural practice in the context of global international property law; its critical import will be to suggest that the legal countenance of "originality" and creativity borne by the designer nonetheless draws on and reinforces the anthropological asymmetry between different kinds of global subject: the modern original and the unmodern *aboriginal*. *Aboriginal*: the term refers to the autochthonous figures already—somewhat inconveniently— present at the origin of narratives of tradition. The usage of the term in this chapter will refer to an anteriority of the modern legal subject, to be slightly distinguished from its common reference to indigenes settled in various parts of the world before the great "Indo-European" migrations.

Reproducing Originals

The transfer of models and templates and the legal complexities as evinced in the carpet industry were not limited to Oriental goods alone. In fact, the "culture of the copy" pervaded the very pedagogical strategy of the Department of Science and Art (DSA), in both the colony and Britain. Ever since their inception in 1835, the Schools of Design had begun to assemble a large collection of casts of European sculpture for use in the classroom. Throughout its history, first at Marlborough House and then at South Kensington, the DSA continued this practice with great enthusiasm. Although the early copies were small and composed mainly of ornamental details of buildings, by the 1860s the DSA was acquiring figure sculpture and eventually entire architectural monuments.[4] A striking remnant of this history in the Victoria & Albert Museum is the full cast of Trajan's column, cut in half to fit within the building height of the cast gallery. Other major pieces obtained at this time were the entire front portal of the cathedral of Santiago del Compostela in northern Spain, the Giovanni Pisano pulpit from Pisa, and the St. Sebaldus shrine from Nuremberg.

Although the SKM was not the first institution to acquire casts in Europe, the DSA's status as a vanguard institution of its time inspired many other institutions to follow suit, thus creating a substantial market and industry in casts. Under Cole's urging, no less than fourteen heads of state from eleven European countries signed a joint declaration at the Paris Exposition of 1867 to legally permit reproductions of monuments and artworks in their possession.[5] The document also explicitly cited South Kensington's as the critical pedagogical model to be emulated by all other European institutions, an opinion seconded by the French Positivist and Comtean Frederic LePlay, the convener of the 1867 exposition. As repository of originals, the museum cannot establish itself without a developed infrastructure of the fake.[6]

The department's interest in artistic reproductions was not limited to casts alone. The DSA promulgated the use of other technologies of reproduction such as electrotyping and chromolithography in provincial and colonial museums and schools.[7] The SKM was the very first state museum to collect photographs and the first to open an independent photographic section in 1856. By 1859 Cole's museum had acquired no less than eight thousand prints, including those by renowned photographers such as Fox Talbot, Baldus, Le Gray, Nadar, Nègre, and Fenton, in addition to contributions from Belgium, Italy, Spain, and the United States. Predictably, many of these were simply reproductions of artwork from the Continent. Yet the SKM was precocious also in its patronage of the medium as possessing artistic value in itself. In 1865, after a sitting, Cole bought eighty prints from a relatively unknown woman photographer, gaining Julia Margaret Cameron her first foothold in the annals of art history.[8]

The DSA's Oriental and Indian collection also consisted largely of reproductions. This was owing to the DSA's immense belief in the sanctity of the original and preservation of artifacts within their place of cultural origin. As a result, India was spared the kind of cultural pillage evinced in the French sack of Italy and Egypt. Initially unable to rouse the East India Company's Nabobs from their disinterest in matters of art policy, the DSA's Indian collections were limited to the work of photographers such as Samuel Bourne.[9] After 1857, however, both the SKM and the Architectural Museum, the latter housed in the Crystal Palace in Sydenham under James Fergusson, were engaged in acquiring a substantial photographic collection of Indian architecture. In 1866 Fergusson published his seminal *History of Indian and Eastern Architecture* based mostly on these photographs. Subsequently, the *History* then became the theoretical and catalogic reference for the museum's subsequent Indian acquisitions.

Nonetheless, the SKM's collection of Indian casts remained miniscule compared to its European acquisitions. To rectify this situation, in 1867, Cole's son, Henry Hardy Cole, a lieutenant in the Royal Engineer's Corps, was sent to India under deputation to the Archaeological Survey of India. In his first year, Cole Jr. wrote back to London outlining an elaborate scheme for taking architectural casts in the North-West Provinces.[10] The administration in India, however, was least disposed toward entertaining the DSA's wishes in this regard, and it was only after Cole wrote an irate letter to the Secretary of State for India, Stafford Northcote (who had been on the 1849 Committee of the Schools of Design), that some progress was made in the following year.[11] With the younger Cole in charge of making casts of important archaeological monuments in northern India, the museum acquired its first large cast of Indian architecture in 1870: the entire gateway to the Buddhist shrine at Sanchi (33 feet 6 inches in height, 11 feet 9 inches in width). In 1872 the museum received no less than 164 pieces of Indian casts, ranging from Gandhara sculptures to Orissan architectural ornaments, the last under the direction of the Indian architectural historian and "Young Bengal" ideologue, Rajendra Lala Mitra.[12] In the next decades, there was a steady infusion of Indian casts into the SKM (many of them made under the supervision of Cole Jr.), with an upsurge during the tenure of Caspar Purdon Clarke as the superintendent of the Indian section in the 1880s.

In the 1886 Colonial and Indian Exhibition, liberal concerns over empire and the ascendance of the Morris circle brought the Cole doctrine of reproduction and original to an ironic pass. In late-Victorian London, there had been increasing criticism of the depredation of colonial craftsmanship by the introduction of metropolitan goods into rural markets. Correspondingly, officials scouring the Indian countryside for objects of "industrial art" deemed the skills of the artisanry in such decay compared to their supposed former grandeur that no contemporary works were deemed worthy of display at the 1886 exhibition. Instead, Indian artisans were commissioned to produce a special series of regional screens based on designs distributed by the officials. The source for these designs was *none other* than Fergusson's photographic collection from the 1860s.

Original and AbOriginal

As the DSA's assiduous enterprise suggests, what is novel about the discourse of cultural provenance in this period is its multilateral—rather than national—scope. To grasp this fully, we need to address the problems faced and the arguments advanced by the Cole circle at its very first encounter with public scrutiny, in the prelude to the Great Exhibition. Before the exhibition, British Parliament, with the connivance of Cole and his free trade cohort, passed a law protecting the rights of international inventors, manufacturers, and designers who would display their products at the exhibition. The legislation was designed to allay the fears of exhibitors about displaying trade secrets in an arena in which the secrets might be exposed to potential imitators. Until this point, the laws governing these rights had been *national* in scope, and the international scope of the exhibition called for quite different approaches. Although these laws were passed by the legislative body of an individual nation-state, Britain's imperial preponderance in this period, the international scope of the Great Exhibition, and the very tenor of the bill, made it the earliest example of a *multilateral* framework for international rights in intellectual property (IP). Cole was prescient about the novelty of this development. In tracts written to refute the protectionist lobby, he boded that the new sphere of IP legislation occasioned by the exhibition would eventually transcend national aberrances of law and become the basis for an untrammeled commercial exchange between nations:

> The beginning of the *reform of our Patent Laws,* or laws for the recognition of the rights of intellectual labor, which I foresee may have great international results on industry, is due to the Exhibition. I say the beginning, for we have only just entered on the very threshold of the subject. Almost as soon as the Exhibition was announced, every one was sensible of the manifest absurdity of inviting exhibitors to display the fruits of their intellectual exertions, whilst at the same time they should be subjected thereby to pillage. ... Imperfect as this law is, it will have important results on industry, both abroad and in our colonies, and will affect inventive rights, more or less *over the whole world.* [e.a.] I am happy to say, that we cannot now go to the Continent, pillage an invention in use, and introduce here as a novelty; and that we cannot prevent a Belgian or French inventor from giving our own colonies the benefit of his skill.[13]

Subsequent world exhibitions became the prime venues where multilateral initiatives on intellectual property rights (IPR) were negotiated, owing to the unprecedented international forums afforded by them in legal, economic, and political terms. In 1865 Britain again led the way by passing a permanent bill for the protection of inventions and designs at all successive industrial exhibitions. This was followed by a spate of IP initiatives on the international front, most of them at the world exhibitions. The first Patent Congress convened at the Vienna International Exhibition of 1873, reconvening at the 1878 exposition in Paris. Ten years after Vienna, the Paris Convention for the International Protection of Industrial Property was signed in by ten industrial nations. Ratified by Britain and three other countries in 1884, these fourteen signatory states became the founding members of the International Union for the Protection of Industrial Property. In Britain the pressures of these international obligations brought the separate domains of IP, that is, patents, designs, and trademarks, under the single ambit of the law of 1883.[14] As for copyright, the 1878 exposition also saw the foundation of the International Literary Association, under the presidency of Victor Hugo. The association spearheaded the international effort to consolidate different bilateral agreements between various nations into the multilateral Berne Convention on copyright of 1886. In some form or the other, both the Paris and the Berne accords remain active to this day; the latter is binding on this book.

The anthropological profiles attributed to artists, authors, and designers were critical to providing an "aura" of creativity and originality to this swathe of legislation and its relationship to the advocates of free trade. In this context, it is not surprising that people like Cole attributed Britain's lopsided trade relationships and export asymmetries with its captive colonies in terms of its vanguardism in design:

> For instance, the designers in this country are just as likely to be called upon to frame a design which will suit the taste or the want of it, of the African savage on the coast of Mozambique, as that which may be necessary to meet the requirements of the inhabitants of Mayfair.

The passage is from Cole's *Report of the Registrar of Designs on Copyright,* written in the aftermath of the passage of the 1851 bill.[15] It makes clear the *global* latitude attributed to the European designer, a profession newly resurgent and redefined in the context of industrial mass production. As such, it reflects both the efforts at cultivation of a domestic mass audience and the innate expansiveness of imagination through which the European aesthete conceived himself as the imperial adjudicator of taste in commodities. This worldview was not simply an imagined chimera; bureaucrats like Cole and his mentor John Stuart Mill, champions of free trade and opponents of national protectionism, were quite directly invested in the formulation of colonial and international law. Circa 1851 the aesthetic thus impeccably frames Britain's trade interests. Thomas Webster, a specialist in design-based litigation, examined the new potentials of IP law in a book published in the same year as the exhibition. Webster hinged the value of artistic and design activity entirely on their commercial ramifications, ones that automatically extended to the colonies:

> Questions of difficulty connected with colonial patents have recently arisen; the same invention has been the subject of grants by the Crown here and by the Legislature in the colony; it is obvious that some means should be adopted of preventing such interference and conflict of rights. ... Patents as heretofore granted do not extend to India; but recent events in connection with the efforts for the promotion of the arts and manufactures, the establishment of railways, the production

of cotton and other articles of commerce in that extensive territory, have called attention to the beneficial effects likely to result from the granting of exclusive privileges for a limited time, and under proper regulations, to the introducer of a new trade, or of inventions tending to the furtherance of trade, in that portion of our dominions.[16]

Notwithstanding this prayer and desire for commercial symmetry in theory, the spread of IP doctrine into the colony would be hard to come by in practice. The tenor of Webster's argument is cast entirely in a unidirectional vein; legal privilege of IPR travels only from European metropole to the colony; the legal situation does not quite travel the same way in the other direction. In the next few sections, we will try to outline some of the anthropological impermeabilities of IP that underlined this legal asymmetry. Following the passage of the 1851 law, even though hundreds of inventors and manufacturers secured short-term registration for their products in the prelude to the exhibition, many were still wary. Some even identified the patent law as a ruse to deprive British manufacturers of their technological advantage. One handbill circulated widely before the exhibition, titled *Industry of All Nations: Be Just before You Are Generous,* warned British manufacturers against the loss of profits from international piracy of the unique qualities of British technology and design:

> Few, if any, who have so liberally subscribed, are aware that their Countrymen are far from entering the Arena upon equal terms, that the law does its utmost to *stifle genius,* to *crush* the efforts of the most valuable members of the industrial classes, or that many of the most important inventions are *irretrievably lost* to the community through the withering influence of the Patent Law.[17]

Because of this unwillingness to put up the actual technology in public view, many of the machines on display at the Great Exhibition were, in fact, made of papier-mâché.[18] As India was Britain's premier colony, the Indian section of the Great Exhibition was second in size only to the British galleries. Nonetheless, none of the extensive deliberations and concerns on matters of IP leading up to the Great Exhibition were deemed relevant to the myriad Indian products, collected at extremely cheap prices by the East India Company through the express intervention of the younger Mill. Both prior to and in the wake of the postexhibition passion for Oriental goods, English designers routinely copied or adapted Oriental designs, copyrighting them under their own name. The global scope of the international exhibition thus imposed its own uneven structures of global legality. In the exhibition's culture of the copy, the facsimile comes face-to-face with the *aboriginal.*

Although the other imperial powers of Europe were amenable to the advantages of the multilateralism sought after in the Vienna, Paris, and Berne conventions, the United States—feeling the aftershocks of near economic ruin in the 1840s and the still smoldering embers of a devastating civil war—resisted subscribing to the free trade dictum underlying the debates on IP at the international level. Citing reasons of economic sovereignty, it persistently refused to protect foreign works or to be drawn into any multilateral accords until well into the last quarter of the twentieth century. The position of the United States in that period closely resembles those of many today in the Group of 77, or "developing" and "least-developed," nations as against that of the G8 nations in the negotiations relating to the TRIPS (Trade-Related Aspects of Intellectual Property Rights) clauses within the World Trade Organization. Ironically, in the 1990s, U.S.-based multinational corporations have been the dominant term setters within the G8 position, aggressively undermining the arguments for IP exceptionalism from the global South. In contrast, in the nineteenth century, when Britain acceded to the Paris and Berne conventions, Europe's colonies were involuntarily conscripted, by proxy, into the signatorial silhouette of authorship dictated by this new legal sphere.

For all the purported association of IPR with individual privilege, the global interface of this dialogue presents us with a paradox. On one hand, the United States, an industrial power, constitutional guarantor of individual freedoms, refused to enter a global regime of rights in order to guard its domestic privileges. On the other hand, India, an administrative entity without political rights, was drawn willy-nilly into this economic regime by the fiat of its colonial masters. Not a single one of the millions of Indian and Oriental objects displayed at the world exhibitions, eagerly copied and exploited by metropolitan purveyors, were deemed to require either patent or copyright. In the monumental implications of this occlusion, and in the harnessing of imperial production to this evacuated authorship of the aboriginal imagination, one begins to sense something of the anthropological parlance within which industrialization is encoded. The aboriginal cannot (legitimately) enter the culture of the copy.

The question that presses itself on us here would not be parried by a retrospective and all too expedient notion of justice that seeks today to simply restore, through a "recuperative" historiography, to the aboriginal artisan of 1851 agency a concept of "rights," rights we see here divested in the very moment of their creation. To do so would mean only to reaffirm nineteenth-century, "liberal" conceptions of creativity, IP, and anthropological subjecthood and their continued legitimacy as global adjudicator. Our questions should rather be as follows: What are the modes of subjecthood through which aesthetic notions of "originality" intersperse with the legal armatures of economic production and political presumptions about rights? What are the conceptual boundaries by which IP rights are deemed to be appropriate for one kind of anthropological formation and not for others? These modalities, we will see, have consequences for different kinds of client groups, the aboriginal as much as the designer, even as these are placed in what appear to be opposite docks in the litigious tribunals of modernity. To respond to these questions, we must examine the mid-nineteenth-century turn in multilateral IP issues, laying out some historical fissures that appear in this complex firmament of aesthetic authorship, legal contract, and political citizenship.

Situating IPR

One point needs to be emphasized here: in the so-called creative disciplines, the key shift into modernity occurs when "imagination" and its predicate "innovation" become less a matter *of* conception or attribution than one *for* legal and administrative discernment.

The Royal Society of Arts was the principal force behind the committee that convened toward the end of 1850 to devise the required legal changes in the patent legislation for the Great Exhibition. Led by Cole, and carried forth by the significant weight of the manufacturers' lobbies, the committee also included the Marquis of Northampton, the Earl of Radnor, Charles Dickens, Owen Jones, Lyon Playfair, and Herbert Minton. In December the society released its *First Report from the Committee on Legislative Recognition of the Rights of Inventors*. Ghostwritten by Cole in its entirety, the urgent tone of the report was occasioned by the imminence of the exhibition.[19] The bill that was consequently passed by Parliament extended the provisions of the Designs Act, offered "Protection from Piracy to Persons exhibiting new Inventions in the Exhibition of Works of Industry of All Nations," and drastically whittled down the torturous bureaucratic maze of the existing system. The act granted provisional protection against piracy during the limited period of the exhibition, pending subsequent registration of the artefact under the normal laws. Within the short period of nine weeks, upward of 765 applications had been made for provisional registration in England alone. Much of the participatory success of the exhibition was owed to this bill and other collateral guarantees offered to exhibitors from the Continent. Many manufacturers enthusiastically took advantage of the act to guarantee short-term profits rather than to submit to the long process of garnering permanent protection. Owing to this success, the 1851 law was made permanent in the following year. In addition, a single patent office was created, based at Chancery, under the direction of a newly appointed commissioner's office.

On Tuesday, October 29, 1850, two days before Cole submitted his Report to the attorney general, he, having spent months working on it and consulting manufacturers and designers, took it to John Stuart Mill for his comments. Later that day, his diary tells us, he incorporated Mill's suggestions into the main of the text.[20] Although that draft and Mill's annotations have probably long been consigned to the dustbin, Cole's deference to his mentor indicates the strong influence of Mill's thought on the actual process of rights legislation of all flavors in mid-nineteenth-century British history. Much of this influence is attributable to Mill's reflections on the individual, which were critical to the DSA's conception of the designer. Mill's landmark essay "On Liberty" contrasted the individual as described in eighteenth-century theories of natural society against its contemporary, servile, socialized variant:

> In some early states of society, these forces [of unbridled passions] might be, and were, too much ahead of the power which society then possessed of the disciplining and controlling them. There has been a time when the element of spontaneity and individuality was in excess, and the social principle had a hard struggle with it. The difficulty then was, to induce men of strong bodies or minds to pay obedience to any rules which required them to control their impulses. To overcome this difficulty, law and discipline ... asserted a power over the whole man, claiming to control all his life in order to control his character—which society had not found any sufficient means of binding. But society has now fairly got the better of individuality; and the danger which threatens human nature is not the excess, but the deficiency of personal impulses and preferences. Things are vastly changed, since the passions of those who were strong by station or by personal endowment were in a state of habitual rebellion against laws and ordinances, and required to be rigorously chained up to enable the persons within their reach to enjoy any particle of security. In our times, from the highest class of society down to the lowest, every one lives as under the eye of a hostile and dreaded censorship. Not only in what concerns others, but in what concerns only themselves, the individual or the family do not ask themselves—what do I prefer? or, what would suit my character and disposition? ... [Rather] the mind itself is bowed to the yoke: even in what people do for pleasures, conformity is the first thing thought of; they like in crowds; they exercise choice only among things commonly done: peculiarity of taste, eccentricity of conduct, are shunned equally with crimes.[21]

Pedagogical exertion must therefore direct itself toward the inculcation, not the harnessing, of dissimilitude in the subject. This instigation of a measure of eccentricity is thus quite at variance from Locke's theory of education, where the subject's uncontrolled "passions" and obstreperousness must be bridled through measures of "external sanctions." Mill's concerns are clearly set out in opposition to these doctrines. Mill's preferences here were not so much philosophical as a cultural response to his times. In Britain universal suffrage was increasingly seen by liberal mind-sets as an imminently feasible reality. Although social unrest remains a persistent feature of this era, the principal danger to the public sphere was no longer perceived to be issuing from the unfettered passions of the "primitive" subject as the lack of socialization between classes. And so it is with Mill and his circle of radicals that we see the early development of a critique of mass culture. In the life of the "crowds," one saw nothing but "conformity ... choice only among things commonly done." The inability to exercise "choice," to articulate aesthetic eccentricity in the savoring of "pleasures" (a theoretically pregnant word in the Benthamite lexicon), also indicated an incapacity for political discretion and ultimately the ineptitude to transcend and therefore undo class interests. It is within this caution against the tendency toward conformity in public life that Cole and the Royal Society of Arts couched their arguments for increased rights of IP. Posed as the apostle of "choice," the designer became a critical ingredient in the ideological slippage between aesthetics and politics in the debate against the protectionists.

Conundrums of Utility

In the previous sections, I have consciously conflated the quite distinct debates on copyright, patents, and design registration in the nineteenth century that might otherwise exercise more fastidious scholars.[22] Nonetheless, at least some of this willed confusion stems from the fact that the terms of distinction between copyright, patent, and design registration were, and are, always ambiguous in terms of ontological description. Firstly, many of the reformers who testified at the different hearings on the different forms of copyright, patent, and other legislation within British parliament were, in fact, the same. Also, as we will see below, the actual history of legislation and litigation demonstrates an irrepressible contamination between the respective domains and definitions of different genres of object and their jurisdiction. The Ornamental Designs Act, passed in 1842, could serve as an example of this ambiguity. One of the first pieces of design legislation to be influenced by Utilitarian thought, this act was also the first to lay out the differences of domain between patent and copyright law. Under its provisions, the law of patents would refer only to "useful" items, whereas copyright would now refer to "nonuseful" items, defined therein as "the 'form and configuration' of any article of utility—in the shape of a steel pen, or a tooth pick." However, as the simpler provisions of the ornamental law (modeled on those of copyright) came into force, the archaic state of the relevant patent laws led many manufacturers *of useful products,* including several mechanical devices, to take refuge under it instead. Cole used the example of the sheer miscellany of objects registered under this act and others preceding it as a cry for patent reform:

> In 1839 an Act was passed to secure to proprietors of designs for articles of manufacture the copyright of such designs, and it was intended that this copyright should apply merely to ornamental designs; but the craving of the public to escape from the persecutions of the old Patent system led them to use this Act, and to take the chance of any protection which it might afford by registering articles under its provisions which were strictly the subject of Patents, and in which ornament was little or no ground for claiming the registration. Even the very first article so registered was a letter-weight, certainly not a very ornamental design. And if the earliest registers of ornamental designs be consulted, they will show that files, horse-shoes, cistern-valves, taps, corkscrews, skates, gas-burners, and even steel-pens were registered as articles of ornament! ... Inventors oppressed by the Patent Laws have taken refuge under [the subsequent 1842] Act [meant to reform the former one], and as we have seen, have registered many inventions as being "forms or configurations"; whereas it is notorious that the object of the claims is the protection of a new mechanical action or contrivance (rather than of ornament).[23]

The immense promiscuity of objects registered under Cole's own provisional law of 1851 did absolutely nothing to dispel this ontological problem of discernment between what constituted "useful" as against "nonuseful." At the Public Record Office in Kew, where every registered design from the period has been meticulously collated and archived, a typical page of the register contains, for example, *drawings* for a needle and a breakfast tray, *photographs* of two different portrait tags, the photographic *elevation* of a bedpost, one *actual* piece of ornamental lace, and three *fragments* of woven fabric consisting partially of Oriental motifs. The term *design* seems to cover over the heterogeneity of quotidian objects in the general; the principle underlying this assembly appears to be one of simple empirical difference rather than an indication of innovative utility per se.

This interchangeability of objective categories, between patentable and copyrightable commodities, had its subjective connotations as well. The important thing to note here is that the *ideological* argument for and

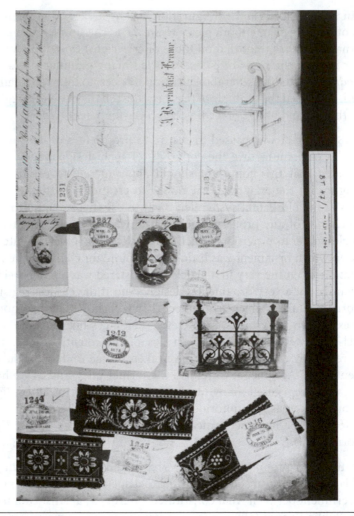

Figure 4.1 Designs registered under the 1851 Act on the Registration of Designs. Courtesy PRO.

against IPR inevitably rested on a remarkably consistent anthropological fiction that survives to this day: of the innovator as somebody who sets his mind to a problem defined by social need and goes about finding the ways and means to solve it. This sequential—I will call this "motivational" —model of directed invention runs throughout all the different turns and twists of IPR law, no matter what their ontological vagary. In the following extract, Cole quotes a parliamentary respondent from 1829:

> It has been stated, that patents may be multiplied to too great an extent; I conceive that idea arises from this circumstance only, that as the law is not clear with regard to patents, so many are obtained that appear

defective in law, which by confusing workmen really do mischief; but if the law be made so clear and defined, that a patent for something really useful, when taken out, would be found to be secure, then I cannot conceive that we can have too many patents, as they are the reward of men's ingenuity. One man has a property in the funds, another in land, a third man in the powers of his head, evidenced by his inventions; and I conceive that if you were to limit the number, you would at once cramp men's ingenuity, and not give those who are clever their fair value in the market, because their brains are the only property which they process.[24]

As we shall see, the dominance of this model acquired substantial adjudicatory and punitive weight when confronted with other provenances of creativity. The ideology of IPR also displaces the relationship of original and copy into one of legitimacy and fraud.

It should not surprise us to find that one of Cole's earliest entanglements in issues of public reform centered on fraud. After his rise to prominence over affairs at the Public Records Office, Cole was invited by the Australian reformer Rowland Hill to join the campaign for Uniform Penny Postage in 1838, an effort to secure a cheap and uniform system of postage that would consolidate the British Empire within a homogeneous circuitry of information.[25] As the movement gained strength, the Society of Arts turned its attention toward the design of a fraud-resistant—yet inexpensive and mass-produced—stamp that could circulate everywhere within the kingdom. The Society's concern was ostensibly humanitarian; earlier in the century, a number of poor artisans had been put to death after being convicted of forging Bank of England currency notes.[26] With the circulation of a cheap stamp becoming imminent, the possible recurrence of a similar scenario of desperate transgression and repulsive punishment once again reared its head. The Committee of the Society of Arts took it upon itself therefore "to enter upon an investigation for the purpose of ascertaining whether there may exist any means within the compass of the fine and mechanical arts" to discourage such temptation on the part of poor artisans.[27]

Defined in the Society's terms, the task was a novel one: to design, through the devices of art, an object that, on one hand, was amenable to mass production, and on the other, resisted forgery or imitation by unauthorized persons. Hill appointed Cole to the Treasury and officially charged him with obtaining a suitable design. The designs that Cole subsequently obtained from various artists, including William Mulready, form an art-historical research field of their own.[28] The process was to result in the composite production of the legendary "Penny Black," whose philatelic uniqueness was testimony as much to the profusion of disparate artistic inputs as to the mechanical processes employed in its creation.

For Cole, this experience inaugurated a lifelong engagement with issues of aesthetics and mass production. Removed from his appointment by a new government, and working largely on an independent basis, Cole subsequently published, in 1844, a scholarly treatise on the series of Dürer woodcuts titled *The Small Passions,* laying out the distinctions between original prints, acknowledged "copies," and unacknowledged "fakes" of these works.[29] It is a fine example of Cole's intellectual powers, in terms of both archival skills honed at the Public Record Office and the ability to discern nuances of artistic and technical verisimilitude. As he was researching the material, Cole came in contact with Charles Dickens in 1843, who was carrying on his own campaign on international copyright against the piracy of his books by American publishers.[30] Using notes provided by Cole on the debilitating process of obtaining a patent, Dickens wrote and published a short story in his weekly magazine *Household Words* about a poor inventor who is deprived of the benefits of his invention in his torturous dealings with the patent office.[31]

The Official Fake

With the 1851 act in force and Cole assuming leadership of the Department of Practical Art in 1852, it was inevitable that the DSA would maintain an interest in matters of IPR. In 1853 the Privy Council of the Board of Trade brought the Registrar of Designs under the purview of the department, directly reporting to Cole. Thus the DSA eventually took on the responsibility of supervising the executive functioning of the 1842 Ornamental Designs Act, the 1843 Non-Ornamental Act (referring to articles of utility), and the 1850 Provisional Designs Act (made permanent in 1852), all of which were extensions of the framework of copyright law. The DSA held this office until 1883, when trademark, designs, and patent registration were consolidated under a single and independent authority of government.

These duties were by no means the only ones the DSA undertook in matters of IPR. In 1851 the commissioners of the Great Exhibition had obtained a number of industrial patent models, which had been submitted to the patent offices in lieu of specificatory documents and had since been kept at Kensington Palace. The palace also housed an additional private collection of models owned by Bennet Woodcroft, a patent agent and former "Superintendent of Specifications" in the Office of the Commissioners of Patents for Invention. When the DSA moved to South Kensington in 1856, the models were also moved to the new site. Using the *Conservatoire des Arts et Métiers* in Paris as inspiration, the DSA grouped the models as a separate Patent Museum, an autonomous institution vested under the Commissioners of Patents. In addition to donations from inventors, the museum contained in its display exquisite models of such landmark inventions as James Watt's steam engine, Stevenson's "Rocket," and Arkwright's "Spinning Jenny,".

As the 1850s wore on, however, the happy accord within the SKM's display between the legal preoccupations of the Office of Patents and its pedagogical purpose of instigating innovation was increasingly ruffled by a growing division over the uses and objectives of IPR. As the interests of manufacturers became more entrenched in the brass tacks of legislation and legal stipulation, the didactic idea of a patent museum to encourage innovation slowly lost its cogency. Patent commissioners were more interested in creating an exhaustive *printed* catalog of all existing patents, a document that would serve as a legal guide and reference for patent applicants, thus making the use of models superfluous in legal terms. Drawing, rather than models, now bore the specificatory abilities most suited for the legal stipulation. On the other hand, SKM curators had become increasingly dismayed by the profusion of models donated to the museum by manufacturers simply as a way of gaining free publicity for their products. In 1864, in front of a select committee formed to decide the fate of the Patent Office Library and Museum, Cole voiced his frustrations regarding the patent models at SKM. His testimony plaintively demonstrated the deviation of intent that the Patent Museum had undergone since its inception:

> I do know that a great many things are there [in the Patent Museum] that have nothing to do with patents: cocoons exhibited by Madame Clemence de Corneillan, a quantity of matters relating to education, such as portable globes, pictures, Chinese sculpture, chemical matters, photographs of men of science who were *inventors and not patentees,* surgery processes, bootmaking, &c. which had no connexion with patents; a loaded pistol fished up off Tilbury Fort, showing the effect of oxide of iron in forming concrete. I merely point out that the scope which the Patent Commissioners had in view in forming this museum was not limited to patents at all; I suppose that these patriarchs of machinery, the locomotive that killed Mr. Huskisson, an earlier locomotive "Puffing Billy," as it is termed and things of that kind, *had little to do with patents particularly;* Arkwright's spinning jenny may have done so, but not the boiler of the "Comet," that went on the Clyde, and things of that kind had not. I consider that through accident, an institution which was originated with the idea that it should resemble the Conservatoire des Arts et Métiers at Paris, has got changed into a little thing called a Patent Museum, such is the drift of my evidence. This Patent Museum, I think that is a complete perversion of the original idea.[32] [e.a.]

Cole's sentiments had certainly come a long way from his strident advocacy in 1851. Why this gradual change of mood, this abject differentiation between "inventors and not patentees"? At least some of the answers can be found in the events leading up to that period. Instead of improving the environmental conditions for technological progress, and far from simplifying the procedural clutter of the old regulations, the new IPR laws had simply produced some of their own. Dickens's "poor man" would still find it an onerous task to reap the fruits of his "intellectual labor." Patent offices were deluged with applications for an array of knickknacks of doubtful utility, a sore point for the progressives who had clamored for change. In subscribing to the motivational model of the innovator that we talked about earlier, it was this specter of indiscriminate circumstance that Cole and his ilk had sought to guard against.

Although it is unlikely that Cole became an outright opponent of IPR, one can surmise that his gradual disillusionment reflected an increasing rift between the technicalities and actualities of IPR procedure and the hortatory earnestness of liberal thought. Cole made it clear before the 1864 committee that the Patent Museum was hardly the embodiment of the idea laid out by the 1851 Commissioners for a Museum of Scientific Inventions. Had those intentions been realized, the primary scope of the museum would have been educational and inspirational, composed of an exhaustive international repository of path-breaking technical innovations.[33] Instead, they had ended up with, at best, an uncurated receptacle for patent specimens and an appendix of specifications for the exclusive reference of patentees and agents. Cole even went so far as to question the educational use of the models: "Patent models are of no use except as information to people who cannot understand working drawings."[34]

This cleft eventually played out into the subsequent history of the models. In the last quarter of the century, as the ideas of the Cole circle lapsed into superannuation, the original aims of the Patent Museum came to be viewed as supererogatory to IPR doctrine. In 1883 Parliament moved to institute a new office for a comptroller-general with increased powers to bring the patents, trademarks, and designs offices (the last hitherto under the DSA) under its single authority. The administration of the Patent Museum, hitherto under the supervision of the Office of Patents, was consigned entirely to the SKM; the import of the models was now relegated to being relics of the recent past. Eventually, as the DSA split up into its constituent divisions of science and art, the patent models were passed on to the Science Museum, in the basement of which they remain to this day, far from the eyes of the public.

Cole's disillusionment with the Patent Museum mirrors the sentiment of other liberal advocates of IPR in other fields as well. If early reformers had sought to define the market as a "natural" determinant that conferred appropriate rewards on resourceful creators of commodities of public utility, another facet of the motivational model alluded to earlier, patenting procedures were increasingly perceived now as only a bureaucratic obstacle in the supposedly self-corrective behavior of the market. The profound conflation by liberal ideologues of the codeterminacy of the market's "natural" behavior and the public good cannot be underemphasized here. Within liberal doctrine, the privatization of ideas was defended on the principle of the public good; both Mill and Cole were vehemently opposed to long-term monopolies that reverted a common resource to private hands for extended periods of time. In more nuanced terms, as a doctrine whose primary function within the state apparatus was to regulate class mobility, liberal thought always based its societal assumptions on the *discriminative* use of rights. Instead, what the deluge of IPR applications in the record books threw up in the 1850s was an indiscriminate scrimmage where causality in relationship to the public good became indistinguishable from accident. A speech given at Edinburgh in 1863 by William Hawes, then president of the Royal Society of Arts, demonstrates exactly how much the stance of that organization had changed from the heady days of 1851. Hawes ruefully contrasted the roughly fourteen-thousand patents granted in the entire 227 years of patent history previous to 1852 to the *twenty-one* thousand that had been granted in the mere ten years since:

> May we not ask whether there is any branch of manufacture so entirely changed by strictly new and useful inventions during the last ten years as such a flood of patents would indicate? Have not these ten years, and I quote from the Jury Reports of the last Exhibition, been remarkable rather for the great majority of the twenty-one thousand patents granted as valueless as they are injurious to the progress of true invention—clogging its course, interrupting the pursuits of the true inventor and taxing his power and genius to benefit those, whose only claim to reward consists in skillfully availing themselves of the operation of a bad law to gather profit from the industry and skill of others.[35]

The motivational model of the innovator subscribed to by the Cole circle therefore presents to us an exact corollary of the suspicion of fashion voiced by the DSA's Richard Redgrave in the previous chapter. For the radical faction, the hope was that more comprehensive IP protection would perform the exact same role that the designer would carry in relationship to taste, which was to reinscribe the indeterminacy of commodity production along an organic impetus of invention, thereby rendering it amenable to both management and perpetuation. In the overwhelming of this organic complex by the proliferation of commodities, we see therefore the critical contradictions that both undermined and underpinned the designer as the privileged director of this heterogeneity. It is to the figure of the designer that we will turn to in the next few sections.

Men of Another Stamp

But it was men of another *stamp* than this that made England what it has been; and men of another stamp will be needed to prevent its decline.

—**John Stuart Mill,** *On Liberty*

If the Society of Art's and the DSA's effort to directly impact IPR manifested itself into unintended failure, this involvement nonetheless had its effects on the evolving culture of design. As we have seen, the search by the Society for a composite design for a cheap postage stamp drew from an earlier suggestion regarding banknotes. In 1789, as a way of guarding against forgery of security documents, Jeremy Bentham had proposed distributing the printing of banknotes among many craftsmen with different stylistic tendencies. Given the identifiable idiosyncrasies of each craftsman, the composite design would thereby become practically impossible for forgers to imitate, presumably because the imitators would be hampered by their own instinctive mannerisms.[36] For Bentham, therefore, psychological (i.e., natural) singularity translates itself into singularity of aesthetic expression; the artistic work bears the inalienable imprint of each individual *as such*. Design, in this reasoning, was simply the outer appearance of irreducible identity. Its verifiability was based on both a differential and a normative logic: in all other respects where A = B, A's work cannot be the same as B's because A is not B. Although Bentham's recommendations were ignored at the time, as we have seen, they found eventual application in the collective design of the Penny Black in 1841. In his *Second Report,* Cole paraphrased the principle in the following way:

If ever there seemed to be a likelihood of unconscious infringement, or an easy road to it, it is here. But the practical working of this Act has been such, that there has not been an average of twenty convictions per annum during the creation of at least fifty thousand patterns. As for unconscious infringement of any one of them, such a thing is hardly possible; no two persons, however alike in taste and education, being set apart to devise a pattern on a given subject, would ever do precisely the same thing, and it would be the same with inventions. It is a law of nature that no two things can be precisely alike. Even manufactures from the same mould present important differences.

There would be sure to be such minute differences as to constitute an independent originality, in all inventions however trifling.[37]

In the previous two chapters, we have examined the post-Kantian complex wherein the pattern was perceived precisely as the outer manifestation of an inner, formative nature. More important, we have seen how this aesthetic/ethical understanding of the pattern was anthropologically differentiated—Kant's particular exemplification of "Greece" and "Egypt" are cases in point—between the *ideal* subject of reason and the subject devoid of it. The Benthamite corpus, in this sense, might be described as a truncation of the ideal subject of philosophy into a practicable anthropology. The individual connotes something of an aggregate, mathematical figure, even an algebraic variable. Paraphrasing Bentham, Mill described this principle in "Utilitarianism" as "everybody to count for one, nobody for more than one."[38]

This mathesis of empirical discernment and psychological variation spilled over into the copyright debates of the 1840s and 1850s. James Emerson Tennent's work of 1842, titled *A Treatise on the Copyright of Designs,* is a landmark if only for the fact that he asks the ontophenomenological question that most writers had ignored up to that point: "What is an original design?" Although Tennent's book was couched in the language of juridical discernment and mostly answered to its commissioners (the textile lobby—Britain's largest imperial exporters at the time), the pragmatism of his solution betrayed the same psychological assumptions as Bentham's. To be able to differentiate between original and imitation, visual quiddity must be taken as a predicate of psychological singularity:

> The essence of originality in a design consists, not in its abstract elements, which may be the property of any one, but in the conception and general effect of their combination and arrangement into new forms, of which, like the notes of music, they are susceptible of in endless variety, whilst each combination will have a character peculiar to the mind of the artist himself. ... It has been demonstrated by experience, that even where precisely the same materials have been given to any number of artists, their several designs have borne little relative similarity to each other, and could each and all be designated new and original; and it is distinctly alleged it is as unlikely, if not more so, that two artists, from precisely the same objects, should produce two separate designs, identical in every point, as that two kaleidoscopes, charged with the same figures, could, in simultaneous turns, produce the same combination of them. In practice, indeed, the most extensive employers of designers distinctly assert, that there never yet occurred an instance in which two artists, working apart,

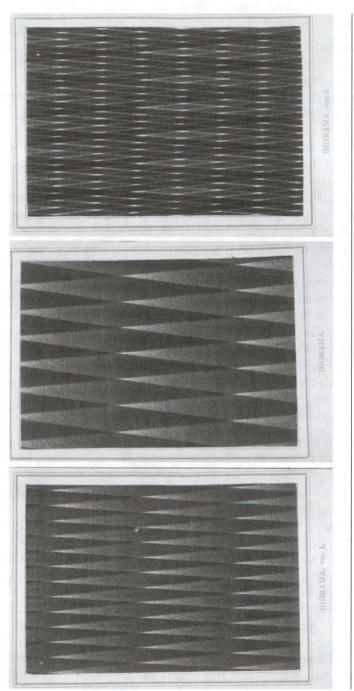

Figure 4.2 Diorama, Variations I, II, and III. These illustrations of fabric patterns were given by James Emerson Tennent as an example of the legal difficulties of ascertaining the original as opposed to variations on a particular principle. From J. Emerson Tennent, *A Treatise on the Copyright of Designs for Printed Fabric; with Considerations on the Necessity of Its Extension: and Copious Notices of the State of Calico Printing in Belgium, Germany, and the States of the Prussian Commercial League.* London: Smith, Elder, 1841.

but from identically the same materials have been known to produce identically the same combination of them.[39]

Two distinct individuals are bound to be different because no two individuals share the exact same thought patterns. Discernment, in this case, proceeds from a negative logic: only where there is intent to copy does the possibility of duplication emerge, whereas the fount of creativity is located in the distinctness of the psychological profile of each individual. Men are "of a stamp," graphable as in the many possible variables of an algebraic formula, presaging more the onset of statistics and demographic science on modern forms of governance. This normativity of the subject should not be confused with the "pinched and hidebound … cramped and dwarfed," infertile automatons produced by restrictive tradition with which the younger Mill took issue in "On Liberty."[40] Bentham's preoccupations are in keeping with their eighteenth-century idiom: to determine the preconditions of "freedom" in the subject rather than to outline the vectors of intentionality itself. By contrast, Mill's pronouncements largely ignore the issues of obedience that beset his mentors. The prime calling of his period, as Mill saw it, was not to curtail the destructive aspects of the individual psyche in a state when human relations appeared as a conflict of interests. The problem, rather, was how to assert the eccentricities of psychological variety in a civil society where "public opinion" was both the prime leveler of individuality and the hallmark of ubiquitous conformity.

If Mill saw the individual as imprisoned by the mediocrity of the collective, the implication is that of the subject as being imbued with a natural fecundity, one that required liberation from the neutering bonds of sociality. Political or aesthetic agency is therefore explicitly conceived of as a state to be attained, to be wrested from the sterilizing forces of present-day modernity. For Marx, by contrast, agency is already *partially* at work in the appropriation of different subjects by means of the different routes of valorization: sociality is thus simultaneously produced and snared in the move to capitalization: "The Negro *is* a Negro. He only becomes a slave in certain relations."[41] [e.a.] Agency is therefore not defined by a finite anthropological attribute defined by any theory of the "passions" or liberty. The subject is always already an agent, whether working in somebody else's interest or one's own. The failure of the French peasants to represent to themselves the organic force of their own revolt lies therefore precisely in its displacement into the political idea of equality and individual rights, thus ensuring the subsumption of their insurgency back into the narratives of the bourgeois state: "the great mass of the French nation is formed by the simple addition of *isomorphous* magnitudes, much as potatoes in a sack form a sack of potatoes."[42] In other words, agency is not an indivisible attribute under the yoke of a repressive society from which the individual could be rescued wholesale. Rather, it is both activated and made visible by the relationships of production, of which the "state" is the protector and "society" is the ideological emblem. For Marx, the failure of the French insurgents to realize the fruits of their revolution stems from the divergence of agency and interest. Agency is the subjective functioning in difference that is set upon by capital. Class consciousness is thus not about "transforming consciousness at the ground level"; rather, it opens up the rupture between agency and interest within the armature of the "individual."[43]

Marx's intuition regarding the irreducibly split profile of the subject is given uncanny substance by the incredible proliferations of multiple personas in the nineteenth century. Hillel Schwartz has given us what we can describe as an exhaustive taxonomy of this proliferation of personas in the modern "cultures of the copy": doppelgängers, alter egos, Siamese twins, mannequins and womannequins, dummies, writing automatons, talking parrots, mimic monkeys, déjà vu, mistaken identities, double blinds, Echo and Narcissus, charges of duplicity, encores. You can say that again. Ditto.[44]

During his career, Cole used at least three different pseudonyms for his different areas of interest: "Felix Summerly" for his persona as designer and aesthete, and "Lee Cromwell" and "Denarius" for use on other fronts. John Lockwood Kipling, the DSA's acolyte "gone native," on the other hand, used the pseudonym "Sadyk Dost" to inhabit the peculiar civilizational conundrums of the British in India.[45] In contrast to the subversive anonymity resorted to by eighteenth-century writers, authorship in the nineteenth century is suffused with subterfuges of signature. Authors sign off with an X, multiply themselves, adopt pseudonyms, and collaborate in collectives or corporations, not to protect themselves but to amplify their voice in the public sphere. In Engel's preface to the second German edition of *The Housing Question* (1887), he describes himself as a *proxy* for Marx, an agreed-on "division of labor" by which he would become a foot soldier in the everyday battles of the workers' cause, allowing Marx to concentrate on the great theoretical opus instead.

> [The proper name] can thus transform itself, at once, and change itself into a more or less anonymous multiplicity. This is what happens to the "subject" in the scene of writing. ... It is a little like the multitude of stockholders and managers in a company or corporation with limited liability, or in a limited, incorporated system; or like that limit which is supposed to distinguish stockholders from managers. Even here, the signatory is no exception.[46]

It is precisely within this split identity of corporate authorship that, as we shall see, a certain legal profile of the designer or architect, indeed, of any profession, becomes possible.

Architecture *Ab Externo:* Framing the Signature

All hail to the vessel of Pecksniff the sire! / And favouring breezes to fan. / While Tritons flock around it, and proudly admire / The architect, artist, and man!

—Charles Dickens, *Martin Chuzzlewit*

The sanctification of the "original" in commodity legislation is the precise justification for the multiplication of subjects and objects in the modern "culture of the copy." As in the case of the "designer," a new legal and corporate figure carved out within the mass-productive rubric of the industrial age, a profession can find its vocation only to the extent that it can translate this multiplication of authorship as a *normative* practice embedded in law. In some senses, therefore, the functional shift of the architectural profession into the era of mass-production epitomizes some of these moves, although only *indirectly,* as we shall see. As Andrew Saint has pointed out, architects in midcentury hardly had the professional status to secure a livelihood based on design alone. Architects typically supplemented their income as land surveyors, real estate agents, property evaluators, building contractors, and so on—a multiplicity of signatorial capacities.[47] Some of them eked out a living as patent agents, because their training in drawing especially suited them to the task of laying out technical specifications. As for the built realm, very little of London's metropolitan silhouette in the 1860s owed anything to the contribution of architects.[48] Perhaps the harshest caricature of the profession was presented by Dickens's Pecksniff, architect and land surveyor, who "had never designed nor built anything," whose "knowledge of the science was almost awful in its profundity," and whose "genius lay in ensnaring parents and guardians, and of pocketing premiums" paid by gullible students who were trapped into becoming his apprentices.[49]

Given the existing state of affairs, it should not be surprising that when the Royal Institute of British Architects (RIBA) was first formed in 1834, the members' interest in shoring up the legal credentials of their profession overtook almost any other considerations regarding taste, style, or aesthetics. Granted with a royal charter of incorporation only in 1837, the history of the RIBA in the nineteenth century offers a revealing comparison with that of the Schools of Design, the first of which was established in the same period. Just as the DSA attempted to normativize the practice of design, the RIBA charter also took on the responsibility of securing "*uniformity and respectability of practice*" for the architect as well as taking "responsibility on behalf of the public for the direction and maintenance of the national character for taste."[50] Plans were set afoot to build up a library and a museum, to introduce a system of formal examinations that would replace the older system of apprenticeship.

In terms of the descriptive function of the architect, therefore, there is a world of difference between the spearheading triumvirate of John Soane, John Nash, and Robert Smirke at the beginning of the nineteenth century and the emerging clout of the RIBA and the Architectural Association at the end of the century. The plaque on the walls of the latter, embedded even today on the western facade of Bedford Square, gives it away: "The Architectural Association, *Incorporated*." If Soane's work with the Bank of England corresponds to the institutional imperatives of a mercantile economy, then the increasing *corporate* legalism that undergirds the term *design* by the turn of the century portends a significant transformation of the architect's professional credentials. During Soane's time, the commercial laws relating to architectural practice were more or less those that governed other trades as well. Legally, therefore, there was nothing to distinguish an architect from a shopkeeper in terms of the intrinsic callings of their profession. Architects were hard put to define their work in formal terms when it came to gaining separate privileges for themselves.

For British architects, the principal obstacle to professional recognition was the overwhelmingly utilitarian bias of law. Although "utility" was one of the principal elements of the Vitruvian triad, the concept of "use" evolving in the shadow of Jeremy Bentham was a far cry from the aesthetic discourses within architecture to warrant the latter's effective deployment within legal or institutional contexts. As a practice, "architecture" lacked its definitive object; on the other hand, different *building* products were always assimilable into the laws governing commodity relations in general. Thus, even if architects were increasingly interested in carving out a separate professional space for themselves, distinct from the other building trades, they were hard put to alleviate the referential indeterminacy of architecture. James Fergusson pointed this out in a talk given to the Royal Engineers in 1863:

> It may at first sight appear comparing great things with small to compare architecture with gastronomy and tailoring, but this is not the question: what I assert most unhesitatingly is, that the useful art of building is refined into architecture by the identically same process

by which cookery is refined into gastronomy, or tailoring into an art without a name. ... The architect has become a man who conceives a design for a building *ab externo,* as a painter conceives the design of a picture; and very rarely indeed a man who works out his forms *ab imo,* or from the real essential necessities of the case.[51]

Even though the name *architecture* was current and in use, it was as if the contemporary activity described by the word was still "an art without a name." Without a well-defined sphere of rights, almost any craftsman or builder could claim to be an architect; indeed this was a common phenomenon until the 1880s, when Parliament finally passed a bill mandating registration for architects. Although building *products* were protected in IPR like any other commercial articles, the ontological description of the architectural "work" proved elusive in terms of legal definition. In a situation where the architect's work could be more plausibly cast into the "nonuseful" rather than "useful" category, architects were hard put to articulate the distinctness of their work or justify its case for legal protection in the manner of inventors or product designers. Without any such sanction and separate legal protection, the signature of the architect as such did not bear any value.

Consequently, when Britain's Parliament moved to extend the laws of copyright in 1861 to embrace artistic objects, a group of RIBA members began pressuring the Copyright Committee to include architecture within the purview of the proposed bill.[52] As a result, architecture was brought within the embrace of copyright for the first time; however, this protection extended only to drawing and not to buildings.[53] Part of this peculiarity came from the fact that copyright laws were understood primarily in terms of literary reproduction. The intuitive analogy between drawings—their stipulatory weight deducible in terms of their syntactic and indexical elements on the sheet—and printed works lent them greater legal force. In the subsequent decades, therefore, the effort to gain more substantial legal rights for architects moved in tandem with developments in the copyright debate. Testifying before the 1878 parliamentary committee on copyright, Charles Barry, then president of the RIBA, described the doleful state of architects in comparison with artists in the following way:

I think the sum of the paper before me, as far as architecture is concerned, is rather given in these two sentences. ... "Upon consideration of this report the Council have freely concurred in the conclusion that the only practical way of supplying the defect in the present law will be to give to all artists copyright in such only of their designs as are authenticated or warranted by their signature, and to make the forgery of such signature an indictable offence, which after all is putting the signature no higher than a trade mark."[54]

In his testimony, Barry strived to differentiate architecture as an *intellectual* activity distinct from the skills-based expertise of builders and craftsmen. In this context, the motivational model inherent within IP doctrine was a useful instrument by which the architect's imagination could be both legitimized and distinguished as a profession in its own right. In creating the image of the architect as an entity whose principal contribution was to be discerned in the work of the directed imagination rather than building activity per se, the RIBA inevitably borrowed the cultural lexicon of the larger IPR debate. It was only within the discourse on IP that a sustained debate could be elucidated in legal terms on the intangible workings of the intellect. Because the profile of the architect in the age of mass production entails a functional *segregation* from the actual work of building, it is at this historical conjuncture that one notices an increased privilege given to a formerly unimportant attribute in the description of the architectural work: innovation. "Novelty" thus enters the professional language through a caprice of the legal-administrative structure. In the nineteenth century, both IPR and the formalization of professional norms are parallel and intersecting developments based on a particular discourse of rights. Thus, if IPR laws reached their conceptual pinnacle in the 1880s through the establishment of multilateral and universal norms, the same decade also saw the first bill introduced in Parliament for the official registration of architects. Oddly enough, architecture could enter the rubric of a profession only under the legal stipulations defining "art."

There is a problem, however, with this scenario. Between the years of 1862 and 1880, we find *only three* applications for plans and sections of buildings recorded at Stationers' Hall, the official design registrar in London.[55] If the number of copyrights granted for buildings are to be viewed as an index of the significance of IPR for architectural practice, the RIBA's exertions to win copyright for architects hardly seem warranted by the actual activity of the architects on this front. As I said earlier, as discrete commodities defined by use, building *products* were more amenably included within the stipulatory boundaries of IPR. On the other hand, the composite nature of architectural construction made mass production of entire buildings unnecessary, because variations were easy enough to incorporate within the schedule of labor with marginal differences of cost. Even during his interview, Barry had undergone considerable difficulty in defining the exact characteristics of architecture that required stipulation. If it was the facade, adjudication on this ground could be easily thrown off track by simply changing the configuration of tiles or even a window. Copyright could be protected only when the entire syntactic assemblage was copied *in toto*. The same logic could apply toward any planar or sectional elements; copyright infringers could infinitely extend the litigation process by incorporating very small changes within any given configuration, making protection very difficult for a profession entirely limited to the small firm category. The last resort, therefore, was simply to set up the judicial process as a case-by-case exercise in discernment of *intention*, precisely on those tenets of empirical difference that Tennent had laid out far back in 1840.

Why then this piggybacking on legislation whose actual concerns only tangentially affected the interests of the profession? I argue that the effect of IPR doctrine on architectural practice should be weighed on quite different terms. Argued within the liberal idiom of individual originality and innovation, copyright does embody a supplementary legal profile for architects in that its stipulations reside *outside of contract*. In most countries today, copyright remains simply an alternative avenue of litigation for architects in cases of reneging clients or contractors. Much more important was the symbolic credence granted by the new form of protection. The architect function simply bolstered its *cultural* credentials by imbibing a juridical principle: how to submit to repetition (normativity) and yet know how *not to copy*. In architecture, therefore, copyright has worked exactly in the opposite direction than in any other sphere of production: it ensures the *singularity and uniqueness* of the architectural edifice rather than creates the conditions for its technical reproducibility. The prehistory of the nineteenth-century copyright debate remains a key reason why architects sign their drawings.

Introducing the New

In the prelude to the Paris Exposition of 1867, James Fergusson gave a speech on the virtues of Indian architecture at the Royal Society of Arts, with Henry Cole in the audience. Fergusson, then director of the Architectural Museum, spent as much time in the address extolling the lessons offered by the subject matter at hand as the methods by which the lessons should be learned. Fergusson repeatedly referred to the tendency of modern architects to copy the styles of the past without understanding the architectonic implications of present-day technology and culture.

> Before attempting to explain to you the importance of Indian Architecture as bearing on our own, allow me to guard myself most distinctly against anything I am about to say being construed into a recommendation to copy any of the forms or details of the Indian

styles. My conviction is, that the system of copying different styles is the great—if not the sole cause of the present anomalous style of the art, and if I thought anything I said would encourage such a practice I would be silent. Although, therefore, I must consider copying the Indian styles as a crime, I feel convinced that there are principles underlying them which cannot be too deeply studied, and that there are many suggestions to be derived from the practice of the Indian architect which cannot fail, if properly used, to be useful to our own.[56]

The argument is directed at the imitation not only of Indian styles but of Greek and Roman styles as well. This theme is recurrent in all of Fergusson's work of the time, including his *History of Architecture in All Countries*.[57] If architects had only recently gotten over the three-hundred-year-old tradition of "servile copying" of classical styles, it had been replaced only by an equally disastrous practice of copying Gothic styles as the new English aesthetic. Fergusson's diatribe against "copying" in and of itself can be considered a relatively new formulation in architectural thought. Architectural discourse until this point had largely revolved on the *appropriate* terms and modalities of antique reference rather than on ruling precedent out altogether. Hardly any argument celebrated change for the sake of the "new" alone. Before Fergusson, perhaps no other architectural writer had put quite such a premium on innovation as a evaluative category for architecture; in the *History* he explicitly offered the Crystal Palace as a much more appropriate encapsulation of Gothic principles than any neo-Gothic building constructed in the recent past.

This emphasis on novelty in architecture is in fact indicative of a larger transformation of commodity and contractual relations in a number of other spheres. "Newness" is new in the context of the nineteenth century. As such, it availed of a unique set of objective attributes that we see simultaneously erupting and acquiring new contiguities in the culture of modernity: fake, copy, novelty, original, prototype, facsimile, reproduction. Fergusson's decrying of the copy is not incidental in an industrial context in which the entire commodity sphere was being transformed by mass reproduction.

Fergusson's call for a "new" architectural ethos uncannily mirrors the cultural fallout of the IP debate. As is well-known, the exposition building of 1867 was realized on a large oval plan. This geometrical arrangement was a specific response to the two principal categorical imperatives of the world exhibition. The radial axes classified the displays by region, whereas the concentric circles classified objects by kind. In August 1865 the *Builder* carried an article reminding readers of a design published in its pages in 1861 and submitted by two architects named Maw and Payne. The design

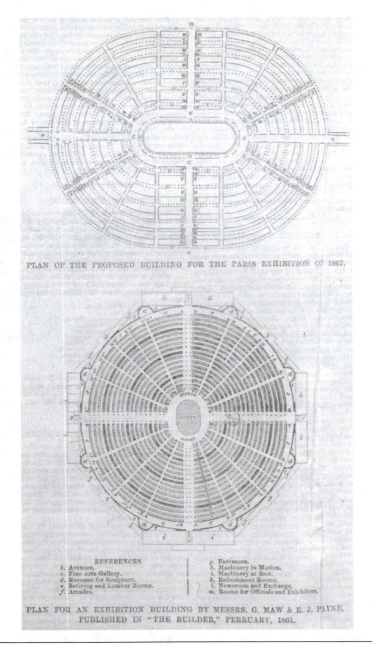

Figure 4.3 Publication in the *Builder* claiming the copyright for the 1867 Paris Exposition building on behalf of Maw and Paine, who had suggested a similar radial plan for the 1855 exhibition. The *Builder,* August 5, 1865. VAA archive file, "Press Cuttings" titled "Paris Exhibition, 1867" in 3 vols., July 1863–July 1867.

was a circular plan proposed for the 1862 exhibition in London, classifying its displays radially by geography and circumferentially by "kindred subjects," uncannily similar to the proposed building in Paris.[58] On the basis of this similarity of "juxtaposition," the *Builder* accused the French government of plagiarism. Although this jingoist claim was refuted by other members of the architectural fraternity, most notably the *Building News* (a rival publication), the force of the former's charge was strong enough for the matter to be taken up on an official level between the British and the French governments. Throughout the course of the 1867 exposition, the *Builder* insisted on its claim to the original and basic "concept" of the plan. Coincidence was taken as *intent* to copy. As we shall see, the IPR framework, dependent as it is on *formal* discernment, is limited by it.

As we noted earlier, at that very Paris Exposition of 1867, Henry Cole was able to push through a multilateral treaty allowing the institutions of European nations to make facsimile casts and reproductions of each other's art collections, thereby setting up the international framework for an industry in cultural property. Invited by Cole to the exposition, Fergusson also supervised an exhibition culled from the extensive folios of Indian architectural photographs he had been collecting from the 1850s. These included photographs made by the Archaeological Survey of India, which was one of the first archaeological bodies to use photography as an official medium of documentation. The 1867 exposition had another pavilion linked with Fergusson's display of photography. Like all the other exhibitions, the Paris Exposition also devoted a substantial portion of its display to machinery. With new laws of IP in place, exhibitors were increasingly emboldened to show actual machines at work. The power for operating these machines was generated by a central boiler unit. In the 1867 exposition, the structure covering the boilers was a full-scale and exact replica in terra-cotta of Syed Usman's tomb in Ahmedabad, India. The details of this building had been deduced from one of the photographic surveys of architecture recently carried out in Gujarat, for which Fergusson had written the introduction.[59] The *Builder* had nothing but praise for this particular copy, devoting two whole articles to the description and aesthetic lessons of this structure.[60]

Of course, a medieval monument with long-dead builders does not qualify for copyright in any case, and Cole and Fergusson were perfectly willing to acknowledge the provenance of the original. The Indian monuments were no different in status than, say, Greek or Roman monuments. Cole was consistent in his approach toward architecture as an inalienable ingredient of national property; his acolytes would do much to set up a preservationist movement in India. The duplicity evinced from the two examples cited previously should not be all too easily transposed into an argument for authentic historical patrimony. The past cannot have

Figure 4.4 "The Boiler Room," a terra-cotta replica of Syed Usman's tomb in Ahmedabad, *Exposition Universelles,* Paris 1867. From Henry Cole, *Report on Terra-cotta,* in Paris Universal Exhibition 1867, British Committee Reports, vol. 2, 1868, pp. 415–23.

any *legitimate* inheritors; rather, this foundational illegitimacy produces the desire for a history. The obeisance to historical patrimony by imperial culturalism instead undergirds a very different function that we need to examine here in greater detail: that of sequestering a different kind of agency or authorship for the aboriginal.

If in the previous example we see the manner in which specific cultural precedents were invoked to create a cosmopolitan patrimony, the following example will demonstrate how such memorializing could militate against the emergence of certain forms of authorship in the contemporary situation as well. In 1882 Abdul Rahman and Rahumtoolah, both "mistrees"[61] from Rourkee in the North-West Provinces, jointly filed a patent claim for the "improvements" they had made on sugarcane mills. After much deliberation on the issue, patent commissioners turned the claim down because of its lack of novelty.[62] The reasons given for rejection adopt a curious logic. The commissioners wrote,

> The slotting teeth proposed in their improvement was invented in 1660, 223 years ago, by Dr. Hooker. It was modified in 1808 by Mr. White of Manchester, *and* has been in use in India from time immemorial to couple and drive sugar rollers made of wood. It is not an improvement on cog wheels properly proportioned, and *is not a novelty*. [These elements can be found] … in almost every village [and are therefore public property].[63] [e.a.]

Authorship for the same object can be attributed to two radically different agencies, in the metropole to the individual ("Dr. Hooker" and "Mr. White") and in the colonial indigene to "time immemorial." What already existed in one place could be marked as "invention" in another; the distinction between invention and noninvention is therefore characterized not by a universal conception of primogeniture but by the difference of applicable discourse to a given situation. If IPR doctrine evolved in the metropole to distinguish the original from the fake, in the colony it devolved to distinguish the original from the *ab*original. By inference then, even if traditional patterns were instrumental in adding value to the metropolitan commodity, their customary practitioners in the colony would not be able to claim rights over their usage. IP doctrine thus sequesters the aboriginal as the figure of tradition that is foreclosed from the modern sphere of rights; as such, the aboriginal is the structural residue of the modernizing discourse in all its contemporariness, not the vestige of some prior state. The aboriginal artisan is the ineluctably *modern* product of an ahistory whose anthropological presumptions thrust an entire set of actors into anonymity.

The Vicissitudes of Verisimilitude

> In principle, *a work of art has always been reproducible*. Objects made by humans could always be copied by humans. Replicas were made by pupils in practicing for their craft, by masters in disseminating their works, and, finally, by third parties in pursuit of profit. But the technological reproduction of artworks is something new. Having appeared intermittently in history, at widely spaced intervals, it is now being adopted with ever-accelerating intensity.[64]

> **—Walter Benjamin, "The Work of Art in the**
> **Age of Its Reproducibility"**

Anonymously and inconspicuously the old tools were transformed into modern instruments. ... But only a fraction of the popular habit of invention is preserved in the Patent Office.[65]

—**Siegfried Giedion,** *Mechanization Takes Command:*
A Contribution to Anonymous History

We have seen three different ruptures in the text of IPR: first, in the Benthamite example, the *contradiction* that is produced within liberal utilitarianism when it attempted to bind together psychological profile with legal stricture; second, the *overdetermination* of the apparatus of copyright to create a legal armor for a professional body—architects—whose mode of production does not quite fit it; and third, the *foreclosure* of a certain kind of subjectivity, manifested in the aboriginal shrouded in anonymity.

Both Benjamin's "loss of aura" and Giedion's "anonymous history" engage in complementary ways the various transmutations of authorship that emerge in nineteenth-century industrialism. Both base their theorization of modernity on the irreversible supplantation of "craft" by the mass-produced object. In *mourning* this transition, Benjamin would get it exactly backward: the "culture of the copy" divests the object from its "aura." As we have seen in this chapter, on the contrary, the copy fosters the aura, it engenders, confirms it. It is the principal paradox of the era of mass reproduction that it engenders a mythology of the "original."[66] On the other hand, Giedion, even as he uses the archive of the patent records, manages to conjure up an *anonymous* history and accord subaltern status to the nineteenth-century history of IP—if anything a story of the *institutionalization of the proper name.*[67]

The examination of the Cole circle's interventions into theories of authorship and originality offers a strong riposte to this obfuscation of the expansion of property rights into the sphere of authorship. Here, once again, is Thomas Webster's account of the principle of legal discernment:

[In] design the subject of registration rests simply in pattern, shape, or configuration; it is, in the language of the geometrician, *strictly linear.* ... A design when transferred to or exhibited on paper is complete; the mind that conceived it and the hand that embodied it must obey the same will; one mind may suggest certain elements to be combined, but no second mind can intervene in the production of the particular design; the assistance of other persons, trial, experiment, and the substitutions of one element for another, are practically excluded. *The design, when complete, is identified by simple inspection; the eye at once decides on the similarity or dissimilarity of two designs.* Thousands of designs may exist of the same style and character, but each different from the other. It may be doubted whether two independent minds ever produced the same design; *identity of design is an evidence of piracy.*[68]

Formal coincidence is thus a map of (criminal) intentionality. The aboriginal is defined as the exception to this rule. The aboriginal (artisan) can only repeat the same. He is structurally mobilized toward a preternatural aesthetic meandering without being able to avail of the reflective apparatus by which his products can be projected into the legally defined field of innovation. The "individual" is the anthropological silhouette through which this convergence of objective singularity and subjective teleology is attained. The individual acts as if a portcullis, culling the anthropological credentials by which certain kinds of subject may or may not enter into modernity. The minimalist (ostensibly universal) attributes of the individual enabled Mill, Cole, and others to tie together fundamentally aesthetic presuppositions with policy and legal prescriptions that impinged on notions of social good. And yet, in Cole's later frustration with the Patent Museum, we see the unraveling of this supposed convergence even as the legal and commercial dimensions of IPR insinuated themselves into the very marrow of industrial capital. In the last chapter we saw the manner in which the pattern appeared not so much as an implement of the artisan as the translational means to decode artisanal production into the global market. Likewise, as liberal activism attempted to legislate IPR by identifying it with the anthropological descriptions of political society, it is the social arrangement that is being inexorably drawn into the primary rubric of economic relations. IPR would operate more as a conduit to expand the realm of property relations into the intangible territories of the mind than as a means of inspiring new domains of creative eccentricity.

In this chapter, we have seen how the metropolitan designer, under the tenets of IPR, is increasingly animated by a model of individualist creativity, even as he or she is bound by the normative outlines of a commercial profession, quite in contrast to, say, authors or artists. However, this transition, basing its fundamental assumptions on the tenets of property rights, also occludes certain forms of subjecthood; we have called this the "aboriginal." These occlusions also become the prophylactic device through which the artisan was restricted from entering the contractually defined arena of "art." The designer cannot abdicate authorship; the artisan is prevented entry into it. Although the artisan occupied the center of aesthetic discourse in the nineteenth century, he or she could not access the liberal legal framework on his or her own terms. What remained for the artisan was the inevitable downward mobility into informal labor, and this is the arena that we will turn to in the next chapter.

Cyborg/Artisan: On a Certain Asymmetry Deriving from the Binary System; or, Notes on a Moment in the Development of a Taylorist Feudalism

I have my hopes, & very distinct ones too, of one day getting *cerebral* phenomena such that I can put them into mathematical equations; in short a *law* or *laws,* for the mutual actions of the molecules of *brain;* (equivalent to the *law of gravitation* for the *planetary* & *sideral* world).

—**Ada Byron Lovelace, 1844**

A portly, pulpy Hindoo, the very type of his unamicable race, with a cat-like gait, a bow of exquisite finish, a habit of sweetly smiling under every emotion, whether they produce a bribe or a kick; a softly murmuring voice, with a tendency to slinking; and a glance which seldom matches yours and when it does, seems not to enjoy the meeting. How timidly he appears at the door! How deferential he slides in, salaams, looks deprecating, and at last is induced to sit down! Might not he be considered a novel kind of automaton, into which you transfer your minds and thoughts—a curious piece of human mechanism in the shape of a creature endowed with all things but a self?

—**Richard Burton, *Sindh, and the Races That Inhabit the Valley of the Indus***

Think of knitting as a pastime. Imagine a white-collar worker who takes to it as a technique of pushing away unwitting reveries, of keeping blank the busy background of incessant and unruly thought. Very likely, this is a woman, even a senior executive who absentmindedly clicks in the purls, moss stitches, slips, and rows, yarns forward and over, and watches for kinks as she participates in a corporate board meeting, expressly asserting her femininity in an overwhelmingly male preserve. Think of the mind–body dialectic in that microcosmic logarithm of power.

Every knit is a pattern. In the past few chapters, we have understood the modern pattern as unveiling some sort of organicist cartography of the mind's internal workings. For nineteenth-century mind-sets, the pattern also signals an elusive contract between heterogeneous commodity and indeterminate taste, between objective motif and cognitive model. Cast in the oscillation of repetition and variation, concrete and abstract, mechanism and naturalism, imprint and image, the pattern acquires the further legal ramifications of original and copy, legitimacy and fraud. In each, the pattern appears to elucidate in outward form the elusive structure of the mind's internal workings.

This chapter grapples with two seminal technological divergences where this two-sided attribute—of internal cognition and external imprint—was famously put to work: the card-based, information-carrying system of the Jacquard loom. Nestled within this dichotomy is the figure of the artisan, a technoanthropological category for whose definition the mind–body dialectic is critical. The Jacquard system was primarily an informational system. In every incarnation, its utility lay in the displacement of some frameworks of variation into an arithmetical matrix. In this chapter, we will explore the ramifications of two quite different historical developments of this displacement.

In the early 1840s, Charles Babbage, philosopher and scientist, proposed a scheme to build his "Analytical Engine," using the punched cards devised by Jacquard to perform certain standard and nonstandard operations. The Analytical Engine was a further development of the ideas underlying his earlier Difference Engine, the incomplete carcass of which was to eventually find its way into the South Kensington Museum. The introduction of the Jacquard system into the Engine is widely acknowledged as a precursor of the modern-day computer.

The other strand of development of the Jacquard system does not lend itself to a narrative quite so progressivist or sanctified in historiographic tone. As is well-known, the Jacquard system became a crucial component of the modern mechanized loom, with different variations becoming integral— given the predominance of the textile sector—to the evolution of national economies and trade across the globe. Even as a national capitalist class in India was incorporating advanced Jacquard powerlooms in the mill sector, colonial officials sought to introduce what was known as a *hand* Jacquard—a rudimentary, eighteenth-century version of the system involving elaborate manual procedures—into the artisanal silk handloom industry. The preservationist approach adopted by the Department of Science and Art (DSA) faction in India was critical to this new formulation of craft. For instance, when the question of moving hand-based silk production in Benares into modern factories was raised, H. Maxwell-Lefroy, "imperial silk specialist," in his *Report on an Inquiry into the Silk Industry in India,* emphasized the higher efficiency of extant custom as opposed to the untested outcome of alien organizational forms: "I am not sanguine as to the [introduction of] small hand-loom factory since here as elsewhere the weaver works better at home."[1] The hand-Jacquard was thus incorporated both to shore up this preternatural domesticity of the Benares weaver *and* to make his output amenable for the colonial market.

In both cases—Babbage's Engine and the Benares loom—the insertion of the Jacquard system effected a cognitive displacement toward a model of greater calculative efficiency but toward quite different ends. Although Babbage's Engine can be thought of as a precursor to the mechanics of the modern computer, its other contribution has also been ideological: to drive the vision of the biomorphic machine displacing, even replacing, the more onerous and repetitive tasks of human labor. To this extent, Babbage's Engines have also attracted attention within the fields of brain and cognitive sciences, although there their exact contribution remains in some dispute.

For Marx the technological transition from artisanal labor to the factory is epitomized by morphotropy: "*The Indian loom is upright, i.e. the warp is stretched vertically.*" The difference from the modern loom is not just a technological one but a shift in the very hierarchy of production. The mechanized loom is horizontal, allowing the passage of the cloth from one section of the factory floor to another such that the workers remain stationary as the cloth comes to them. By contrast, the Indian artisan has to move about from one stage of production to another.[2] Given his limited and hardly unbiased sources, it should come as no surprise Marx's dialectical view is not borne out by historical evidence. The traditional Benares loom was not vertical; however, given the implications, it *is* surprising that in the intermingled history of what has been termed "craft," "art industry," "artisan," or "small industry," the kind of sociological transitions, that might have occurred with the introduction of the Jacquard in Benares—and caused Marx to sit up and take notice—have hardly attracted any attention. Where an account of this shift appears at all, it is described only in passing within general technoanthropological descriptions, or alternatively, as an inconsequential aberration of or within methodological approaches whose concerns are elsewhere, say the relative improvement or non-improvement of the artisanal sector under the colonial economy. Oddly enough, not a single account in the quite enormous compendium of studies on traditional textiles in India provides the exact date of the introduction of the first Jacquard apparatus in India.

Generally speaking, most accounts gloss over the shift signaled by this introduction either in the mode of the inevitable (the "modernizing" narrative) or the always has been ("tradition"). An example is the government of India report of 1950, flushed with the spirit of a modernizing independence, describing the Jacquard, introduced only thirty years earlier, as emblematic of the *unchanging* nature of the artisan: "The Benares gold thread saree and brocade weavers are still sticking to their old Benares looms with their intricate harness for their Jacquard."[3] A more recent, technoanthropological study on the weavers of Benares observes (only incidentally) that the Jacquard mechanism had done away with the intricate arrangement of technological contraptions and workers that undergird the very complexity of the sociological relationships that are the focus of his research. And yet the study paradoxically insists that this technological transformation has changed little in the traditional dispensation of the craft. "Much of the complication has since been eliminated by the incorporation of the jacquard to the looms. Still the hereditary arrangement of unknown antiquity persists almost in its original form."[4]

These tacit elisions are surprising, given that the introduction of the Jacquard, when it did happen, was neither incidental nor unconsidered: Indian artisans had consistently opposed the introduction of the Jacquard throughout the nineteenth century. The potentially negative social reverberations of deskilling much exercised and confounded colonial officials entrusted with supervision of economic production in the customary sectors. Official reports on mechanization in these contexts were therefore routinely qualified by detailed anthropological observations on the social interrelationships underpinning artisanal labor. In this context, what is significant about the introduction of the hand Jacquard is that it can be seen primarily as a response to an anthropological understanding, reflecting administrative and policy preoccupations, rather than an "economic" transition from a nonmechanized situation to a more "efficient" one.

The divergence between the two trajectories of Babbage and Benares can therefore be formulated in the following two ways: on one hand, the *unrealized* dream of an impeccable substitution of the body by the machine, and on the other, the actual insertion of an *obsolete* technology to suit a realpolitik agenda of traditionalist continuity. The two terms of this divergence could be made to approximate an ongoing intellectual battle in British academe and polity in the nineteenth century, as William J. Ashworth has described it in an essay on Babbage:

For ... analyticals [such as Babbage], human culture progressed through the development of human reason, while for the Burkean mind culture preceded reason, the social order antedated the human intellect and thus defined the conditions of human interaction.[5]

In Benares, the introduction of the Jacquard loom constitutes a *Burkean* transplant rather than the "normative," mechanistic subsumption. It is a mechanical atavism nestled within an anthropological atavism. The particular terms on which the Jacquard system appears as a common point of reference in these two divergent situations therefore require some reflection, given the master-topos of a unitary modernization spelled out at the beginning of this book. To this end, this chapter first addresses the context of the Jacquard's application to Babbage's Engines and, subsequently, to traditional looms in India. The chapter argues that this differentiation can be better encapsulated by a theory of the cyborg than one of straightforward technological progressivism. A theory of "woman", as paradigmatic construction of the body as error, will be critical to establishing the abconstructed efficiency of the cyborg. The chapter concludes with a postscript delineating the implications of this formulation on other spheres of design and production.

Difference in the Difference Engine

Some ideas about a calculating machine may have been on Babbage's mind as early as 1812, when he founded the Cambridge Analytical Society with his friends John Herschel and George Peacock. The earliest official intimation, however, of the Difference Engine can be dated to Babbage's 1822 letter to Humphrey Davy, president of the Royal Society, asking for financial support to build the machine.[6] The impetus behind the machine was Babbage's discovery of errors in the Board of Longitude's astronomical tables in the course of using the forty-foot reflector telescope belonging to Herschel's father, the renowned astronomer William Herschel. Babbage's concern can be placed in the context of an increasingly widespread awareness of pervasive errata then being discovered in various statistical tables in use at the time.[7]

For his part, Babbage identified these errata with human error. The Engine was thus conceived with the ambition of replacing certain kinds of "menial" mental procedures by what he deemed the infallibility of mechanization. Babbage compartmentalized cognitive activity into two principal faculties:

Those labours which belong to the various branches of the mathematical sciences, although on first consideration they seem to be the exclusive province of intellect, may, nevertheless, be divided into two distinct sections; one of which may be called the mechanical, because it is subjected to precise and invariable laws, that are capable of being expressed by means of the operations of matter; while the other, demanding the interventions of reasoning, belongs more specially to the domain of the understanding. This admitted, we may propose to execute, by means of machinery, the mechanical faculties.[8]

The passage above is the very first in an essay on the Engine published in 1842 by an Italian military engineer, Luigi Frederico Menabrea, in whose writing Babbage had more than a guiding hand. The segregation of the menial and repetitive tasks of mensuration as the "mechanical" faculty of the brain is significant.[9] In many ways, the Difference Engine was a giant mechanical calculator. Its mathematical principles drew from a then-popular technique for calculating polynomials, called the "method of differences" (hence the name) wherein difficult numerical functions were reduced to the simple operations of addition and subtraction. The principle can be illustrated by the following two tables, the one on the left pertaining to the squares of integers, and the right one pertaining to the cubes.

	a	b	c	d			a'	b'	c'	d'	e'
1	1					1	1				
2	4	3				2	8	7			
3	9	5	2			3	27	19	12		
4	16	7	2	0		4	64	37	18	6	0
5	25	9	2	0		5	125	61	24	6	0
6	36	11	2	0		6	216	91	30	6	0
7	49	13	2	0		7	343	127	36	6	0

If a number is taken from column a and deducted from the number immediately below it, such that the difference is tabulated in column b, and then again the difference is taken between numbers in column b to produce column c, the difference between the numbers in the third column c is the same: the number 2. In the table of cubes, this number (6) is reached in the fourth stage, d'. Further differentiation yields the uniform value 0 in columns d and e', respectively. In tables listing the series of integers raised to the power four, five, and so on, the standard difference would thus be reached in the fifth and sixth stage, and so on.

To crudely describe Babbage's Engine, each column would correspond to a mechanical column of wheels, each cog bearing a number x, along with a mechanism that moved the wheel next to it by x number of places.

With the initial differences and values set by the operator, the engine could be turned to generate the entire series. Babbage understood well that this arithmetical procedure, requiring considerable expertise and financial investment, could only perform a certain kind of calculation. Nonetheless, the machine could be used to generate a number of very useful tables: logarithms, sines, tangents, square roots, the positions of the several moons of Jupiter, and insurance rates based on mortality statistics.[10]

The links between economic uses and mathematical tables are not incidental. The immediate precedent for Babbage's Engine was neither mathematical nor mechanical but a model of labor. In 1792 Gaspard Clair François Marie Riche de Prony, director of the *Bureau du cadastre,* had compiled an enormous table of logarithmic sines, ratios, and tangents, calculated to between fourteen and twenty-nine decimal places.[11] Prony accomplished this stupendous task by assembling a unique tripartite hierarchy of mental labor. The first tier was composed of Prony and other elite colleagues, who devised the various formulas and easiest methods of calculating the tables in question. The second tier, consisting of six to eight mathematicians, took the formulas provided by the first tier and input the numbers to be calculated, in addition to providing the third tier with the proper intervals or "differences" between each value. The third tier, composed of seventy to eighty laborers who could only add or subtract, did the actual computation using only those two methods. Hairdressers, formerly catering to the aristocracy and whose profession was now in severe recession owing to the identification of hairstyling with the ancien régime, formed a significant faction of the "workers" thus employed in the third tier. With more than seven hundred results produced each day by this arrangement, the final work contained eighteen large folio volumes.

Prony's own inspiration for this arrangement had come from a chance reading of Adam Smith's famous description of the pin factory in the first chapter of *The Wealth of Nations:*

> I suddenly conceived the notion of applying the same method to the enormous work with which I had been charged, and to manufacture logarithms as one produces pins. I have reason to believe that I had already been prepared for this idea by certain parts of mathematical analysis, on which I was then lecturing at the *Ecole Polytechnique.*[12]

The Difference Engine would further automatize this hierarchical attitude. In his letter to Davy, Babbage described his Engine as carrying out the labor of the third tier, thus employing only about twelve trained mathematicians, rather than a hodgepodge ensemble of a hundred people. The principal impetus was of saving costs, but it reveals an elemental aspect of mathematics that is shared by Prony: mathematics is an economic theory of numbers, of producing value in numbers, of putting them into use and exchange, and of making them function more efficiently in desired directions.

Throughout the 1820s, Babbage became an inveterate observer and visitor to factories and manufacturing units across the industrialized world. His sojourns became the basis for a unique set of formulations regarding the current state and future potential of different aspects of mass production. He assembled these in a book titled *The Economy of Machinery and Manufactures,* which addressed in great detail the state of mechanization and engineering, division of labor, motive power, capitalization, material capacities, taxation, and extraction of resources.[13] The strident advocacy of mechanization in Babbage's volume is not unlike—although with fewer sociological insights than—its more well-known contemporary, Andrew Ure's *Philosophy of Manufactures* of 1835, which wove its account of technological transformation with views on its improved effects on social conditions.[14] Both Babbage and Ure based their radicalism on the machine's power to ameliorate menial labor.

Marx used Babbage's and Ure's formulations to organize his thoughts on mechanization and the division of labor in the notes for *Capital.*[15] In his manuscripts of 1861–63, he clubbed them together with an anomalous —and more recent—source: Charles Darwin's newly published views on the differentiation of organs in the *Origin of Species.*[16] Marx inserted a passage from Darwin as the exordium to his notes; in the passage, Darwin speaks of two different kinds of differentiation within organs: first, elements whose low level of organization did not necessitate any significant degree of variation to perform their tasks better, therefore permitting a wide range of generalized variations, and second, higher degrees of organization that necessitated more pronounced manifestation, through greater degrees of differentiation, of singular functional characteristics. Darwin compared the former to a knife, which being of the same shape could cut any manner of object, as opposed to the azygos "tool," which reflected in its form its singular purpose. Marx's identification of the machine with an organology aligns the unstated materialist implications of Babbage's formulation with an organicist view; the emphasis here—paradoxically in the context of an exegesis on differentiation—is on the whole or the unifying element within differentia.

> *Differentiation*—difference of forms and crystallization of these forms. *Specialization,* that the instrument which now only serves a particular purpose is only effective in the hands of labour which is itself differentiated. Both things imply the simplification of the instruments, which only have to serve now as the means of a simple and uniform operation. … Babbage calls the machine … a "union of all these tools,

actuated by one moving power." He is not speaking here of the mere combination of different elementary mechanical forms, such as those mentioned above. There is hardly even a simple tool which is not a combination of several of these forms. Babbage here speaks of the union, the combination, of all the different instruments which e.g. within the manufacture of the same commodity are appropriate to different, separate modes of operation, and therefore to different workers; and also of the setting in motion of this combination of instruments by a *single* motor, whatever this motor might be, whether the human hand and foot, animal power, elemental forces, or an automatic mechanism (mechanical propulsion).[17]

Or, if the chain of causation is followed back, the "single motor" is capital in the abstract. Marx's emphasis on a single and unifying agency in this scenario of infinite parcelization—the machine pounding labor down to its atomized elements—presents an antiphony to Babbage's thesis of mechanical substitution, if only by way of corollary. The machine replaces artisanal labor in its specific dimensions only to reintroduce it elsewhere as labor in the abstract. Capital as difference engine differentiates labor into a unifying substrate, in the paradigm of the knife rather than the tool. Labor is displaced, not replaced, along a more extended and compressed organum. The organological underpinnings of the following paragraph are difficult to avoid:

A vast automaton, i.e. a *system* of connected productive mechanisms, receiving their motive power from a self-acting central motor. This system of machinery, with its *automatic PRIME MOTOR,* forms the body, the articulated body of the mechanical workshop. The cooperation of various *classes* of worker, distinguished mainly by whether they are adult or not, *differences of age and gender.* These workers themselves appear as merely the intellectual organs of the machinery (the machinery does not appear as their organ) who are distinguished from the inanimate organs by consciousness, and who work "in concert" with the latter, acting, like the inanimate machinery, in subordination to its moving force and equally uninterruptedly.[18]

Marx's organicism is explicitly posed against organicism's romantic or archaic manifestations that would oppose the mechanical to the organic: it is the machine that sets the terms for understanding the human body.

Analysis and the Analytical Engine

Babbage's conception of the Analytical Engine—which followed the abortion of the Difference Engine in 1832—represents a better recognition of the problems of comprehensive thinking than the mechanistic approach adapted in the Difference Engine. The earlier model simply sought to break down the object of analysis into its component parts. If for Marx the machine-like element in capital was a theoretically synthesizing force, then the Analytical Engine was in theory a machine designed to grapple with the problems of infinity, continuity, and synthesis. Inasmuch as it was meant to address concrete mathematical problems, the Engine was also conceived as a demonstrative condenser of a significant epistemological debate then developing within the English intellectual landscape.

Babbage's early campaigns in Cambridge were marked by his advocacy of the Leibnizian notation system in calculus as against the native English proclivity toward Newtonian notation. According to some accounts, British mathematics had been characterized by a nationalist refusal to adopt Continental techniques significantly advanced by the French, a legacy of the contested paternity of calculus between Leibniz and Newton. Newton's preference for geometry as an ontological prop to aid explanation in calculus had hardened through the centuries. The principal objection to Leibnizian calculus lay in its use of algebra, an exotic, Oriental system of manipulating symbols without objective reference. The English anathema for negative and imaginary numbers has been explained in the context of an ingrained cultural paternalism for whom algebraic calculus connoted a dangerous regression into imaginative fantasy.[19] Any reference to Leibniz was especially fraught at a moment when an intellectual, "abstract" incursion with French antecedents was bound to draw aspersions of Jacobin tendencies. The image of continental calculus as a supersensory system, an apprehension hardly mitigated by formulations such as the following from Marx's remarkable historical analysis of calculus, was sure to stand English hairs on end:

> First making the differentiation and then removing it therefore leads literally to *nothing*. The whole difficulty in understanding the differential operation (as in the *negation of the negation* generally) lies precisely in seeing *how* it differs from such a simple procedure and therefore leads to real results.[20]

The anathema toward such "sublative" abstractions grew as the "Analytical faction"—named after Babbage's small and short-lived Analytical Society of 1812—increasingly came to describe its mathematical preoccupations as presenting a cognitive model in themselves, a surrogate for the operations of the mind. The investigation of analysis was described as an autonomous set of operations within itself—there is more than an echo of Kant here—rather than as an explanatory framework for natural philosophy. The Analyticals' interest in algebra and its symbolic system was therefore in league with a more general intellectual thrust at the turn of the nineteenth century to concoct or find a unifying ("universal") media of communication.

The Analyticals' persistent referral of calculus to linguistic models, in the shadow of mathematicians such as Joseph-Louis Lagrange, Pierre-Simon Laplace, and the philosopher Étienne Bonnot de Condillac,[21] sparked an interest in notations that was claimed to bear the characteristics of a full-fledged semiology. Babbage's contribution to this runaway "inference" is marked by a string of essays with very suggestive titles, often more linguistic than mathematical in thrust.[22] The connection envisaged between theories of language and mathematics—and the accompanying argument for an epistemological generality—is evident in the following extract from a manifesto for the Analytical Engine published in 1842. (The extract is quoted here at length, with italics from the original.)

It were much to be desired, that when mathematical processes pass through the human brain instead of through the medium of inanimate mechanism, it were equally a necessity of things that the reasonings connected with *operations* should hold the same just place as a clear and well-defined branch of the subject of analysis, a fundamental but yet independent ingredient in the science, which they must do in studying the engine. ... It may be desirable to explain, that by the word *operation*, we mean *any process which alters the mutual relation of two or more things,* be this relation of what kind it may. This is the most general definition, and would include all subjects in the universe. But the science of operations, as derived from mathematics more especially, is a science of itself, and has its own abstract truth and value; just as logic has its own peculiar truth and value, independently of the subjects to which we may apply its reasonings and processes. Those who are accustomed to some of the more modern views of the above subject, will know that a few fundamental relations being true, certain other combinations of relations must of necessity follow; combinations unlimited in variety and extent if the deductions from the primary relations be carried far enough. They will also be aware that one main reason why the separate nature of the science of operations has been little felt, and in general little dwelt on, is the *shifting meaning* of many of the symbols used in mathematical notation. First, the symbols of *operation* are frequently *also* the symbols of the *results* of operations. We may say that these symbols are apt to have both a *retrospective* and a *prospective* signification. They may signify either relations that are the consequences of a series of processes already performed, or relations that are yet to be effected through certain processes. Secondly, figures, the symbols of *numerical magnitude,* are frequently *also* the symbols of *operations,* as when they are the indices of powers. Wherever terms have a shifting meaning, independent sets of considerations are liable to become complicated together, and reasonings and results are frequently falsified. Now in the Analytical Engine, the operations which come under the first of the above heads are ordered and combined by means of a notation and of a train of mechanism which belong exclusively to themselves; and with respect to the second head, whenever numbers meaning *operations* and not *quantities* (such as the indices of powers) are inscribed on any column or set of columns, those columns immediately act in a wholly separate and independent manner, becoming connected with the *operating mechanism* exclusively, and re-acting on this.[23]

"Shifting meaning," a "retrospective and prospective" deferral of signification, a structure of citationality where numbers can become other than numbers (symbols of operations, e.g., indices), and the notion of a (semiotic) "chain":[24] the Analytical Engine operates as much as a grammatological gearbox even as it translates mathematical conventions into a polysemic enterprise. As opposed to the engineering deficiencies that led to the abandonment of the Difference Engine, the failure to build the Analytical Engine would stem from the enormity of its epistemic claims. The previous tract is taken from the copious notes appended to Menabrea's essay on the Analytical Engine and was written by Ada Augusta Lovelace, daughter of Robert Byron and Anne Isabella Milbanke and something of an amanuensis and publicist for Babbage. The following passage by Lovelace makes the polemical claim of the Analytical Engine clear:

> The Analytical Engine [as opposed to the Difference Engine] is not merely adapted for *tabulating* the results of one particular function and no other, but for *developing and tabulating* any function whatever. In fact the engine may be described as being the material expression of any indefinite function of any degree of generality and complexity.[25]

The Analytical Engine was thus imagined to be able to compute through the logic of any syntactical arrangement. The Engine's claim to superiority over its precursor and to epistemic comprehensiveness in general lay in its adaptation of the Jacquard card system and the mechanism of "backing up": the ability to repeat certain functions when necessary. Menabrea and Lovelace used the following formula to explain this mechanism:

Given two equations

$$mx + ny = d$$
$$m'x + n'y = d'$$

we can deduce , $x = \dfrac{dn' - d'n}{mn' - m'n}$, while $y = \dfrac{dm' - d'm}{m'n - mn'}$

In the machine, the value of x can therefore be calculated by breaking down the equation into its component parts, each of which are composed of a card V. Initially, cards V_0, V_1, V_2, and so on are prepared, composed of variables and constants, where $V_0 = m$, $V_1 = n$, $V_2 = d$, $V_3 = m'$, $V_4 = n'$, $V_5 = d'$. A further series of cards are prepared that perform operations on the basic set already available, to give the products in the equations; thus, $V_6 = V_0 \times V_4 = mn'$, $V_7 = V_1 \times V_3 = m'n$, and so on, as in the following table. Eventually, V_{15} gives the value of x, whereas V_{16} gives the value of y.

To run a calculation of this kind, Babbage envisaged three categories of cards: "Operation" cards, which would actually carry out the operations of the calculation; "Directive" cards, which would convey values to their proper place in the Engine where other operations could be carried out on them; and "Number" cards, which assigned particular numerical values to the variables. As opposed to the Difference Engine, the Analytical Engine could also perform multiplication and division. (Anyone who has operated a sliding- or manual-gear transmission in an automobile will have a rough sense of how this might have worked.) In this equation, the operations of multiplication, division, addition, and subtraction are repeated several times. Hence, these Operation cards would be used several times, requiring the process of "backing up"; hence the notion of a "retrospective or prospective" faculty or "chain" alluded to earlier. Other numbers, variables or products, may be needed to be used several times, such as the binomials mn' and $m'n$ in the denominators' place in the previous equations for x and y.

The Directive cards would convey them to a place where they could be accessed at different times. Babbage, true to form, used an industrial analogy for this place; he called it the "Store," as opposed to the "Mill," where the actual operations were carried out. To make sure that complex results were not wrongly transcribed owing to human error, Babbage also envisaged a printing apparatus at the end of the process to ensure accuracy.

The Algebra of Weaving

The most significant breakthrough in this retrospective account, by far, came from Babbage's adaptation of the Jacquard system to his Engine; it marks the introduction of the binary code into cognitive thought. It is important to note that the evolution of the Jacquard loom marks one manifestation of the mind–body, or cognitive–physical, limit. It is not coincidental that the essential element of the Jacquard loom—its card mechanism—was first devised by Vaucanson, creator of several pseudo-intelligent automatons. Both the Jacquard loom and de Prony's logarithms are thus products of Revolutionary temperament. The mind–body characterization becomes clearer if one examines the specific changes wrought by the Jacquard mechanism on traditional looms. Indeed, the specific character of these transformations dictated also the forms of resistance to it—and there were many—because the cognitive alterations contained in the machine implied quite concrete divestitures of particular kinds of skilled labor.

As is well-known, cloth is composed of weft and warp in the x and y dimensions, respectively. The warp—the y dimension—is stretched first longitudinally on the frame of the loom, and its threads create the "field" or "ground" condition of the design. The weft—the x dimension—is carried by the shuttle moving to and fro across the warp; this constitutes the "motif," "figure," or counterfield to the warp. To weave plain, monochromatic cloth, the weaver raises every alternate thread by means of a heald A. The shuttle passes beneath the threads raised by A and above the other remaining threads, connected to another heald B. In the second sequence, A is lowered while B is raised as the shuttle moves back across the warp, thus effecting the weave. In traditional looms, the healds are moved by means of pedals operated by the weaver's feet.

This simple arrangement of two healds holding alternate threads undergoes further degrees of complexity when figures or chromatic effects are desired in the piece. The more the variation desired in the cloth, the larger the number of healds required; the numerical finitude of healds, levers, and pedals also limited the complexity of the pattern. (The maximum documented number of healds on a single frame was ninety-six.[26]) This complexity was supported by a number of vocations that supported that of the master weaver, including the "draw boy," who was assigned with the specific task of raising the correct heald at any given point.

Exhibited first at the Paris Industrial Exhibition of 1801, the Jacquard apparatus was the historical culmination of efforts at increasing the complexity of the loom, yet its principle was markedly different from earlier models. Adopting an algebraic rather than the arithmetical exponentiality described above, Jacquard's system radically simplified the functioning of the healds, even as it extended the number of possible design variations into infinity. Instead of multiplying the number of healds, Jacquard's innovation made it possible to vary the configuration of "sheds" (or "picks") on each heald, therefore requiring very few healds. The shed is opened by means of cords that link, through a series of connectors, to wire hooks that are manipulated by the Jacquard attachment.

In the Jacquard attachment, the information regarding the design—resolved into x and y coordinates—is carried onto the loom using a series of punched cards. A series of needles, with their positions corresponding to the punches in the card, are attached by means of springs to a needle board. In the middle of the needles, a little loop interlocks them loosely with the hooks connecting to the warp. The hooks, on their part, are moved up and down by a blade. Each card corresponds to one weave of the shuttle, and each designated hole corresponds to one pick of the warp. At each tread of the loom, the needles move toward the card, the perforated holes allowing their corresponding needles to pass through, while the imperforated holes arrest the movement of the other needles, thereby compressing the springs at their base. The needles that pass through the holes carry the hooks forward with them; the latter thus attach to the blade, which moves up carrying them, and the warp moves with it. The hooks attached to the needles that are held back do not attach to the blade, and so their picks remain in place. After the shuttle moves through the warp, the blade moves down again, releasing all the hooks and needles. The cylinder holding the cards rotates, putting the next card—bearing the sequence for the next weave—in place. The raising of the individual warps, the picks, and the needles are thus all resolved into a place-marked binary logic—hole or no hole. A perforated hole thus leads to the raising of its corresponding pick, each rise of the heald can then correspond to an entirely different configuration of the warp.

The mechanism thus encapsulated a series of functions that earlier required a combination of mental and manual faculties encapsulated in the word *skill*. The deskilling that was wrought by the Jacquard innovation was patent to both its apologists and its opposers. In a late nineteenth-century textbook on textile manufacturing, Thomas R. Ashenhurst identified this deskilling with the onset of a new economic role, the designer. Even as he chastised the "jealousy" of the machine breakers, the new designer, he confessed, had very little to do with design, if the term signified any exercise of intentionality and imagination:

> The arrangement of patterns for weaving is generally performed by one man for a large manufactory, and is dignified by the title of designing, whether or not the class of goods manufactured require any of the skill of the designer, or whether there is anything in the nature of the pattern which can give it any claim to the dignity of a design.[27]

Functionally contrasted against the artist's license to play with the imagination, the Jacquard designer in Babbage's Engine is the precursor of the programmer. Babbage's objective was to rule out indeterminacies in the carriage between different mathematical operations; he was fond of quoting "The *Erratum* of the *Erratum* of the *Errata* of Taylor's Logarithms." In this subtle displacement from the human *in* error to the human *as* error, we see a bifurcation of the faculties of "skill": of the manual into the mechanical and of the conceptual into a calculus. The management of error is here cited as "efficiency." In this emphasis on efficiency, the human is not erased; rather, the attempt is to govern, calibrate, manage its tonality, to continually revisit the boundary between the quantitative and the qualititative. I will suggest shortly that the artisan is in the mode of the human as *felicitous* error.

Uneven Patterns

Babbage's vision of efficiency in the machine parallels the early mathematization of political economy inaugurated by theorists such as Augustin Cournot in the first half of the nineteenth century.[28] The shift to the machinic from the artisanal thus impeccably went hand in hand with the transition from the ethical frames of the old political economy to the generalized calculus of what Alfred Marshall first termed the new science of "economics." For Babbage, this new abstraction introduced the labor equation into a calculus that could be extended to a relationship between nations. Writing in his book *The Exposition of 1851*, Babbage articulated this model of efficiency as the principal economic justification of the exhibition:

> It is found by experience that the upper-leather of boots made in France, is better and more durable than the upper-leather manufactured in England. On the other hand, it is found that the leather prepared in England for the soles of boots is less permeable by water, and more durable than that made in France. ... *Let us assume, for the sake of simplicity, that in each country the upper-leather and the soles have the same value.* Then it is equally clear, if England were to give to

France a million pair of soles in exchange for a million pair of French upper-leathers, that one million of the inhabitants of each nation would find their boots last during fifteen instead of twelve months.[29]

As we saw in the first chapter, imperialism is the attempt to promulgate precisely this kind of uneven equivalence. As I have argued, the insertion of the Jacquard system into the Benares loom in the early twentieth century represented a technological *regression*—more a conditioned response to a situational demand than an inevitable move to mechanization.[30] Although it is clear that both demand and production of Benares silk increased in the nineteenth century owing to the availability of new markets, the lack of state support and public debt mechanisms hindered the formation of either a strong capitalist class or a significant technological transformation of the industry.[31] In addition, the industry's position in the luxury goods sector, including its special use in customary rituals, reinforced its characterization as craft, based in piecework. This characterization also underlay the resistance to new technology from both above and below. In 1900 Yusuf Ali, a colonial officer, compiled a detailed anthropological and technical monograph on the silk fabrics of the province. Compare his description of a Benares designer to the passage by Ashenhurst cited earlier:

> The design of a cloth is first worked out by the designer. Every *kárkhána* or factory has a designer retained by it who draws up designs to order or invents new ones according to his own ingenuity ... new designs are made every day at Benares, but they are as a rule wanting in originality. They are mostly variations on old designs.[32]

The DSA's tentacles could be felt this far afield; Ali advocated that innovation be set into motion by applying "the principles laid down by Mr. Owen Jones in his Grammar of Ornament."[33] On the basis of the contrasting thrust of other reports published since 1900,[34] and my own fieldwork done in the Madanpura area of Benares, Ali's emphasis on the *factory form* as the organizational scaffold of labor extraction rings off-key. Although a significant portion of the silk industry was located in large manufactories, the dominant mode of production has continued to be informal, largely contained within the domestic household. Certainly, the industry has undergone critical changes at different points in its history. Today, almost all the various labor components of the silk industry are parcelized into discrete, independent occupations. In Madanpura, for instance, silk production is carried out in shops facing the main street, in narrow bylanes, on converted ground-floor workshops, and in the inner spaces of bedrooms.

The most renowned product of Benares silk is the brocade, known as *kimkhwab* in Hindustani, anglicized as kincob. The fabric's uniqueness draws from its interweaving of metal—gold, silver, copper—wire, known as *kala-battun* or *jari*, in its patterns. Obtained as skeins of raw silk, the material is twisted by various procedures, called "throwing," into yarn. The yarn is treated with chemicals, dyed and thickened into warp. The warp is then stretched out and arranged between stakes in the sequence required by the loom. This is done on the street, thus accounting for the quintessential character of bylanes in this area. The warp is then delivered to the weavers' workshops, which also receive the designs for the cloth from independent designers. This enchanting urban sight—much rhapsodized by culturalists—is in diametrical opposition to the invisible economic activity of women in this community, who pursue a host of preparatory and finishing trades, including appliqué and sequin work.

The activity of silk weaving is thus divided into dozens of occupations, and each ramification of the industry is organized into a discrete domestically practiced profession, which affects the larger organizational character of the trades as well. Guilds and kinship structures are horizontally rather than vertically ordered, along each particular occupational specialization rather than compositely along the entire division of labor. The division and hierarchy of labor are kept in place by relationships of custom and finance rather than by the spatial constraints of a composite factory. Debt, kinship, and gender relations are crucial in qualifying employment relationships, often demonetizing and disguising what are otherwise clear economic hierarchies.[35]

One remembers Adam Smith's canonical invocation of the pin factory as the spatially efficient reorganization of the division of labor. Poised against a convoluted portrait of tangled customary relations in traditional economic activity of the eighteenth century, this rationalizing invocation appeared to announce the critical form of modernization in industry. In modern Benares by contrast this efficiency is achieved through the *mobilization of customary relations* rather than through a conversion to the factory system. In the current "conjuncture," this customized mobilization is the less-than-visible model on which the norms of industry are being reshaped according to the dictates of finance capital the world over. An examination of transitions in the "design" function will perhaps make this clearer.

The nineteenth-century framing, exemplified by Ashenhurst and Ali, saw the designer in the scene of production as abjectly constituted by the translation of art(istic motifs) into the coordinates required by technology. Before the introduction of the Jacquard loom in Benares, the designer's activity comprised more the elements of a significant *rehearsal* or duplication of the weaver's manual skills than a role created by the segregation of its intelligent and motor functions. The pre-Jacquard designer or *naksha* maker (*naksha*, meaning map, pattern) first drew out the design on a paper, on which a grid was drawn to approximate the warp and weft. This approximation was then transferred to a small frame with a warp whose number of threads equaled the number of threads in the pattern. The designer's job was to resolve the design into the number of threads required for each motif; in contemporary computer parlance, this could be called the degree of pixilation of the pattern. Composed of cotton thread, the *naksha* was placed vertically above the actual silk warp where—with the assistance of a draw boy who sat on a plank over the warp—it served as a template for the actual weave.

The Jacquard system eradicated the need for such a rehearsal of the weave. The shop of Ahmed Tahir, "Designer," opens out to one of the principal bylanes leading off of the busy Sonapura/Madanpura road in Benares's downtown Ramapura area. On a wintry afternoon in January 2002, two teenage boys were sitting hunched over a table, filling in color on a design drawn on graph paper. They were learning the designer's trade as apprentices, and they no longer attended formal schools. For his part, Tahir ascertains from vendors and traders the popular or current designs in the bazaars. In addition to this market research, Tahir also uses, for reference, a number of tattered fragments or photocopies of pattern books with obvious Victorian provenance. The designer's end product is limited to the drawing on graph paper. After this, the design goes to the shop next door, where

Figure 5.1 Child assistants to Ahmed Tahir, "Designer" of silk sarees. Madanpura, Varanasi, January 2002. Photo: Author.

a number of (visibly poorer) workers punch holes into the cards required for the Jacquard. The cards are prepared using a perforated metal template that marks out all the possible hole positions. The workers place the graph paper in front of them and—using a long wooden ruler to ensure correct alignment—punch in holes corresponding to the design thus pixilated on the graph paper. As can be imagined, each card computes the picks on one weft; the sequence of holes (or absence thereof) determines the sequence of warp threads that are lifted. The cards are then strung together, in a

Figure 5.2 Artisan punching holes in Jacquard cards. Each saree can require up to thirty thousand such cards. Varanasi, January 2002. Photo: Author.

chain that often comprises as many as thirty thousand such cards for a single *saree*.

The procedure is the laborious re-creation of an *already existing* mechanical process. In both popular and aesthetic perceptions, the appreciation of craft work emphasizes an extreme fineness of detail in the product, necessitating constant supervision and calibrated readjustment of the mechanized element of production. This frame is not merely a romantic chimera; it keeps Tahir Ali in place in Madanpura, diamond cutters in Antwerp, circuit-board assemblers in Indonesia. Detail in this sense is defined as

Figure 5.3 Informational format supplementing the brain: a child carries on his head the Jacquard code for one saree. Varanasi, January 2002. Photo: Author.

Figure 5.4 Jacquard loom attachment. Varanasi, January 2002. Photo: Author.

variation from the programmed, what I have termed earlier as "felicitous error"—I remind you of Babbage's determination to eradicate error in the so-called mechanical faculties of the cognitive brain. The artisan's work is defined as (potentially) error through and through, where every pick bears the possibility of an incomputable deviation from the norm, the precise point where the computational principle—however regressive in actuality—is deemed to require supplementation by the "human" in the mode of a fecund miscomputation. In this sense, the artisan is the prototype of which the designer is the final form.

Cyborg/Artisan

> It is the rationalizing and ordering imposed by technology that makes us forget that machines have their origin in the irrational. In this area as in all others, it is necessary to know how to accommodate the irrational, even when—and especially when—we want to defend rationalism.
>
> —**Georges Canguilheim,** *Machine and Organism*

The global proliferation of personal computers (or PCs) in the 1990s has triggered a novel form of collapse between Marx's Department I and Department II, namely the production and consumption circuits.[36] It is perhaps because of this conflation that the supposedly elective tenets of Department II have allowed the dissembling of the tremendous socializing power of digitally networked capital as bearing the anthropological scaffold of a Robinsonade. Take, for instance, the following pronouncement, typical of many such that offer the pedagogical manifesto for computational teaching in design schools across the world, and think of the Benares hole puncher and the knitting executive in its idiom:

> The hand works in two directions: part effector and part probe. When enhanced by a tool, the hand remains such a two-way conductor, but its powers become narrowed and intensified. That is, when using a tool we can sense some things better, and we can alter some things better, but others not at all. … Ultimately the computer is a means for combining the skillful hand with the reasoning mind. We never had such a tool. If designed and used properly, this already lets us apply something about what we know of symbolic processing to using tools, and this alone should become more enjoyable than industrial automation. But at the same time computers let us turn the tables—to apply something of what we know about using tools to achieve richer symbolic processing. Metaphorically, they let us get a hold of our ideas. Concepts become things. We can't touch them yet, but already we can look at them, point at them, and work on them as though with hand-held tools. All this is ultimately more interesting than automation. Our use of computers ought not be so much for automating tasks as for abstracting craft.[37]

What is more interesting in the above comment is not the supposedly cybernetic interreliance of man and machine, of correspondence between prehensile digits and electronic digitality, but the curious reversion of the designer to the figure of craftsman. In previous chapters, we have come to recognize this reversion as a signpost for the customized differentiation of labor produced by the technological transactionality of drawing. In the following sections, I will attempt to describe this techno-customization as engaging not only conceptual differentiations but the body itself as the scene of error, differentiation and the residual. To do so, a certain understanding of the phantasmatic identification of women's bodies as the scene of functional differentiation and of biomorphic abconstruction might be necessary. This is for two reasons. "Woman" offers the primary template for the description of the body molded as if in error. And, by the 1990s, with the progressive hold of digitally networked capital over different forms of labor, it is "woman" who has come to bear the mantle of the artisan, as we shall see. The artisan is defined not by any particular definition of work but as an autochthonous residue, a functional placeholder in capital.

The artisan hovers at the limit of the machine. In this we see a reframing of the mind–body dialectic. In the past three centuries, this dialectic has followed a well-mapped course, reaching a particularly radical enunciation in the writings of the eighteenth-century materialist Julien Offray de la Mettrie. In his 1748 essay *Machine Man*, de la Mettrie characterized the human body and nature as an agglomeration of mechanical and chemical processes, purely a sum of its parts. As we saw in chapter 2, this mechanistic presumption was contested by the Romantics, who restored the older, theological idea of the soul—as repository of intention—in the teleology of the "whole" in nature. This later faction received its strongest vindication with Darwin's 1859 *The Origin of Species,* where this teleology of the whole was reconceptualized precisely from the point of the deviation—as errata—from the sum of the parts. In his theory of "natural selection," Darwin restored a larger intentionality to variations that were unintended; nature became the template for the felicitous management of error.

As a rule, nineteenth-century intellectual thought inevitably related its theories of biological change to some model of technological change. Samuel Butler's *Erewhon* shares with the dystopian future worlds of H.G. Wells, Jules Verne, or William Morris (in *News from Nowhere*) the apprehension of the eventual souring of the dependence between man and machine. Arriving in Erewhon ("nowhere" in reverse), the narrator discovers a land where "antimachinists," some five hundred years before, have destroyed the machines of the land or have forbidden their use. Seeking an explanation, the narrator comes upon a manifesto written at the time of the revolt, whose premonitions of a future world—where machines would overpower men—present a startlingly Darwinian perspective on technology. The manifesto's fear of the increasing power of machines over humans hinges on their eventual acquisition of a reproductive capacity. In the quest for self-propagative abilities, machines are aided not by their estrangement from humans but by their functional reliance on them. Even if machines cannot reproduce themselves, machine and man constitute an intimate symbiosis in which humans, by their irrepressible need to outdo each stage of technology, assist the reproduction of new machines just as insects assist the reproduction of flowers:

> Surely if a machine is able to reproduce another machine systematically, we may say that it has a reproductive system. What is a reproductive system, if it be not a system for reproduction? And how few of the machines are there which have not been produced systematically by other machines? But it is man that makes them so. Yes; but is it not insects that make many of the plants reproductive, and would not whole families of plants die out if their fertilization was not effected by a class of agents utterly foreign to themselves? ... Each one of ourselves has sprung from minute animalcules whose entity was entirely distinct from our own, and which acted after their kind with no thought or heed of what we might think about it. These little

creatures are part of our own reproductive system; then why not we part of that of the machines.[38]

Nature is the support—both metaphorical and actual—for the fecundity of the machine. The technological universe is not distinct from the biological but an extension of it. The machine partakes in evolution through the precise kind of discontinuity given teleological intention in organic thought by Darwin. It is also subject to the principle of felicitous error. Butler's portrait of the organic as a prosthesis of the machine is diametrically opposed to the general tendency of scientific thought in this period. Nineteenth-century science is defined by its reconceptualization of the organism as an analogon of the machine. "Applied" theories of entropy, energy, work, circulation, and mechanics modeled the organism into the ever-evolving paradigm of an ulterior efficiency. Helmholtz's neurological studies, Marey's photographs of living automatons, and Taylor's hive of workers all epitomize this dramatic recasting of the human along the lines of a system with computable variables.[39] This dystopian view allows us to review what is at the heart of the Cartesian sleight of hand, where, in the words of Michel Serres, "a technological anthromorphism has been substituted for a political anthropomorphism":

> Turner's canvases expose or faithfully represent this new world: no longer the space of statues, but the working (of engines) ... Lamarck, ... Darwin, ... Hegel, ... Marx, ... Freud, ... [and] Nietzsche. ... They all assembled engines.[40]

Erewhon's dystopic reversal enacts the inverse of this procedure. Machines would acquire supremacy not by means of their individual superiority over humans but by mimicking the hierarchies of human society. To the extent that these hierarchies were deemed to reflect the "natural" order of things, the functional differentia of organs and organicisms are here accorded an import for social order. It is this *biomorphic* differentiation of machine and human that Donna Haraway suggests has remained unperturbed in the productive ideologies of the twentieth and late twentieth century, even as theories of mechanical differentiation as espoused in conventional Marxism or Taylorism have fallen by the wayside. In Haraway's view, the historical differences posited between man and machine were indexes of power relations in the nineteenth-century registers of class, race, and gender. The conceptual limit of the reproductive machine was thus only the "caricature of [a] masculinist reproductive dream."[41] Today, however, the increasing miniaturization and pervasiveness of machines responding to every pore of organic life—Butler's specter of machines that talk to each other through humans is eerily palpable—call for a radical reunderstanding of these power relations.

Haraway's "Cyborg Manifesto" paints the picture of an autonomous "grid" of global technological transformation that, notwithstanding its origins in the military-industrial complex, appears to be undoing the binaries of geography, class, race, and gender. Interested in delineating the political agency of the lower-class laboring woman, Haraway argues that no such singular agency exists. "Woman," "black," "Third World," and "labor" are today irretrievably differentiated by the micrologies of technology. To encapsulate these differentiations, and displacing the fantasmatic organicism of the "working class," Haraway offers an alternative, equally fantasmatic, agency: that of the "cyborg," an infinitely adaptive, politically less dogmatic yet potentially recalcitrant global figure. The cyborg is a futurist creature, encompassing the characteristics of both (wo)man and machine. Its individuality is less a biological attribute or culturally derived identity than the function of an efficient differentiation within the technological realm. Writing before the establishment of the World Wide Web, Haraway spoke of this realm in the managerial class lingo of the "network," thus reconciling it with the feminist invocation of weaving as women's preferred activity: " 'Networking' is both a feminist practice and a multinational corporate strategy—weaving is for oppositional cyborgs."[42]

Weaving Sex, Patterning Algebra

We may say most aptly, that the Analytical Engine *weaves algebraic patterns* just as the Jacquard-loom weaves flowers and leaves.

—**Ada Augusta Lovelace,** *"Note A"*

For Lovelace, the Jacquard apparatus's provenance in weaving machines allowed a poetic association between the imaginative and mensurational aspects of patterns, thus precisely undoing Babbage's attempt to differentiate between different faculties of the mind. As we shall see, this poetic association was more than just that. It expresses a force of analogy whose power operated precisely to associate faculties of the mind with theories of corporeal and social organization, leading to some very far-reaching ramifications. Many of the allusions that have attracted contemporary cyber utopians and cognitive theorists to Babbage's work are actually in Lovelace's hand, including the passage quoted at the very beginning of this chapter. Lovelace's annotative female voice, effacing herself in the footnotes of the primarily male provinces of mathematical knowledge and technological innovation, has drawn the attention of technofeminists such as Sadie Plant.[43] The classic Victorian narrative of women's work in the shade of male accomplishments rings particularly true in Lovelace's case, a sickly child of an abandoned (albeit wealthy) mother, who learned calculus as an adult and carried out research amid furtive visits at odd hours to the library of the Royal Society, then restricted only to male membership. It is no small irony that the cry for the imaginative sanction of the techno-utopia envisioned in Babbage's Engine comes couched as a gendered desire for poesis in the machine. In the following sentences, Lovelace may well be imploring as much the aloof rectitude of the sciences as the male preserves of Victorian society: "You will not concede me *philosophical poetry*. Invert the order! Will you give me *poetical philosophy, poetical science*?"[44]

The scene of gendered weaving—and its metaphorical use in the image of the World Wide Web and the Internet—also appears in Sadie Plant's techno-feminist retrieval of Ada Lovelace.[45] Seizing on Babbage's adaptation of the Jacquard system and Lovelace's poetic invocation to weaving in her manifestos for the Analytical Engine, Plant relates their collaboration to Freud's theory of femininity, the latter posed against the tableau of his daughter Anna's regular habit of weaving at her loom. This dual relegation—of Lovelace by techno-logical history and of daughters by psychoanalysis—figures, in Plant's mind, an unresolved, and ultimately elided, conjuncture at the very beginnings of the digital revolution. The unresolved entity is gender, taken here—as in Haraway—as a metonym for differentiated identity in general.

Freud marks a significant turn in the Western understanding of the mind–body dualism. As Charles Shepherdson has pointed out, the many culturalist readings of psychoanalytic theory in a variety of disciplines have tended to obscure its resolute beginnings in *clinical* practice. Emerging from an intellectual milieu riven by the nature–culture opposition, Freud's grounding in clinical practice allowed him to locate as the special province of psychoanalysis a kind of phenomenon that infinitely complicated this opposition: physically observable pathologies whose causes could not be attributed to natural dysfunction alone. Shepherdson describes this new disciplinary province as a historical conjuncture that already divines the exhaustion of the division between the "natural" and "human" sciences, a division that has been accorded renewed weight in recent times by the debate between the respective votaries of "essentialism" and "representa-tionalism" in theories of identity. "Representation," in psychoanalysis, is defined precisely as an impact on the organism that leaves no biological trace:

> In a "Comparative Study of Organic and Hysterical Motor Paralyses," for example, [Freud] explicitly spoke of hysterical paralysis as "repre-sentation paralysis," and noted with some surprise (in keeping with his neurological training) that unlike organic paralysis, in which a physical cause—and indeed a material "lesion"—can always be found, in hysterical paralysis by contrast one finds a concrete, bodily dis-turbance in which the organism itself remains undamaged. "I will

try to show," Freud writes, "that there can be a functional alteration without a concomitant organic lesion."[46]

Encapsulating the various etiologies of these "alternations" into a transcendent category, Freud locates "sex" *at work,* producing difference (identities) in the subject. Sex is thus—to return to our discussion on Kant and flowers in chapter 2—a *causal principle:* "sexual difference is [therefore] neither [biological] 'sex' nor [cultural] 'gender,' "[47] neither essence nor representation but the analytical a priori of psychoanalysis. The (causal) reflexivity of sex produces the heterogeneous effects of gender. Although in this technical sense the psychoanalytic body has no cultural provenance, Freud inevitably models the prototype of this principle of sex on the bourgeois European family. From this anthropological reduction, we see a rupture in the analytical frame that will trigger a reversal in the late Freud's attempts—quite like the late Kant's attempt to fashion anthropologies—to diagnose larger civilizational propensities. The ruminations on Judaic origins or da Vinci's childhood and the 1929 lecture on "Femininity"—cited by Sadie Plant—are in this genre.

In "Femininity," Freud uses the psychoanalytic complex to make a historiographic, although consciously tenuous, predication:

> It seems that women have made few contributions to the discoveries and inventions in the history of civilization; there is, however, one technique which they may have invented—that of plaiting and weaving.[48]

The relationship of sex to invention is rather like the prophylaxis inserted between the aboriginal and IPR in the previous chapter.

It is important to note that this technological provenance is *neither gendered nor sexual, cultural, or biological;* it rather configures a body that can properly be called (psycho-)*analytical.* The elements of this formulation are well-known. Women's "genital deficiency" causes "shame" as a structurally feminine emotion. "Nature" offers a respite, by growing pubic hair that conceals the genitals. Women thus only actuate this latent natural predisposition by taking this matted filament and weaving it over the vagina, thus hiding their lack of a penis. Given this part-natural impetus to weave, (natural–cultural) origin soon becomes (cultural–technological) historical provenance. Women must thus be credited with the invention of weaving. Marx's criticism of Mill's political economy is easily transferable here: bourgeois gender relations are being recodified as world transformative history. For technofeminists, this functionalist fable has presented the mixed terms of a dubiously granted identity: both the terms of an (incarcerative) originary, part-natural divestment and that of the (liberative) irreducible difference of woman. Plant invokes weaving in her resurrection of two muffled amanuenses to two father figures: Ada Lovelace and Babbage, Anna and Freud.[49]

Both women appear as midwives at the founding of two master analogues of human thought: psychoanalysis and information technology.

Both Haraway and Plant position their analyses against the backdrop of the transfer of sweated labor to the global economic South. In this transfer—whether in the traditional "finger-work" industries such as garments or newer sectors such as electronic circuit boards—it is *women* who have emerged as new economic actors, even if only as the superexploited labor base of global trade. Against this backdrop, it is important to make some qualifications: Plant's understanding of woman as preternaturally identified with weaving as a *social* activity is largely a legacy of the European bourgeois household. In global historical terms, women have not necessarily been the primary actors in weaving as an economic activity—especially in areas where surplus production was directed toward supplying nonlocal markets. In areas with substantial extraregional trade, domestic divisions of labor within customary patriarchy usually relegated women to secondary economic roles, as in Benares. The onset of industrial capitalism—with bourgeois relations as its ideological vanguard—reorganized contractual relations to push women in weaving even further into shadow. This is patent as much in the silk-weaving districts of nineteenth-century Lyons as in northern India. Although metropolitan France—with the wherewithal to set its own macroeconomic policy—industrialized to carve out new economic spaces for women, women in artisanal sectors in the nonindustrialized world entered an extended period of invisibility under colonialism. It is this invisibility that is being harnessed by both transnational subcontracting (production) and microcredit (finance) in today's context. Old-style "feminism"—to the extent that it employs the European bourgeois household as the norm to be opposed—only offers a ruse for this new form of harnessing into extramural, superexploited forms of economic agency in its insistence on the (economic) visibility of women in the South. Haraway's manifesto for cyborgs is a brilliant attempt to reframe the norm in the light of this new globalized apparatus.

Along the same lines, Jacques Donzelot and Gilles Deleuze have berated the personalist reception of Freudianism, urging rather an analysis of the manner in which psychoanalysis proves amenable for the institutional management of families for capitalism.[50] For Donzelot, Freud is symptomatic of capitalist socialization in the focus on the family as the source of crisis, the flip side of which is the demand-generating theory of John Maynard Keynes.[51] Deleuze and Guattari's cry for schizoanalysis rather than psychoanalysis thus takes aim at a symbolic apparatus of supplementing production that psychoanalysis only bolsters through its alternating narratives of Oedipal presence and lack; the critical precursor being Engels's *The Origin of the Family*.[52] In place of the mythical castration of a phallic totality,

Deleuze and Guattari's retort is to construct (female) difference as the interminable assimilation and rejection of multifarious and unexceptional *part-objects;* the operative inspiration here is Melanie Klein. For Klein, Oedipus is only one of many formative—not foundational—stages, the ground for which is established much earlier in the infant's development, by his or her relationship to the mother's breast. This part-for-whole substitution where the detachable organ/breast (the site of a *natural nurture*) is substituted for the organic entirety of the mother locates the formation of character in an ever-persistent *binary* affective apparatus, which Klein designates as the conflicting, and originary, impulses of "love" and "hate." This particulate binarism allows Kleinian analysis to read an anterior multiplicity into the Oedipal theater. Symbolic lack is thus displaced into an interminable series of desire and repudiation, reparation and responsibility; Deleuze and Guattari have called this "code," in the analogue of both informational technology and genomic analysis. Gayatri Spivak has written of this serial processing in the analogue of weaving; objective determination is here seen in the image of particulate points subsumed within a topology:

> The human infant grabs on to some one thing and then things. This grabbing (*begreifen* as in *das Begriff* or concept) of an outside indistinguishable from an inside constitutes an inside, going back and forth and coding everything into a sign-system by the thing(s) grasped. One can call this crude coding a "translation." In this never-ending shuttle, violence translates into conscience and vice versa. From birth to death this "natural" machine, programming the mind perhaps as genetic instructions program the body (where does body stop and mind begin?) is partly metapsychological and therefore outside the grasp of the mind. Thus "nature" passes and repasses into "culture," in a work or shuttling site of violence.[53]

The analogy between organology and machine is not easy to dislodge.

Translation, Pattern, Code: The Artisan and Neo-Asiatic Modes of Production

In the different allegories of weaving in the above sections, we have come to an understanding of error as neither "natural" nor "cultural" in a preformed sense, but determining differentiation within a socializing rationale. Why does capital retain this place of error? Why does the technological differentiation of labor, even as it subsumes the human in the name of a greater efficiency, retain the "human" as the place for the potentially laborious substitute for the machine? Let us return to the scene of the hole punchers in Benares, with their shop next to the "Designer's," manually recreating a mechanical process well established elsewhere. The process is the reverse of Babbage's deductive logic, recalling that Babbage scrupulously located the Analytical Engine as a prosthetic for the *quantifiable* elements of qualitative thought. The artisan producing the cards for the Jacquard extension constitutes a *qualitative reconstruction of a quantitative process*.

This reconstruction manifested in the hole puncher—inscribing manageable error as felicitous in the interstices of the machine—is critical in that it uses the grain of custom as a conduit to socialize itself. The Taylorist division of labor into human bodily actions has appended to it a neofeudal comportment. The hole puncher is readable only as a place marker in a generalized, antithetical system; an entire "reterritorializing" grain of capitalist socialization. As such, this presents a reassembly of the Fordist assembly line, where mechanization was seen to graduate the worker into a demand-generating consumer of their "own" product (there is an impeccable affinity between Ford and Keynes on this terrain) along a theory of a "way of life." This arrangement has its own usefulness for the contemporary conjuncture, marked once again by capital flight from the North to the South. In this situation, the custom-branded hole puncher can appear as a totem for a new socializing apparatus characterized precisely by its calls to a socially cohesive ("Confucian")[54] "Asia" as opposed to a Europe "alienated" and made indolent by its experience with welfarism. We could term this, in the wake of Marx, the "*neo*-Asiatic mode of production." Here, a certain coding of "woman," wherein finance capital claims to rescue women from precisely the kind of symbolic structure of lack laid out in the Freudian family, can be pressed into efficacy. "Woman," in transnational capital, figures both the site of a fracture within the socius—thus the site of economic penetration—and the adhesive that binds its particulate elements into an organic cohesion. Patriarchy is not undone but displaced, and supplemented, in this globalizing move.

The *transnational differentiation* of labor, itself morphed from the "international division" of labor spelled out in the Third International, can be covered over in this phenomenological restoration of humanism at the core of technological capital. The Kleinian weave is a better mechanism to read this part-appropriation than is the torn portrait of the Freudian family. Gender—the image of CAD-CAM facilitating women's home working in the South needs to be kept in mind here—is in the weave of this differentiation. "Sex," with its motifs of plenitude and lack, is here only the handmaiden of a new global axiomatic whose principal thrust is to effect a Taylorist "reform" of the part-feudal.[55]

In the previous section we saw the intimate analogy between the intricacy of weaving and the indeterminacy of psychic identity. The analogy is archaic, but in Babbage's wake it acquires a new cognitive predication that makes it readable as "code" for the efficiencies and counterefficiencies, the warp and weft, of the human. In chapters 2 and 3, we looked at the "pattern" in this way; I called it the mnemotechnological supplement that operates in the place of *writing,* as a coding that both preserves and renders absent the artisan. The pattern is an instrument through which the traditional artisan is deciphered from its archaic speech and *translated—* what Spivak depicts above as the infant translating from below can also apply here to capital translating from above—into *qualified* labor power, the site of value addition. We remember that for Marx the qualitative-to-quantitative transition is epitomized by the transition between use-value and exchange-value. In chapter 2, we came to understand the pattern as the unifying imprint, in the context of the industrial revolution, of both qualitative and quantitative labor in the commodity. The indeterminate determinacy of the pattern allows it to be read as a map of cognitive schemas or concepts.

The pattern thus encapsulates the vitality of a *part–whole* relationship, where the absolute scale of phenomenality ("nature's" irreducible wholeness, in Kant's words) is held against a divisible measure (by a series of syllogistic relationships) that is in itself infinitely extendable. The pattern comprises both a fragment whose entirety signals an organicist relation to the nongraspable whole and the divisible element that is readable only through composite iterations. As such, we have seen how the embrace of the organicist pattern connotes a move away from the simple or mechanical repetition in nineteenth-century thought.

The cyborg can also be read in this register. The Romantic conceptualization of a new efficiency predicated by an open-ended relationship between parts and wholes displaces a theory of the automaton whose antecedents go as far back as Descartes and of which Marx was a late adherent. In this sense, Darwin's theory of natural selection marks a displacement in the understanding not of the organism but of the machine. The automaton is merely the machine whose sum of parts is equal and subservient to the whole. The cyborg, on the other hand, is the functional apotheosis of the Darwinian phenotype, in that it can both autogenerate variation and maintain the unifying telos, an anterior intendedness, within random transformations. The cyborg is an "organic" entity whose parts can both posit a radical independence from, as if in "error," and maintain a (dis)continuity, a "felicity," with its undetermined whole.

The parcelization produced by class formation, which is always the necessity and the bane of mechanisms and inherent in all the pedagogical and socializing programs commensurate with the industrial revolution, can thus be supplanted by the singular and morphogenetic efficiency of the cyborg. The cyborg autosocializes, whereas the artisan, also having bypassed class formation, is coded as perennially socialized; the nature–culture dyad is deemed to have been superseded in both. Unlike the worker, whose anthropological profile will be always be susceptible to the wear and tear of the machine—producing the "insouciance, suffering and revolt" within the socius that Keynes and Freud wanted to manage—the artisan will bear within itself the autogenerative kernel of a nonalienated socius. Like the cyborg, the artisan restores within the heart of the technological imagination the *idea* of the socius-as-whole, if only as a fragment. This part–whole organicism will resolve itself into the very body of the cyborg/artisan.

Teleproduction and the Artisan

In 1922, while teaching at the Bauhaus, Laszló Moholy-Nagy ordered five paintings on porcelain enamel from a sign factory. Keeping the factory's color chart in front of him, Moholy-Nagy sketched out the design on a graph paper. Using the telephone, he dictated to the factory supervisor, who had a similar paper in front of him, the color-coded coefficients of each square.[56]

The colonial abconstruction of labor in the nineteenth century already bears the brunt of this teleproduction. By the end of the nineteenth century, "Oriental" patterns referred to a slew of interchangeable motifs that were commercially traded across the breadth of the imperial system. Thomas Holbein Hendley, curator of the Albert Hall Museum in Jaipur, giving his presidential address to the Lahore Art Conference of 1894, noted how, traveling in Istanbul, he was offered, as "Persian pottery," a vase that had been produced in the Jaipur School of Art. The motif had been copied from an oil painting in Amber Palace. For Hendley, this confusion indicated in fact an inherent transcultural replicability of the Oriental artifact, in which inlaid wood done in Mainpuri in the North-West was deemed identical to traditional work from Broussa in Asia Minor.

> We in India, who know what facilities for interchange of ideas and spread of the arts are secured by pilgrimages to distant shrines, can understand this easily enough, especially in these days of copying and of imitating the arts of one part of the country in the workshops of another, perhaps a thousand miles distant, but many mistakes have been made in Europe for want of this knowledge. For these reasons I think that we should encourage the accumulation and record of all facts, however small, which seem to bear on the history of our *presumably* local arts. … If we wish to have new ideas and new manufactures [in India], I would suggest that we should … seek fresh models from Byzantine or Moorish art—the parents of our Indo-Saracenic schools—or from Hungary where are still to be found many ancient

Oriental designs. The museum at Buda-Pesth, for example, will, I believe, afford much that would be of value to use in India.[57] [e.a.]

By the end of the century, the DSA had become the principal archive supplying patterns and information about different artisanal techniques to different production centers. In addition, DSA officials such as Caspar Purdon Clarke also sent models for the most economical or aesthetic resolution of picks and weaves on any given pattern.[58] The DSA coterie both in India and in Britain thus institutionalized and provided a research backbone for what was an already widespread and busy commercial practice. Inasmuch as the DSA's textbooks, booklets, catalogs, and journal publications were published as pedagogical apparatuses, they were significantly more influential in reorienting artisanal production toward the aesthetic mores of imperial trade. The South Kensington Museum and DSA's enterprise in documenting, cataloging, and publishing patterns became critical handi-kits for less aesthetically trained officials in distant regions. The specificatory tone of the DSA tracts was particularly suited to the policy modalities to which bureaucrats were beholden, which explains their widespread referencing in official reports and correspondence. Both Babbage and the DSA therefore represent two different part-appropriations and recodings of the artisan: the first toward a productive use of the part-cognitive, and the second toward a part-universalization of culture as counteraxiom for production.

Opus Criminale: The Prison of Custom

In the metropole, the primary motivation for the schools of design was to preempt workers' dissent through the valorization of the self-realizing artisan. In exhibition after exhibition, the displays of industry iterated this caprice, according both singular, "free" agency to the worker and yet seeking to manage this freedom through a regulative discourse on taste. In India, by comparison, the DSA's intervention through the art schools turned on a conceptual blindness toward the functional difference between traditional and neotraditional industry. The absolute reliance of colonial capital on traditional forms of labor was dissembled by a metropolitan conceit that associated industrial capitalism primarily with machine production.

If customary authority within the trades and the mercantile class presented itself as a convenient armature through which to mobilize the output of labor, the mores that marked this appropriation also posed significant obstacles to the full-scale integration of this production system with market imperatives. A classic example of this patent discrepancy is the metropolitan perception of Oriental lassitude. Throughout colonial literature, the perception of a predisposition toward "lassitude" on the part of Indian artisans permeates European accounts of native productivity. Baden Henry Baden-Powell epitomizes this perception in the following paragraph: the Indian artisan is pathologically lacking in enterprise, unable to adapt himself to changing demands of the market:

> The lack of enterprise and the unwillingness to work everywhere met is the more astonishing because Indian workmen, if "driven to it," can work with exemplary diligence and endurance. The prospect of steady money-making seems either uncertain or too remote to furnish a stimulus. In giving orders for native work, even when the order is accepted, the inevitable "to-morrow" must always be borne in mind. The smallest thing will never be done to-day, but to-morrow. All over the East it is the same—"*farda*" drawls the Cairene workman just as readily as his Indian brother says "*kal*." Then, besides the time required for meals, for the *huqa*, for prayers and for holidays, there is always the convenient fever, the sick mother, the inevitable grandmother who has died, and the daughter to be married, and so, alas, Posthumus! "fugaes labuntur aunni."[59]

This Oriental lassitude indexes a schism in the chronotope of imperial production.

This mismatched tempo of the artisan in the imperial economy, in this strict sense, is not unlike Marx's view of "domestic industry": a household-based, anachronistic holdover of precapitalist organizations in contemporary capital. In the colony, the transition to the modern factory-form was occluded as incongruous, culturally limited by its inability to mobilize the intricacies of custom. Nonetheless, in passages such as the previous one, the abstractive chronotope of the factory is implicitly invoked as the primary *measure*—and here one could reflect on the profound politics regarding measurements in the nineteenth century[60]—as the model of productivity. In relation to the myriad forms of labor, the factory-form acts like a sliding scale, as if locating correspondences between rational and irrational numbers in arithmetic. The factory-form sets up an analytical structure of *interiority,* a parenthetical apparatus by which ("*ceteris paribus*") the spatialization of the factory becomes the temporal measure of labor. (The nineteenth-century expression for domestic industry was, symptomatically, "putting out.")

Through this abstractive spatiotemporal measure, a series of impertinent, anomalous, *differential* models, calculations, formulas and programs can be set in place to drive the socializing engines of modernity in all its formal manifestations: household, nation, workplace, farm, and industry. In the ensuing section, I will argue that if the factory-form was the primary enclosure through which waged labor could be submitted to a calculus,[61] then the intramural apparatus *extraordinaire* that served as the nineteenth-century caliper for *nonwage* (superexploited) labor was the prison. More important, in the colony where the factory-form remained a distant chimera, the disciplinary instruments of the prison—a key modernizing instrument of the colonial state—also served an indirect economic function of reorchestrating work practices in informal sectors. For observers such as Baden-Powell, it was obvious that some of the so-called failure of Indian artisans to conform to metropolitan norms could be attributed to the philosophical assumptions underlying those very norms. The Benthamite credentials of the statement are clear:

> A traveller in India, who did us the honour to visit our Punjab Exhibition in 1882 remarked jokingly that it seemed as if the only way to get native workmen to do anything was to shut them up in a jail! It is certainly instructive for those who pride themselves on a ruthless and inflexible pursuit of what are called "principles of political economy," to notice how some of the fundamental ideas of that science fail to prove false in the case of the native craftsman certainly in the Punjab, probably all over India. But in fact the maxims of political economy are based on the assumption that human motives and human desires work or act in certain ways and directions: and if it should be observed that in some countries human motives do not so work as is assumed, then what becomes of the maxims?[62]

The visitor in question was very likely Caspar Purdon Clarke, superintendent of the Indian section at the SKM. As we saw in chapter 4, the same Clarke had offered to make available patterns and technologies of carpet manufacture gathered from all over Asia in the SKM repositories to the burgeoning "Jail and Bazar factories" of India. The SKM was unique in that many of its floor decorations were made by female convicts from Woking prison in an effort to undercut industrial prices quoted by the Staffordshire potteries. This so-called social experiment, gleefully described as the museum's *Opus Criminale* by Cole and his cohort, is a lesson in the manner in which deskilled work was incorporated as an element of "craft."[63] The functional conflation between sweated prisoner and artisan, so that incarcerated subjects could, "with little instruction," carry the mantle of craft, is not in this case simply a question of deskilling customary work and training noncustomary entrants through the disciplinary ambit of the prison. The apparatus of the prison was not a replacement for artisanal work in the conventional sense. Rather, it needs to be read as a dominant calibrating mechanism for informal labor.

In India the gradual transition of prison work from the early idea of inculcating industrious "habits" to the later introduction of full-scale industries involving complex skills and machinery are reflective as much of the changing discourses of the value of labor as shifts in disciplinary dominance. In the earliest examples of the introduction of "industry" into prisons, the "Thuggee" reformatories in Jabalpur, administrative ethnocriminology combined with conventional political economy to infuse "approvers" within these (economically) disruptive tribes with "useful" and "remunerative" skills. The Thugs (the famed Central Indian tribes whose colonial characterization became a descriptive word in English) entered the political–administrative lexicon not as regular criminals but as *criminalized by custom*. The history of the Jabalpur Manufactory therefore offers us an example as much of economic modeling as of ethnosurveillance.[64] Supervised by military officers, young male Thuggees were first trained in brick making, bricklaying, carpentry, and masonry and then set to work building the manufactory. Within a decade of its establishment, the manufactory was producing tents, table linens, woolen and "Kidderminster"[65] carpets, gun wadding, and paper in quantities that not only offset the costs of running the reformatories but also turned profits for the administrators. The bricklayers and carpenters, classed as "unprofitable labor," were subsequently employed in government works. As the history of the Jabalpur school attests, the reformative thrust was not primarily interested in upgrading customary skills to new market conditions. Rather, "custom" was the mode of appropriation by which the indigene was submitted into a semiautonomous hierarchy of work control. *Craft* functions therein as a new term introduced to map the schism between extant customary conditions and colonial political economy:

> From approvers of the Mooltan Bunjarah class of Dacoits, we have lately succeeded in turning out good rope-makers and leather-workers, and from the Berriahs, a still ruder tribe, tent tailors and weavers; but the Bhudducks continue to baffle all efforts to teach them any particular trade or calling. They profess great contempt for all artisans, and prefer seeing their sons employed as day-labourers in the Lac Manufactory, or even begging in the bazaar, to learning a trade, which they consider derogatory to them as "men of sword and spear."[66]

The recoding of *craft* as a new term to appropriate vagrant spaces— places actually cast *out* of customary privileges—also resonates in Alex Hunter's Madras School of Industry, established in 1850. Before coming under the sway of the DSA agenda in the late 1850s, the school's constituency reflected an affinity between industrial work and a kind of anthropological rarefaction. Orphans, Eurasians, blind paupers, prisoners, "idiots and lunatics"—the consigned subjects of both colonial and traditional society—offered a custom-free anthropological foil in which to instill a rarefied concept of industry, defined as the human's moral inclination toward diligent labor. Just as the pedagogical techniques of Pestalozzi and Dyce purported to break down drawing to its constituent elements, the craft work done by the Madras students in the school's early stages can also be defined in terms of a notion of hand work pared down to its automatist facets: pottery for orphans, rope and string making for the blind and mentally challenged. All of these were subsequently sold on the local market to meet operational costs.[67] In conflating this rarefied model of industry with a vagrant and unmoored constituency, the school acted as a vestibular theater: an actual rehearsal of the rudimentary "Robinsonades" at the heart of liberal theories of political economy. The notion of craft in this context is not a lapsarian entity paling in the face of the inexorable advance of mechanization. It is rather a localizing and nested facet of socialization at the capitalist periphery. Observe the peculiar coding of the term *artisan* and its use in the following document on the display of machinery at the Dacca agricultural exhibition of 1864:

> It must be remembered, that all such Machinery is brought out only in component parts, which require to be put together and set up by professional men, who, labouring under the difficulty of procuring a sufficiency of manual labour, are often unable to complete the work undertaken by them within the stipulated time. ... Though owing to a greatly increased rate of ordinary wages a number of artisans were secured to push on the work in the Machinery Department, nothing would induce them to work beyond the ordinary hours, and when on a particular occasion more than double the pay was given to them for night work not one of the artisans made his appearance the next day, and it was impossible to procure substitutes at any price.[68]

Tradition is defined by both its immediate availability and its economic intransigence. It is not coincidental, therefore, that the DSA's entry into art-industrial pedagogy in India impeccably coincides with the introduction of basic machinery and complex crafts into colonial prisons. From the 1860s onward, in the name of reformative industry and economic self-sustenance, prisons increasingly became experimental venues for the introduction of both modernized artisanal skills and their relay to and from the market. Typically, jails turned out a plethora of products for local and international markets, such as furniture, carpets, and cloth, in addition to supplying labor *gratis* for local public works projects. Because, unlike traditional sites of manufacture, most of this work was carried out under official supervision, prisons were also a key site for the introduction of specificatory standards. The following extract from a report made by officials of the Moulmein division of Burma in 1860 bears out the relationships between incarcerated labor, interiority, and specification:

> The value of labour, skilled and unskilled, is so high at Moulmein, that under proper management the Jail far more than pays its own cost. The Department of Public Works can employ a thousand more prisoners than they now do, and [some of us are] of opinion that, if this number were added to the Jail [by expanding the framework of criminality?], the whole of the works in the Department of Public Works could be executed *without any cash disbursements* being required for labour. ... I desire it be particularly noted that no prisoner has under me gone out of walls, except to a regularly estimated project. *These are not works taken up at the fancy of a Magistrate merely desiring to work his prisoners,* even although as usefully as possible, but are most necessary works of regular engineer plans and estimates, most of which have received the sanction of Government, and *all* [i.o.] of which have gone up in their several Departments, and been well considered and approved of by the Commissioner and Chief Engineer of these Provinces.[69][e.a.]

Prison labor was therefore critical in folding the antieconomic rubric of tradition onto the infrastructure of the colonial economy. Correspondingly, with the midcentury shift in the configuration of penal work from extramural to intramural labor, perhaps the most remarkable case of industrial activity within prisons was that of carpets. From 1862 onward, Indian prison-made carpets with Oriental patterns were a consistent feature of all the major international and regional exhibitions. Carpet manufactories were introduced in prisons throughout India.[70] For colonial officials, the orchestration of this work lay very far from the wellsprings of traditional imagination, although prison-made carpets were in fact marketed as part of and competed with artisanal production, thus driving down prices in the wider market. Prison manuals such as Marshall Upshon's distanced the imaginative factor of "design" from the prisoners' executive function in realizing the commodity. In the prison, "design" is largely defined by the conformity to specification:

> It should be borne in mind that by "Designing" is not here meant the invention of new designs or patterns, but the correct method of expanding or contracting a design so as to exactly fill a carpet of the required size. The invention of new designs is the business of the artist, and it is not proposed to attempt it here. But if a customer has seen a carpet of a certain design, say, 18′ × 9′ and orders one of the same design, but of another size, it is obvious that the problem of expanding that design, or of contracting it, is to be faced, so that every portion of design may

be repeated sufficiently enough to exactly fill the size required. Some Carpet Foremen think they are clever enough to do without a fresh design, and will start off reducing or expanding out of their heads; the result is, that, when the carpet is nearly finished, they find that it is too short or too long; so, proceed to enlarge or contract that part of the pattern, which, needless to say has a disastrous effect.[71]

Figure 5.5 Carpets disinterred from royal palaces by colonial aesthetes in order to reuse their design. Courtesy: V & A Images.

In directly addressing the interrelationships between art and industrial education, penality, reform, free markets, subsidies, and the role of government in fostering new industrial sectors in the periphery, the interwoven dialogue of industries within the prison system is illuminating for the manner in which the distinction between modern industry and craft was played out by different interlocutors within the debate.[72] Generally, both art school and jail policy makers found themselves torn between two conflicting agendas. On one hand, it was important to increase productivity so as to reduce government outlay in educational and penal apparatuses. On the other hand, when introducing industries into schools and prisons, while areas of artisanal, nonmodern, expertise went uncontested

Figure 5.6 "Entrepreneurial" prison officials circulated large tracings of carpet patterns, such as the ones shown in the figure, between prisons to orient prison manufacture for the international Oriental commodity market. Curator in image is Dr. Graham Parlett. Photo: Author. Courtesy: V & A Images.

and colluded in price-reduction of artisanal commodities, colonial officials had to be careful not to tread on the hallowed grounds of nongov-
ernmental interference and zealously defended arenas of investment by
British-owned, mechanized industries. The brouhaha raised by British
metal-working firms over "free trade" upon the introduction of aluminium manufacture into Madras prisons offers an example of the latter.[73] In
characterizing art schools and jails as pedagogical institutions to inculcate industry rather than as industrial installations, the officials found
themselves addressing the contradictory aims of both free trade and governmental intervention into the economic sector.

In the next chapter, we will look at the figure of Gandhi as posing a critical
involution of this indigenizing force of error, wrenching it from its colonial
dispensation into a nationalist mobilization. With their "materialist" identification of the body with the tool, Descartes and de la Mettrie launched a
crisis within humanism that would—during the industrial revolution—
come to be identified with different models of efficiency. The drawings of
different trades in Diderot's *L'Encyclopédie,* the new conceptualizations
of systemic efficiency in the Napoleonic period, and the factory imagery
of the factory in Adam Smith and Andrew Ure all appeared to forecast
the ultimate substitution of the body by the machine. The challenge, then,
was to mould the body in accordance with these concepts of efficiency.
Taylorism was the totalitarian apotheosis of this intellectual movement.
It also exposed the significant deficiencies of this mechanizing impetus
and its inability to fully encompass the socialized body. The industrial
"worker"—an anthropological type purely reflecting the demands of the
production line—was merely a chimera of the nineteenth century. The
modern conceivers of industrialization were always hard put to effectively manage the "secondary" spheres thrown up by industrial capitalism on which it was nonetheless reliant: the insouciant arenas of sex,
tradition, culture, and sheer animalistic physiology that were so critical
to the progress of the industrial revolution. The very extraeconomic factors that reproduced the body of the worker outside the factory so that
it could reinsert itself in the production line once every three shifts were
ciphers to the managerial and administrative mind-sets, even to the
so-called mavens of "reform," who saw these extraneities as incidental
effects rather than as constitutive of the factory system. The compliance
of the worker was always at risk, and his body, alienated from affective
sustenance, always susceptible to breakdown. The convulsive twitches
of Chaplin's body in *Modern Times* would only confirm in the popular mind what had been long patent to captains of industry: that the
socializing apparatus of mechanistic industry was susceptible to wear
and tear.

With this realization, the materialist view forges a new convergence with the organicist. Efficiency is conceived of in the mode of the machine as not substituting the body but rather *supplementing* it, increasing its potency and resilience to locate it at the core of value production. It is here, I argue, that the artisan, conceived in the nineteenth-century frame as asymptotic to the trajectories of mechanization, returns in this new organicist concordance as the felicitous subject encompassing both the internal and the external vectors named earlier. The pattern books circulated by the DSA apparatus in artisanal sectors suggest that the cyborg is not a late entrant but a parallel development, a counterstrain within the industrial revolution. The anachronism of the Benares hole puncher and the expansion of industrial production into colonial prisons are significant if this is kept in mind. The cyborg is the culturalized "human" recoded into value. The cyborg, in this sense, is a conservative figure. Or, it is rather a figuration that differentiates and reveals the schisms between the "biological," the "social," and the "technological" (and we could think of other categories) as something *conserved* and therefore to be decoded from its erstwhile antediluvian moorings and recoded as a node of valorization. The cyborg is thus persistently misread by the vanguardist expropriators of modernity, who invest in it a posthistorical agency shorn of the internecine baggage of the past. Quite to the contrary, the cyborg figure gathers up the autochthonous, the primitive, "the feudal," the organic, the customary, the extrahistorical, the *aboriginal residues* circumvented or overcome by the dominant. The cyborg mines the many "lags" of historicity as openings for its myriad futures; it eschews any singular telos. Gandhi would be the name for one such artisan/androgynous cyborg.

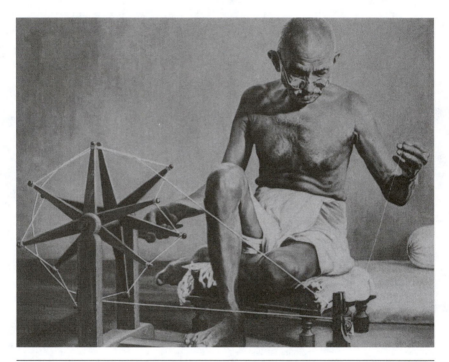

Rendering of Margaret Bourke-White's iconic photograph of Gandhi. Courtesy, Navjeevan Trust, Ahmedabad.

CHAPTER **6**

Congress: Gandhi at the World Exhibitions

The seventeenth annual session of the Indian National Congress,[1] held in Calcutta in December 1901, hosted an industrial exhibition in conjunction with its proceedings. For the first time, the session also devoted a considerable amount of time to a resolution on the state of industry in India, a motion given heightened political urgency by the recurrence of famine in the preceding years.[2] The presidential address left no doubt as to the forces behind this new feature of the Congress:

> We have opened an Industrial Exhibition in connection with the Congress, which, I hope, will in future be a permanent feature of our annual meeting. We cannot live in ignorance of the supreme importance which industry has assumed in modern civilization. In these days every political question is at bottom an economic one. It seems that hence forward markets are to be the battle-fields where destinies of nations will be decided. With the average European, it is a fixed idea that in the pre-established harmony of the Universe, Europe is to sell and Asia to buy. But *we* cannot help feeling that our thoughts and energies cannot be better employed than in the work of effecting a revival and development of our industries. The Exhibition that we have got up cannot fail to be useful in that it will keep the industrial problem before our eyes: and the poverty of the show will impress us with the "little done and vast undone."[3]

The denunciation of "deindustrialization" here goes beyond the routine charge of civilizational and cultural decline that suffuses both colonial and native thought of the nineteenth century. The criticism by and rather concentrated on the infrastructural inadequacies of the colonial economy, marking a turn in focus from lamenting the loss of tradition to one of failed parity within the modern. To the extent that this failure was gauged primarily in terms of the lack of modern industry in India, these (d)enunciations signal a new convergence of native capitalist interests with the nationalist agenda. Henceforth, each of the annual Congress conferences would include an industrial exhibition. This twinned staging signalled a new assertiveness on the part of Indian capitalists, one that matched the vociferousness of the political factions in the next half-century. Political slogans would borrow from economic agendas, and vice versa. Accusations of colonial commercial monopoly were now routinely voiced alongside criticisms of nonrepresentation in government.

From 1905 the industrial exhibitions within Congress conferences became the stage for the Indian Industrial Conference. In 1915 the Congress-aligned Indian Merchants' Chamber hosted the first Indian Commercial Conference, which later combined with the Indian Industrial Conference to form the Indian Industrial and Commercial Congress in 1920. The interwar period of heightened anticolonial activism thus dovetailed with unprecedented aggression on the part of Indian capitalists on the industrial front. Nationalist sentiment was critical in breeding solidarity among Indian establishments against colonial firms. This solidarity also bred a new confidence in Indian business to graduate from primarily commercial enterprise to industrial ventures. Businessmen such as Ghanshyam Das Birla helped to transform these various organizations into the Federation of Indian Chambers of Commerce and Industry (FICCI) in 1927. Subsequently, FICCI was able to consolidate the significant differences of caste, religion, and region within Indian business to formulate a reasonably cohesive nationalist agenda. At the same time, British capitalists in India suffered significant decline in the uncertain financial climate of the period following World War I, habituated as they were to nineteenth-century patterns of colonial enterprise based on racial privilege and proxy management.[4]

By the end of World War II, both wartime profits and these concerted efforts of the Indian business communities and other convergent factors resulted in indigenous enterprise obtaining 72 to 73 percent of the domestic market and 80 percent of deposits in the organized banking sector. In the view of a recent FICCI publication, this transformation was crucial for the nascent Indian state—unlike so many other decolonizing states where economic domination by Western capital continued uninterrupted—in that it was able to resist neocolonial interference after the attainment of formal political independence.

> The result was that [the Indian national movement] was able to evolve a comprehensive critique of imperialism in all its manifestations: whether direct appropriation through home charges, exploitation through trade, finance, currency manipulation or foreign investments, including in their sweep the now globally celebrated concept of "unequal exchange" where transfer of surplus is seen to occur through trade between countries with widely different productivity levels, even when the trade occurs at free world market prices. [FICCI] monitored complex national and international developments that had a bearing on imperial domination and Indian economic development, and forcefully argued the national position.[5]

It is important to note here that FICCI's constituency was primarily limited to the "modern," derivative, Western industries in India. The "national position" being argued here never extended to the total gamut of industry and economic agency in India. This qualification is critical. At the time of independence, the manufacturing sector accounted for a mere 17 percent of national income and employed barely 10 percent of the country's workforce; the modern factory sector accounted for only 9 percent of net domestic product.[6] Despite the global claim, native industrialists or FICCI could hardly claim to have representative authority over, or were their economic interests necessarily aligned with, the vast majority of India's population. This factional character replicated the political arrangement. At the time of the first industrial exhibition in the 1901 Congress, the politicians who claimed to represent "Indian" interests were hardly entitled to that claim, restricted as they were to a select elite of business leaders and intelligentsia. In the nationalist historiography of India, decolonization is defined as the unilinear and slowly maturing processes by which these vanguard "factions"[7] could, in the next few decades, reconcile their disparate and contradictory interests behind a unified discourse. Generally speaking, the terms of consent to this process by the broad swathes of nonelite or subaltern sections of society, outside of these vanguard factions, remain more than glossed over.

That some claim of broad consent could indeed be affirmed at the moment of independence rested, and rests today, much on the performative transformation of a young Gujarati lawyer who also made his political debut at the 1901 conference, reporting on the political travails of the colored peoples and Indians of South Africa. On his part, Mohandas Karamchand Gandhi was none too impressed by the modus operandi of the various sessions. A painfully self-critical thinker, he had meticulously prepared for his speech, which requested a resolution supporting the Indians in South Africa. In his mind, the unreflective enthusiasm that prevailed among the participants gave the Congress a facile solidarity:

> The procedure was far from pleasing to me. No one had troubled to understand the resolution, everyone was in a hurry to go and, because [the senior leaders] had seen the resolution, it was not thought necessary for the rest to see it or understand it! ... There was no question about the passing of the resolution. In those days there was hardly any difference between visitors and delegates. Everyone raised his hand and all resolutions passed unanimously. My resolution also fared in this wise [sic] and so lost all its importance for me.[8]

Gandhi's famed reinvention of his persona upon his permanent return to India reflected as much his alienation from this early form of Congress as his desire to encompass the vast gamut of subaltern politics within the nationalist ambit. This new persona represented an exceptional convergence of critical aspects of late-Victorian, colonial, and Indian societies. As we have seen in this book, colonial administration dissembles its messages within a nativist argot, deriving strongly from customary and religious idioms. Gandhi's nativist self-reinvention against this argot constitutes an involution of this colonial conception of Indian society. This involution manifested itself not only in Gandhi's thought but also in a reinvention of his very body, incorporating severe corporeal regimens of rigorous fasting, dietary constraints, daily disciplining rituals, and physical exercise. Some scholars have sought to portray the analytical rigor of these somatic regimens as a form of full-fledged experimentalism, comparable with a laboratory schedule.[9] In addition, it is also important to appreciate these experimentations as a form of internalized, empirical confrontation with the colonial discourse on hygiene.

And if the colonial discourse on hygiene was a form of periphrasis to naturalize a new economic condition, Gandhi's bodily reinvention had economic dimensions as well. So far, this book has looked at the staging of the artisan as the crux on which change within the modes of production could be mapped as a continuum. In this context, Gandhi's self-iconization as a *spinner,* a figurehead for subsistence-based economic agency in the colonial polity, is testament as much to the particular form of colonialism's hold over its subjects as to Gandhi's acute analytical ability to decipher these skeins. This chapter examines how Gandhi's pursuit of spinning as a daily activity constituted a unique convergence of the political and economic factions within Congress and a banner behind which native capital could dissemble its quest for industrial parity under the mask of an alternative, "protected" identity.[10]

This chapter looks at two different historical junctures where the artisan was invoked as nationalist icon in India, the first being the consolidation of "swadeshi" capitalist interests behind Gandhi, and the second being the spectacular showcasing of artisans during the 1980s Festivals of India held in Britain, France, Japan, and the United States. If Gandhi's guise as artisan fronted a consolidated attempt to force out foreign economic dominance of the Indian market, the Festivals of India were instruments for reinviting foreign investment after a three-decade experiment in a command economy.

Exhibiting Audiences: Reflexive Anthropology and the Customary Fair

The 1886 Colonial and Indian Exhibition marked a significant departure from the earlier world exhibitions. If the "free trade" ecumenism of the early exhibitions bound together the complementary factions of reformist voluntarism and *laissez-faire* commercialism, the 1886 exhibition concentrated entirely on the imperial construction of craft. Various reasons can explain this shift. For one, the organization and strategies of labor activism in Europe had progressed to the point at which unions were no longer attracted to the midcentury reformist nostrums that underlay the early exhibitions. At this moment, the colonial craftsman was the only anthropological type that could, at least in the metropole, be safely endowed with these nostrums. The 1886 exhibition thus marks an anomalous moment in the broader shift from the imperial paradigm of the early world exhibitions to the nationalist emphasis of the twentieth-century world fairs.

The labor delegations and conventions that were part and parcel of the early exhibitions were not immune to significant labor activism in these years. Louis Bonaparte—the object of Marx's trenchant derision in the *Eighteenth Brumaire*—and Cole's Society of Arts were instrumental in the travel of a French delegation of workers to the 1862 exhibition in London. Bonaparte's patronage of the delegation was an attempt to counter rising discontent against his regime; it had the unintended effect of fostering the connections between French and British workers that led to the formation of the International Workingmen's Association, Marx's "First International" of 1864.

If the world exhibitions signaled a new integration of industrial operations among European nations, an integration that remained resilient and ever expanding in spite of the intermittent bouts of protectionism and war, the First International too emerged from a rare agreement over workers' shared extranational interests in the 1860s. The First International was undergirded by a general tendency toward increased participation by national trade unions

Figure 6.1 Customary artisanal tools from India collected by the South Kensington Museum. Left: tiling and pottery tools; right: plasterer's tools. Photo: Author. Courtesy: V & A Images.

in foreign struggles. The consolidated support by both English and French workers of the Italian Risorgimento and the Polish insurrection of January 1863 are examples. This newfound cosmopolitanism was not necessarily without self-interest: one of the principal reasons for the British trade unions' support of the First International was to secure the cooperation of foreign unions against British employers' constant threat to bring in foreign "blacklegs" during strikes.[11]

Against this turbid backdrop, the Department of Science and Art's (DSA's) staged displays of craft are conspicuous by their elision of these workers' struggles in favor of their quiescent emphasis on "taste" as the principal yardstick of industrial reform. Quite against the grain of the image of exhibitions painted by contemporary aficionados of Walter Benjamin, midcentury exhibitions tended to emphasize the categories of industry and labor, hallmarks of the *production* circuit (Marx's Department I), rather than the *consumption* circuit (Department II). The DSA factions saw their world exhibitions as a criticism of petty, fashion-led commercialism, aiming instead to establish broad principles of morality and aesthetics for political economy. Thus the exhibition was a venue both for the exchange of information about technological advances and for the propagation of qualities of diligence, honesty, self-privation, abstinence, and obedience mediated through popular culture. Self-indulgent consumption was anathema to this ethos.

The 1886 exhibition was the last gasp of the DSA's dolorous emphasis on the exhibition as a pedagogical venue for workers. Its emphasis on *Indian* industry was a sign as much of the significant alienation of this pedagogical agenda from British labor activism of the period as of the figuration of the colonial artisan as the last vestige of the organic union between labor and taste. As such, the exhibition represented as much of a nostalgia for the mid-nineteenth-century intellectual complex of "industry" as of the spectralization of an "other" Asiatic mode of industry per se. Its chief architects were the diasporic acolytes of the Cole circle in India: George Birdwood, John Lockwood Kipling, Ram Singh, Swinton Jacob, Thomas Holbein Hendley, Caspar Purdon Clarke, Henry Hardy Cole, and George Watt. If the Great Exhibition triggered the foundation of the DSA, the catalog for the 1886 exhibition displays would evolve into the handsome *Journal of Indian Art,* with a run of twenty-five years. The *Journal of Indian Art* was the final apotheosis of the DSA complex, lasting well beyond the demise of its distant metropolitan progenitors. The *Journal of Indian Art* also provided the aesthetic counterpart to the scientific nomenclature of the six-volume *Dictionary of the Economic Products of India,* initiated as a systematic register for providing primary commodities for the different world exhibitions from the 1870s onward. The *Dictionary* was the principal

Figure 6.2 Models of artisans made for the 1886 Colonial and Indian Exhibition under the direction of John Lockwood Kipling, now kept at the Lahore Museum. Detail. Photo: Author.

Figure 6.3 Models of artisans made for the 1886 Colonial and Indian Exhibition under the direction of John Lockwood Kipling, now kept at the Lahore Museum. "Weavers at Work" detail. Photo: Author.

reference source for captioning the collections of the different regional museums established by the DSA faction in India.[12] The colony would be the prime field for the experimental afterlife of the critique of commercialism crafted in the midcentury metropole. As we shall see, the Indian National Congress's critique would engage this very anticommercialism as the ruinous ideological basis for colonial deindustrialization.

Peasants in the Architecture

That was also part of his routine: to watch the places where the watchers watched. The church, where the ebb and flow of the local population is a ready topic; county hall, register of electors; tradesmen, if they kept customer accounts; pubs, if the quarry didn't use them. In England, he knew these were the natural traps that watchers automatically patrolled before they closed in on you.

—**John le Carré,** *Tinker, Tailor, Soldier, Spy*

In Europe the audiences that the world exhibitions gathered unto themselves were by no means members of a homogeneous working class. The use of the railway to bring rural audiences to world exhibitions demonstrates the extremely uneven construction of the exhibition visitor. The average exhibition-goer was as likely to be a peasant, rural worker, landowner, and urban and rural craftsman as a factory worker. At the same time, in countries such as France and England, instead of undergoing a decline in the face of increased mechanization and urbanization, the frequency of rural fairs underwent a *fourfold increase*.[13] Thus, not only did the world exhibitions tap into a long-standing tradition of congregation in these fairs but these calendrically regular, usually annual, rural events proliferated the agenda of the sporadic world exhibitions that were typically held once in a decade. The vanguardist architecture of the world exhibition is directed at peasants.

When the British first started to host exhibitions in India, colonial officials drew strongly on rural tradition. Most colonial fairs were grafted onto customary fairs; the prototype for the colonial government's exhibitions was the cattle fair or rural agricultural fair. Like their many European counterparts, traditional fairs in India tended to be inseparable from religious congregations. Even when fairs were devoted to commercial transactions, such as cattle fairs, the schedule followed the religious rather than the farmers' almanacs. More often than not, they were held in places of regional or transregional pilgrimage. The religious subtext of these events offered only an ambivalent tool for an administration that was otherwise wary of the mobilizational power of religion. On one hand, the customary lines of solidarity that underlay these congregational sites offered administrators a ready-made audience, a premodern "public sphere" to be modulated from above. As the extrarational guarantor of social cohesiveness, religion, properly used, offered a managerial device whose prepolitical character could at the same time defer the emergence of a political (rights-demanding) audience. On the other hand, this very extrarationality made religion into a double-edged knife, because its mobilizational power could easily spill out of the administrative calculus and overwhelm its manipulators. The colonial "separation" of church and state therefore implied both a process of heightened control and acute appropriation of religion.

With the fraught topics of "native agency" and religious sensibility rife after the 1857 Mutiny, customary fairs came under renewed scrutiny in terms of their propagational power. Initially, colonial officials were uncertain as to the means by which to address the religiosity of the fairs. This terminological uncertainty had the effect of undermining colonial authority over the functioning of the fairs, a lack of legitimacy that officials gradually began to undo by evolving an alternative phraseology that focused on the hygienic and commercial elements of these events. Note how, in the following extract from 1868, the religious is estranged by way of sanitational discourse and moved into the realm of the commercial:

> A [major] cause [for the congregation] appeared to be a desire to worship at certain Hindoo temples quite near to Gurhmooktessur town, and about a mile from the fair; to bathe in and drink of the water of a holy well attached to the temples. Many thousands of people bathed in this water; and the plan of bathing I saw pursued was, that after the bather had washed his body by throwing water all over and well rubbing it, he proceeded to wash his cloths, and this having been satisfactorily accomplished, as a last act the bather drank one or two handfuls of water. On the last days of the fair it was noticed the water in this well had an oily look, and was, I should say, a very unwholesome water to drink.
>
> [Another] cause appeared to be a desire to trade, the articles offered for sale being principally food and sweetmeats, toys, trinkets, beads, brass and iron vessels, articles of clothing, English ware, walking-sticks and bamboos. The sellers of such articles had furnished themselves with small shops situated at the margins of the principal thoroughfares, the sites of the shops being let during the continuance of the fair at an average rate of 2 annas per foot of frontage.[14]

Religious activity was translated, by way of periphrasis, into concerns of sanitation and public order. As the religious subtext of fairs was increasingly underplayed by the administration, their commercial potential became central to the official interest in expanding markets for metropolitan goods ("English ware") in rural regions. Fanning out to the remotest areas, officials energetically sought to bring these arenas under government revenue and appropriate them for the sale of metropolitan commodities. In the administrative reports produced on these events, the *geo*economic thrust behind what might otherwise look like a localized description is unmistakable. In 1874 British Parliament was presented with a number of reports on a series of fairs, some customary and others organized by the British, held in the preceding years on the northern frontiers of India.[15] Officials strongly emphasized to parliament the geopolitical and geoeconomic importance of these fairs, especially of two that were held by the British at Palampur in the Punjab and the military encampment of Sudya on the borders of Assam, to open up for trade the vast "uncharted" territory that lay between the British Empire and its contenders Russia and China: the area stretching from Afghanistan through Central Asia into Tibet. The fairs were used by the British to set up a permanent set of "marts" for tradesmen coming out of these strategic regions.

Held annually, these fairs parallel the series of four exhibitions held by the DSA in London between 1871 and 1874.[16] The Society of Arts, a key sponsor of the London exhibitions, also supported these remote fairs in India, urging the British government to build more roads, bridges, railways, and shelters, as well as to make new commercial treaties with local potentates in these remote areas.[17] At the Palampur fair, the commercial elements were supplemented by an elaborate "durbar," a ceremonial gathering where rajahs and *raises* (local satraps) presided over diverse games and sports. In addition, a regional conference of participating traders deliberated on the manner in which trade routes could be made more secure and chartable. Beset by inclement weather, merchants nonetheless came from as far away as Yarkand, Ladakh, and Central Asia. Typically, the imports from Central Asia consisted of opium and Pashm wool bound for the carpet manufactories in Amritsar, whereas the exports from British-held territories consisted of English piece goods, country cloths, metal vessels, and plantation-grown tea. Generally, exports tended to be higher than imports, and each year the sale of English piece cloth went up from the preceding one, both points of satisfaction for colonial officials. Given the interest of the Society of Arts in these proceedings, the following observation by a government official was nearly tailor-made for the predilections of the DSA:

In selecting goods for the Yarkand market patterns with figures of birds or animals should be eschewed; stripes find more favour than checks; bright colours are much preferred by people here; black is not at all approved; tweeds are not appreciated. Glaces, chintzes, and all kinds of cotton goods are in great demand.[18]

At many of these fairs, civic, revenue, and military officials sought to further dramatize these forms of commercial exchange as unique sites of encounter with anthropological figures whose shadowy silhouettes had not been fully captured by the colonial encyclopedia. Anthropological probing was thus another key agenda of these fairs. At the Sudya fair, for instance, the military officer in charge documented the different participating tribes in great detail. Many of these came from areas outside British control, and Major Clarke, the officer in question, spent many hours interviewing them and gleaning information about the customs and geographical features of their homelands. The official report on the fair therefore reads more like a primary ethnographic account, including demographic descriptions of tribesmen from each tribe, lists of their chieftains, and the commodities they brought for trade.

Colonial officials by no means understood this description as an exhaustive one. What is remarkable about the tone of these reports is its thrust toward a *partial* rather than a complete manipulation of the customary sphere; the colonial role is seen as activating custom rather than transcending or transgressing it. At Sudya, officials laid the groundwork and were the primary motivators behind the hosting of the annual fair, and yet customary modalities were scrupulously followed throughout the proceedings. Tribesmen came and congregated according to their own mores, conducted councils and meetings on their own schedule, and dispersed at their own leisure. The disciplinary apparatuses of sanitation and "the preservation of order" were advanced as enabling diversity rather than inhibiting it:

Owing to the immense number of persons assembled, their uncleanly [*sic*] character, the want of being able to make them attend to convenient as well as sanitary arrangements, and the expense of their entertainment, the fair only lasted for one day instead of two;[19] and it was found more advisable to let them sell their commodities at their own pleasure and time, and in their own manner, instead of appointing a particular day when all who wished to trade with the hill tribes might assemble together with them at an appointed place, and the whole be subject to some surveillance, for the preservation of order, as also for their *mutual* protection.[20] [e.a.]

Colonial control thus legitimized itself as a guarantor for a peaceful diversity to flourish rather than to allow differences to descend into internecine conflict.

Charting Difference: The "Pure Vernacular of Empire"

If the unavowed purpose of the colonial fair was to chart difference, then, like the metropolitan exhibition, the fairs also introduced metropolitan commerce and industry as a new term within traditional transactions. Thus, even as colonial administrators struggled to establish a terminology to properly mobilize these indeterminate transactions on the periphery, the format of the exhibition also required radical reformulation. Given this indeterminate encounter, the very *name* of the exhibition became uncertain terrain for the organizers of the Punjab Exhibition of 1864. The Exhibition was held, barely fifteen years after the British annexation of the region, to have the local potentates "acknowledge by their presence [in the exhibition] the supremacy of the British Government which they have found too just to hate, and too strong to withstand." Through the exhibition, empire descends into the vernacular:

> What's in a name: now that Nature has overcome the work of man, and the anomalous legend in the Persian and Hindee character affixed to the walls of our Great Exhibition has been effaced by the saline efflorescence, which murders the vegetation and will not even spare the latest specimen of nondescript architecture at Lahore, we put it to the united wisdom of the half hundred *savants* and philosophers on the Exhibition Committee, whether that legend is worth restoring. Would it not rather be as well to try and find a more sensible and accurate translation in the native languages for what the Committee wish to express, viz. "The Great Exhibition of Arts, Products and Manufactures of the Punjab." The first attempt of Ajaibgah [*sic*], in Persian means only the "Place of Wonders"; and repeated in Hindee, it is simply an absurdity. The English name might as well have been put up in the Greek character, or in Egyptian hieroglyphics … is there no Orientalist who will come to the rescue, and give us a decent and correct designation for the Exhibition *in the pure Vernacular of the Empire*?[21] [e.a.]

It is as if the colonial fair is an encounter without language, without a terminology that can graduate this nameless babble and its gesticulations into a determinable syntax. The language thus evolved would assist not only colonial cognition but native self-cognition as well. In this sense, custom is not so much "made" or "invented" as is made operational as the effective vehicle through which change must be managed in the indigene. The otherwise indeterminate indigene could thus be self-stratified into a cohesive chart of difference. On the eve of the Delhi Durbar of 1903, Curzon characterized this extravagant event, following immediately on the heels of the great famine of 1900, as an arena in which Indians could arrive at a transcendent comprehension of their own diversity; in short, a "hydraulic state," to use Karl Wittfogel's expression:

> The weak point of India is what I may call its water-tight compartment system. Each province, each native state, is more or less shut off by solid bulkheads even from its neighbour. ... It cannot but be a good thing that [members of these different states] should meet and get to know each other, and exchange ideas, and yet no opportunity of meeting on a large scale is possible, unless it be afforded by a state occasion such as this. ... [Even amongst British administrators] there is many a man in Madras who has never seen the Punjab, or even in Bombay who is wholly ignorant of Bengal. ... People are apt to complain of uniformity in government. I can assure them that the differentiations of system and plan in India are amazing. I am not the person to wish to blot them out; but I do say confidently that an occasion like the Delhi Durbar, when soldiers and civilians from all parts of India will meet, not for a few hours or a day, but for a fortnight, and can compare notes and exchange ideas with each other, will be fraught with incalculable advantage, both to the participants and to the administration which they serve.[22]

It is only through imperial ventures such as the exhibition that the indigene could map out the unified schema of its own differentiated anthropological and administrative silhouette.[23] The DSA was directly implicated in this pageantry. For the 1877 imperial durbar, John Lockwood Kipling had designed heraldry for Indian potentates, the banners being produced in Indian silks and satins by Indian tailors under the direction of his wife, Alice.[24] It hardly needs to be reiterated that such a display would have been unthinkable in the older "weak" tributary feudalism that characterized the Islamic empires. Kipling's designs, reverting the model for the arrangements of decentralized imperialism in India to systems of vassalage in medieval Europe, are a direct index of the stronger hierarchies imposed in the colonial transition to neofeudalism.

If Curzon's sumptuous culturalism marked a posthumously Victorian epitomé of the principle of separate spheres and divided governance, then Indian nationalism would hone alternative currents within Victorianism to mobilize a contending culturalist vision. Here then, in the following passage from his *Autobiography*, is Gandhi's criticism of the emasculating

ostentation of the colonial durbars while attending Curzon's durbar immediately after the 1901 Congress conference. At issue is precisely the *obliga-
tory* frame of custom through which native culture is asked to represent
itself at these fetes. The description is remarkably masculinist, quite out of
keeping with the androgyny generally attributed to the later Gandhi:

> I was distressed to see the Maharajas bedecked like women, silk pyja-
> mas and silk *achkans,* pearl necklaces round their necks, bracelets on
> their wrists, pearl and diamond tassels on their turbans and, besides
> all this, swords with golden hilts hanging from their waistbands.
> I discovered that these were insignia not of their royalty, but of their
> slavery. I had thought that they must be wearing these badges of
> impotence of their own free will, but I was told that it was obligatory
> for these Rajas to wear all their costly jewels at such functions. I also
> gathered that some of them had a positive dislike for wearing these
> jewels, and that they never wore them except on occasions like the
> *darbar* … it is distressing enough to have to attend viceregal *darbars*
> in jewels that only some women wear. How heavy is the toll of sins
> and wrongs that wealth, power and prestige exact from man![25]

Congress and Exhibition

Gandhi's criticism of the durbars could as well have been posed against the
early phase of the Indian National Congress. The impetus behind the creation of the Indian National Congress in 1884 by British liberals was very
much in keeping with the turn toward "native agency" in the last quarter
of the nineteenth century. The Macaulayan dictum of creating an intermediate elite "English in taste, Indian in blood" translated here into a form
of pseudoparliament where the customary clothing of the participants was
perceived to be of greater interest than their locutions on particular issues.
W.S. Caine's turn-of-the-century tourist guide *Picturesque India* described
this tokenism quite clearly:

> The Congress meets at different centers each year. European visitors
> are always made very welcome, and seats in the best portion of the
> auditorium are reserved for them. Apart from its political interest,
> the spectacle is impressive and remarkable, being an assemblage of
> three or four thousand persons gathered together from every part
> of India, all attired in the characteristic dress of their districts. … It
> will greatly increase the interest which an English traveler must feel
> in his Indian fellow subjects, to have some surface knowledge at any
> rate of those social and political problems which are exciting them
> from time to time.[26]

As we have seen, at the 1901 Congress, Gandhi's dissatisfaction was directed precisely against this form of staged locution. Gandhi was not unfamiliar with the context of the world exhibitions. In 1889 he had visited the Paris Exposition, fondly describing the new Eiffel Tower as a "trinket" that appealed to the inner child within all adults. Gandhi was not particularly enamored by the glitter of the late-century world exhibition, and at least some of this ambivalence drew from the contradictory imperatives of the exhibition itself. As Paul Greenhalgh has pointed out, the liberal objective of educating workers through the exhibitions was persistently at odds with the exhibitions' more hedonistic treats, and the latter trend was definitely on the upsurge by the end of the century.[27] It can be assumed that Gandhi, called more to the midcentury discourse on reform rather than to the late-century embrace of entertainment, might have preferred the more somber objectives of the early world exhibitions.

Born to a trading community, Gandhi's engagement with labor issues was only initiated by his well-known encounter with John Ruskin's *Unto This Last* on a twenty-four-hour train journey between Johannesburg and Durban in October 1904. Spending a sleepless night mulling over the implications of the book (later summarized by him into the Gujarati *Sarvodaya*) Gandhi found at least one précis that was to stay with him for the rest of his life: "that a life of labour, *i.e.*, the life of the tiller of the soil and the handicraftsman, is the life worth living."[28] Gandhi resolved immediately to found a commune based on the principles of the book, which was subsequently established on the outskirts of Durban under the name of Phoenix Settlement. If the Ruskinian lesson was etched deep on his mind, we do not see further manifestations of it until much later in 1917, two years after his arrival in India, when he was well ensconced in the turbulence of its politics. In his proposal for setting up a "National School" that year, Gandhi urged setting aside several hours of the curriculum to learning the manual skills of agriculture, weaving, and carpentry. Gandhi also wrote up a full program and appeal for funds for his Satyagraha Ashram—a further development of the Phoenix idea—which he planned to use as the headquarters for his political work. His view of Ashram life envisaged various rigors of manual labor, including weaving and cleaning.

At this point, Gandhi advocated weaving mostly as a disciplinary tool to regulate the day of Ashram inmates, although in various funding appeals he tried to portray the Ashram's activity as creating a community of weavers that would arrest the national decay in the artisanal sector.[29] Gandhi's vision of the Ashram here was more in keeping with the Victorian suspicion of a life devoted exclusively to cerebral pursuits and its premium on labor as a prime element of life. Neither Gandhi nor the inmates were particularly apprised of the skills or the finer technological points of weaving looms. Eventually, a weaver was finally procured from out of town who, by Gandhi's own admission, only imperfectly taught the inmates some weaving techniques. These faltering experiments in microcosm were nonetheless crucial in bringing Gandhi to his well-known epiphany realization, that a guild of hand-based weavers would only strengthen the hands of mechanization in their ultimate reliance on mill-produced yarn. The Ashram had unwittingly "made [itself] voluntary agents of the Indian [mechanized] spinning mills."[30]

Gandhi's identification of colonialism with industrialization and his iconic emphasis on spinning and early commoditization as the bifaceted instrument of economic and political liberation was therefore exactly contrapuntal, as we have seen, to the consensus achieved between the political and industrial leaders within Congress. Gandhi's vision of the Ashram as an economically self-sufficient commune whose members would both spin and weave their own cloth further emphasizes this contrapuntal characteristic given that the Ashram was consciously located in one of India's key centers of modern textile industry, Ahmedabad. This contrapuntal characteristic notwithstanding, the modern industrialists' immediate embrace of Gandhi, with the resultant further iconization of the spinning wheel into its deified place as the central emblem of the new Congress flag of 1921, is hardly paradoxical. Rather, it underscores for us once again the peculiar involution of craft that the DSA had sought to institutionalize so many years ago and that a nationalist class of industrial competitors would find useful in their identification of colonialism with deindustrialization.

The transition of the spinning wheel from communistic instrument to nationalist emblem thus reflected a series of displacements whose provenance cannot be located within the persona of Gandhi alone. More significant is how Gandhi's persona is produced as an intersecting terrain between the elite mobilization of subaltern resistance, the colonial management of native political ambitions, native capitalist interests, and the uneven strata of colonial political economy. From 1921 onward, Gandhi's thought underwent a significant transformation from the experimentalism of the Ashram to a full-scale nationalist strategy for economic mobilization. The shift toward direct economic action evolved in two directions: first, in the shape of exhortations to native capitalists to take up their "national" responsibility to more fully harness indigenous resources and redress economic grievances of workers, and second, the devising of "swadeshi" programs comprising the burning of foreign cloth and the establishment of Khadi (homespun) workshops across the country to combat mass mechanization. If the former effort handily sanctioned the surging ambitions of native capital, the latter would provide tremendous symbolic weight in the anticolonial struggle.

The Village Community—Colonial and Swadeshi

The arrival of direct economic action at the heart of the nationalist agenda in the mid-1920s indicates the maturation of an ideological revolution that had been simmering for a half-century. In 1901, the same year that the Indian National Congress brought on board industrial exhibitions as part of its annual conventions, Romesh Chandra Dutt completed his landmark two-volume *Economic History of India*. Dutt had been the president of the Congress conference of 1899. In page after page, Dutt detailed his arguments against the discriminatory economic policies of the British, accusing them of applying "free trade" nostrums more dogmatically in the colony than manufacturers' interests in Britain would have allowed their own government.

> [The British government] taxed the coarse Indian fabrics with which Manchester had never competed and never could compete. It threw a burden on Indian mills which competed with no mills in Europe. It raised the price of the poor man's clothing in India without the pre-text of relieving the poor man of Lancashire. ... In India, where an infant industry required protection, even according to the maxims of John Stuart Mill, no protection has ever been given.[31]

For Dutt, if the modern sectors of the economy were thus stifled through unequal taxes and tariffs, the bedrock of the traditional economy that had been despoiled was the "village community" of precolonial India. Formu-lated by a number of theorists from the colonial officer Thomas Munro to the jurist Henry Maine,[32] the village community offered, for both colonialist and nationalist, a parenthetical exigency—equivalent to the interiority of prison and factory—of an organically knit political entity, where the divi-sion of labor was orchestrated by customary rather than contractual law. As a construct, the village is an *active* machine, the Asiatic equivalent of the factory-form through which colonial production can be mobilized. Even before Maine's lectures or the establishment of the DSA agenda in India, the early colonial exhibitions were in any case principally directed toward agricultural consumers and primary production, composed mainly of dis-plays of agricultural machinery, seeds, produce, and livestock. The rep-resentation of Indian production in the European world exhibitions and the regional colonial exhibitions in India thus charted two very different paths. Inasmuch as the regional agricultural exhibitions in India tended to be onerous exercises foisted on often unwilling regional officials—many hav-ing to go through the drudgery of requisitioning heavy machinery all the way from Britain—they usually tended to be unidirectional affairs. Unlike the broadly internationalist or comparativist thrust of the metropolitan exhibitions, the explicit purpose of the colonial exhibitions was to repro-gram the economic basis of regional markets:

> Here the object is not so much to exhibit specimens of the most perfect ingenuity as applied to industry or art, or to bring them into contrast or comparison, and thus stimulate competition—here it is rather that we may impress upon the vast body of our native fellow subjects the great advantage of bringing science to the aid of labour. Our object here is not so much to perfect as to teach, and I am sure that the results of an exhibition such as this—which I hope is only the precursor of many other such exhibitions in other parts of the country—will be to teach our native fellow-subjects the advantage, not only of industry, but of applying all the science, and all the newest machinery to the improvement of the productions of this country.[33]

Farmers would see new mechanical implements only for farming, artisans would purvey advanced tools for their respective trades, and native chiefs would be recognized by having official titles conferred on them.

The *Journal of Indian Art* and the *Dictionary of the Economic Products of India* thus represent the two axes of the dual initiative manifested in the regional exhibitions in India and the 1886 London Exhibition: secondary production in the metropole and primary production in the colony, with the artisan offered as the mystical continuum between the two. With artisanal wares and craftsmen presented together in impeccably cataloged dioramas, the 1886 exhibition in a strict sense belonged *neither to industry in the metropole nor in the colony* but rather as an ideological program aimed at working through the contradictions of global capital in its impe-rial manifestation. The exhibition appeared as both the pinnacle and the otherworldly imprint of an aesthetic and economic complex that operated as an antiphon at the heart of industrial capitalism.

The nationalist agenda turned this management of contradiction on its head. The 1902 Ahmedabad Congress, although reiterating the despo-liation wrought by British industry on native craft, directly criticized the DSA agenda in India, arguing that this agenda was only a ploy to deem-phasize the emergence of modern industry in India. The organizers of the Ahmedabad industrial exhibition contrasted it sharply against Curzon's impending durbar in Delhi. In his opening address at the exhibition, Pherozeshah Mehta spoke of his experience at the Paris Exposition of 1900, where "what struck me most profoundly was the enormous dif-ference between India and Europe to-day." Dazzled by the shining steel work and the textures, artistry, and sophistication of the machines, Mehta turned to the discrepancy between the commodities of the Indian and the

European home. An "enormous gulf" separated the "comfort" of the European cottage and the spare Indian home, the former subject to a "merciless tide that was ... sweeping and eddying around ... drawing its needs from a thousand machines ... and gathering its comforts from the four quarters of the globe."[34] Given such a spectacle of industrial change, Mehta argued, the Curzon durbar could only be a nativist blinder for the lack of British investment and encouragement of Indian industry. Echoing the same sentiments, Surendranath Bannerjea in his presidential address took aim at the craft-based "technical education" system advocated by the DSA acolytes in India, arguing that the pedagogy operated more as cover for colonial underdevelopment than as an instrument of actual change within the economy:

> Technical Education is indeed a red herring trailed across the path of industrial reform by Government in order to divert public attention from the real chase (hear, hear). Technical Education is in the West a very useful and indeed indispensable means of maintaining industry at a high standard of efficiency. We must have industries first, and then Technical Education to perfect them. ... The subject of Technical Education has been attracting greater attention every year during the last decade. But there are many whose idea of Technical Education does not soar above petty industries, others there are who want art-work, a third class, more sensible than the rest, yearns for the large manufacturing industries. Not a little confusion is frequently caused by jumbling all these together. Every sensible person would admit that there is not much room for expansion at present in the petty industries such as tailoring, shoe-making, carpentry, etc. Our wants in these directions are well enough supplied at present. As regards art-work the extinction of art industries would be a great loss to such a poor country as India. These are the days of rapid and cheap production. Considering the present wants of India it is apparent that in this country the utmost attention should be paid to the development of manufacturing industries because while the art industries deal with the beautiful rather than the useful, the manufacturing industries deal exclusively with the useful, and increase the wealth of the country (hear, hear). The principal means by which industrial development may be effected are joint-Stock organizations and Technical Education. The kind of Technical Education that is being imparted now in Bombay [at the J.J. School, a DSA outfit] is not the one that we want; it is a sham. It is merely an apology from Government for doing nothing in the name of industrial reform. ... Our chief want now is the manufacture

on an extensive scale of cheap articles of daily household use. Utility and not beauty must be given preference.[35]

As early as 1902, therefore, given what it perceived as continued deindustrialization and economic stagnation in India, the nationalist elite had turned fully in favor of modern, technocratic industrialization. Only large-scale industrialization, Congress leaders claimed, could ameliorate the significant depopulation and pauperization of the Indian countryside. The response of the DSA faction brings out the irony of this inversion. In 1910 Ernest Binfield Havell, DSA graduate and principal of the Calcutta School of Art, accused the Swadeshis of falling into the trap of Anglocentrism and Western demagoguery and of not fully appreciating mechanized industry's tendency to produce "conditions healthy and dangerous, bad for mind and body, making women unfit for motherhood, cursing the children, and causing the people to deteriorate."[36] A *true* Swadeshi would be one who, rather than "disloyally" expending his lungs at political forums, would recognize the centuries-old and permanent underpinnings of India's laboring population in the inculcation of its craft.

Even if not couched in precisely those terms, Havell's argument pointed out an important asymmetry in nationalist pronouncements on the economy. Drawing mostly from a Macaulayan stratum versed in the liberal arts and restricted entirely to bureaucratic, legal, or professional careers, early Congress critics of colonial policy drew more from *macroeconomic* pronouncements—based on colonial reports themselves—than from an empirical grasp of economic realities. In adopting the oppositional language of the pastoralists and protectionists of liberal Britain (note Dutt's invocation of John Stuart Mill), statements by Congress ideologues equally demonstrated the lack of grasp of the terra incognita of the unmodern economy of the hinterlands. Economic historians have described this preindependence rhetoric as "overdeveloped" and "overdetermined" with respect to its "objective" economic basis,[37] a characteristic that can be attributed to a terminology borrowed first from European oppositional factions and later from the steady infusion of Leninist literature into the country. (As early as 1921, the communist S. A. Dange had published his landmark *Gandhi vs Lenin*.)

The discrepancy between material understanding and macroeconomic rhetoric is easily discernible in both the relative meagerness of products and the lack of a clear curatorial discourse at the Congress exhibitions. It is ironic that it is the DSA-influenced reports and exhibitions of these years that give us a better picture of material work and skills of the nonmodern sectors. Indeed, contemporary historians have relied on these reports to reconstruct a more accurate picture of the artisanal economy in this period. R.C. Dutt's treatise is considered the propaganda piece.

The absence of the microeconomic picture within Swadeshi ideology was particularly suited to the aspirations of the emerging capitalist class within India. The reasons for this felicity are manifold. Moving out of the restricted "bazaar capitalism" of the nineteenth century, the new ambitions of native capitalists focused largely on the existing outposts of metropolitan industry in India rather than on areas of native competence. The principal emphasis was on areas of import substitution. These early features established a permanent attribute of industry in India that continues to the present day: unlike the industrial revolution in Europe where technological innovations in machinery drew from artisanal crises, technological transformation in India has been wrought largely by way of seeking compatibility with first-world systems. Then, as now, native capitalists banked on raw materials and cheap labor as the primary source of capital, while all machinery was imported. "Modern industry" in India would permanently retain the characteristics of a hothouse economy. In spite of their alignment with the nationalist economic agenda, therefore, native capitalists shared the exact shortcoming of their political counterparts. In their overdetermined discourse, this modernizing created a rift from the unmodern sectors of the economy that both factions were hard put to bridge, this despite the capitalists' long incubation within those sectors. This conceptual lack between a limited capitalist sector and the undercapitalized majority of the Indian economy created along with it a corresponding lack of political sanction. Gandhi was crucial in building that sanction.

From Weaving to Spinning

Gandhi's idealistic conception of industry evinces greater empirical comprehension only from the time of the invitation extended to him in February 1918 by Ahmedabad mill workers to arbitrate on their behalf over a wage dispute. The failure of the arbitration attempt led to a lockout by the workers and a stronger leadership role for Gandhi in relationship to the workers. The particular characteristics of this dispute established certain permanent features of what would come to be called "Gandhian" trade union politics. The Ahmedabad mill industry in this period comprised fifty-one native-owned "composite" mills (involving spinning and weaving operations) that were owned by families from a limited number of castes, dominantly Jains. Capital was raised on the basis of long-established kinship ties, and the mills were run with great personal investment with management kept within family and kinship frameworks; technological expertise remained a foreign province to a community whose interests remained primarily business oriented.[38]

Customary connections would be preeminent in the mill owners' reposing of trust in Gandhi's arbitrative intervention on behalf of the workers, not a little of it owing to the latter's shared Bania roots with them. In the Ahmedabad dispute, the paternalism of the mill owners' families played out in complex ways. Anasuyaben Sarabhai, sister of the leader of the mill owners' faction Ambalal Sarabhai, took a leading role on the part of the workers, opposing her brother on the issue. Gandhi's intervention—he went on fast—resulted in both a 35 percent wage increase and a permanent dispute-settlement mechanism. Gandhi's role here shows the multifaceted persona he represented to the many opposed factions of the nationalist struggle. On one hand, Gandhi's Ruskinian tenets against mass production and mechanization kept him at a distance from endorsing the competitive zeal of native capitalists, a factor critical in the workers' adopting him as their leader. At the same time, Gandhi relied on the Sarabhais and other native capitalists for his campaigns and the establishment of his Ashram at Ahmedabad.

This twofold legitimacy is evinced throughout Gandhi's relationship with native industry. Gandhi's early politics of active moderation made him attractive to a business class that had much to lose financially by visibly involving itself in nationalist politics. As Gandhi's hold over the nationalist movement grew greater, so did his influence over the new industrialist faction. A complex relationship developed. Gandhi routinely used the estates of the industrialists in his travels around India as bivouacs. (He was assassinated in Ghanshyamdas Birla's Delhi mansion in 1948.) Industrialists financed Gandhi's myriad ideas for movements, institutions, and other initiatives. Gandhi thoroughly revolutionized Congress's treasury and accounting, transforming fund-raising into an essential political element of the nationalist struggle. Gandhi single-handedly drew in a significant cadre from the business families into direct participation in anticolonial movements; from 1920 onward Jamnalal Bajaj was to remain the "working treasurer" of the Indian National Congress for twenty years. On the part of the industrialists, there was selective affinity on Swadeshi when it referred to questions of discriminatory tariffs and economic-rights recovery, characterized by public deference to and private dismissal of Gandhi's criticism of mechanization. Understanding this dynamic well, Gandhi adopted what might best be described as a critical intimacy in his relationship to industrialists. In the years before and after the Ahmedabad dispute, Gandhi wrote a number of leaflets, accosting native merchants and traders on their implicit collaboration with the colonial economy.[39] This admonitory tone is seldom found in his personal letters to individual industrialists, many of whom, notably Bajaj and Birla, considered him their family counselor, on several occasions inviting him to intercede in family disputes.[40] This mixture of personal closeness and political cageyness reflected a sense of mutual utility on many campaigns of both Congress and family-owned businesses. At the time of independence, this long-standing, strategic codependence led to the particular format of the Indian command economy where the traditional family firms were placed in a position of predominant advantage in their access to both native resources and international capital.

The years of Gandhi's deepening involvement with modern industrialists exactly coincided with his heightened interest in spinning as the device to undo the deleterious effects of modern industry. His emphasis on spinning now evolved from a microeconomic device for inculcating autonomy of individual character to a full-fledged macroeconomic prescription for national regeneration. In June 1919 he wrote to the Indian Industrial Conference, asking them for detailed figures on the production, prices, and subsequent processing of cotton into cloth. His subsequent arguments for Swadeshi were routinely reinforced by the weight of statistical data. In a series of articles and speeches, Gandhi further elucidated formulas to analyze the economically unutilized time in the day of poor peasants. Advocating spinning in this spare time as a supplement to income and as a buffer for the subsistence economy, Gandhi's arguments on spinning thus took the anticolonial argument beyond a merely protectionist rhetoric and imbued it with an econometric basis for economic regeneration.

After his emergence into the national limelight after the 1920 Congress, Gandhi sought to integrate his ideas on homespun cloth into the basic functioning of the Congress. The Khadi movement of this period advocated the public burning of foreign goods and cloth, the establishment of spinning and weaving centers countrywide, and the attempt to create a sales and distribution system for Khadi goods. Congress passed resolutions to make Khadi wearing compulsory for all its members. In a series of open letters, Gandhi accused Indian mill owners and cloth merchants not only of collaborating with British industry and impoverishing their own brethren but also of myopically bypassing a greater business opportunity: of harnessing the bulk of India's resources for themselves.[41] Gandhi's insistence on Khadi as an essential core of Congress activity came to a head with his program for the "Khadi franchise," which sought to displace regular membership fees by the obligation on each Congress member to produce two thousand yards of yarn per month. The proposal bore within it an implicit criticism of Congress rhetoric, indeed an acute consciousness of the "overdetermination" mentioned previously: the leaders debated and made statements on platforms and in legislatures, whereas the ground cadres, if they could afford it, paid up the four-*anna* membership fees and "sat around" for the rest of the year.

> You do not quite realize what Congress is. Today it happens to be an ill-defined and disorganized institution. ... Our country today is

a country of idlers and dreamers. I refer, not to the dumb millions who are groaning under poverty and slavery, but to ourselves—the so-called intelligentsia, the talkers. How can I engage all these in some kind of national work except through the spinning-wheel? In what other manner could the Congress be made a practical organization?[42]

The spinning wheel had reverted back from economic profession to a disciplinary tool. In the event, this commandment ended in failure at the 1924 Ahmedabad session, where Congress workers clearly demonstrated their reluctance to participate in the Khadi franchise. After this point, Khadi remained a symbolic caveat within the national movement, where Congress workers all wore Khadi but seldom produced it. At the time of independence, it was very far from the economic contract being carved out by FICCI and the new government.

Gandhi as Cyborg

You must find a Gujarati equivalent for "workshop." Will *karakhanu* do? Some had mentioned "metric system" in the curriculum. Henceforth, we should be careful about using such terms.

—**M.K. Gandhi,** *Letter to Sankalchand Shah,* **May 30, 1917**

I have discovered that man is superior to the system he propounds.

—**M.K. Gandhi,** *To Every Englishman in India,* **1921**

In both popular and scholarly perception, the evaluation of Gandhian Khadi has turned on a series of often-opposed frameworks and attitudes. Economic analyses variously present it as out of step with modern industry or, alternatively, as an antidote for the underdeveloped rural periphery. A more "romantic" appraisement, with its emphasis on reformative ideals, looks at Khadi as a moral, disciplining instrument, part and parcel of a larger somatic and social regimen underpinning Gandhian ethics that extends to dietary and other habits as well. In critical ways, these opposing modes of analysis do not transcend the nineteenth-century topos of posing the relationship to industry as a choice between an affirmative pragmatism and an abnegatory idealism. In this position of choice, the critical *functionality* of Khadi in weaving together the heterogeneous, potentially divisive, inevitably contradictory trajectories of political and economic interests, elite competitiveness and subaltern insurgency is ignored altogether. Khadi in this sense is less an industrial proposition or medieval tableau, more so a barometer of intractable difference. For Congress, Khadi thus became a vehicle for Congress to graduate the temporal asynchrony of the colonial economy into an effective political and economic attitude. As captains of industry, the Sarabhais, the Birlas, and the Bajajs, took to wearing this coarse cloth in solidarity with the nationalist struggle, through Khadi the undercapitalized, traditional periphery could be symbolically deciphered as the contrapuntal fuel for nationalized capital. The figure of the cyborg is useful to understand this countermovement.

In the previous chapter, we saw the cyborg emerge as a counterfigure within the twin revolutions of rationalism and industry, taking up the seemingly irrational and aboriginal residues that those revolutions cannot directly encompass. In Gandhi's reinvention of the Congress activist as spinner, we see an attempt to mobilize precisely this apparently antediluvian—and *demographically major*—residue within discourses of the imperial economy and its nationalist opposition. The spinning cyborg can be described as the conceptual bridge for the twin movements of nationalism and competitive native capitalism to forge an alliance with subaltern, decolonizing movements from below.

The Gandhian cyborg is therefore not in opposition to the industrializing ethos or the aspirations to power of India's political elite. Rather it gathers up the contradictions of their specific overdetermined and overdeveloped historical conjuncture. The Gandhian cyborg reassembles the asymmetries, reframes them as a unifying organon encompassing the irrefragable and anachronistic elements thrown up by colonial modernity. Productive inefficiency is recoded as efficient agency; the Gandhian cyborg recenters the frames of *unmodernity* in India—caste, rurality, religion, and craft—as fundamental rubrics through which any path to capitalist accumulation would have to pass. Note the phenomenological and antiethnographic tenor of the following extract from Gandhi's *Village Swaraj*; the last portion uncannily mirrors—and is uncannily contemporary to—Husserl's description of the discovery of platonic forms in his *Origin of Geometry*:

> Take the instance of spinning. Unless I know arithmetic I cannot report how many yards of yarn I have produced on the *takli*, or how many standard rounds it will make or what is the count of the yarn that I have spun. I must learn figures to be able to do so, and I also must learn addition and subtraction and multiplication and division. In dealing with complicated sums I shall have to use symbols and so get my algebra. Even here, I would insist on the use of Hindustani letters instead of Roman. Take geometry next. What can be a better demonstration of a circle than the disc of the *takli*? I can teach all about the circle in this way, without even mentioning the name of Euclid. ... I am elaborating the instance of spinning because I know it. If I were a carpenter, I would teach my child all these things through carpentry. ...

Let me further elaborate the idea. Just as a biologist, in order to become a good biologist must learn many other sciences besides biology, basic education, if it is treated as a science, takes us into indeterminable channels of learning. To extend the example of the *takli,* a pupil teacher, who rivets his attention not merely on the mechanical process of spinning, which of course he must master, but on the spirit of the thing, will concentrate on the *takli* and its various aspects. He will ask himself why the *takli* is made out of a brass disc and has a steel spindle. The original *takli* had its disc made anyhow. The still more primitive *takli* consisted of a wooden spindle with a disc of slate or clay. The *takli* has been developed scientifically, and there is a reason for making the disc out of brass and the spindle out of steel. He must find out that reason. Then, the teacher must ask himself why the disc has that particular diameter, no more and no less. When he has solved these your pupil becomes a good engineer.[43]

Khadi is therefore both a reconstellation and an undoing of the attitudes of the DSA and the more contemporary Arts and Crafts movement. Rather than revert to a fullness of ethnographically derived "community," the Gandhian cyborg rather pares the productive apparatus down to an alternative *phenomenological* minimum, an Indic "Robinsonade" through which a nonmetropolitan condition can be activated. The Gandhian village requires not preservation but imaginative *reengineering.*

The range of Gandhi's writings on rural India include not only ruminations on its autonomy but also detailed prescriptions on pedagogical attitudes, production techniques, wage benefits, systems of credit, and the political relationship with the state. Gandhi's suggestions for village industries encompass what he considered the plurality of village life, his specifications therein based substantially on personal experimentation and practice.[44] His observations on economic life ran the gamut from improving the production of *gur* (jaggery), the knowledge of chemistry required for tanning, the state support of dairy industries, the preparation of compost manure, the advantages of handmade paper, the bankruptcy of oil *ghanis* (customary cooking-oil mills), and beekeeping to the hand pounding of corn and rice. Even the kind of toothbrush the villager should use, to stem the onset of foreign and city-made imports into the village, did not go unexamined.[45]

The village exhibition was crucial to Gandhi as a potential demonstrator to display these sorts of economic experimentation. His conception of exhibitions offers interesting comparisons and contrasts with the early agenda of the DSA. In some aspects, Gandhi's stipulations read almost like Henry Cole's. "An exhibition should not become a *Tamasha* (sheer entertainment)," he wrote, emphasizing the role of the exhibition as a medium of education and self-upliftment for the villager. No sales should be conducted at the exhibition site. "It should also teach how to make village life artistic." On the other hand, in contrast to the DSA's overtly commercial agenda, Gandhi was opposed to the use of the village exhibition as a venue for advertising or as a source of income. The exhibition would show two models of villages— "[the decaying] one as is existing today and the other an improved one."[46] The improved model would show a clean village, offering with the aid of books, charts, and pictures models of village conduct, including diet, sanitation, comparisons of village and machine industry, animal husbandry, educational systems (nai taalim), and health care. Last, but not least, the exhibition would be useless without a strong showing of village industries and handicraft.

By the time of independence, this political contract founded on the *figure* of the Gandhian spinner and artisan as economic agents was institutionally tokenized in the Village and Small Industries sector of the many Five-Year Plans, which encompassed a significant network of co-operatives, registered institutions, and sales outlets throughout India. The establishment of the Khadi and Village Industries Commission in 1957 and the All India Handlooms and Handicrafts Board in 1981 in the wake of the Gandhian Morarji Desai–led government of 1977–79, among others, provided important milestones in the history of the artisanal sector in postindependence India.[47] This tokenized infrastructural network eventually took on the function—much in the grain of its colonial forebears—as a client-faction of the socialist state.[48] These institutions would be critical in providing the productive infrastructure for the Festivals of India.

The Neoliberal Rebirth of Craft: Festivals of India

Gandhi was internationally in the news again in 1982, this time owing to the multiple Oscar-winning film by Richard Attenborough. Marked by its overt privileging of the Ben Kingsley-played character's conversations with those played by Western actors such as Martin Sheen and Candice Bergen at the cost of much more important Indian historical figures, the film inaugurated a sudden spurt of films on the British Raj in the early 1980s: *Heat and Dust* (1983), David Lean's *Passage to India* (1984), and the television serial *Jewel in the Crown* (1984). This abrupt conjuration of the Raj was not a coincidence. The reinvocation of Gandhi marked a serendipitous tango with a critical turn of post-independence Indian history, namely the economic détente initiated by Indian premier Indira Gandhi with the new supply-sided consensus then being forged in Washington and London.

These foreign media events also spoke to a new form of cultural politics adopted by the Indira-Congress government after Congress's first ejection from central government since independence. The unprecedented access afforded by the Indian government to these film crews impeccably mirrors a greater investment into the power of spectacle riding on the back of a wave of foreign commodity inflow into the Indian economy. The 1982 Asian Games, with its accompanying launch of satellite-borne color television programming across the country, and the Festivals of India are of a piece with this new investment into spectacle. The Festivals were outright attempts to invite foreign investment into the Indian economy after a three-decade experiment in *dirigisme* initiated by Indira's father Jawaharlal Nehru. The paradox here is the reversion to a pre-lapsarian ethnicism and craft as the hallmarks of Indian contemporaneity evinced in these exhibitions. Indeed, the official promoters of the exhibition specifically posed this paradox as the face of an Indian "complexity":

> It's a perfect moment for India to cash in, to change existing prejudices about India in the western world and to signal a new era of Indo-American cooperation and exchange.

And then,

> These are the things that we want but cannot get until we alter our image. We are still trapped in the *Heat and Dust* and *Indiana Jones* syndrome. We have to show that India is *not only exotic but contemporaneously exotic* as well as modern and competent.[49]

Gandhi was critical to producing this simultaneity of tradition and modernity. In every letter written by Smithsonian officials to potential corporate funders for the Festivals, the popularity of the film was cited as indicative of a new openness of American audiences to the Indian market. If the Colonial and Indian Exhibition of 1886 marked an anomalous moment in the transition from pedagogical paternalism to consumptive spectacle, from colonial calibration to nationalist assertiveness, the dioramas of artisans displayed in the Festivals of India a hundred years later were designed, I argue, to produce a similar seal of abchronous consent in a transaction whose impetus lay elsewhere.

After independence, the particular combination of family-based business, political nationalism, and widespread underclass insurgency that underlay the freedom movement had led to a command economy structure marked by import substitutive and distributive mechanisms, significant domestic macroeconomic control, strong planning exercises based on the Soviet Five-Year Plan model, state-owned enterprise, and delinkage from international financial agencies. The measures resulted in significant protection against the desperate economic conditions and inequities in which the British left the peasantry and subaltern populations of India.

Yet the major beneficiaries of the postindependence arrangement were the family-owned businesses that moved in to take over formerly Anglo-owned concerns. After independence, these companies continued to operate as licensed units of foreign and multinational firms, producing local variants of multinational commodities. Ironically, it was the progressive structure of the command economy that laid the groundwork for the perpetuation of this kinship-based (in ownership terms) and quasi-feudal (with respect to employment) character of the industrial elite. One scholar has called this form of institutional organization "Bungalow-*Chawl-Haveli*" capital-ism, referring to the respective domiciles of the bureaucrat, the migrant laborer, and the hereditary industrialist.[50]

The Festivals of India were a partial response to the absolute breakdown of this postcolonial arrangement. The festivals have to be seen in the con-text of the Indira Gandhi government's tussle over legitimacy with the cultural politics of the Jayaprakash Narayan-inspired socialist–dissident Janata government of 1977. In the early 1970s, the Nehruvian formula of infrastructure development and welfarism transmogrified in the hands of his daughter Indira—under threat of imminent Congress breakup—into the populist "Garibi Hatao" ("Remove Poverty") slogan of the early 1970s. In the absence of any structural strategy for redistribution, the promise of providing more purchasing power in the pockets of the poor was financed by a ballooning deficit, one that became unmanageable with a series of monsoon failures and the global oil shock of 1973.[51] With political dissent spilling over in the streets under the Jayaprakash Narayan banner and loom-ing economic crisis, Indira declared an Emergency in 1975, suspending civil society rights and political processes, curtailing freedom of expres-sion, and surreptitiously reversing not only her own economic policies but also the broad policy thrust of the past thirty years. The reaction to this development was the short-lived Janata government of 1977–80, the first time when Congress lost its monopoly over the government of India since independence.

At the time of the initial meetings for the festivals, in 1979, Indira was very much engrossed in playing off various factions of the Janata govern-ment against each other. Her return to power in 1980 with an overwhelming majority found an unchanged economic situation from her earlier tenure, with native capitalists and bourgeoisie restless with undercapitalization in the domestic market. Indira's response was to contract a record loan from the International Monetary Fund in 1981, thus strongly integrating the Indian economy with international finance agencies and inching India toward the supply-ended consensus being forwarded by the rise of Rea-gan and Thatcher in the West. With this move, Indira effected what has been described in the Latin American context as the "neoliberalization of populism."[52] To consolidate her political base, she adopted a strategy of aligning herself with traditional—religion- and caste-based—sources of authority. The Festivals of India gave this quite concrete traditionalist vector an ecumenical sanction. The festivals therefore simultaneously accomplished a competitive indigenism with her domestic detractors on the cultural front and a new fiscal détente in relations with the major centers of foreign direct investment—Britain, France, the United States, and Japan—in addition to the Soviet Union.[53]

"An Inspiring Set Piece"

In the immediate aftermath of independence, the aesthetic manifestation of the "Bungalow-*Chawl-Haveli*" arrangement is best exemplified by the institutions established in Ahmedabad by the very patrons of Gandhi's berth in that city. Le Corbusier was invited to design the headquarters of the Millowner's Association, the same organization against which Gandhi had been invited to intercede on behalf of the workers. A Sarabhai descendant—Gira Sarabhai—was critical in the decision to invite Charles and Ray Eames to write the "Ahmedabad report", the manifesto for founding the National Institute of Design. The Sarabhais also invited Le Corbusier to build one of their residences, Louis Kahn to design the Indian Institute of Management, and Frank Lloyd Wright to design an unrealized showroom for their Calico brand of textiles. Later, Frei Otto built a Calico showroom. In 1957 an institute of "Indology" was designed by the Corbusier acolyte and CIAM/Team X participant Balkrishna V. Doshi.

The indigenist design sensibilities articulated in the Eames's Ahmedabad report were to have a crucial role in the aesthetic framing of the Festivals of India. The National Institute of Design would have its own show in the British component of the festivals, held at the Commonwealth Institute. At another exhibition at the Museum of Mankind, Vasna, one of the then-outlying villages of Ahmedabad, was presented as the quintessential Indian village. Long-standing relationships between the Ahmedabad patrons, their local designer/architect clientele, and designers such as Bernard Rudofsky, Frei Otto, and Ivan Chermayeff were reactivated for the Golden Eye exhibition held at the Smithsonian's Cooper-Hewitt Museum of Design in New York as part of the 1985 festival in the United States. In the prelude to Golden Eye, a Smithsonian News Service team sent to India to produce publicity material for the festival wrote an article on the National Institute of Design in consultation with its director. The formulation is uncannily DSA-like. The colonial dichotomy of elite/metropolitan aesthete and "community-based" artisan was reproduced in the very marrow of the globalizing agenda of the festivals:

Western errors are imported. Home-brewed soft drinks proudly hail the artificiality of their flavouring. Asbestos roofing is cheerfully promoted. Plastic goods are introducing India to the world of permanent trash. [The National Institute of Design's] goal is to train design professionals who will use Western design technology and concepts to improve India's living standard and quality of life, but without loss of Indian cultural identity. … The West has had more than 150 years to become familiar with the Industrial Revolution and the new sciences, arts and follies that accompanied it. … Once, "design" in India was the almost-unconscious heritage of the community or the craftsman; things were made for personal use or for sale in the village market or the shops in a nearby town. … Much [of the students'] time is spent with Indian craftsmen. Sometimes that simply involved suggesting a new product, as with the woodcarver whose business got a new lease on life when he started making cricket bats. … Projects may be more complicated, as in the case of a village of weavers losing their market. Here an NID designer—from a traditional weaving family in the same community[54]—advised changes in the looms, developed new products using traditional textiles and suggested the production of cotton shirtings, the better to serve India's market in Western-style men's clothing and the export market that provides Americans with summer wardrobes.[55]

The resonance with the DSA agenda is not entirely coincidental. The Festivals of India were first conceived in discussion or correspondence between the British High Commissioner in India and Victoria & Albert Museum official Tim Scott. Scott and Robert Skelton, keeper of the Indian Department at the Victoria & Albert Museum, then visited India for discussions with the Indian Ministry of Education and Culture, which set up a "high powered committee" (effectively a separate ministry) to oversee the functioning of the exhibitions.

The festivals were primarily an attempt by the Indian government to invite investment. As such, the bulk of the work and budget of the Festivals of India in terms of actual conceptualization, realization, and preparations on the Indian end was borne by the Indian government.[56] The scale of the festivals was immense; the events in the United States, for instance, included more than a hundred events organized by museums, libraries, and universities across the country coinciding with the events hosted by the Indian government. The causes for the governments of Britain, the United States, France, and Japan to play "host" to the festivals were different and complex. On the British front, internal foreign ministry communiqués from the British high commission in India leave no doubt as to the objective of the festival:

Trade: To build on the MOUs signed during the PM's visit here and to advance our commercial interests generally, clinching any deals that are ripe. …

If we are to get the big commercial deals we have to get the atmosphere right. Because of our difficulties over the substance of many of the political issues we must compensate in presentation. Mrs. Gandhi responds to this. … *To meet the first objective we have an inspiring set piece in the Festival of India.* The importance of its success cannot be over-emphasized. … A possible way around some of the objections would be to avoid immediate political context (for, like the French [Festival of India] example, the text would be notable for what it did not say).[57][e.a.]

The documents reveal quite patently the agendas that "should not be said" in this "notable" way to the Indian government. The addendum to the letter contains a long list of potential companies interested in investment contracts and defense deals with India. That this "inspiring set piece" was explicitly thought of as a proxy for a new economic interrelationship was evident in the fund-raising pattern of the different institutions involved in the festivals. On a research trip to India, Carla Borden, project director of the Office of Smithsonian Symposia and Seminars, obtained lists of the Indian operatives for American firms with the intent to request funding from their parent companies in the United States. In a handwritten note written to her immediate superior Wilton S. Dillon, Borden suggested particularly approaching Union Carbide and its chairman Warren Anderson (later indicted and absconding), assuming Carbide's need to mend relations with the Indian government in the immediate aftermath of the Bhopal gas genocide of 1984.[58] Dillon, on his part, also wrote to chairmen of different corporations, laying out the potentials for their products in the Indian market and urging them to use this opportunity to ingratiate themselves with the Indian government. Told repeatedly by corporations that India was "off their map," Dillon took the initiative to convince them that this event was not to be viewed as a normal "cultural" event. The following epistle to the Bechtel Corporation strongly emphasizes the real stakes:

The language used in your second paragraph leads me to think that I have failed to communicate that the Smithsonian was not asking for a philanthropic grant. Rather, we were offering Bechtel an opportunity to identify the corporation with a project much valued by the Government of India on whose pleasure Bechtel operates in that country. Thus I had hoped that Mr. Allen might have referred our offer to the advertising department or to those in Washington with discretionary funds aimed at "lobbying" or government relations.[59]

The British government also invoked a similar "enlightened commercial self-interest."[60] *Culture* was not only the indirect term used to circumvent the direct agenda of the economic but also the umbrella for a curatorial strategy that emphasized the old colonial exhibitive strategy of organic dioramas—now resurrected as Indian tradition—over the Western art-historical preoccupations of "history" and "style." The cultural apparatchiks of the Indian government were particularly insistent on this organizational motif of the displays in their interaction with Western curators:

> [Indian officials] expressed misgivings about the separation of the continuum of Indian art and culture into the compartments indicated by the exhibition programme and said the Indian view was of the inseparable relation of art and function. Hence a conceptual and thematic approach was more appropriate than an assembly of objects according to historical or stylistic criteria.[61]

Culture thus comprised not only the face of an ill-concealed economic project but also, more important, the antiepistemological thrust of the traditionalist organum. This construction is patent in the curatorial strategy adopted throughout the festivals. The centerpiece of the British and the U.S. festivals was a diorama called "Aditi—The Living Arts of India," first held in New Delhi and later at the Barbican Center, London (1982) and the National Museum of Natural History at the Smithsonian, Washington, D.C. (1985). In this exhibition, the material world of the artisan first formulated by the DSA was now relocated along a cosmogony of individual growth from childhood to adulthood in India. Change was conceptualized as the multiple responses of "Indian life" to present-day, "modern" exigency—in other words, "history"—as constantly shaped by the parallel, autonomous, adaptive, *regulative* continuum of the self-evolving noumenon of tradition. "Most of what *Aditi* presents is still part of a living tradition in India, *or that which is within easy recall.*"[62]

Every one of the different exhibitions and events conceived in the context of the Festivals of India unerringly replay this abchronous curatorial strategy. A mere list of the titles of the different exhibitions of the festivals should suffice to show the antidisciplinary and ethnofetishistic approach taken by the exhibitions: *The Canvas of Culture—Rediscovery of the Past as Adaptation for the Future; Sringar—A Pageant of Indian Costumes, The Living Arts; In the Image of Man; Vasna—Inside an Indian Village; Kham—Space and the Act of Space; Vistara—The Architecture of India;* and *From Village to City in Ancient India.*[63]

If a consciously unselfconscious ethnosensibility offered the basis for the construction of "culture" at the above exhibitions, then design and its relationship to the artisan was the keystone of the Golden Eye exercises and exhibition at the Cooper-Hewitt Museum in New York.

Golden Eye: Raising the Same Questions

With the Festivals of India in the 1980s, the Gandhian institutions catering to craft would have a paradoxical rebirth. The antihistorical thrust of the Golden Eye exhibition did not prevent its unwitting reliance on the historical influence of the DSA's influence in India, one equally beset by an antihistorical ethos. The introductory note to the catalog written by the exhibition's convener Rajeev Sethi opened with a full quotation from William Buick's own preface to the *Arts and Industries Manual* of 1883. The formulation is unmistakably that of the DSA:

> There are both in England and abroad men whose devotion to and intimate acquaintance with oriental art are not exceeded, sometimes not equaled in India itself. It is to such experts that an appeal is now made to assist the authorities in India, through the medium of this journal, both to direct progress in a right groove and to prevent the decline of Indian art by pointing out of when and how [*sic*] to check degradation. One of the most important matters in connection with the extension of a demand for Indian artware is to decide how far it is legitimate to adapt oriental workmanship and designs to articles of modern utility in Europe and America. ... The anklets and nose-rings of an Indian beauty cannot be worn by a lady of fashion in Europe. To what extent then can Eastern designs and workmanship be applied to Western forms?[64]

Sethi follows, "One hundred and one years later we are raising the same questions." On the right of the entrance to the exhibition, the panel describing the objectives of the exhibition was framed in stone marquetry; the tremendous pedagogical and experimental apparatus assembled by John Lockwood Kipling and his acolytes in the Punjab was symptomatically reduced to a nameless cipher: "The designs were inspired by pictures of the now-vanished 16th century tiles of Lahore fort found in a 100-year old British book."[65] We remember the screens reproduced under the direction of DSA officials for the 1886 exhibition using Fergusson's photographs from the 1860s.

To entice designers to take on the Golden Eye project, Rajeev Sethi traveled to different metropolitan centers outside India with suitcases filled with an exhaustive array of craft samples from different Indian regions.[66] The list of elite designer participants is impressive: Charles Moore, Bernard Rudofsky, Ivan Chermayeff, Mary McFadden, Frei Otto, Jack Lenor Larsen, Mario Bellini, Milton Glaser, I.M. Pei, Hans Hollein, Ettore Sottsass, and Hugh Casson.[67] Some of these—Sottsass, McFadden, Rudofsky, and Chermayeff—were old India enthusiasts. Their zeal is evident in the correspondence with both the Cooper-Hewitt and Rajeev Sethi, some of them mutually

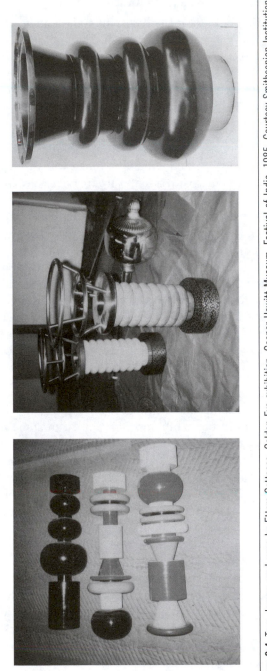

Figure 6.4 Toys, lamps, and vase by Ettore Sottsass. Golden Eye exhibition, Cooper-Hewitt Museum, Festival of India, 1985. Courtesy Smithsonian Institution Archives.

collaborating on projects. Participants were expected to travel to India a year before the designated opening of the show in September 1985 and to produce a design within three months of that date. The Handicrafts and Handloom Exports Corporation of India—one of the tokenist Gandhian institutions—superintended the production of the prototypes in India. Other than travel expenses, designers were not paid for the project, the quid pro quo being that they kept royalties from future sales of the objects after they went into production.[68] The craftsmen, on the other hand, were paid piece-work wages for their labor at low Indian wage rates; some of them were taken to New York where they were displayed along with the objects in the classic tradition of the nineteenth-century world exhibitions.

Some designers produced objects that are reminiscent of the Victorian penchant for using patterns as infill panels between structural elements. We could include the objects designed by Frei Otto, Hugh Casson, Mary McFadden, Ettore Sottsass, and Jack Lenor Larsen in this category. Pattern-producing techniques that would have been familiar to the DSA faction—marquetry, inlay, brocade weaving, bidri-ware, and carving—were used copiously to produce jewelry, furniture, garments, rugs and durries, bags, wall panels, containers, and other domestic objects. Frei Otto's canvas tents used a geodesic bamboo structure with appliqué work from Gujarat or can-vases painted by the Pichwai painters of Rajasthan.

In another category, we could place the objects whose outlines were otherwise well in keeping with the concerned designers' ongoing preoccu-pations of the time, except that they employed craft patterns to produce a certain grain of material (we remember Christopher Dresser here). Mario Bellini's stone bench would perhaps be the best example of this type, where Rajasthani marble-carvers were used to produce a piece that would have fitted seamlessly into an exhibition of contemporary Italian design. Like-wise, Charles Moore's miniature temple enclosures in painted wood are in keeping with the kind of post-Pop, "classical" symbolism evinced in his *Piazza d'Italia*, finished in 1979. Chermayeff and Glaser's animal/vehicle toy-boxes in Kashmiri papier-mâché also speak to the playful, post-modern sensibility of the time. I. M. Pei's wall-lamp dovetailed well with his gen-eral aesthetic of using chamfered platonic forms in his designs.

Of all the work, the footwear and foot jewelry by Bernard Rudofsky require a separate category. It can be safely asserted that Rudofsky was by far the most enthusiastic of the participants, spending a significant amount of time traveling and doing research in India and eventually producing the largest number of objects in the exhibition, including, in addition to the footwear, numerous pieces of furniture.[69] Explaining his design rationale, Rudofsky drew on the formulations propounded in his 1944 show "Are Clothes Modern?" at the Museum of Modern Art, especially in his section

Figure 6.5 Left: chair by Frei Otto; middle: toys by Ivan Chermayeff and Milton Glaser; right: toy models of Hindu temples by Charles Moore. Golden Eye exhibition, Cooper-Hewitt Museum, Festival of India, 1985. Courtesy Smithsonian Institution Archives.

on the "Unfashionable Human Body." The argument was that fashion—both modern and traditional—imposed illusory "symmetries" on the human body (we remember Christopher Dresser's formulation of *bimana* here); the natural forms of the body, however, are beset by irregularities and asymmetries. The shoe *never* fits. Rudofsky designed a series of asymmetrical pairs of shoes with the highest point at the big toe rather than in the middle as with conventional shoes; a number had a separate compartment for the big toe. The implication was also that the left foot was also essentially asymmetrical with the right:

> They are as asymmetrical as the foot itself and thus differ radically from today's pointed, symmetrical shoes. In other words, they run counter to the demented notion that the foot has to fit the shoe, instead of the other way. (... our shoes are made for feet that have a big toe in the place of the third toe.) Furthermore, Golden Eye shoes are flat, much like genuine Indian footwear, and therefore represent the opposite of the spike-heeled shoe, symbol of woman's submission to man. Should the nation have a change of mind and abjure current shoe fetishism, time will tell whether men will be able to procreate without the aphrodisiac of the High Heel.[70]

It is important to understand here that unlike the prototypes designed by the others, Rudofsky's work was not primarily reliant on the "decorative" strength of traditional artisanry. They rather pointed to a different premise that brings the mode of production in synch with the biological, even the "aphrodisiac" and the copulative: the one-off product of the artisan mirrors the asymmetrical singularity of the body. In its functional *customization* of the customary, the alignment of labor and social differentiation with biological difference, Rudofsky's formulation would hardly have been amenable for either the DSA's or the Golden Eye's vision of export-oriented Taylorized craft. Rather, with its intractable emphasis on the irreducible differences of biological singularity, it points to an extreme customization, whose proper province is only that of the cyborg.

Despite this infelicitous match of biology and craft, it is important to note Rudofsky's conception did not so much undo the presumptions of the exhibition as reveal its deepest conceptual kernel. More than being merely showcased, in the Festivals of India, the skills of Indian artisans were being appropriated into a transitional field where the hierarchy of production within the protectionist welfare state was being subsumed into new exigencies of investment. If Golden Eye once again invoked the master-*topos* of the managed modernization of tradition, the ruse hidden within this topos is revealed by the fact that none of the objects displayed in the Golden Eye exhibition were ever sent into production in the manner touted by its

Figure 6.6 Shoes by Bernard Rudofsky. Golden Eye exhibition, Cooper-Hewitt Museum, Festival of India, 1985. Courtesy Smithsonian Institution Archives.

conceivers. As desired, the festivals, for all their traditionalist framing, were the "inspiring set piece" for massive transmutations of financial arrangements and *high-technology* industry rather than the creation of formulas for any significant infrastructural infusion into artisanal production. The infelicity of Rudofsky's objects for export replicability exposes once again both the economic peripherality and the functional centrality of craft in building consent for a transformed geoeconomic environment.

The Time of Beauty

In putting together customization with organicism, Rudofsky's chimerical construct yields up the lie in Golden Eye. The bifaceted complex of subjective infelicity as the basis for an economic felicity is not just notional. For the DSA, the artisan represented the face of a preformed division of labour to tie together unguarded colonial production to the global economy. In this chapter, we have come to understand Gandhi as reversing this physiognomy, reverting the artisan to a customized totem of the post-independence welfare state. The artisan is therefore a centrally-poised figure in the long history of modernization, within which nation-formation was tied to a valorizing project under both exogenous and indigenous command economies. With the dissolution of the command economy envisaged in the Festivals of India, this totemizing centrality of the artisan, inaugurated a century and a half ago by an ornamental artist in the Alhambra, would find an emblematic burial. On July 3, 2001, the body of Jangarh Singh Shyam, a thirty-seven-year-old Pradhan Gond tribal artist, was found hanging in his room in a village in Niigata Prefecture, Japan. Shyam had been invited as an artist in residence (at a salary of approximately $270 a month) at the relatively unknown Mithila Museum there, a museum dedicated to the aesthetic artifacts of the aboriginal populations of the Mithila region in northern India. During his lifetime, Shyam's career had passed through some of the iconic institutions of Indian art and tradition of the late twentieth century. At the age of seventeen, in 1981, he had been spotted by the seminal painter J. Swaminathan in the village of Patangarh in Madhya Pradesh, the very village adopted by the equally seminal British clergyman and anthropologist "gone native" Verrier Elwin. Swaminathan invited Shyam to create murals on Charles Correa's arts complex in Bhopal, Bharat Bhavan, then nearing completion. Shyam's work was subsequently recognized in shows at the Surajkund Crafts Mela and the Pompidou Centre. Shyam's output thus caught a curatorial wave of interest both in India and abroad in work putatively outside of the formal-theoretical preoccupations of postwar art in the West, such as the Festivals of India and the Pompidou's *Magiciens de la Terre* (1989).

In eulogies published by well-known artists, apparatchiks and former patrons, Shyam's career was characterized as being caught between market and institutional asymmetries, "trapped in crossing" between "folk" and "urban" art, artisanal and artistic genres. Obituary after obituary narrated the incident along the plotlines of the Fall, the story of an autochthonous inspiration, an innocence "corrupted" on its arrival into the urban and global marketplace.¹ I have suggested in this chapter that the artisan is the magical (in/felicitous) counterfigure on the shoulders of which colonial and national industry transacts with global capital. This counterfiguration is driven by both its use as a lever for the mobilization of custom and its identification as contrapurposive loci for accumulation. Jangarh Singh Shyam's career points less to modernity's inability to sanction tradition than to the abconstructed place of tradition within it. In this sense, his "discovery" and his suicide do not belong to two separate, incompatible frames of reference but are of one piece. Shyam's suicide points us to the realization that these geoeconomic transactions are actually productive of subjecthood, of "selves" that can often only be affirmed by self-effacement. This suicide indicates less the failure of a premodern ethos to emerge into a sanctioned modernity than the expendability of cyborgs.

In the next chapter, we will look at another expendable figure of felicitous illegitimacy in the colonial and post-colonial dispensation of culture: the *fine* artist. As we have seen, in its focus on industry and industrial reform as the prime canvas of aesthetics, the Department of Science and Art's (DSA's) curriculum strongly inveighed against fine art. In both Britain and India, the late onset of "modern" art can be attributed to the long day (and shadow) of this imperial attitude. In invoking the artisan as the primary fount of formal culture, both colonial and anticolonial imaginaries in India saddled fine art practice with providing the supplementary terms of a civilizational quest, the perennial resolving of the conceptual ruptures of modernity and tradition, of elite and popular, to which the nation will appear as the response. The "individuated" numen of fine art practice in India is both institutionally centralized and formally undone in this mutual affirmation between artist and nation, for although liberal art practice benefits from the indirect imprimatur of the liberal state in the postcolonial era, unlike the avant-garde elsewhere it cannot negate the broad civilizing frame within which it is set. (This practice continues to its present-day appropriation in the "global" and "multicultural" biennales.) Posited against the colonial project and its "perpetual deferral" of the political sphere (as we have seen in chapter 1), the nationalist artist is encumbered with fashioning an aesthetic that will motor the *perpetual anticipation* of an imagined future. At the moment of independence, the enigma of Indian nationhood and the indeterminacy of art are inevitably placed as analogues, as codetermined in a joint quest for "civilizational parity", to use Geeta Kapur's phrase, among the nations of the world.[71]

If Kant described the aesthetic as the place of unverifiability, as the motor of thought without recourse to referent, then it is not coincidental that in the anticolonial imaginary the conundrums of an ever-elusive anterior nationhood should be aligned with the themes of the aesthetic. For a certain form of nationalist aesthetic, the transition from colonialism to postcolonialism effects something like the slippage between figure and referent, between unverifiability and the lie. The passage from anterior to present, from potentiality to actuality, opens up an atemporal abyss whose memory can only be narrated as the loss of beauty. The passage to the modern is inexorably experienced as the loss of the modern.

The next two chapters each focus on two memorials—mnemotechnical apparatuses—whose purpose it was to institute through particular conceptions of "history," particular relationships of beauty and memory. The above account of Jangarh Singh Shyam's suicide can serve as a memento, as we shall see, of other kinds of effacement produced by these sorts of instituted memory.

CHAPTER 7

Unmaking Beauty: Aesthetics
in the Shadow of History

Sikandar-ne Porus se ki thi ladhaai, jo ki thi ladhaai, to mein kya karoon? (Alexander (the Great) fought with Porus, and so if he did, what is it to me?)

—Hindi song lyric from the film *Anpadh* (The Illiterate)

Yeh daag daag ujala, yeh shabghazida sahar, woh intezaar tha jiska, yeh woh sahar to nahin (This tainted light, this benighted dawn, that which was awaited, this is not that morning.)

**Faiz Ahmed Faiz, *Subhe Azaadi – Agast Saitalis*
(Morning of Freedom, August 1947)**

What of beauty, then? Why beauty *now*? Now, at this late stage of the game? Alternatively, *when* was beauty? The question seems out of step, more so in a book such as this in which "context" and a certain historicity might appear to be privileged over the *punctum* of the beautiful moment. Congress, exhibition, capitalism, ruses, liberalism, nationalism, subalternity, cultural politics, strategy, bureaucracy, custom, ideology, the tired clichés of an emasculating "anti-essentialism"—no longer, it seems, does beauty launch arrows, no longer does it wound. Indeed, to ask the very question might draw consternation from the tired troops on either side of some well-worn barricade, who would rather that the battle lines be taken elsewhere, to allow a moment's repose to imagine that they were now inured to these darts.

The battle lines are old. Archaic philosophy construed beauty as ahistorical, as eternal and outside the realm of human affairs; precisely that which historiography cannot encompass. Beauty operates outside, and reveals, the limits of history and the historical imagination. Modern philosophy, at its inception defined by an epoch called "Romantic," inaugurates a project of historiography that appears to subsume this externality. Historiography, in this modern sense, thus begins to track the various *figures* of beauty—mimesis, perception, ideality, and so on—to bring beauty within the historical canvas. Beauty is historical, the claim goes. All transcendentality can be historicized in terms of its provenance in particular epistemic conventions. This modern, Romantic conceit ironically only *confirms* archaic convention: beauty cannot be grasped *by* human hands, only grasped *at*.

True to their Romantic upbringing, both university scholar and salon artist will profess to have competing claims to a beauty that both will describe as indefinable. This professional partisanship seems to mimic, in institutional terms, the theoretical fallout of what Schiller described as "beauty-as-Idea" as the equilibrium (*Gleichgewicht*) between a determining reason and an emotive reception in history: "The utmost that experience can achieve will consist of an oscillation between the two principles, in which now reality, now form, will predominate."[2] The impossibility of actualizing this Idea therefore becomes the irreducible condition for a perennially bicephalous state that will predicate the institutions of modernity *as such:* thought/feeling = historiography (criticality)/aesthetics.

This schism of European modernity will find its institutional locus in the program of the museum. It is no coincidence that the birth of the modern, *public* museum emerges at the same that the Romantic dichotomy is posed between categorical analysis and an aesthetic sensibility grounded in phenomenality. Consequently, the museum also bears the burden of that other hidden or tertiary imperative that is concealed within the idealist dichotomy. We described this in chapter 2 as the *pedagogical or acculturative imperative* within Kantian and post-Kantian thought. Schiller's conception of an "Aesthetic Education" can be illustrative here: not everyone, in fact humanity as such, is capable of apprehending the cutting edge of the bicephalism described above. Not everyone thinks or feels with philosophical rigor. For Schiller, this is the principal fallacy that leads to the fact of any history at all. Humanity's lack of critical rigor leads its members to tilt toward either an unfeeling rationality or an irrational emotionality, resulting in the ever-swinging pendulum of human events; history is the incommensurable narrative of the endless play of such unmethodical lurching.

The idealist critique of the aesthetic invites a caveat—a supplement—in the shape of pedagogy that will engineer the improper anthropological

Figure 7.1 Vivan Sundaram, "Journey towards Freedom: Modern Bengal." Victoria Memorial, Calcutta, 1998. Photo and courtesy: Vivan Sundaram.

subject toward the subject of aesthetics proper. Kant is impelled to formulate his *Anthropology* at the end of his life—the afterthought in which he will qualify the three *Critiques*.[3] As if by coincidence, the anthropological (or ethnographic) museum, the materialist (or industrial) museum, and the art (or aesthetic) museum map between themselves a differentiated anthropology of the European subject in the nineteenth century: a typologized orientation of all humankind toward the privileged and abstract locus of criticality that is occupied and desired by philosophy.

The objective of this chapter is to revisit these ever-appearing conventional boundaries—between historiography and aesthetics, between rational empiricism and sensuous subjectivity, between reflective thought and spontaneous feeling—and their harnessing into a pedagogical or acculturative imperative whose elements constitute a series of notions about modernity that operate in the form of an intense traffic across these boundaries. The chapter moves from more general philosophical framings of beauty in modern thought to the empty frames addressing historiography in an installation set up by the Indian artist Vivan Sundaram in Calcutta's Victoria Memorial Hall. The memorial was commissioned by the same Curzon in whose feudalizing pageants Gandhi had so bitterly felt the emasculating force of colonialism in India.

Sundaram's installation offers a synoptic acccount of aesthetics in a particular period in a particular region. Titled "Journey towards Freedom: Modern Bengal," the installation was set up in 1998, commemorating fifty years of Indian independence. The subtitle invokes a well-known topos in Indian cultural politics and political history: the Bengal "renaissance" of the nineteenth century. It also describes the content of the exhibit. This renaissance, like its European namesake, evokes a febrile arena of dialogues regarding the aesthetic, politics, history, and subjectivity, with the qualification that this arena is carved out by and under British colonialism. Owing to this acknowledged miscegenation, unlike the European renaissance, this one will have trouble basing itself on a phantasmatic, unruffled historical lineage from antiquity onward. This chapter will argue that Sundaram's commemorative installation in a *rememorative* space such as the Victoria Memorial both stages and rehearses this troubled recuperation of the past in Indian modernity. Implicated in this diorama is a critique of the divergent institutional histories of the museum.

"Modern Bengal" attempts a renegotiation of the museum as a critical apparatus, especially given that the dominant institutionalization of the aesthetic in India derives from the DSA-type museum and its further development through the Festivals of India. If the Golden Eye exhibition can be described as unwittingly commemorating the colonial DSA's policies in India, Sundaram's installation explicitly engages its "nationalist" counterstrain. Tapati Guha-Thakurta has shown how the "Bengal school" was the privileged locus for the nationalist position of a resurrected imitative and symbolic "art" against the antiart policies and proartisanal policies of the DSA.[4] In the later association of Ernest Binfield Havell, DSA-trained superintendent of the Calcutta School of Art, with the nationalist Bengal school, we can gauge the transition from artisanal production as the lodestone of culture to the construction of a numinous tradition, with its attendant themes of organicism and informality, as the founding inspiration for the modern fine artist in India. The following is Havell's interlocutor Nandalal Bose, professor of art in Rabindranath Tagore's Santiniketan school in Bengal, writing in his pedagogical treatise *Śilpakathā*:

> The European artist starts with an analysis of the parts and moves towards the whole; the Oriental artist starts with the whole and comes to the analysis of the parts. One climbs up from science and grammar towards the understanding of life-movement; the other moves down from an understanding of life-movement to the study of science and grammar.[5]

The schemas of German romanticism and the DSA are unmistakable in this creation of a nationalist Orientalism, even if pitched against the privileging of the artisan.

Let us return to the question, "When was Beauty?" Raymond Williams had asked a comparable question: "When was Modernism?"[6] For Williams, the question was rhetorically poised, a ploy revealing his desire to extricate modernism from its historically reified forms and to restore to it an extrahistorical demiurge that fights free of the confining labels conferred by historicism. One must return to the *spirit* of the modern precisely to get beyond a canonized and formalized modernism.[7] Formal inquiry must transcend historical forms to produce (new) form; modernity must supersede any given modernism. The circularity is palpable.

This circular schema—filtering a spirit from a prescriptive formalism— approximates the underlying agenda of Hegel's *Lectures* on aesthetics.[8] Art, the domain of beauty, fails to exude any "life" or "truth" in its present time, having reduced itself to the transcendental realm of *ideas,* or reflective thought. Hegel's gesture is toward Kant, who rigorously works against aesthetic judgment having any programmatic implications for the art *object.* From what Hegel construes as this subjective and transcendental morass, a new vocation will be found for philosophy: to guide art to its genuine fullness by constructing a conceptual framework for history composed of an alternating series of subjective ideas and object motifs, each surmounting the last.[9] The intimate strife of art and the idea plays out in the mode of externality and internality: of the idea as a persistent and self-evolving inner essence and of art as the ever-atrophying, external manifestation. This exteriority also lends to art a certain geoaxiomatic element. In examining the development of aesthetic thought,

Hegel surreptitiously slips in a territorial history of the world. The question of "when" and temporality will be displaced by the thematics of place and "where"—history is a logicogeographical, not temporal, discipline in this conception. History, distilled as the succession of so many "ideas," is staged as the superseding renaissance of one region after another. The progression of time is played out as the dynamic of place. The art of Zoroastrianism in Persia is therefore equated with the conceptual development of an "unconscious symbolism," "Mohammedan poetry" is equated with a "sublime symbolism," and so on. Global history unfolds as the conceptual development of the Idea. This terrestrial strife plays out until Hegel approaches the culminating scenario of his underlying, *and unerringly local,* reference point: the overcoming of the irreducibly subjective import of Kant's critique of aesthetics by the *eidaesthetics* of Goethe, Schiller, and members of the Jena circle.[10] Hegel cannot label his contemporaries as "Romantic," having already reserved the term for Christian medieval art.

The Force of Analogue

Hegel's conception of the aesthetic is a gesture toward, against, Kant. As we have seen, Kant arrives by beauty on his way to the sublime. Indeed, the sublime becomes necessary as the internal transcendentality of subjective reason, the topic of the First Critique, contemplates the exteriority of the object world at/as its limit. The Second and Third Critiques are thus two different openings toward that which is deemed as external to reason—in the respective elucidation of moral and aesthetic judgment. Kant is aware of a structural analogy between the two. He speaks of the former as the exercise of a "lawfulness without law" and the latter in terms of a "purposiveness without purpose."[11] In elucidating this analogy, he strictly warns against an easy equation between the two.

Kant's interdiction will be repeatedly ignored, triggering different sets of disciplinary careers. One strand, passing through Hegel, will perceive the art object as the material locus through which the moral–ethical dynamics of epoch, place and concept are worked out. The art object will be put on the dock as evidence, as a form of juridical testimony for a historiographic "science." Another approach, refuting the prescriptive possibilities of any such juridical science, will persistently force the analogue open, drawing on its bipartite strife as the engine driving a perpetual, antimaterial, and antiformal speculation. Romanticism marks the enduring legacy of this latter approach in modernity. The artwork—and in this case it is art as work, not as object—signals only the ever-elusive resolution of the moral and ethical conundrums of the age. A proper handle on the analogy will forever seem just outside the grasp of the work of art.

Although this bipolar strife will overdetermine many choices of career in modernity, a tertiary lesson will be persistently ignored in the history of modernity. This tertiary axis can be encapsulated as follows: Kant's careful positioning of morality and beauty as heterogeneous and logically *unrelated* terms within an analogy (Lyotard has called this a "differend"), on the other hand, belies his *reliance* on the analogy as bearing the critical *force* for the *effectivity* of the Third Critique. There, the critique of aesthetics acquires veracity not from itself, for aesthetic intuition is after all unverifiable on its own grounds, but because *it feels similar to,* invokes comparison to, the exercise of morality. It is in the *manner* of its operation that aesthetic sentiment reminds one of the submission to morality in accordance with the transcendental principle of freedom, that the understanding of beauty acquires its "critical" comportment. One gives in to beauty *as* one does to morality. But unlike the latter, Kant admonishes us that it is impossible to chart a course of behavior to lead the aesthetically fulfilled life.

Taking up one of Kant's words, Derrida has described this analogical force as that of the *parergon*—the framing device that, although being deemed alongside and outside (*para-*) the work (*ergon*), motivates it from within.[12] The parergon prises open, makes effective the play of the circular schema of abstract and particular, of inner spirit and external manifestation. At different points in the three Critiques, Kant seems well aware of this play. The caution regarding the analogy is a parergonal insight, a subtle yet strong riposte to the archaic argument that would otherwise equate the beautiful with the good. Nonetheless, the analogy appears as (but only just) a temptation to attempt a crossing between the triadic schema of the three critiques, between truth, goodness, and beauty. This temptation will be taken as license for a crude conflation, to collapse the abyss between these heterogeneous analytics in a ploy for power.[13] Perhaps the following characterization of this abuse from Lyotard will suffice:

> The way [between the critiques of morality and beauty in Kant] being thus opened, more than one thinker, hastily concluding the Good from the beautiful, has rushed forward and succeeded in crossing the bridge (despite the many warnings of Kant) in order to reimplant the metaphysical bridgehead on critical soil, in order to reaffirm the archaic argument, archaic for Western thought, according to which the outcome, having moved from the beautiful to the Good, is the Good and that in *feeling* the Good, one will *do* Good. Furthermore, in making the beautiful felt, one will make others do good. In shaping the given according to the beautiful, with taste, one preaches the individual *ethos* or the community *politikon*. The way toward

an "aesthetic education," which was lost for a moment, is reopened without taking any account of the explicit reservation Kant incessantly opposes to a conclusive use of analogy.[14]

Many paths are forged in this kind of crossing, the collapse of the analogue—this equation between truth, the good, and beauty—that will acquire the name of this or that "modernity" or "modernism."

Figures in the Crossing

"Nationalism" must be one of these bridges, even a cluster of such crossings. Paul de Man has spoken of the modern nation-state as conceivable precisely in the passage from the philosophical imaginary of Kant to the pedagogical psychology of Schiller, and not only in the German context.[15] I think of this conceivability as I view the video *Structures of Memory* by Sundaram, his own interpretation of the installation inside Calcutta's Victoria Memorial.[16] "Modern Bengal" is a topos in the cultural politics of Indian nationalism, a term redolent with pleasant and noxious aromas, like "antebellum Low Country" or "Louis-Phillipe furniture." As a palpable field of associations, it defines a period and a place: the nineteenth century and early twentieth century in the lower Ganges delta in the environs of Calcutta, where a new society of letters, arts, and science emerged as a result of the unique interaction between European colonial officials, liberal thinkers, and members of the native gentry and elite. This new society can be considered as complicit in the colonial apparatus—many of the personalities involved were zamindars and government officials—even as it devised a discourse that led to colonialism's formal demise. An array of institutions emerged during this period, institutions that we would associate with "modernity": liberal arts colleges, universities, literature clubs, magazines and journals, movements for religious reform, and institutions for the social and human sciences. The explosion of print media was paralleled by a convulsion of divergent, contradictory opinions and debates. The fretful cerebrality of this culture would incite the likes of Rudyard Kipling to caricature the Bengali as an effete type perennially scheming to undermine the muscular demands of Indian administration.[17] This paroxysm of culture was accompanied by the worst economic depredations of colonial rule in the same province: recurrent famine, relentless agrarian depopulation, land divestment at the subsistence level, and the superexploitation of labor. At the turn of the century, Calcutta was the geographical linchpin of both the print revolution in India and the asymmetries of resource-extractive colonial "trade." In this situation of disparity, the nationalist factions ensconced in the previously mentioned institutions could acquire the status of a(n overdetermined) "vanguard," both in terms of the formation of a nationalist imaginary and with regard to the underclass.

Sundaram's installation reflects various ramifications of this epoch. At several points, the installation explicitly juxtaposes the emergence of elite literacy and cultural discourse with scenarios of superexploited plantation labor. Sacks of grain, piled high, have inscribed on them the dates and short descriptions of myriad peasant and worker insurgencies of the era. Skeins of jute, Bengal's prime colonial export, are arranged on the floor; the economic trajectories of primary production are staged throughout as artwork. Tea chests—containers for both new modes of labor and a new mode of sociality—frame illuminated images of the neo-Baroque dome and arches that frame the Victoria Memorial.

Walter Benjamin appears to be a significant influence for Sundaram; the installation brings in multiple reproductive techniques to supplement these dioramas of primary production. The nineteenth-century obsession with "mechanically" reproduced images—calotypes, collodion prints, and the like—is reproduced by photocopying images and visual materials of the period onto acetate. A picture frame without its backing holds a transparent image of the sedentary Victoria *on* the protective glass, superposed against a contemporary molded plastic chair. The assembly travesties the resplendent statue of the empress that sits on the memorial's northern side.

Figure 7.2 Vivan Sundaram, "Journey towards Freedom: Modern Bengal." Victoria Memorial, Calcutta, 1998. Photo and courtesy: Vivan Sundaram.

The installation is replete with such papery reproduction and Warholesque iconization, of faces and physiognomies, vanguard figures in a century of intensely innovative cultural politics, the burgeoning nineteenth-century cult of portraiture and personification.

A life-size replica of a freight wagon rests on rails through the center of the hall. The video calls this the "spine" of the show, emphasizing the tremendous impact of this infrastructural element on economic and social life in the colonial period. The visual armature is complemented by the timbre of aural devices. Inside the darkened, visionless interior wagon, speakers emote lines from, in addition to other texts, Deenabandhu Mitra's 1860 play *Neel Darpan*, promptly banned by the British for its stark depiction of the travails of indigo farmers on British-owned plantations.[18] Indeed, Sundaram seems a little overwhelmed by the profusion of voices. "There is an *enormous* production of text and print," the video announces. Well-known quotes from the period are scrolled on the walls. The mystic Ramakrishna Paramhansa's pluralist aphorism, "As many opinions, that many paths (*joto mot, toto poth*)" is lit up in neon, reminiscent of the work of Bruce Naumann.[19]

"Journey towards Freedom": the subtext is that of a syncretic cultural politics as prolegomena to nationalism. Chugging along with the politicoeconomic and cultural-anthropological locomotive is the bogie (pun intended) of the aesthetic. "Modern Bengal" is also a tale about the search for beauty. One question acquires some importance in this regard. *Why does nationalism,* with its seemingly more urgent themes of shared narrative, political enfranchisement, and infrastructural and economic parity, *invoke the question of beauty?*

The Function of Place

> If man is ever to solve that problem of politics in practice he will have to approach it through the problem of the aesthetic, because it is only through Beauty that man makes his way to Freedom.
>
> —**Friedrich Schiller, "Second Letter,"**
> **On the Aesthetic Education of Man**

It is not coincidental that as this or that nationalism crops up here and there, the question of beauty is invoked specifically in the mode of "Romanticism,"[20] a Romanticism that remains as unnamed within nationalist practice as in Hegel's nudge toward his contemporaries. In the case of Bengal, it would be a plausible task to trace a genealogy from German Romanticism by way of English Romanticism into an indigenous arena of letters and aesthetics that articulates incipient nationhood precisely in these terms.[21] I suggested earlier that Kant's tripartite schema is a pretext for a theory of anthropology. Not everyone can appreciate the productive telos from the sensuous toward reason that is implicit in the proper understanding of beauty and the sublime. In the abyssal analogy between beauty as a sensuous impulse "without interest" and the "free" exercise of morality, nationalism is a template of the pedagogical "work" that is required to nudge the sensuousness of the prepolitical (Kant's Savoyard peasants and Eastern voluptuaries) across the abyss into the "formative" impulses of the political.[22]

Nationalism can be thought of only through the analogue of the aesthetic.[23] Within anticolonial nationalism, the indeterminability of beauty appears to mirror the a priori of "freedom" as ontological absence. The conflation produces strife in both senses of the word, as internal dissonance and of striving toward a decolonized future. It is an enduring irony of this futurist project that it has no past beyond the imported impetus of Eurocentric capital. The strife is therefore also a temporal one of bridging irreconcilable teleologies. The anticolonial desire for an authentic "history" therefore harnesses heterogeneous narratives by an exotic structure of causality. Sundaram's installation includes a quote by Bankimchandra Chattopadhyay, key progenitor of the nationalist aesthetic in India, that underscores this point: "When the sahibs come out to kill birds it becomes a subject of history, but there is no history of Bengal."

It is precisely through the aesthetic impulse that nationalism can be characterized as the identification of a heterogeneous people with a shared historiographic narrative. Bankimchandra's lament about a lack of history will launch a historicizing vanguard in nineteenth-century "Young Bengal." As might be expected, in the early phase the desire for historiography is routed through an aesthetic apprehension of the unformed. It is a while before the infrastructural prescriptions of Romesh Chandra Dutt's *The Economic History of India* emerges as a riposte to the Mills—*pater and filius*—and Macaulays of British thought. For James Fergusson, architectural historian, the importunity of the "Young Bengal" intellectuals lay in their amalgamation of an inflated sense of identity with an inexpert indoctrination into the European methods that had fostered the identity in the first place:

> When I left India the Mutiny had not occurred to disturb the relations between Europeans and natives, and more than this, the party usually designated as "Young Bengal," did not then exist. These are the creation of another age and another state of things, and are one of the most unsatisfactory results of our attempts to force our civilization on a people not yet prepared to receive it. One of the first effects of educating any set of men beyond anything known in their

own class, and of treating them as equals before they have acquired any title, morally and intellectually, to be considered as such, is to inspire them with the most inordinate conceit in themselves. They soon learn to consider themselves not as equal to their former masters, but as superior, and they turn round and glory in their own fancied superiority.[24]

As I have said before, nationalism must be the outcome of many such, necessary, miscegenations. Bengal becomes an incubator for such miscegenation.

Some caution needs to be voiced here, a care for organicist terms such as *incubation*. I have said that Romanticism prefigures "this or that nationalism," without rigor, without specificity, as if all nationalisms were the same, isogenic. Until this point, we have followed a common topos of historiography: imbuing particular events with *causal* characteristics so that a given narrative can then be seen to proceed more or less as the links on a chain. We have not escaped a certain Hegel. From German aesthetics to British colonialism to Bengali cultural politics to Indian nationalism, each stage appears to determine the next. We shall not have been the only ones. It has been argued, not without substance, that the colonial history of Bengal has often been passed off as the history of India, and Bengali historians, to their professional detriment, have subsequently theorized Third World geopolitics from the standpoint of the restricted cultural dynamics of these rural–urban settlements around the lower Ganges delta.[25]

This *parochial* claim to vanguardism rivals the hubris of the declaration of universal human rights following a regional brawl atop the ramparts of the Bastille. This pervasive blueprint, however, cannot be undone simply by positing other regionalisms or geographic categories in its place. The problem is the framing of historiography rather than of the objects it purports to study. Even as the installation commemorates a remarkable explosion of cultural and individual genius, Sundaram's video emphasizes a narration that gets beyond "the homage mode of history-writing." How does one escape this commonplace conundrum? To understand the global implications of a phenomenon without producing a globalizing blueprint? How does one both acknowledge vanguardism and critique the hegemonism on which all models of vanguardism are based?

"Modern Bengal" is a *function* in accounts of nationalism, a name filling a crucial "empty place" in the intimate counterpositioning of nationalism and global arrays of power. In this sense, the place-name is not merely a nomenclature for a geographic trait, such as a population with such and such ethnic and socioeconomic characteristics, a bustling city on a teeming river, or a hot sun beating down on a humid troposphere, but a place marker, a signifier within an imperial dispensation. It becomes coherent only in a structure of difference, as an element in a discontinuous "sign chain," in the sense that this term indicates a system of corollaries *without axiom*.

Bengal is a name in such a chain—cultural, political, and economic— through which concepts of nation-state and region, the relationship between the local and the global begins to take hold, to adhere together. Other functions will engender other place-names that draw coherence from other logics: *the* Punjab, *a* Bombay, *a* Paris, *a* Chicago, *a* Shanghai. Kant's example of the Cape of Good Hope as a threshold of knowledge rather than a geographical place-name comes to mind.[26] In the next chapter, we will look at Afghanistan as such a place marker for a function of being caught between contending empires. Functionality thus describes as much a discontinuity within place-names as a passage from the old to the new: Hegel's continuist construction of place as conceptual stage needs to be crosshatched by the differentiating map of capital, or as Marx would put it, "turned on its head".

Some clarification of the term *function* is crucial here, in the sense that it appears to invoke a programmable, even if arabesque, causality. It is important one does not mistake Kant for Hegel. Kant invokes the cause-and-effect relationship in his discussion on beauty. Beauty is an instance of effect without reference to cause. "Causality" describes a procedure where the phenomenon, the effect, is given first; the process of reflection must extend back through the exercise of reason toward the generality of a principle. As Lyotard has put it, "The 'action' of the cause that 'produces' the effect is only a principle of the *unintelligibility* of the phenomena."[27] Causality is therefore not an event in time, but the statement of what remains in the end a discontinuous, unrelated principle. "Determination" describes the inverse of this procedure. The generality (i.e., the rule, principle) is made available first, and from this it works down toward the particular. Marx follows the trail of capital as cause rather than as determinant—it is important that one does not mistake Marx for Hegel either.

If this extremely nuanced formulation is kept in mind, then the functionality of Bengal comprises a certain chiasmus, a crossing to-and-fro, similar to the crossing of the triadic schema outlined by Kant. *"Capital" is the cause, "India" is the effect, and "Europe" is the determinant.* Nationalism emerges to cover over the unintelligible origins of modernity: the discontinuity of the global chain covered over by a call to the supposed continuist, unifying essence of the local. It is in this sense that we can speak of "this or that nationalism" in terms of a logic that does not erase the specificities of the local but depends on it to produce the discontinuous generality of the system. Power in this globalizing sense is underpinned by the force of analogue not unlike that between beauty and truth: a comparative structure where the effects of the causative power of capital are tied back to the abstract frame of "Europe" by both colonized and colonizer. In its idealized construct,

"Modern Bengal," the installation and the epoch, is the provisional locus through which a certain Eurocentric and globalizing "humanism"—of rationalism supplemented by Romanticism—sets foot on non-European soil, through which a mutual contract is set up between the protonational and the imperial and through which a certain imaginableness of an "India," even "Asia," and subsequently *a* "Third World," becomes viable, imaginable. An analogue between Eurocentric Enlightenment and the capitalist periphery, two distinct yet related trajectories, can be put into play.

To repeat, Bengal will not retain this place function forever. The move from cultural politics to realpolitik, from protonationalism to nationalism, from an aesthetic imagination to a moral one, as India uses Bengal to think itself, will result in the withering away of "Bengal". It will putrefy as an unripe fruit even as the vine takes hold. The radicalism of its cultural mo(ve)ment cannot be infinitely kept center stage as it increasingly begins to threaten the incipient myths of nationalism. Sundaram's invocation of Ritwik Ghatak's films, which we will examine very shortly, is extremely significant in this regard.

The Aesthetics of Historiography

Sundaram is part of a coruscating group of artists and writers, loosely clustered around the recently terminated periodical *Journal of Arts and Ideas,* who have made a formidable research field out of Indian popular culture, art, media, and aesthetics in the postindependence period.[28] I venture that Sundaram—in the critical company of some of the writers in the journal—receives his principal revelations about the Bengal school, and by extension about "Modern Bengal," through the dual lenses of the filmmakers Satyajit Ray and Ritwik Ghatak. The two are very different legatees of the epoch, and the dichotomy between them is now an accepted staple of discussions of postindependence aesthetics. Sundaram's installation reiterates this dichotomization. Scenes extracted from the films of the two auteurs are continuously played on a television set sitting between the two pillows at the head of a four-poster bed from the period.

As Geeta Kapur has pointed out, Ray's films routinely sidestep historical events of the tumultous postindependence years in which they are set.[29] Modernity is parsed into "thresholds"—ethical and situational conundrums encountered by the aesthete protagonists. The aesthetic is hypostasized in individual narratives of autopoesis, through which the macroscopic moral conflicts posed by political and economic decolonization are worked through as if in microcosm. Kapur calls this nationalist or ethnographic "allegory." Ghatak, on the other hand, reveals the fractures of the nationalist allegory through its most immediate and devastating effect on Bengal's history: "partition." The term refers to the vivisection of Bengal into West Bengal and East Bengal, now Bangladesh, a process set into play by Curzon's partition of 1905. (Bengal's poet-savant Rabindranath Tagore is thus the only person in history to pen the national anthems of *two* nation-states, India and Bangladesh.) The voice of a character from Ghatak's film *Komal Gandhar* intones inside the rail wagon, "It crossed my mind that the [rail] tracks which had been a sign of union, have become a sign of disjuncture. There, the country (*desh*) has been cut into two parts." The character thus reverses the colonially derived nationalist motif of the railway as unifying network. The vivisection of freedom is experienced as the loss of beauty.

This divergence can be seen in the quite different aesthetic approaches of Ray and Ghatak and, consequently, in the differences in their reception. Ray's cinema is more in the genre of "realism," in the sense this genre describes both a preference for visual empiricism and the distancing of the cinematic tableau away from any particular historical conjuncture. The perversity is Sade-like in its sublimity; the upheavals and complicities of anticolonial or postcolonial modernism are routinely played out as "philosophy in the bedroom."[30] Unlike Ray's naturalized tableaus, the estrangement of Ghatak's characters with their historical situation is signaled by conspicuously formalist techniques of defamiliarization and melodrama. For Ghatak, historical alienation is translated into labored dramatic contrivances that hem his characters, whereas for Ray, this alienation is resolved through the character's self-shielding, heightened aestheticism. The old schoolteacher in Ghatak's *Meghe Dhaka Tara,* confronting the realization that his family's economic mobility has been predicated on the ruining of his daughter's body, points his index finger into the air and cries, in English, "I accuse!!" The crucial cathartic moment of the film is thus carried by an abstruse (for Bengal) quotation from Zola. His son remonstrates, angrily, immediately, "Who?" The (causative) agent of history is absent in the tragedy of the present. And the daughter, recognizing that the transition from petit-bourgeois to bourgeois society—the primary ruse of the nation–state—has made of her ipseity a ritual sacrifice, bitterly regrets this smothering museumification: "Make for me a glass case, and display me like a wax doll!"

The reception of Ray, first abroad and then at home, culminates the vanguardist function and the canonization of "Modern Bengal." Appropriated by cultural mandarins as the face of postindependence art, Ray's cinema immediately secured sanctification abroad and sanction at home as representing an other avant-garde, honing the emerging sensibility of a "humanist" Third World. By contrast, Ghatak's cinema will putrefy on the vine. Ghatak's last feature film, *Jukti Takko Aar Gappo* (Reason, Debate, and Gossip), was realized under dire economic struggle and a losing battle with alcoholism. Self-consciously, he put his own persona in the juridical dock, playing a persona barely distinguishable from himself, the political presumptions of whose art are ruthlessly eviscerated by the other characters. Over the years, Sundaram and the group mentioned previously have crafted an intricate critique and aesthetic of this sort of ruining, of lament.

Memorial, "Not a ... Museum"

The informal character of Sundaram's mnemonic fragments explicitly contrasts with the monumentality of the Victoria Memorial. Designed by William Emerson and realized between the years of 1906 and 1921, the building's design marked an important point in an intense debate about architectural representation in India. Curzon's choice of European classicism for the memorial was markedly incongruous with his general predilection toward drawing from the sources of Indian "tradition" in administrative, aesthetic, and architectural matters.[31] The Victoria Memorial is therefore the singular exception to a reign otherwise marked by its emphasis and encouragement of Indian architectural styles and local craft practices, most famously manifested at the Delhi Durbar of 1903. This anomaly, in Curzon's view, was not a contradiction with his broader attitude; rather he argued for this stylistic interloping as presenting the latest term in the successive schema of India's many historical pasts. Just as India had flourished under a series of empires that had left their imprints through their distinct architectural monuments, so too would the British leave their distinct emblem in the capital of this newest empire. As if to push the analogy further, Curzon chose the same Makrana marble for the Victoria Memorial as for the Taj Mahal, whose preservation he initiated in addition to a number of Mughal sites.

In the memorial, the programmed spaces, the trophy, sculpture, and picture galleries, are huddled into the tightest spaces on the plan. The bulk of space in the building is by comparison undefined. These include the two quadrangles, the Queen's Hall, and the durbar. The logic is impeccably baroque: the most grandiloquently articulated spaces, including the domed hall in the center, are programmatically void. The used spaces appear almost as if inserted by hindsight, interstitial infills hidden within the plastic undulations of the building envelope. The billowing emptiness of the memorial thus shares a critical facet of the ongoing discourse on monuments in the early twentieth century, as embodiments of *pure* architectural expression without programmatic constraints, parerga without prescribed content or referent. Curzon would hint at as much in his explanatory speech to the Asiatic society:

> [The Victoria Memorial] will not be an industrial museum. ... It will not be an art museum. ... It will not be a geological, or ethnographical, or anthropological, or architectural museum.[32]

A memorial is a museum with no exhibits other than itself. I repeat: the museum is the precise place of an impossible crossover between conceptions of history and of beauty, that is, between a historiographic disciplinarity that models itself on the critique of reason and an aesthetic that cannot have a model. It is because of this impossibility of crossover that the museum, more than others, is a building type without typology, or rather comprises an empty typology—it transforms itself to suit the shifting discourses of the aesthetic and the changing formal definitions of the artwork. Inserting new forms of content into the memorial's empty, unpopulated halls, Sundaram hints at the ever-possible reprogramming of the monument. As we saw in the first chapter, railway stations in colonial India were often used as exhibition venues. Here, memorial is converted into a railway station, a godown, or lumberyard, reinscribing the theaters of labor and production that the marbled palace was designed to gloss over.

As if to reinforce this (re-)programmable aspect of the memorial, in one part of the installation, Sundaram alphabetically arranged empty file boxes labeled with the names and photographs of prominent men and women of the era. Visitors were invited to scour their own domestic archives and genealogical collections and drop newspaper cuttings, memorabilia, or other associated items relating to any of these personalities into the file box bearing their name, an archive in reverse. The limitless authority of the archive, premised on its open-endedness, lies in its metonymical relationship to the bottomlessness of memory. In this sense, memory is not history. Belonging to temporality, it is inescapably *intuitive*, indiscernible, internalized, and temporizing-of the same order as the aesthetic. The project of history, of historiography as discipline, is to *institute* memory as if *intuited*. The empty file boxes point out this institutionalizing prerogative of history: it must reorganize memory to establish itself.

As we will see in the next section, it is in this difference between memory and history, between intuition and institution, that Sundaram's work realizes both its ultimate limitation and its greatest possible potential. I offer two audience responses, then, before moving on. After showing Sundaram's video in an advanced graduate seminar on "The Aesthetics of Decolonization" at my university (MIT), a visual arts student, intimately versed in the critical culture of the American art scene, voices his reservations: "It seems to have a bit of everything." In other words, it is a work not controlled by the exploration of a singular aesthetic problem and hence without methodological rigor, without critique. One is reminded of Schiller's misgivings. On the other hand, there is the verdict of the formidable coterie of Bengali Indian historians in India and the West, many of whom dismissed the work as sententious nostalgia about a rather well-documented place and period. Schiller's other pole: an irrational emotionalism. To the extent that both these judgments offer particular bridges between aesthetic and critique, one cannot measure the legitimacy of these viewpoints. Neither of these criticisms, however, are being attentive to the specific institutional trajectory of the museum and art practice in India and, by extrapolation, to the different functional trajectories and the rubrics of judgment, of beauty in the postindependence realm.

Intuition and Institution

We must then ask, History for whom? The difference between subaltern and elite in their respective approaches toward either art or history is oriented precisely by their relative *access* (or lack thereof) to institutionality. One could call this notion of access the theory of an "audience," an audience that is given the moral authority to judge and *to be judged*. For Kant, this coterminous faculty should ideally be codetermined: one should judge others as one judges oneself. To do so, judgment must wrest itself from external constraints or duress. The model here is the internal autonomy of "critique," defined not as negation or condemnation but as Derrida has put it, "judgment, evaluation, examination that provides itself with the means to judge [art or history]."[33] Judgment can come only from within, but with one caveat. Freedom is the a priori of able judgment. And for Kant, the institutions of the state must constantly calibrate their behavior and that of the polity such that freedom becomes available, accessible. Pedagogy, incorporating the panoply of universities, schools, museums, and exhibitions, is one of the tools for such calibration, and the police are another. Both Hegel and Marx will point out the asymmetry developed in the idealist codeterminacy between subject and the state by focusing on the latter's monopolization of the tools of coercion.

I have said that the asymmetry of elite and subaltern can be gauged by their relative access to institutional support and indoctrination. Colonial ideas regarding education present some of the critical attributes of this discriminative entry point into the micrology of power. As ideological vehicles and pedagogical devices of the state by means other than literacy, the colonial museums' approach toward their audiences inevitably brushed against the asymmetrical anthropologies within which colonized subjects were cast. The ethnographic strategies of the border exhibitions described in the previous chapter characterized the DSA-type museum as well. In Europe the conduct of museums, inasmuch as they reflect desires to orchestrate public taste, offer us indexes of the ongoing debates on citizenship.[34] To the extent that colonial museums bore this "burden" as well, they inevitably confronted the fact that political citizenship was absent, even as the museum became a crucial vehicle for post-Enlightenment attitudes to organize the colony.

In India only 105 museums had been established by the period of completion of the Victoria Memorial. This meant that each museum served a population a hundred times as large as its European counterparts, and ten times
that of other Asian states such as Japan and Egypt. Given this institutional
minimalism and the supposed anthropological heterogeneity that appeared
to militate against the idea of anything like a unifying impulse in the audience, the concept of an "aesthetic education" produced quite unique problems
for the colonial context.[35] This in addition to the fact that mass education for
the colonial population was never engaged even as a nominal claim.

Rather than bring attention to their own *institutional disinterest* in creating broad subjective parity, colonial administrators wrung their hands
at the obstructions thrown up by the intuitive differences among natives,
pointing to what was deemed as their preternatural disposition toward
inequality. This fretting and fussing dovetailed well with the feared fallouts
of directing mass education towards decisive moral autonomy. The "civilizing" process thus camouflaged within itself an uncivilizing vector. In India
the fraught question "What is worth teaching?" was (and continues to be)
thus continually compromised and complicated not only by the asymmetries
of class and gender (as in Europe) but also along other anthropological and
cultural vectors: the colonial and postcolonial epistemologies of caste, religion, and so on.[36] The hegemonies fostered by colonial pedagogy need to be
understood not only in the complex European–native dyad and the emergence of an indigenous governing class but also in the bolstering, exacerbating, and institutionalizing of traditional inequities within Indian society.

Museums were a natural extrapolation of these attitudes. Although the
tepidity of the colonial policy debates on museums does not compare with
the ferocity of the arguments on general education for Indians, the former
does parallel the latter in one significant respect. The grandiosity of the discourse is matched only by its perfunctoriness and irrelevance for the large
breadth of the population, another facet of the "overdetermination" referred
to in the previous chapter. Museums in India were primarily motors of specialized knowledge, assembled for shoring up the expertise of the privileged
benefactors and administrators of the state rather than the conduits for
broad-based education. Markham and Hargreaves's 1936 report on museums of India acknowledged as much. In the same breath, mass illiteracy,
even as it is bemoaned in terms of liberal anguish about the many failures
of colonialism, was attributed to a "natural" propensity of Indian subjects
toward ignorance rather than to administrative failure or disinterest:

In America, Germany, and in Great Britain, museums have been
established by the hundred as adjuncts to elementary and secondary education, but in India few museums have been established with

this object in mind. ... Perhaps the greatest problem which confronts the Indian museum curator keenly desirous of popularizing his museum is the question of how to deal with illiterates. ... For, if the vast majority of the visitors are illiterate it follows that if the museum is to be used as an educational institution *no amount of labeling* will reach the majority of the visitors. ... To these visitors, therefore, the museum is a peep-show, a wonder house, a mansion full of strange things and queer animals, and the main appeal is to the Indian sense of wonder and credulity. ... In this way and perhaps in this way alone can the illiterate visitor be given any conception of the world beyond his village or its nearest town. His mental horizon cannot be expanded through the medium of books because of his illiteracy, *or even through the cinema* [if only they had known!] because of his poverty, but the museum skillfully parades before him the accumulated treasures of a province; though the interpretation of it is left to his native wit.[37]

Pervasive institutional and infrastructural neglect across the colonial system could thus be covered over by the ascription of civilizational lacunae on the part of the audience. British concerns over native agency therefore worked themselves into a fastidious attention toward institutionalizing vernacular languages in educational and official policies. This fastidiousness played out in museum discourses as well. In their discussion on museum captions, for instance, Markham and Hargreaves referred longingly to the polyglot faces of British Indian currency, printed in English and eight other vernacular languages.

Markham and Hargreaves's anxieties about the cognitive deficiencies of local museum visitors reflect a general concern on the part of colonial government that cognitive competence must be routed through the vernacular. As is well-known, in its desire to manage the local with greater degrees of efficiency, educational strategy in British India was defined by the formalization of dialects into defined regional "languages," a process that had its fallout in the many linguistic nationalisms witnessed in modern Indian history. This phenomenon parallels the trajectory of the regional "sign chain" that I laid out earlier. "Enlightenment" Bengal, as the "effect" of the other Enlightenment, is thus also defined by a language where the "mother" culture and "mother" tongue are reinscribed within a rule-bound provenance. "Mothers' mouths are made to practice till *ü* no longer sounds like *i* and *g* no longer sounds like *ch*"; the provincial tongue of mothers is ventriloquized into a national voice.[38] We looked in chapter 3 at the paradox of the mother tongue in our examination of the DSA's pedagogy: the mother tongue is precisely that which is *not* learned according to a set of rules. One cannot learn the mother tongue; either one has a mother tongue or one cannot learn. *Teaching* the mother tongue, what we can call instituting the vernacular by the means of orthography and grammar, is rather a way of instilling the boundaries of statist morality into the precognitive intuitive apparatus.

Language is thus parsed into an oral system involving determined exercises of the mouth and tongue. But this corporeal regimentation is not enough. Linguistic literacy is inevitably bound up with the sort of visual literacy alluded to by Pestalozzi, even as he allegorizes the pedagogical mother function in the character of Gertrude:

The art of writing, to be taught consistently with nature, ought to be treated as subordinate to that of drawing, and to all its preparatory acquirements, especially the art of measuring. Writing is no more, nay even less, than drawing, to be taught without a previous proficiency in the measuring of lines; for in the first instance, writing itself is a sort of linear drawing, and that of stated forms, from which no arbitrary or fanciful deviation is permitted.[39]

Education in the mother tongue is primarily a matter of pictorial processing of absorbing patterns. Pestalozzi therefore skirts a pervasive conceit of the European nineteenth century that emerges precisely at the moment that universal literacy is being contemplated as a mass acculturative device: that of drawing's visuality as the primordial, universally understood, and naturally translatable language.[40] As we saw in chapter 3, drawing education for the working classes predated linguistic education by at least a century. The same can be said for the museum with relation to the establishment of school boards.

In the 1990s, under the guidance of the fiscal mechanisms laid down by the International Monetary Fund and the World Bank, therefore, mass pedagogy has been largely defined as the instrument to increase the industrial employability of Third World subjects. As opposed to the colonial emphasis on physically skilled "industry," the postfordist workforce is defined by its literate ability to decipher information. If under colonialism literacy is fended off precisely because of its associated indoctrination of the subject into political society, in contrast McLuhanesque neocolonialism requires "literacy" as the minimal attribute to be admitted into economic society. Consequently, international global "development" agencies have defined literacy standards largely in the context of teaching subalterns the alphabet—writing their own name, printing a phonic pattern—so that they can be provided with the means to countersign their access to monetization and the lowermost stratas of cyber labor.

The alphabet remains a *pictorial* apparatus rather than the inculcation of a dexterous ability to manipulate the hold of power over language.

Museum, Concept, Caption

The late-imperial mind-set manifested in the Victoria Memorial offers an early example of this bypassing of the infrastructural demands for parity. Let us reprise our story so far: an installation about well-known facets of Bengali history in the heart of Bengal, a pedagogy for Bengalis already well apprised of this history. If this art is the indirect vector of a pedagogy, what is being taught here? Raymond Williams's perplexity in his experience in postwar adult education in Britain would not be irrelevant here: "*What is this?*"[41] The redundancy replicates the redundancy within pedagogy we saw earlier.

Curzon's address to the Asia Society outlining the purpose of the memorial might make the colonial response to this paradox more palpable:

> Let us, therefore, have a building, stately, spacious, monumental, and grand, to which every newcomer in Calcutta will turn, to which all the resident population, European and Native, will flock, where all classes will learn the lessons of history, and see revived before their eyes the marvels of the past. ...[42] I believe that it will teach more history and better history than a studyful of books. I believe that it will appeal to the poor people just as directly as to the rich; and that they will wander, wondering perhaps, but interested and receptive, through its halls.[43]

The Victoria Memorial is historiography without captioning, a history book without need for literacy. The logic of the memorial occasions a spectacular collapse of the analogue of beauty and morality: it is the aesthetic-visual, in its claim to affect a universal subjecthood, that will introduce the illiterate colonized into the historical telos of colonial subjecthood. Curzon was emphatic that the history displayed in the paintings, sculptures, and trophies in the various chambers would not be one of British triumphalism but reflect an Indian viewpoint as well. He proposed the inclusion of "those who had fought against the British," including ones who had become important for the nationalist countercanon: Shivaji (for Lokmanya Tilak's Hindu patrimony in Maharashtra) and Tipu Sultan, if shown only in defeat at Srirangapatnam (as a hero of India's Muslim population). History would thus be shown not as one of British civilizational superiority but as a series of stages of which British ascendance was the latest. It is through this synthetic frame that the Victoria Memorial became the first edifice in India to bring modern historiography within the ambit of the museum.[44] It is also by far the most spectacular, a riposte to the nineteenth-century curatorial mind-set that confined colonial museums in India to primarily two types: the economic–materialist museum moulded on the South Kensington model[45] or alternatively the archaeological museum that housed a comparative discourse on civilizations.[46] To complete this willful myopia, colonial curatorship occluded any contemporary "modern," "artistic" practices from being displayed within Indian museums. We note once again that the Victoria Memorial, this repository of history, was designed to be primarily empty.

There is enough material in the archives to reveal Curzon's ecumenism as mere posture. He consulted no Indians in the design of this monument to an Indian "viewpoint," even though the funds mostly came from native elites and princely estates. In many cases, money was actually diverted from private philanthropic kitties that had been intended for famine relief; at Victoria's death, India was recovering from yet another periodic throe of these recurrent and manmade events that were the leitmotif of her regime. In his address, Curzon even suggested that the Victoria Memorial would be a much more valuable enterprise than the otherwise laudatory and myriad attempts at economic reform and technical training. The memorial thus refuted the DSA agenda in more ways than one:

> Some people talk and write as though technical instruction were going to solve the Indian agrarian problem, and to convert millions of needy peasants into flourishing artisans. Long after every one in this room has mouldered into dust the economic problem will confront the rulers of India. It is not to be solved by a batch of Institutes or a cluster of Polytechnics. They will scarcely produce a ripple in the great ocean of social and industrial forces.

Ideological inculcation, Curzon seems to say, by way of rememorating a national history, is more important than material infrastructure. What is significant is the mode under which "modernity" is launched here. Routed through the visual as a default form of literacy, historiography is being inculcated as a form of self-knowledge that must be represented for the masses, precisely because this self-knowledge defines a nationhood that claims to speak in their name.

Sundaram's installation, in engaging the history of nationalism and nationhood, necessarily confronts this long history of display in the postcolony. In a situation of institutional minimalism, of curatorial rarefaction, the postcolonial artwork therefore cannot abandon its desire for institutional support as the basis of its freedom. This is in contrast to the foundational ethos of the European avant-garde. During the period of the Victoria Memorial's construction, Marcel Duchamp will precociously launch a critical practice that is directed against the museum as the critical frame of the artwork. R. Mutt's "Fountain" reframes the museum as a discursive apparatus of the aesthetic—an overdetermined captioning mechanism—as opposed to a passive receptacle for objects attributed with an extradiscursive "beauty." By contrast, there will be no Indian Marcel Duchamp; the colonial and postcolonial museum foregrounds the "wonder" invoked by its displays *in place* of the pedagogical force of caption. In the absence of an omnipresent institutionality or a strong market, the oppositional format of the avant-garde cannot take root as the basis for a negational modern*ism*.

The state museum in India is therefore inordinately weighted toward providing the positive basis of culture rather than the contrapuntal terms of "art." Geeta Kapur has described the postindependence cultural strategy of the nationalist state as a process where

> culture was sought to be institutionalized precisely in order to carry out the overall mandate of modernization. ... In fact [the nationalist state] would privilege culture above art as well, precisely because the intrepid claims of art always exceed, or subvert, even the more progressive rhetoric of institutionalized culture. ... Indian modernism has developed without an avantgarde. A modernism without disjunctures is at best a reformist modernism. The very liberalism of the state absolves the left of confrontational initiatives on the cultural front.[47]

The model for producing such a "Nehruvian" cultural self-image without avant-garde, modernity without modernism, is Satyajit Ray.

Postrepresentational Dioramas

In India the potentials of art as institutional critique are excised in both colonial and postindependence official culture. For the postindependence Indian artist, therefore, it is not that modernism in this particular sense is absent but that it is rather played out in a *mode* of absence, a "lack," as ever-palpable but never-realized vectors of historical possibility. Vivan Sundaram is of the generation that specifically lives out this liberal-statist horizon of art practice. "Modern Bengal" thus indicates a practice that seeks to *supplement* the *absence* of modernity rather than to *supplant* its presence. It produces a surrogate institutionalization of historicity even as it undoes an entire history of institutions.

Sundaram appears conscious of the asymmetry of subaltern access to the institutions of the liberal state, an asymmetry within which any work such as his would be implicated. This asymmetry is signaled in his work by an uncertain sensibility toward cultivating the "popular," manifested in the installation by its picturesque layout or plan, a determinate naturalism of ambulation through the venue. The visitor is characterized as if shorn of anthropological determinants, relying rather on his or her phenomenological instincts. The spectator is expected to wander about the hall, bumping into the different components of the artwork in non-orchestrated series of encounters. The connoisseur or the historian is no more privileged in this whimsical assembly than the chance peanut vendor drawn by curiosity into the hall. It is another point altogether that picturesque whimsy is precisely the imprint of an elite aesthetic dating from the eighteenth century. This apparently fancy-free layout as a shared ethos of subaltern and elite certainly signals what Geeta Kapur has sympathetically described as the postindependence artists' inevitable "political naiveté."[48] The anxiety about the pedagogical power of the historical diorama is disingenuously resolved by a professed absence of schema for the exhibition. As we have seen throughout this book, such romantic indeterminacy hides within it an organic kernel whose function is to dissipate the appearance of power. Sundaram's formal intuitions both draw from and critique this indeterminate legislation.

Given this organicistic approach, Sundaram appears uninterested in positing any strong formal strategies. The hybrid devices used in the "Modern Bengal" installation borrow from any number of conceptualist, minimalist, and media art strategies crafted around the world in the past three decades. Photographs from the era are photocopied onto transparent acetate and flutter in the breeze, shorn of the verificatory rectitude of the picture frame. Jute sacks piled high, filled with grain, remind one of the massive presence of the steel plates of Richard Serra's *One Ton Prop* (1968–69), even as their surfaces are covered over with chronological dates and short captions in the manner of conceptual art, listing the myriad anticolonial insurgencies of the era. The amorphous skeins of jute, arranged neatly in a cubic shape, establish an inverse relationship to the "formless" felt and waste pieces of Robert Morris, Barry Le Va, or (Sundaram's preferred inspiration) Arte Povera. Sitting on top of this amorphous and light ensemble is a very indurate nineteenth-century glass display cabinet. The frame is offered as display, as minimal object without content. And like any number of "site-specific" productions in post-1970s global art, the video intones that in this installation gallery and studio are one. The differentia of the archival catalog is presented as much as a catalog of different artistic techniques.

The force of the installation does not lie in its claim to creative negation, the kind of claim that is the staple of the avant-garde. Indeed, the subject matter of Sundaram's dioramas appears to betray a tepid nostalgia, as many detractors have argued. Nonetheless, I reiterate my argument that this estimation is misplaced within the careful historical understanding of display within which Sundaram's artwork is produced. Indeed, I suggest that the brunt of Sundaram's work is directed entirely elsewhere. Taking on the museumization of a period of tremendous aestheticism overdetermined by its political and socioeconomic encumbrances, Sundaram's *weak* formal attitude takes aim instead at the postindependence artist's *inability to achieve a historically authentic oeuvre.*

For Ghatak, the failure of morality is experienced as the loss of beauty—the analogue is still operative albeit in absence. We remember here that for Kant, beauty is an intuition grounded entirely in subjectivity, without objective referent. There is no beautiful *thing.* As installation, Sundaram's "Modern Bengal" frames a discourse about beauty in a certain period. *It frames nothing,* or rather it frames a certain historical dispensation of anti-colonial desire whose wistfulness will never find its positive fruit, quite unlike the way that European cosmopolitan Enlightenment could be commemorated by European empire. Historicity beyond "the homage mode of history-writing" is revealed in the multiplication of empty frame upon empty frame, parergonal viviparousness without referent. In the tea chests that frame views of the Victoria Memorial, the envelope of the building itself is revealed as frame. The file boxes, bearing the place of the archive's epistemic weight, are empty. A "library" providing a bibliography on the period contains only photographs of the spines of books on the face of its vacant shelves.

Memory is an empty exercise of thought. Again and again this trope of reversal, of the weight of the framing device and the emptiness of content, is played out, unsystematically, haphazardly, yet consistently enough not to invite notice in its omnipresence, or omniabsence, throughout the installation. "Modern Bengal" therefore enacts an *intuitive* displacement

Figure 7.3 Vivan Sundaram, "Journey towards Freedom: Modern Bengal." Victoria Memorial, Calcutta, 1998. Photo and courtesy: Vivan Sundaram.

of institutionalized history into art, a making visible without objective referent of the indeterminate relationship between history and memory, between archive and sensibility.

The asymmetry of audience is therefore addressed through what one could term a *postrepresentational diorama,* one that simultaneously engages the uneven trajectory of museological devices in the colony and neocolony, of the variegations of audience, of artwork and discourse, of historiography, and of the conventionalizing frames in which all of these are set. In Sundaram's appropriation of conceptual art conventions to assemble quotes, media reprints, catalogs of personalities, and lists of historical events, the museum is reduced to catalog. Words are *displayed* to gawk at rather than written to be read and understood. The work of art, traditionally perceived as the transcendence of knowledge, is posed as the nebulous conduit of estranged letters and incommensurable information.

The asymmetry is understood here as that of simultaneously devising a history *and* posing a critique of the "objective" premises of historiography and the museum in a situation of pervasive institutional minimalism and neglect. The asymmetry is that of posing a critique of logocentrism in the midst of a crying need for literacy, of questioning the primacy of the word even as the transition from colonial/national frames of illiteracy to postfordism is marked by a patent emphasis on an antihistorical, homeostatic literacy. "Homeostatic" here describes contemporary capital's propensity to produce populations that "live very much in a present which keeps itself in equilibrium or homeostasis by sloughing off memories which no longer have present relevance."[49] The asymmetry is that of rememorating a history that can animate claims to (a decolonizing) justice without acquiescing to the vectors of power that inevitably accompany such a pedagogy. (Toni Morrison has described "rememoration" rather aptly for our context—Sundaram's artwork strewn around the floor of the memorial—as a history that one "bumps into.") The asymmetry is that of remembering beauty as *loss* where it is constituted as (historical) *absence.*

The question must be repeated: What is being learned here? What is being remembered, framed as history? The response is: *nothing.* What is being learned is a lesson about learning, remembering about how questions of history are only questions and must always be foregrounded as questions rather than as narratives of fact. Freedom is not an ontological condition; beauty reminds us of its ghostly memory. In Sundaram's exhibition, beauty is only invoked as absence; context is invoked as mere place function. Working within a rarefied institutional context, the ever-multiplying aesthetic frames of history approximate a parergon rather than a paragon of the artwork; in this, there might be lessons yet for the critique *and necessity* of institutional privilege.

"He sat, in defiance of municipal orders, astride the gun Zam-Zammah on her brick platform opposite the old Ajaib-Gher——the Wonder House, as the natives call the Lahore Museum. Who hold Zam-Zammah, the 'fire-breathing dragon,' hold the Punjab, for the great green-bronze piece is always first of the conqueror's loot. There was some justification for Kim——he had kicked Lala Dinanath's boy off the trunnions——since the English held the Punjab and Kim was English" (Rudyard Kipling, *Kim*). Photo: Author.

Infinite Justice:
An Architectural Coda

Tum karo zulm, to woh sarkari hai? Hum kare fariyaad, to woh gaddari hai? (You oppress, and that is government? And if we should complain, that is treason?)

—Hindi film *Pukar*

We end, or begin, with that which cannot be encompassed in the two terms of the contest, between tradition and modernity, between colonizer and native, between custom and contract, between morality and aesthetic, between truth and artifice, between memory and archive:

> As distinguished from a litigation, a differend [*différend*] would be a case of conflict, between (at least) two parties, that cannot be equitably resolved for lack of a rule of judgement applicable to both arguments. One side's legitimacy does not imply the other's lack of legitimacy. However, by applying a single rule of judgement to both in order to settle their differend as though it were merely a litigation would wrong (at least) one of them (and both of them if neither side admits this rule). Damages result from an injury which is inflicted upon the rules of a genre of discourse but which is reparable according to those rules. A wrong results from the fact that the rules of the genre of discourse by which one judges are not those of the judged genre or genres of discourse.[1]

There are the questions voiced in the previous chapter that need repeating. Whose judgment? Whose history? Whose memory? Whose architecture? Whose modernity? Lyotard's exergue on the "differend" gives us a name for the residual or excess element in the scene of the encounter, any encounter, between heterogeneous modes of discourse. To be attentive to the differend is to bear witness to the irreducible alterity of the other, at the very point where both parties seem to resist the very terms of the encounter. Lyotard opens the framing of the differend with a European example—the problem at hand is juridical, posed as a problem of evidence. Those who witnessed the gas chambers in action, those who could testify to their existence and use, died in them. In their absence, how are others to convince the tribunals that the gas chambers did indeed exist or, more important, who is owed justice, by what translation of injury, when the victims no longer live to phrase their testimony? Because the rest of the world did not die in the gas chamber, who could legitimately claim to be a beneficiary of such justice? Whose justice, but also justice for whom? In its ultimate unwillingness to address these questions within its own territories, Europe exports the Jewish differend to Asia.

We will reframe the differend through an Asian example. The place: Hopetown, part of the penal colony founded by the British in the Andaman and Nicobar islands, in the middle of the Bay of Bengal. The time: the evening of February 8, 1872. A visiting dignitary, an Irishman named Richard Southwell Bourke, steps off the boat along with his official retinue. The group is here to inspect the programs set underway to reform the convicts. As they head back to the ship after having toured the island, a man creeps up behind Bourke, stabs him in the back and kills him. The murderer's name, as far as we are able to determine, is Sher Ali. He is a Pashtun native of Jamrud, near Peshawar, at the foot of the Khyber Pass. After 1901, having miserably failed to conquer the entirety of the Pashtun homelands, the British will call this area the North-West Frontier Province, a name that remains to the present day. Its strategic geopolitical importance as the frontier toward the vast Tsarist Empire to the north takes precedence over local place-names. To its immediate west is Afghanistan, much of whose population is composed of the same ethnic background as Sher Ali's. Between 1838 and 1919, Britain and Russia fought three major wars and many small battles in this region, using several local warlords as proxies and dupes. Mukulika Banerjee has documented in detail the subjective fallout of this simultaneously pacificatory and puissant administrative-military policy in the North-West Frontier Province:

> In comparison with other areas of India, the North West Frontier Province was heavily militarized, oppressively policed, in possession of fewer civil liberties and democratic concessions, weighted with a particularly large taxation burden, and had fewer schools and sanitary facilities. In addition, the Pathans had been doubly divided

by the British, who in the classic manner of "divide and rule" had sought to transform an open frontier into a closed border. The Durand Line sought to prevent communication between the Frontier Pathans and the Pathans in Afghanistan. Further restrictions sought to prevent communication between the Pathans of the Settled Districts and their brethren in the Tribal Areas. In general, the Pathans were closely watched over by a colonial regime which was simultaneously scared, dismissive and admiring of them, and occasionally even desirous.[2]

Sher Ali's first arrest straddled this bifaceted, bihanded bisection in all its contradictions. A subaltern in the Peshawar police, he had been arrested for avenging the murder of a kinsman by killing the assailant, a practice justified in tribal custom under certain conditions. British jurisprudence, which forbade the individual from taking the law into his own hands, deemed Ali's act a criminal infraction. The trial was carried out on what was at best questionable jurisdiction—had Ali incidentally carried out the murder outside of the porous borders of British-held territory, he would not have come under the purvey of British or Afghan criminal law. Taking these circumstances into cognizance, the magistrate handed out what he considered a lenient sentence—transportation to the Andamans. It is precisely because of the importance given to custom in British jurisprudence and political thought that the penal subject has to be removed from its "traditional" surroundings. Edmund Burke is as much the progenitor of the penal colony as Jeremy Bentham is. Considering this symbolic ignominy rather than legitimate punishment, Sher Ali asked to be put to death rather than be incarcerated in a foreign land. This voluntary offer was, of course, ignored. In the Andamans, Ali now set about planning his own death, but this time he would factor in British imperial justice in an entirely new equation.

When Sher Ali killed Bourke in 1872, he had waited four years for the opportunity, four years of planning and waiting not only for a significant victim to arrive but for his own death as well. And the murdered victim was the ideal one; indeed it was an assassination and not just a murder, because Bourke was none other than the Earl of Mayo, Benjamin Disraeli's appointee as the viceroy of India, the *Laat Saaheb* of Britain's eastern empire. The incident triggered shockwaves across the world, including a corresponding burst of nationalism in Britain. Many commented on how mourning had "united" the country from its usual fractious internal rivalries. Newspapers opined and ruminated, editorialized and investigated the possible geopolitical implications of this event. The British-run *Friend of India* helpfully suggested that the government "send the scoundrel to perdition in a pig skin to break his caste."[3] When asked to divulge his accomplices, Sher Ali refuted any larger plot: "*Merá sharík koí ádmí nahín; merá sharík khudá hai*" (No man is my companion, my companion is God).[4] His disclaimers notwithstanding, almost everybody was intent on wrenching global meaning out of this singular act. Liberals, nervous as to not sound antipatriotic, made ineffective noises attributing the act to disaffection over Britain's economic and taxation policies. Some pointed out Mayo's oppressive treatment of Wahhabism, an insurgent and millenarian movement that had recently emerged in India. The *Times* in London darkly hinted at the existence of a secret "fraternity of hatred," of a secret Wahhabi plot to undermine the British Empire. Originally founded in the eighteenth century in the Nadj area where the Saud tribe had established a kingdom on its literalist emphasis on the reading of Islamic scriptures, the Wahhabi movement in India had no direct connections to its Arab counterparts. Its beginnings stemmed from conversions to the cause in the eastern city of Patna. Its early campaigns had been directed against the Sikh Kingdom, under which Muslims tended to be badly discriminated against. Because the British were fighting the Sikhs at this time, they found it convenient to encourage them in the early stages.

However, with the annexation of the Punjab in 1848, the Wahhabis had increasingly become a thorn in the side of the colonial administration. After a spate of police crackdowns on the insurgent sect, tensions came to a head when the officiating chief justice of the Calcutta High Court was assassinated by a man affecting Wahhabi sympathies on September 20, 1871, barely three months before Mayo's assassination. The specter of an international insurgency with sectarian adherents as far distant as Mecca and Calcutta unnerved many who saw all manner of conspiracies being hatched to destabilize the British Empire. It hardly helped that the Duke of Edinburgh, Victoria's second son, had been shot at by an Irish Fenian on the way from India to Australia in 1868. After Mayo's murder, officials searched for letters that Sher Ali might have received from the "Patna malcontents," hoping to establish links with the larger Wahhabi movement. No such proof was forthcoming.

The British administration commemorated Mayo's short-lived career in India through a spate of institution building that would bring home the message of the intended persistence and tenacity of the Empire. Officially, the administration described Sher Ali's act as an individual act of discontent, dismissing speculation that Mayo could have been assassinated for political reasons. Every official action they took, however, thereafter reflected precisely such apprehensions. This memorializing impetus realized its apogee in Lahore, capital of the erstwhile Sikh kingdom in the Punjab, traditional enemy of the Afghan rulers, with the construction of the Lahore museum and the Mayo School of Art. Both the program and the form of these coupled institutions reflected the transformed attitude of the administration toward accommodating "native agency" in the policies of governance, especially after the 1857 Mutiny. The spate of localized insurgencies that continued throughout the nineteenth century was to keep the question of native agency alive in debates over colonial policy.

As we saw in chapter 1, the creation of the Punjab as a "non-Regulatory" province in 1849 had already signaled the turn toward the institutionalization of native customary agency.[5] This turn derived as much from economic considerations as from political ones. A minimalist administration that left the terrain of domestic and personal law for native adjudication also absolved itself of the infrastructural costs of a full-fledged state apparatus at the periphery. Punjab's administrative arrangement thus contrasted sharply with the early "regulatory" provinces (such as Bengal), where personal and domestic laws were brought directly under the purview of colonial jurisprudence. Recurrent insurgency from below owing to colonial interference in domestic and personal laws thus only appeared to justify a general tendency toward minimalism in colonial governance from above. This dual rationale was instrumental in shaping a decentralized and two-tiered policy where customary jurisprudence devolved to native authorities and the colonial administration retained control over political, criminal, and economic policy. Imperialism resolves the problem of the differend by affecting a relativism.

Colonial architecture reflected these concerns of governance at almost every level. The Mayo School and museum were designed along the lines of the emerging official architectural style of the British administration in India, the so-called Indo-Saracenic style incorporating elements of Islamic ornament. As we have seen, this representational motif was consistent with the general thrust of colonial policy in economic, political, and cultural fields. India would have her antiquity resurrected and restored to her through the recuperative stability of the empire. In the imperial periphery, the monument is not so much a mute testimonial as a machine for subject formation.

Let us cut to a scene happening within the Lahore museum, which the British have renamed Jadoo-Ghar or Wonder House, adopting native vernacular as official terminology.[6] The time: indeterminate. We cannot be quite sure. The North-West is restive again. Beyond Afghanistan looms the vision of an all-pervasive Russian Empire that threatens to infiltrate the core of Britain's territories in Asia. Soon there will be a war. At this time, a Tibetan lama arrives at the gates of the museum. A boy playing outside takes him in to meet the elderly curator, a white-bearded, gentle, learned Briton empathetically expert in the ways of the East. A peculiar encounter then unfolds, peculiar because it signals a shift in sign systems.

The lama has come to the museum because he has heard of the renowned Buddhist statuary kept there. At the sight of an image of Sakya Muni Buddha, the lama breaks down, overcome by piety. The secularized ruins and fragmented museum display of a lost Buddhist civilization in South Asia suddenly become activated into a palpable and living revelation. Sculpture once again becomes idol. Curatorial canon becomes religious pantheon. Seeming to acknowledge the East's greater profundity in these matters, the European curator defers his sense of rationalist historiography to the lama's transcendentalist understanding. Both the curator and the lama through their respective powers of knowledge and faith appear to share a stupendous secret that both must realize in their separate ways. "We be craftsmen together, thou and I," the lama tells the curator, in their respective quest for a redemptive destiny. The history of the past encapsulated in these lifeless images augurs a future British India where knowledge and religion will impeccably coincide in a time of peace to come. As proxy agent for the curator's epistemological project, Kim, the little brown-skinned boy loitering outside the museum, will accompany the lama on his sacred search to realize this convergent prophecy.

The scene is, of course, from Rudyard Kipling's *Kim*.[7] It is well-known that Kipling based the character of the curator on his father, John Lockwood Kipling, Department of Science and Art alumnus, professor of architectural ornament, founding principal of the Mayo School, and founding curator of the Lahore museum. In addition to his South Kensington training, Kipling Sr. also derived his creed from the ongoing scholarly effort by the British to unravel the native's frame of action and ethics through the extraordinary interdisciplinary collaboration between quite distinct professional endeavors. Tapati Guha-Thakurta has written at great depth on the collaboration between two such fields, archaeology (architecture as alternate form of the written archive) and ethnology (extraarchival recovery of past custom as motor for contemporary agency).[8] James Fergusson's book *History of Indian and Eastern Architecture* (1876), developed as part of his landmark world history, periodized the different stages of Indian history as the successive ascendancies of different ethnic and racial groupings.

Fergusson's views were already well formed and publicized in the 1860s. In his wake, Alexander Cunningham, explorer and the first head of the Archaeological Survey of India, began to group the various effects of his research as "Buddhist," "Jain," "Brahmanical," "Indo-Scythian," "Pathan," or "Moghul." The institution of the Archaeological Survey underlined a series of parallel initiatives in museology and preservation. At least part of the concern over colonial archaeology and preservation stemmed from the fact that Indians seemed to be least interested in either recovering or preserving their own past. Under a recuperative imperial epistemology, the contemporary Indian (or, for that matter, Greek or Egyptian) unable to gauge his sense of historical agency, would gain a sense of his ethical present through the colonialist excavation of the past. Memory must be instituted *as if* intuited. We are in *Blade Runner* territory here—historical memory is always already an implant. Eldon Tyrell's description of his replicants could well be paraphrased as the programmatic manifesto of empire:

> Commerce is our goal. ... More [native] than [native] is our motto. [India] is an experiment, nothing more. We began to recognize in them strange obsessions. After all they are emotionally inexperienced with only a few years in which to store up the experiences which you and I take for granted. If we give them the past we create a cushion or pillow for their emotions and consequently we can control them better.

This is the secret, the fabulous normalization of complicity between colonizer and colonized, that is shared by the curator and the lama—the curator desires to *institute* what the lama *intuits*. The lama's character is significant for another reason as well. As we saw in the previous chapter, the miniscule ratio of Europeans in comparison with the native population necessitated the creation of a native gentry and bourgeoisie who would act as imperialism's agents at the periphery. It is the native bourgeoisie's political consciousness, ever susceptible to European notions of political action and opposition, that must be circumscribed by this form of history. In *Kim* Hurree [Hari] Babu, the Bengali Hindu spy and aspirant to membership of the Royal Geographical Society, the figure held most in contempt by Kipling and who holds India more in contempt than does Kipling, approximates the subjective outlines of this emergent figure. In the affairs of British India, Buddhism, more or less a political nonentity, could therefore also be invoked as a major alibi in the establishment of *Pax Britannica*, precisely to counter this politically emergent subject (both Hindu and Muslim) militantly recuperating its religious identity as instrument for sedition.

With the transition of mercantilism to industrial capitalism in Europe, transcoded in philosophy and culture as the "Enlightenment," European states could dissemble their identity as triumph of the political state over religion. However, the basic identification of every European state with one particular religion remained a dirty little secret that could be made visible or covered over at will.[9]

In the nineteenth century, this fear of an insurgent nationalism driven by religion is the reason why imperialist politics acquires its secular face in the global arena. The secularism of European polity would be used not to battle religion in Europe but to circumscribe it in the colony. Religion would therefore be undone in its insurgent potentials, even as some of its elements would be transcendentalized into proxy ideologies for the imperial agenda of keeping the peace. The political script of empire could now be read as *our* Benjamin Disraeli, *your* Gautama Buddha, *our* Winston Churchill, *your* Mahatma Gandhi. (Indeed, Gandhi's most significant critical achievement was the ability to overturn this repressive pacification, out of keeping with the unbroken precedent of European bourgeois states established by war, into the basis for a bourgeois state.) Through this political reframing of the economic theater of imperialism as a cultural conundrum, as a conflict between religion and customs, the colonized native bourgeoisie would be pried away from attending to the most depredatory effects of the British imperial system. The skeletons of the thirty million Indian dead from starvation alone in the period between 1870 and 1947 would be covered over by the bourgeois staging of a conflict between cultures and civilizations.[10]

In the context of colonial archaeology, these claims of culturalist ethnography invoking an identification between native agency and the romantic evocation of place found itself at odds with the contending demands of scientific epistemology and research. The claims of the museum, repository of the latter strategy and of the Enlightenment principles of disinterested study of objects removed from their context, began to be squared off in the 1860s against the countervailing principle of preserving artifacts and buildings in situ. Even as the introduction of reproductive techniques such as photography, casts, and drawings appeared to satisfy museumatic demands, colonial archaeologists and architectural historians now began to see India as an open-air museum. The categories created in the museum were now extended to the geographical map. Henry Hardy Cole, son of our Cole and first curator of the Department of the Conservation of Ancient Monuments founded in 1880, therefore reclassified the Indian map, marking different sites as B (Buddhist), H (Hindu), J (Jain), or M (Muhammadan).

> It has been the policy of the Government of India to keep the small and movable antiquities, recovered from the ancient sites, in close association with the remains to which they belong, so that they may be studied amid their natural surroundings and not lose focus by being transported [e.g., Sarnath, Pagan, Taxila, Nalanda, Mohenjo-daro and Harappa, Sanchi, and Khiching]. *Although the population at most of these excavated sites is scanty, the maintenance of these museums is entirely justified, for the objects preserved in them are all-important to the student if he is to visualize aright the conditions of life in Ancient India and to infuse life and colour into his picture.*[11]

Imperialism places the differend within relativism—but this relativism is limned precisely by figuring a transcendentalist identity larger than the peoples who presently inhabit it. In the context of the Indian North-West, the largely neofeudal character of the colonial administration, borne out of political expediency, was thus supplemented by competing claims to the transcendent influence of Islam and Buddhism in the region. Thus, the many open-air preservational sites of the Gandhara region and the Bamiyan Buddhas complemented the establishment of the Lahore and the nearby Kabul museum—thus explicitly encoding the region's contributions to global civilization within a Buddhist identity. Charles Allen's adulatory study of the supposedly enlightened British who "discovered India's lost religion" inadvertently exposes this opportunistic reinvention of Buddhism in its very title: *The Search for the Buddha.*[12] The Buddha is a research product and administrative insertion of the nineteenth century.

It is important to note here that this dyad of regional transignification and global particularity is the principal thematic invoked in the first wave of anticolonial nationalist imaginaries. It is because of the noncoincidence of transcendentalist imagination and geographical map that the nationalist project can be said to be a kind of longing for an origin that is inevitably located "elsewhere." Nothing epitomizes this better than the case of the two states carved out of British India. The Indus Valley civilization, perceived fount of Indian history, has most of its archaeological remains located inside Pakistan, whereas the principal imperial remains of Pakistan's presumed cultural forebears, the Islamic emperors, are located inside India. In the aftermath of so-called political decolonization, the complicity between this flawed transregional imaginary and a derivative Eurocentrism can be said to be underpinned by the creation of the United Nations, the old cosmopolitan specter of a global community of nation-states. Correspondingly, institutions such as UNESCO and the World Heritage project can be considered to be the direct legatees of the Fergussons and the Cunninghams in that they activate cultural pasts to secure a global *pax.*

In contemporary South Asia, this has had some interesting ramifications. On December 6, 1992, gangs of the Hindu religious right destroyed an abandoned mosque, named after the first Mughal emperor Babar, in the northern Indian town of Ayodhya. Even as this symbolic affront created ripples across Asia and the Islamic world, the mavens of Eurocentric global "cosmopolitanism" and agencies such as UNESCO kept quiet. The destruction of a mundane mosque was an affair *too regional* to be of import to the concept of World Heritage. In the subsequent national election, the political party responsible for the destruction—the Bharatiya Janata Party, subsequently responsible for increased military cooperation with the United States—was voted into power in India's federal government.

In the beginning of 2001, the Taliban government, enraged at what it perceived as the global community's apathy toward its economic desperation, blew up the ancient Buddhist sculptures in the province of Bamiyan. B reverted to M on the map. The spark appears to have been ignited by UNESCO's offer to provide expert assistance and funds to preserve the sculptures when the Taliban was desperately seeking international funding, in the face of economic sanctions, to stabilize its government. Militia leaders also pointed to the destruction of the Babri Masjid as precedent. The international community's reaction was distinctly different from the Babri Masjid incident. In a signal moment of triumphalism after the fall of the Taliban in the face of the U.S.-led attack on Afghanistan in 2001, the anti-Muslim Bharatiya Janata Party government staged an exhibition in New Delhi's Indira Gandhi National Center for Arts on the "Arts of Afghanistan." Only representations of Buddhist antiquities were shown, with a prominent replica of the Bamiyan Buddhas guarding the entrance.

In the context of the history that I have narrated, how are we to read these apparently corresponding acts of iconoclasm and ostentatious iconophilia? As identitarian fundamentalism against capitalist cosmopolitanism? As comeuppance for a historiographic strategy set in place by imperialism? As the revenge of the local and particular against the global and the universal? Not quite. First of all, under the dispensations of modernity realized by imperialism and neocolonialism, the global can hardly be equated with the universal. Conversely, the local is hardly the particular. In this case, the difference was that with its statal dispensation conforming to the model of a liberal nation-state and ideology of macroeconomic dismantlement, India occupied a quite different position in the system of nations. Similarly, in the aftermath of the fall of Baghdad to American-led troops in 2002, as crowds ransacked and looted Iraqi museums, the occupational forces described this lost heritage as less important than other ground objectives, quite in contrast to the same government's indignation at the Bamiyan demolitions. The heritage discourse is an element of geopolitical realpolitik, nothing more, nothing less.

With this two-faced legacy of the Enlightenment in mind, I would like to return us to the concept of the differend and with it the singular case, both juridical and historiographic, of Sher Ali. As we have seen, he had requested to be executed by the British administration rather than be transported to a distant place. In the following section, I will suggest that Ali's request can be said to unravel the adjudicatory claims of European humanism. There are a few more determinants, however, to consider along the way.

One question cannot be ignored, especially after close to two hundred years of a repetitive history: Why Afghanistan?

Peter Hopkirk's extraordinary series of books on Central Asia have highlighted the incredible history of the contestations over the region by the great imperial powers. Written from an Anglocentric perspective, these six books explicitly seek to recuperate a sort of Kiplingesque romance of imperial espionage, the keystone among them indicatively titled *The Great Game*.[13] Reading these books not entirely against their grain, I would like to explicate the question "Why Afghanistan?" through Louis Althusser's invocation of the Leninist theme of "the weakest link": "A chain is as strong as its weakest link."[14] In the previous chapter, we looked at the nomenclature "Bengal" in the context of a "sign chain." In the aftermath of the October revolution, Lenin attempted to theorize its inexplicable early triumph by asking the question "Why Russia?" Lenin calculated that the overwhelming contradictions articulated in Russian society, the overlap of advanced industrialism in the cities and exacerbated feudalism in the rural areas, the crepuscular "ignorance" of the peasantry and the enlightened cosmopolitanism of its exiled political elites, derived as much from internal determinants as from its external relationship with regard to the other imperialist states. Given the particular stage of global history in the aftermath of the war, "Russia was the weakest link in the chain of the imperialist states." Although it is these contradictions that fuel the revolution, in its aftermath it became clear that the bourgeois revolution could not coincide with the peasant revolution. It goes without saying therefore that Stalin sought to sew up these maximized contradictions through the vision of a bourgeois "Communist Party that was a chain without weak links."[15] The contradictions were erased rather than worked through.

As we saw in the previous chapter, Lenin's theorization is here a product of a common imperial refrain of the period; the British Empire was described by many of its proponents as a chain of weak links that needed to be strengthened. With this frame in mind, I suggest Afghanistan's status as a "weak link" *in the chain of colonized states*. Its locus is defined by *maximum overdetermination* in the context of Eurocentric imperialist geopolitics and *maximum undermining* of the project of Eurocentric modernity. Suspended in the cusp, the no-man's-land and buffer state between two superpowers, it was therefore the global nonplace that not only was not colonized but *could not be* colonized. (The Balkan states play out a comparable thematic on the European side, with the difference that their proximities to the countries of the Enlightenment locate them *within* the boundaries of Europe as a cosmopolitan superstate.) Barnett Rubin has recounted in great detail the multiple fractures opened up in Afghan society in the 1980s by the conflict between a puppet government of the Soviet Union monopolizing the tenuous state apparatus in the absence of a strong nationalism and the tribalist strategy adopted by the CIA-funded Pakistani Inter-Services Intelligence to organize insurgency. The global "balance of powers" could only grasp at the possibility of the *national* sovereignty of Afghanistan as a cipher. In this context, the Taliban effort to secure national integrity was therefore as much a Stalinist eradication of weak links as an instance of theocratic oligarchy.

In September 1996, one of the first acts of retribution by the Taliban after the conquest of Kabul was the execution of Najibullah, former head of the genocidal secret service agency Khad, responsible for the deaths of thousands of Afghans, and communist president during the Soviet era. Before he was dragged out from the UN compound where he had sought refuge after the defeat of his government by U.S.-backed Islamist rebels in 1992, Najibullah had told UN officials that he was translating Peter Hopkirk's *The Great Game* into Pushtu.[16] After the U.S. invasion of Afghanistan, Hopkirk explained the reason for this effort: "He had told friends that every Afghan should be made to read it so that the terrible mistakes of the past would never be repeated."[17] This last ditch, and failed, attempt to institute for Afghans a national narrative, even if by way conveying the extraordinary overdetermination of this territory by external powers, has the pathos of Vivan Sundaram's empty frames in the previous chapter.

If the bourgeois-communist Najibullah waited for his death by unsuccessfully attempting to forge a nationalist, therefore modern, historiography, Sher Ali's wait for death marks the failed relationship to modernity in a slightly different way. As a Pashtun, Sher Ali's linguistic-ethnic matrix is split between imperial extraterritoriality (Afghanistan) and the terra firma of British justice (North-West Frontier Province)—it is here that his case can be seen to approximate the differend between neofeudalism and the Enlightenment subject. British officers were well aware that their Pathan subalterns conformed to tribal codes outside British territory, but they effectively tolerated these practices as a realpolitik strategy. At least one commentator on the Mayo assassination described Sher Ali's behavior as typical of the clan-feuds endemic to mount dwelling populations, comparing it to Scottish vendettas. Justice thus is the institutional monumentalization of power over territory, but power is a response to cultural differences both within and without any given territory. In this sense, Afghanistan is also the "free trade zone" of imperialist ethics.

> The British territory is free to all, and by implied compact all are bound to forego their feuds and animosities when on British ground. This principle of the sanctity of the neutral ground afforded by our territory is well known and recognized by all the tribesmen on our borders. I have frequently had men, and parties of men, sitting on the same carpet before me who directly they [*sic*] crossed the border could only meet as Montague and Capulet.[18]

In his dying confession, Sher Ali stated that the slaying of a hereditary foe was no crime in his eyes. In spite of this disavowal of culpability, however, he had preferred to be executed rather than to be transported and kept alive. Operative in this is a robust sense of submission to justice, even when justice is enacted through the law of the other. On the other hand, the British magistrate's decision to transport him cannot be seen as anything less than a humane act. Embedded in this act is the exemplary tolerance of British liberal humanism toward the nuances of customary and common law. And yet, for Sher Ali, the core of the injustice lay in the decision to keep him alive rather than to kill him. On the level of singular acts of justice, this asymptote epitomizes the differend—the honorability of either side cannot be doubted at the level of singular intention. Two systems of justice seek to compete not by undoing but by outdoing the other.

In his next crime, however, the murder of the viceroy, Sher Ali put this very singularity, and therefore this presumed honorability of intent, into question.

European pluralist humanism can unfold as a global ethic only under the cocked rifle hammer of British imperialism. Sher Ali's lunge with the knife undoes this coerced complicity. It is here that his revolt becomes systemic, the unraveling of a protocol of power rather than merely an intuitive opposition. Islam acts here as customary *constraint* rather than as messianic injunction; a qualification in terms of the ethics of the hashishi/ assassin code is perhaps best left here to more competent commentators. Nonetheless, this reading is further intensified by his response to a telegram sent by Mayo's children on the eve of his execution. On hearing their message "May God forgive you," Ali became enraged, saying that if they had sent a message ordering him to be cut to pieces he would have been glad, but he could not accept from them a prayer for God's forgiveness.[19] I grant you the right to punish but not the right to forgive. I accept your law but not your justice.

It is because the origins of modernity in the colony are inexplicably tied up with the ends of imperialism that its outlines operate as a historical teleology in reverse: *first* the institution of the neofeudal-capitalist/disciplinary apparatus (even within the postcolonial "independent" state), while the "Enlightenment"—we can turn Kant's phrase "*Sapere Aude!*" here: know your subjection as your subjecthood—of the native is a project that can be deferred endlessly. But the assassin and the insurgent are more functions of discursive difference—the activators of the differend—than they are representations of a "nonmodern" native will or symptoms of some "other" manner of being. It is the managerial force of imperial pluralism that is unraveled by the assassin.

Sher Ali's action produced a crisis at the geopolitical level. At the same time, his narrative singularity could neither be embraced by statist historiography (colonial or nationalist) nor be appropriated by narratives of "political" insurgency. Sher Ali's ethical trajectory is *in* the great apocalyptic master narratives of modernity but not *of* it. Within the province of law, Lyotard points out that the "humanist" assumption of innocence on the part of the accused primarily benefited hegemonic power, because its victims could never formulate their testimony into a cognizable "phrase." Sher Ali's singular narrative could not therefore be recognized by colonial power as full-fledged "political" consciousness. This is why in the first historiographic account we encounter of his story, in Mayo's biography, his name is willfully written out: "Neither his name, nor that of his village or tribe, will find record in this book."[20] The early Subaltern Studies collective in India read the colonial archive to tease out precisely such irruptions in its textual protocols. In the colonial records of anticolonial insurgency, subalternist historians saw these insurgencies as necessarily failing (because colonialism could always muster enough force to stamp them out physically) and yet leaving their trace as a crisis in the textuality of colonial historiography.[21]

But the differend also plays out in one other aspect. It was Walter Benjamin who pointed out that the otherwise unnecessary procedure of formulating "peace" treaties in the aftermath of wars derived from the necessity of imposing the victor's law as the new status quo for the vanquished in the peace to come.[22] Sher Ali's plea for his own execution reveals death as the keeper of the differend. If I cannot live according to my norms in your (triumphalist) juridical frame, then let me die so that the norm can be preserved. Bury the differend so that it can be mourned "properly"; do not rationalize it away and leave it to fester as the province of the irrational. Humanistic justice, willfully noncognizant of its complicity with imperialism, cannot honor this plea as a desire for modernity, a plea for *accession* to a universal justice, a justice that could also be the name for a modernity yet to come—a modernity and a justice that the Christianized *pax imperialis* and regime of *sympatha* can never bear. Unlike Western Europe, *internal* revolutions, the necessary "working through" that leads the ancestors to their proper burial, continue to be interdicted across the (neo)colonial world. The differend must invoke other forms to win recognition.

Notes

Introduction

1. Henry Cole. "On the Facilities Afforded to All Classes of the Community for Obtaining Education in Art" (November 24, 1852), in *Addresses of the Superintendents of the Department of Practical Art, Delivered in the Theatre at Marlborough House* (London: Chapman and Hall, 1853).
2. The extract is by Timothy Mitchell: "A plan or framework would create the appearance of objectness ... by seeming to separate an object-world from its observer. This sort of framework is not just a plan that colonialism would bring to Egypt, but an effect it would build in ... the colonial process would try and re-order Egypt to appear as a world enframed. Egypt was to be ordered up as something object-like [as depicted in the world exhibitions]. In other words it was to be made picture-like and legible, rendered available to political and economic calculation. Colonial power required the country to become readable, like a book, in our own sense of such a term." Timothy Mitchell, *Colonising Egypt* (Berkeley: University of California Press, 1988, 1991), 33. On the same lines also see Zeynep Celik, *Displaying the Orient: Architecture of Islam at Nineteenth-Century World's Fairs* (Berkeley: University of California Press, 1992); Paul Greenhalgh, *Ephemeral Vistas, The Expositions Universelles, Great Exhibitions and World's Fairs, 1851–1939* (Manchester: Manchester University Press, 1988); and Gyan Prakash, *Another Reason: Science and the Imagination of Modern India* (Princeton, NJ: Princeton University Press, 1999).
3. See Sumit Sarkar, "The Decline of the Subaltern in Subaltern Studies," in *Writing Social History* (New Delhi: Oxford University Press, 1997), 106.
4. Gyan Prakash, *Another Reason*, 19.
5. Martin Heidegger, "The Origin of the Work of Art," in *Poetry, Language, Thought*, trans. Albert Hofstadter (New York: Harper and Row, 1971), 25–26, 50.
6. Ranajit Guha, "The Prose of Counter-Insurgency," in *Subaltern Studies II: Writings on South Asian History and Society* (New Delhi: Oxford University Press, 1983, 1992), 1 (emphasis mine).
7. See Ranajit Guha, "On Some Aspects of the Historiography of Colonial India," in *Subaltern Studies I: Writings on South Asian History and Society* (New Delhi: Oxford University Press, 1982, 1991). Also see his "The Prose of Counter-Insurgency," in *Subaltern Studies II* (New Delhi: Oxford University Press, 1983, 1992).
8. Gayatri Chakravorty Spivak, "Can the Subaltern Speak?" in *Marxism and the Interpretation of Culture*, ed. Cary Nelson and Lawrence Grossberg (Urbana: University of Illinois Press, 1988).

9. See Paul de Man, "Kant and Schiller," in *Aesthetic Ideology* (Minneapolis: University of Minnesota, 1996).

10. See Gayatri Chakravorty Spivak, "Subaltern Studies: Deconstructing Historiography," in *In Other Worlds: Essays in Cultural Politics* (New York: Methuen, 1987). A speech-act is a phrase where the very utterance of a sentence simultaneously performs an act. The encounter between Derrida and John R. Searle, votary of the speech-act theory laid out by J.L. Austin in his landmark *How to Do Things with Words* (Cambridge, MA: Harvard University Press, 1962, 1975), is put together in Jacques Derrida, *Limited Inc.* (Evanston, IL: Northwestern University Press, 1988). Also see John R. Searle, *Speech Acts: An Essay in the Philosophy of Language* (Cambridge, UK: Cambridge University Press, 1969, 1999).

11. Ranajit Guha, "Dominance without Hegemony and Its Historiography," in *Subaltern Studies VI: Writings on South Asian History and Society* (New Delhi: Oxford University Press, 1989, 1992), 232.

12. Vladimir Ilyich Lenin, *Imperialism: The Highest Stage of Capitalism* (1917) (New York: International Publishers, 1990); John Atkinson Hobson, *Imperialism: A Study* (1902) (London: Hyman, 1988); and Rudolf Hilferding, *Finance Capital: A Study of the Latest Phase of Capitalist Development* (1912) (London: Routledge and Kegan Paul, 1981).

13. Jean-François Lyotard, *Lessons on the Analytic of the Sublime* (Stanford, CA: Stanford University Press, 1994), 133.

14. Siegfried Giedion, *Architecture and the Phenomena of Transition* (Cambridge, MA: Harvard University Press, 1971), 1.

15. Paul de Man, "Kant and Schiller," 133.

16. Mark Swilling, "Rival Futures," in *blank—Architecture, Apartheid and After,* ed. Hilton Judin and Ivan Vladislavić (Rotterdam: NAi Publishers, 1998), 297.

17. The figures are taken from the following: John C.L. Sparkes, *Schools of Art: Their Origin, History, Work and Influence. Printed and Published for the Executive Council of the International Health Exhibition, and for the Council of the Society of Arts* (London: William Clowes, 1884).

18. See Henry Cole, *Fifty Years of Public Works of Sir Henry Cole, Accounted for in His Deeds, Speeches and Writings* (London: George Bell and Sons, 1884); and Elizabeth Bonython, *King Cole: A Picture Portrait of Sir Henry Cole, KCB 1808–1882* (London: V&A, 1982).

19. Elizabeth Bonython and Anthony Burton, *The Great Exhibitor: The Life and Work of Henry Cole* (London: V&A, 2003).

20. Commonly used name for the Society for the Encouragement of Arts, Manufacturers and Commerce, founded in 1754 and granted a royal charter in 1847.

21. See the following: Quentin Bell, *The Schools of Design* (London: Routledge and Kegan Paul, 1963); Janet Minihan, *The Nationalisation of Culture* (London: Hamish Hamilton, 1977); Arnold S. Levine, "The Politics of Taste: The Science and Art Department of Great Britain, 1852–1873" (PhD diss., University of Wisconsin, 1972); Stuart Macdonald, *The History and Philosophy of Art Education* (London: University of London, 1970); and Sparkes, *Schools of Art.*

22. Raymond Williams, "Contrasts," in *Culture and Society 1780–1950* (New York: Columbia University Press, 1983).

23. Adrian Rifkin, "Success Disavowed: The Schools of Design in Mid-Nineteenth-Century Britain (An Allegory)," *Journal of Design History* 1, no. 2 (1988): 93.

24. In its midcentury avatar, the term *taste* is best qualified by Ralph Nicholson Wornum's prize-winning essay written for the Great Exhibition, "The Exhibition as a Lesson in Taste," in *The Crystal Palace Exhibition; Illustrated Catalogue, London 1851,* special issue, *The Art Journal* (1851; repr., New York: Dover Publications, 1970).

25. Minihan, *Nationalization,* 114. A detailed account of the history of the museum's collection is available in Anna Somers Cocks, *The Victoria and Albert Museum: The Making of the Collection* (Leicester: Windward, 1980).

26. Mark Wigley, *White Walls, Designer Dresses: The Fashioning of Modern Architecture* (Cambridge, MA: MIT Press, 1995); and Zvi Efrat et al., eds., *Fashion: In Architecture* (New York: Princeton Architectural Press, 1994).

27. For a detailed study of the audience reactions to the Indian section of the Great Exhibition, see Lara Kriegel, "Narrating the Subcontinent in 1851: India at the Crystal Palace," in *The*

Great Exhibition of 1851: New Interdisciplinary Essays, ed. Louise Purbrick (Manchester: Manchester University Press, 2001).

28. Ruskin decried the exhibition as much for its celebration of industry as he dismissed the Oriental wares therein as the work of a primitive, unthinking imagination. See John Ruskin, *The Opening of the Crystal Palace, Considered in Some of Its Relations to the Prospects of Art* (London: Smith, Elder & Co., 1854).

29. *Journal of Indian Art* 2, no. 23 (July 1888).

30. Norma Evenson, *The Indian Metropolis: A View from the West* (New Haven, CT: Yale University Press, 1989).

31. *Proceedings of the Art Conference Held in the Technical Institute at Lahore on the 1st, 2nd, 3rd, and 4th of January 1894* (Calcutta: Govt. Central Printing Office, 1894) [IOL: DPI files].

Chapter 1

1. See Peter Hopkirk, *Trespassers on the Roof of the World: The Race for Lhasa* (Oxford: Oxford University Press, 1983); also see Timothy Richards, *The Imperial Archive: Knowledge and the Fantasy of Empire* (London: Verso, 1993).

2. Henry Cole, *History of a Tea Cup and Saucer* (Privately printed, [1878?]), SNAL.

3. John R. Seeley, *The Expansion of England: Two Courses of Lectures* (Boston: Little, Brown, 1905), 10.

4. Michel de Certeau, *The Practice of Everyday Life* (Berkeley: University of California Press, 1984, 1988), xiii.

5. See Felix Summerly (Henry Cole), *Travelling Charts: or, Iron Road Books* (London: Railway Chronicle Office, 1848).

6. The correspondence between Marx and Engels (who was in Manchester) at this time mostly addresses matters on the Continent and the possibility of Marx traveling to America to take up the editorship of a newspaper, which Engels discourages. Engels's letter of May 1 suggests that they meet in London for the exhibition, whereas his letter of May 9 complains of being disturbed continually by tradesmen who have crossed over the Channel for the exhibition (Engels was taking care of his father's business in Manchester). In Marx's letter of August 22 to Hermann Ebner, a German journalist, in actuality a secret agent who was passing on Marx's correspondence to the Austrian secret police, he even seems dismissive of the "phantasmagoric" character of the glass architecture of the Crystal Palace and its relationship to audience: "From the foregoing you will have seen how [Gottfried] Kinkel [little-known German poet living in London who sympathized with the revolutions of 1848] now advances, now retreats, now embarks on an undertaking, now disavows it, always in accordance with the way he believes the popular wind to be blowing. In a piece for the short-lived *Kosmos*, he expressed particular admiration for a gigantic mirror exhibited in the Crystal Palace. That's Kinkel for you; the mirror is the element in which he exists. He is first and foremost an actor." MECW 38: 430.

7. Karl Marx, "The Eighteenth Brumaire of Louis Bonaparte," in *Surveys from Exile: Political Writings*, vol. 2 (New York: Penguin Classics, 1992), 227.

8. Is it tendentious to talk of the newspaper side by side with the exhibition? The British Section of the 1867 *Exposition Universelle* in Paris exhibits no less than twelve hundred contemporary specimens of "Periodical and Ephemeral Literature" published in the United Kingdom during the preceding year. The collection contained representative specimens from all the English provincial areas, in addition to Irish, Welsh, and Scottish examples. Periodical exhibitions were to become a constant feature of the ensuing exhibitions. The 1871 Exhibition had its own newspaper, *The Key*, announcing daily events and occurrences, and was published out of one of the printing presses on display. The temporal celerity of the newspaper can become a subject of display. See *Catalogue of the British Section, Containing a List of the Exhibitors of the United Kingdom and Its Colonies, and the Objects Which They Would Exhibit*, I and II (London: Spottiswoode, 1867). Also see *The Key: Programme and Record of the London International Exhibition, the Royal Horticultural Gardens, the Royal Albert Hall, the Schools of Science and Art in the United Kingdom, and the South Kensington Museum* (Newsletter of the London International Exhibition, 1871), NAL.

9. Husserl uses the term in his "Origin of Geometry," where he equates the readership of the newspaper with something like an original, "passive" reception of meaning, which then awaits a subsequent "active production" that is the domain of judgment. Husserl's larger thesis on how certain knowledges (science, geometry) become communal and self-evidential will be further analyzed in chapter 3. Husserl describes newspaper reading as follows: "A passively emerging sentence (e.g., in memory), or one heard and passively understood, is at first merely received with a passive ego-participation, taken up as valid: and in this form it is already our meaning. From this we distinguish the peculiar and important activity of explicating our meaning. Whereas in its first form it was a straight-forwardly valid meaning, taken up as unitary and undifferentiated—concretely speaking, a straightforwardly valid declarative sentence—now what in itself is vague and undifferentiated is actively explicated. Consider, for example, the way in which we understand, when superficially reading the newspaper, and simply receive the 'news'; there is a passive taking over of ontic validity such that what is read straightway becomes our opinion." Edmund Husserl, "The Origin of Geometry," in *Edmund Husserl's Origin of Geometry: An Introduction*, ed. Jacques Derrida (Lincoln: University of Nebraska Press, 1978), 167.
10. Marx, "The Eighteenth Brumaire," 229.
11. A contemporary account of the daguerrotype appeared in the Welsh newspaper *The Cambrian*, on September 20, 1839: "The Daguerrotype ... apparatus is similar to that employed in the camera obscura. The invention is a great improvement on photogenic drawing, inasmuch as the representations of existing objects are more perfect, the minute details are accurately preserved, and to a slight degree the tints of colours secured." q. Mark Haworth-Booth, *Photography; An Independent Art: Photographs from the Victoria and Albert Museum 1839-1996* (Princeton, NJ: Princeton University Press, 1997), 16.
12. Although Benjamin's "Work of Art in the Age of Mechanical Reproduction" begins with a reference to Marx and his supposed prognosis of the dissolution of capitalism, his analysis of the photographic and cinematic image is largely confined to the period after 1900. The essay begins as follows: "When Marx undertook his critique of the capitalistic mode of production, this mode was in its infancy. Marx directed his efforts in such a way as to give them prognostic value. He went back to the basic conditions underlying capitalistic production and through his presentation showed what could be expected of in the future. ... The transformation of the superstructure, which takes place far more slowly than that of the substructure, has taken more than half a century to manifest in all areas of culture the change in the conditions of production. *Only today* can it be indicated what form this has taken." [e.a.] Walter Benjamin, "The Work of Art in the Age of Its Reproducibility," second version, in *Selected Works* 3, 1935–38 (Cambridge, MA: Belknap Press, 2002), 101.
13. William Whewell, "The General Bearing of the Great Exhibition on the Progress of Art and Science," in *Lectures on the Results of the Great Exhibition of 1851, Delivered before the Society of Arts, Manufacturers, and Commerce* (London: David Bogue, 1852), 8.
14. Ibid., 9.
15. Eugene Rimmel, *Recollections of the Paris Exhibition of 1867* (Philadelphia: J.H. Lippincott, 1868), 3 (emphasis mine).
16. Moncure Daniel Conway, *Travels in South Kensington; with Notes on Decorative Art and Architecture in England* (New York: Harper, 1882), 27.
17. Louise Purbrick, "South Kensington Museum: The Building of the House of Henry Cole," in *Art Apart: Art Institutions and Ideology across England and North America*, ed. Marcia Pointon (New York: Manchester University Press, 1994), 26.
18. q. *The Museums Area of South Kensington and Westminster, Survey of London* 38 (London: Athlone Press, 1975).
19. Purbrick, "South Kensington Museum," 26.
20. Conway, *Travels in South Kensington*, 26.
21. J.C. Robinson, *An Introductory Lecture on the Museum of Ornamental Art of the Department* (London: Chapman and Hall, 1854), 17–18 (emphasis mine).
22. Henry Cole, *Plans for Laying Out the Quadrangle at South Kensington: Proof by Cole*. HCM, IX (emphasis mine).
23. Kenneth Frampton, "Industrialization and the Crises in Architecture," *Oppositions* 1 (September 1973): 65.

24. See Tom Peters, *Building in the Nineteenth Century* (Cambridge, MA: MIT Press, 1996), 349–50.

25. Lance E. Davis and Robert A. Huttenback, *Mammon and the Pursuit of Empire: The Political Economy of British Imperialism, 1860–1912* (Cambridge: Cambridge University Press, 1986, 1987), 38.

26. See David R. Green, *From Artisans to Paupers: Economic Change and Poverty in London, 1790–1870* (Aldershot: Scolar Press, 1995), 5.

27. Prabhat Patnaik, *Whatever Happened to Imperialism and Other Essays* (New Delhi: Tulika, 1995), 90.

28. Michael Hebbert, *London: More by Fortune Than Design* (Chichester: John Wiley, 1998), 38.

29. See M.H. Port, *Imperial London: Civil Government Building in London, 1850–1951* (New Haven, CT: Yale University, 1995), 5.

30. Port, *Imperial London*, 5.

31. John Summerson, *The London Building World of the Eighteen-Sixties* (London: Thames & Hudson, 1973), 7.

32. See Henry Cole, *Expediency of Combining the Advantages of English and Continental Management on the London and North-Western Lines; A Letter to Robert Stephenson, Esq. Engineer of the London and North-Western Railway* (London: James Holmes, 1846) [in HCM VII].

33. J. Holmes, *An Account of the New Docks at Great Grimsby, and of the Manchester, Sheffield and Lincolnshire Railway. Prepared on the Occasion of Laying the First Stone of the Docks by His Royal Highness the Prince Albert, on the 18th of April 1849* (London: J. Holmes, 1849) [in HCM VIII].

34. Frampton, "Industrialization," 65.

35. Cole writes to a General Grey from Geneva (dated November 23, 1858): "You see that there are two competitors making a Railway to connect the Railways on the North & South of the Thames at Chelsea. This Railway involves accommodation for the South Kensington Institutions—which is of great importance to their future progress. So the question of the mode of supplying the accommodation ought to be well watched" [in HCC I: Part 1].

36. HCM XII: 171.

37. "I think I can make you best understand ... by showing you what now happens to a Hanley student who comes up to London to visit the British Museum and the South Kensington Museum. We will suppose that he comes up to town towards the end of the Christmas holidays. He arrives at Euston station. No railway terminus is within a mile of the British Museum, so he has to take a cab, or walk. He goes there on a Tuesday, he finds the gates closed. He asks for admission. He is told that the Museum is not open on Tuesdays, except to party of fifty [... etc. etc.]. ... Now, let me contrast these antiquated obstructions with the facilities which the Hanley student will find at the Kensington Museum. He comes up by the railway from Hanley, not to Euston, but to South Kensington Station, which puts him down within some 200 yards of the Museum. He finds the place open every day in the week at ten o'clock. It is never closed for cleaning and repairs." Henry Cole, *Threatened Suppression of the South Kensington Museum. Address Delivered 20th October, 1873 to the Students of the Hanley School of Arts* (London: W. Trounce, 1873), 13–14.

38. Henry Cole, *The Functions of the Science and Art Department* (London: Chapman and Hall, 1857), 27.

39. "The main building, for arts and manufactures, consisted of parts of a railway shed disposed in the form of a cross. The iron work was lent by the East Indian Railway Company to the Central Committee, and its Chief Engineer ... gave a plan for its arrangement. When this plan was handed over to me the foundations had been nearly completed, and shortly after, [an official] of the East India [sic] Railway Company, arrived with a gang of trained workmen to superintend the erection of the iron work, which was then gradually being delivered on the ground." See *General Report of the North-West Provinces Exhibition, Held at Agra, February 1867* (Roorkee: Thomason Civil Engineering Press, 1868), SNAL.

40. Theodore C. Hope, *Report on the Broach Exhibition, 1868–1869* (Bombay: Education Society's Press, 1869), 2.

41. *Report of the Nagpore Exhibition of Arts, Manufacture and Produce* (Nagpore: [Central Provinces Printing Press], 1865), 29.

42. The vulgar conception of time is the complete covering over of Heidegger's demand of "ontological and ontical priority." This priority is the acknowledgment that the question

of being and beings comes before all subjective insight, before all disciplinary inquiry, before the investigation of historical beings. The Hegelian "moment" tends toward the vulgar conception of time in that it too concentrates on the now; however, in being fully self-cognizant of its temporal transition from past to present, it is both too resolute for the "authentic" temporality of being and too authentic in its temporal framing for the vulgar conception. One lives in vulgar time when the now is frittered away in both an inauthentic and an irresolute manner. Its epitome is the subject who says, "I have no time." There is an "aporia" between the vulgar conception of time and authentic temporality (where being is acknowledged). Because one is already ontological in vulgar time, the way toward authentic temporality, toward acknowledging the priority of the ontological, cannot be defined by necessity or need, "one either looks for the problem of the continuity of time, or one leaves the aporia alone." Martin Heidegger, *Being and Time,* trans. Joan Stambaugh (Albany: SUNY Press, 1996), 386, 390–91.

43. See John Gallagher and Ronald Robinson, "The Imperialism of Free Trade," *The Economic History Review* VI, no. 1 (1953).

44. Ramachandra Guha and Madhav Gadgil, *This Fissured Land: An Ecological History of India* (New Delhi: Oxford University Press, 1992, 1996), 117.

45. Davis and Huttenback, *Mammon and the Pursuit of Empire,* 10.

46. John Stuart Mill, "A Constitutional View of the India Question," (1858) in *Writings on India,* vol. XXX, *Collected Works* (Toronto: University of Toronto Press, 1990).

47. Karl Marx, *Grundrisse: Foundations of the Critique of Political Economy,* trans. Martin Nicolaus (New York: Penguin, 1992), 86–87.

48. Karl Marx, "Economic and Philosophical Manuscripts," in *Early Writings,* trans. Rodney Livingstone and Gregor Benton (New York: Penguin, 1992), 354.

49. A substantial part of my argument here is derived from Gayatri Spivak, *A Critique of Postcolonial Reason* (Cambridge, MA: Harvard University Press, 1999). Spivak discusses Marx's notion of the AMP and historical multilinearity in detail between pages 71–105.

50. Spivak, ibid. The distinction between the slave–serf systems of feudal Europe and "oriental systems" are found in the *Grundrisse* between pages 462–79.

51. Karl Marx with Friedrich Engels, *The German Ideology* (New York: Prometheus Books, 1845, 1998), 58.

52. Marx's understanding of *global* competition gives us a glimpse of imperialism's role in binding together different temporalities of production. It must be pointed out that he frames competition in the context of global trade and not "colonialism," which for him is the *territorial,* and not necessarily economic, conquest of one nation by another. Marx gives a very different treatment to *domestic* competition in chapter 50 of the third volume of *Capital,* titled "The Illusion Created by Competition." Karl Marx, *Capital,* III (New York: Penguin Classics, 1990). Marx's interest concentrates on the relationship of prices in relation to surplus value.

53. Marx writes in his short essay for the *New York Daily Tribune* of June 7, 1858, titled "Lord Canning's Proclamation and Land Tenure in India," "In speaking of the landed interest at home, they always refer rather to the landlords and rent-receivers than to the rent-payers and to the actual cultivators; and it is, therefore, not surprising that they should regard the interests of the zemindars and talookdars, however few their actual number, as equivalent to the interests of the great body of the people. Here indeed is one of the great inconveniences and difficulties in the Government of India from England, that views of Indian questions are liable to be influenced by purely English prejudices or sentiments, applied to a state of society and a condition of things to which they have in fact very little pertinency." MECW 15: 548.

54. Mill, "A Constitutional View," 174.

55. John Stuart Mill, "The Petition of the East-India Company," (1858) in *Writings on India,* 84.

56. "Yet I have no doubt of being able to make out, to the satisfaction of all reflection minds, that the man who should bring to the composition of a history of India the qualifications alone which can be acquired in Europe, would come, in an almost infinite degree, better fitted for the task, than the man who should bring to it the qualifications alone which can be acquired in India; and that the business of acquiring the one set of qualifications is almost wholly incompatible with that of acquiring the other." James Mill, *The History of British India* (New Delhi: Atlantic Publishers, 1817, 1990), 6.

57. John Stuart Mill, "The East India Company's Charter," (1852) in *Writings on India*, 33.

58. Ibid., 51.

59. Continuing his critique of Mill in the *Grundrisse*, Marx writes, "All production is appropriation of nature on the part of an individual within and through a specific form of society. In this sense it is a tautology to say that property (appropriation) is a precondition of property. But it is altogether ridiculous to leap from that to a specific form of property, e.g., private property. (Which further and equally presupposes an antithetical form, *non-property*.) History rather shows common property (e.g., in India, the Slavs, the early Celts, etc.) to be the more original form, a form which long continues to play a significant role in the shape of communal property." Karl Marx, *Grundrisse*, 88.

60. Edmund Burke, *Reflections on the Revolution in France* (London: Penguin, 1968, 1986), 153.

61. See Edmund Burke, "India and the Impeachment of Hastings," in *Edmund Burke: Selected Writings and Speeches*, ed. Peter J. Stanlis (Gloucester, MA: Peter Smith, 1968). For a more critical evaluation of this supposed embrace of difference, see Uday Mehta, *Liberalism and Empire: A Study in Nineteenth Century British Liberal Thought* (Chicago: University of Chicago Press, 1999).

62. Edmund Burke, *Reflections on the Revolution in France*, 278.

63. John Stuart Mill, *Mill on Bentham and Coleridge* (London: Chatto & Windus, 1950), 154.

64. John Stuart Mill, "Practical Observations of the First Two of the Proposed Resolutions on the Government of India," (1858) in *Writings on India*, 188.

65. Mill, "A Constitutional View," 175.

66. Mill, "A Constitutional View" and "Practical Observations" (both 1858).

67. "The greatest part of Asia is under Mahomedan governments. To name a Mahomedan government is to name a government by law. It is a law enforced by stronger sanctions than any law that can bind a Christian sovereign. ... That the people of Asia have no laws, rights, or liberty, is a doctrine that wickedly is to be disseminated through this country. But I again assert, every Mahomedan government is, by its principles, a government of law. ... Mr. Hastings has no refuge here. ... Let him fly where he will, from law to law; law, I thank God, meets him everywhere. ... I would as willingly have him tried by the law of the Koran, or the Institutes of Tamerlane, as on the common law or statute law of this kingdom." Edmund Burke, "India and the Impeachment of Hastings," 399–400.

68. q. John Stuart Mill, *Writings on India*, 116.

69. Mahmood Mamdani, *Citizen and Subject: Contemporary Africa and the Legacy of Late Colonialism* (Princeton, NJ: Princeton University Press, 1996).

70. See footnote 9.

71. Jacques Derrida, "*Différance*," in *Margins of Philosophy* (Chicago: University of Chicago Press, 1982), 3.

72. Rafael Cardoso Denis, "The Educated Eye and the Industrial Hand: Art and Design Education for the Working Classes in Mid-Victorian Britain" (PhD diss., the Courtauld Institute, University of London, 1995), 174–77.

73. David Lindsay Crawford, "The Provincial Obligations of South Kensington Museum, or, a Note on the Circulation Department of South Kensington Museum," *National Review* (London: 1899), 886.

74. Henry Cole, "Observations on the Organization of the Permanent Civil Service" ([London?]: 1854), 7.

75. Henry Parris, *Constitutional Bureaucracy, the Development of British Central Administration since the Eighteenth Century* (New York: Augustus M. Kelley, 1969).

76. R.G.S. Brown, *The Administrative Process in Britain* (London: Methuen, 1970).

77. Henry Cole, "On the Facilities Afforded to All Classes of the Community for Obtaining Education in Art," (November 24, 1852) in *Addresses of the Superintendents of the Department of Practical Art, Delivered in the Theatre at Marlborough House* (London: Chapman and Hall, 1853), 8–9.

78. Henry Cole, *The Functions of the Science and Art Department*, 31.

79. John Stuart Mill, "The East India Company's Charter," 33.

80. For a critique of official colonial writing, see Ranajit Guha, "The Prose of Counter-Insurgency," and Homi Bhabha, "Sly Civility," in *The Location of Culture* (London: Routledge, 1994).

81. The Romantics thought of "system" primarily as a way of realizing the fiction of a "collective movement" in the shape of a poetry composed of "fragments." The disjunctive form is read

as a sign of transcendental continuity. Mill, the bailiwick-holding bureaucrat doubling as philosopher–aesthete and political–economist, reading Bentham through Coleridge, will translate a manifesto for aesthetic poesis into a norm for official prose. As for the theorization of "systems," I refer, of course, to the collectively and anonymously scripted "Earliest System-Programme of German Idealism" (1796), q. Andrew Bowie, *Aesthetics and Subjectivity: From Kant to Nietzsche* (Manchester: Manchester University Press, 1990). Also see Phillippe Lacoue-Labarthe and Jean-Luc Nancy, "Overture: The System Subject," in *The Literary Absolute: The Theory of Literature in German Romanticism* (Albany: SUNY Press, 1988).

82. Home files, Education, July 1893, 193 [IOL].

83. q. Mahrukh Tarapor, "John Lockwood Kipling & the Arts and Crafts Movement in India," in *AA files,* 3 (January 1983): 13.

84. Jejeebhoy is said to have controlled at least one-third of the supply of "Malwa" opium, largely grown out of Company territory in Central India, to the Jardine, Matheson, and Company warehouses in Canton. See Asiya Siddiqi, "The Business World of Jamsetjee Jejeebhoy," in *Indian Economic and Social History Review* 19, no. 3–4 (1982).

85. "The people of India, as your lordship in council is well aware, possess a delicate physical organization and seem to be peculiarly fitted to excel in every kind of industry that required the patient application of length and skilful manifestation. Even now their ingenuity albeit often erroneously directed, produces specimens of very appreciable excellence which as was apparent at the late great exhibition, their skill in the harmonising and adoption of colour was such as to excite the admiration of finished artists in England and France." Quoted in *The Story of Sir J.J. School of Art, 1857–1957* (Bombay: 1957), 14.

86. John Griffiths, "Report Called for in Government Resolution in the Educational Department, No. 1957, Dated 13th September 1892, on the Question of the Restoration and Maintenance of a Higher Standard in the Art Industries of the Country," in *Proceedings of the Art Conference Held in the Technical Institute at Lahore on the 1st, 2nd, 3rd, and 4th of January 1894* (Calcutta: Govt. Central Printing Office, 1894), 32.

87. Writing at the time of his retirement, Kipling notes the indigenizing mission of the school: "In establishing a School of Art at Lahore in 1875, the idea of the authorities was rather the revival and encouragement of indigenous means of Art than the importation of European notions, and your Memorialist [Kipling] has wrought steadfastly on this idea." Kipling Archives, Special Collections, University of Sussex, Box File: 3/11.

88. See, for instance, vol. 2, no. 19 (July 1887) of the *Journal of Indian Art,* which contains a special report on Wazir Khan's Mosque in Lahore, with illustrations done by Kipling's students. The next issue, no. 20 (October 1887), was a special issue on "Industries of the Punjab," with districtwise reports entirely researched and written by Kipling. This was followed up by substantial entries under the same title in issues no. 23 (July 1888) and no. 24 (October 1888).

89. Home files, Education, July 1893, 189 [IOL].

90. "A Bombay [Photographic] Amateur," in a letter to the *British Journal of Photography* (August 1, 1862); q. Ray Desmond, *Victorian India in Focus* (London: HMSO, 1982), 38 (emphasis mine).

91. Uday Singh Mehta, "Liberal Strategies of Exclusion." Also see Mehta, *Liberalism and Empire.*

92. W.H. Moreland and B.C. Burt, "United Provinces Agricultural and Industrial Exhibition, Allahabad 1910," *Northern India as a Market for Agricultural Machinery* (Allahabad: [Superintendent Government Press], [1910?]), 3–4.

93. Gareth Stedman Jones, *Outcast London: A Study in the Relationship between Classes in Victorian Society* (Oxford: Clarendon, 1971), 159.

Chapter 2

1. Marx renders this aspect of the money form through Shakespeare's *Timon of Athens.* Karl Marx, "Economic and Philosophical Manuscripts," in *Early Writings,* trans. Rodney Livingstone and Gregor Benton (New York: Penguin, 1992), 376–79.

2. Charles Dickens, *Hard Times* (New York: W.W. Norton, 1990), 11.

3. "Dickens' Working Plans," in *Hard Times*, 224.

4. Immanuel Kant, *Critique of Pure Reason*, trans. and ed. Paul Guyer and Allen W. Wood (Cambridge: Cambridge University Press, 1997), 107.

5. Kant, *Critique of Pure Reason*, 108. On the inventor's name, also see Werner Oechslin's account of the Renaissance tendency to attribute every curve and shape to singular classical individuals. Werner Oechslin, "The Vitruvian 'Science' of Architectural Drawing," *Daidalos* 1 (September 15, 1981).

6. Edmund Husserl, "The Origin of Geometry," in *Edmund Husserl's Origin of Geometry: An Introduction*, ed. Jacques Derrida (Lincoln: University of Nebraska Press, 1978), and Derrida, *An Introduction*.

7. Achille-Constant-Théodore-Émile Prisse d'Avennes, *The Decorative Art of Arabia* (London: Studio Editions, 1989), 10.

8. René Descartes, "Optics," in *Selected Philosophical Writings*, trans. John Cottingham et al. (Cambridge: Cambridge University Press, 1988).

9. Jules Bourgoin, *Les Arts et le Trait Général de l'Art Arabe* (1873), in Prisse d'Avennes, *The Decorative Art of Arabia*, 18.

10. Susan Stronge, ed., *The Decorative Arts of India* (London: Studio Editions, 1990), 9.

11. Caspar Purdon Clarke, "Moghul Art in the India Museum," in *Transactions of the Royal Institute of British Architects*, vol. 4 (London: [s.n.], 1888), 10–11 (emphasis mine).

12. Oechslin, "Vitruvian 'Science,' " 21.

13. J.M. Coetzee, *Waiting for the Barbarians* (New York: Viking Press, 1982), 16.

14. DSA, *The Introduction to the Drawing Book of the School of Design, Published in the Years 1842–43, under the Direction of W. Dyce* (London: Chapman and Hall, 1854), 42.

15. Extracted from George Eduard Biber, *Henry [sic] Pestalozzi and His Plan of Education* (London: Thoemmes Press, 1831, 1994), 332.

16. Ibid., 334.

17. See P. Woodham-Smith, "History of the Froebel Movement in England," in *Froebel and English Education: Perspectives on the Founder of the Kindergarten*, ed. Evelyn Lawrence (New York: Schocken Books, 1969).

18. William Dyce, *Report Made to the Right Hon. C. Poulett Thomson, M.P., President of the Board of Trade, on Foreign Schools of Design for Manufacture* (March 3, 1840), 39.

19. q. Rafael Cardoso Denis, "The Educated Eye and the Industrial Hand: Art and Design Education for the Working Classes in Mid-Victorian Britain" (PhD diss., the Courtauld Institute, University of London, 1995), 57.

20. Mr. Gradgrind and the unnamed gentleman may even be citing Proposition 13 of Owen Jones's *Grammar of Ornament*: "Flowers or other natural objects should not be used as ornaments, but conventional representations founded upon them sufficiently suggestive to convey the intended image to the mind, without destroying the unity of the object they are employed to decorate." Owen Jones, *The Grammar of Ornament* (London: Day and Son, 1856), 10.

21. Immanuel Kant, *Critique of the Power of Judgment*, trans. Paul Guyer and Eric Matthews (Cambridge: Cambridge University Press, 2000), 114.

22. Ibid., 93.

23. Ibid., 107.

24. He cites George Christoph Tobler, "Nature! We are surrounded and embraced by her—powerless to leave her and powerless to enter her more deeply. ... She brings forth ever new forms: what is there, never was. ... We live within her, and are strangers to her. She speaks perpetually, with us, and does not betray her secret. We work on her constantly, and yet have no power over her." See Johann Wolfgang von Goethe, "Nature [A Fragment by Georg Christoph Tobler]," in *Scientific Studies*, vol. XII of *Collected Works*, trans. and ed. Douglas Miller (Princeton, NJ: Princeton University Press, 1988, 1995), p.3.

25. See Goethe, "The Experiment as Mediator between Object and Subject," in *Scientific Studies*.

26. Ibid., 15.

27. Ibid., 16.

28. Goethe, "Introduction to Comparative Anatomy," in *Scientific Studies*, 118.

29. Kant, *Critique of the Power of Judgment*, 139.

30. Ibid., 143.

31. Jean-François Lyotard, *Lessons on the Analytic of the Sublime* (Stanford, CA: Stanford University Press, 1994), 149.
32. See Lyotard, "The Sublime as Dynamical Synthesis," in *Lessons,* 133–46.
33. Kant, *Critique of the Power of Judgment,* 148.
34. Ibid., 148.
35. Martin Heidegger, *Being and Time,* trans. Joan Stambaugh (Albany: SUNY Press, 1996), 388.
36. Georg Wilhelm Friedrich Hegel, *Aesthetics: Lectures on Fine Art,* vol. I, trans. T.M. Knox (Oxford: Oxford University Press, 1998), 128–29.
37. Goethe, "Fortunate Encounter," in *Scientific Studies,* 20.
38. Phillip C. Ritterbush, "Organic Form: Aesthetics and Objectivity in the Study of Form in the Life Sciences," in *Organic Form: The Life of an Idea,* ed. G.S. Rousseau (London: Routledge and Kegan Paul, 1972), 39.
39. Ritterbush, "Organic Form," 37.
40. See Goethe, "Observation on Morphology in General," in *Scientific Studies.*
41. Goethe, "The Purpose Set Forth" (From *On Morphology*), in *Scientific Studies,* 63.
42. Ibid., 64.
43. Barbara Whitney Keyser, "Ornament as Idea: Indirect Imitation of Nature in the Design Reform Movement," *Journal of Design History* 11, no. 2 (1993). On this topic, also see David Brett, "The Interpretation of Ornament," *Journal of Design History* 1, no. 2 (1988).
44. DSA, *Introduction to the Drawing-Book,* xvi–xviii.
45. Ibid., ix.
46. q. Ritterbush, "Organic Form," 41–42.
47. DSA, *Introduction to the Drawing-Book,* xviii.
48. See William Dyce, "Lecture on Ornament Delivered to the Students of the London School of Design," *Journal of Design and Manufactures* I (March–August 1849): 27–28.
49. See Richard H. Drayton, *Nature's Government: Science, Imperial Britain and the "Improvement" of the World* (New Haven, CT: Yale University Press, 2000); and Ray Desmond, *Kew: The History of the Royal Botanic Gardens* (London: Harvill Press and Royal Botanic Gardens, 1998).
50. See Widar Halén, *Christopher Dresser* (Oxford: Phaidon/Christie's, 1990); also see Michael Whiteway, *Christopher Dresser, 1834-1904* (London: Skira, 2002).
51. Christopher Dresser, *Unity in Variety* (London: James S. Virtue, 1859), 158, 159, 162.
52. Christopher Dresser, *Truth, Beauty, Power: Principles of Decorative Design* (London: Cassell, Petter & Galpin, [1859?]). The volume is a compendium of Dresser's articles in *Technical Educator.*
53. Also see John Lindley, *The Symmetry of Vegetation: And Outline of the Principles to Be Observed in the Delineation of Plants; Being the Substance of Three Lectures Delivered to the Students of Practical Art, at Marlborough House, in November, 1852* (London: Chapman and Hall, 1854).
54. Kant, *Critique of the Power of Judgment,* 126.
55. These are kept today in the Victoria & Albert Museum's Prints and Drawings section.
56. Goethe, "Excerpt from 'The Spiral Tendency in Vegetation,' " in *Scientific Studies,* 105.
57. Goethe, "Introduction to the *Propylaea,*" (1798) in *Essays on Art and Literature, Collected Works,* vol. III (Princeton, NJ: Princeton University Press, 1995).
58. Richard Redgrave, *On the Necessity of Principles in Teaching Design, Being an Address at the Opening of the Session of the Department of Science and Art, October 1853* (London: Chapman and Hall, 1853), 21.
59. Ibid., 23.
60. Gottfried Semper, "Science, Industry and Art: Proposals for the Development of a National Taste in Art at the Closing of the London Industrial Exhibition," (1852) in *The Four Elements of Architecture,* trans. Harry Francis Mallgrave and Wolfgang Hermann (Cambridge: Cambridge University Press, 1989).
61. Ibid., 141.
62. See Nancy J. Troy, "Transition: The Problem of the Corner," in *The De Stijl Environment* (Cambridge, MA: MIT Press, 1983).
63. Le Corbusier, *The Modulor: A Harmonious Measure to the Human Scale Universally Applicable to Architecture and Mechanics,* trans. Peter de Francia and Anna Bostock (Cambridge, MA: MIT Press, 1954, 1968).

64. Karl Marx, *Capital*, vol. 1, 164.
65. Semper, "Science, Industry and Art," 141.
66. See Marx, "The Eighteenth Brumaire of Louis Bonaparte," in *Surveys from Exile: Political Writings*, vol. 2 (New York: Penguin Classics, 1992), 146–47.
67. DPA (Great Britain and Ireland), *A Catalogue of the Articles of Ornamental Art Selected from the Exhibition of the Works of Industry of All Nations in 1851 and Purchased by the Government for the Museum of Ornamental Art at Marlborough House* (London: Chapman & Hall, 1851), 6–7.

Chapter 3

1. Christopher Dresser, *Truth, Beauty, Power: Principles of Decorative Design* (London: Cassell, Petter & Galpin, [1859?]), 3–4.
2. Dresser's call for truth in material expression and against "[mere] taste" is therefore also a ruse for transforming the basis of taste itself. Take for example the following exposition of the principle of truth in materials: "All graining of wood is false, inasmuch as it attempts to deceive; the effort being made at causing one material to look like another which it is not. All "marbling" is false also: a floor-cloth made in imitation of carpet or matting is false; a Brussels carpet that imitates a Turkey carpet is false; so is a jug that imitates wicker-work, a printed fabric that imitates one that is woven, a gas lamp that imitates an oil lamp. These are all untruths in expression, and are besides, vulgar absurdities which are the more lamentable, as the imitation is always less beautiful than the thing imitated; and as each material has the power of expressing beauty truthfully, thus the want of truth brings its own punishment." Dresser, *Truth, Beauty Power*, 16. Note also how the argument against "false" ornament also carries within it an argument against the *direct imitation* of patterns and textures.
3. Richard Redgrave, *On the Necessity of Principles in Teaching Design, Being an Address at the Opening of the Session of the Department of Science and Art, October 1853* (London: Chapman and Hall, 1853).
4. J. Forbes Royle, Appendix 3, "On the Exhibition of Raw Products and Manufactured Articles from India," in *Report Made to His Royal Highness the Prince Albert, President of the Society of Arts, etc. etc. etc., of Preliminary Inquiries into the Willingness of Manufacturers and Others to Support Periodical Exhibitions of the Works of Industry of All Nations*, ed. Henry Cole and Francis Fuller (London: [?], 1849).
5. Redgrave, *On the Necessity of Principles in Teaching Design*, 8.
6. John Stuart Mill, "On Liberty," in *On Liberty and Utilitarianism* (New York: Bantam Books, 1994), 77.
7. John Stuart Mill, "Utilitarianism," in *On Liberty and Utilitarianism*, 164 (emphasis mine).
8. The passage continues, "These forms and lines of beauty are all, it is true, to be found in the objects commonly placed before the artist; but artistical imitation, so far from leading directly to their discovery, is, on the one hand, calculated to inspire a distaste for the abstractive process by which they are made to assume a positive and independent character; and, on the other, is for beginners about as bad an exercise as can be conceived for the attainment of the sort of accuracy and precision of hand in the delineation of superficial form, or of the patience in minute details of execution, which are indispensable to ornamentists." DSA, *Introduction to the Drawing Book of the School of Design, Published in the Years 1842–43, under the Direction of W. Dyce* (London: Chapman and Hall, 1854), xix–xxi (emphasis mine).
9. The DSA's formulations follow a widely prevalent strain of thought regarding artisanal training with its inception in the eighteenth century. Thomas Sheraton's 1802 *The Cabinet-Maker and Upholsterer's Drawing Book*, for instance, has the following to say about the use of geometry for carpenters: "As it is possible for a man of sound sense to reason well without knowing the rules of logic as they are taught in fine and regular systems, so I apprehend it is also possible for a workman of no learning, but what is common, to attain to a useful knowledge of geometrical lines, without the trouble of going through a regular course of Euclid's definitions and demonstrations, &c." Thomas Sheraton, *The Cabinet-Maker and Upholsterer's Drawing-Book in Four Parts*, 3rd ed. (London: T. Bensley, 1802), 16.
10. Dresser, *Truth, Beauty Power*, 23.

11. T.W. Good, *The Science and Art Geometry. Section I: Geometrical Drawing. For Students Preparing for the Elementary School Teacher's Certificate "D"; the Second Grade Drawing Certificate; the Art Class Teacher's Certificate* (London: George Gill and Sons, 1888), 185 (emphasis mine).

12. Dresser, *Truth, Beauty, Power*, 1 (emphasis mine).

13. Ibid., 3.

14. "It has to be annihilated, it is annihilated. Its annihilation, the transformation of the individualized and scattered means of production into socially concentrated means of production, the transformation, therefore, of the dwarf-like property of the many into the giant property of the few, and the expropriation of the great mass of the people from the soil, from the means of subsistence and from the instruments of labour, this terrible and arduously accomplished expropriation of the mass of the people forms the pre-history of capital." Karl Marx, *Capital*, vol. 1 (New York: Penguin Classics, 1990), 928.

15. "Lifting the lid of that seemingly unified concept-phenomenon [i.e., money], Marx uncovered the economic *text*. Sometimes it seems that cooking is a better figure than weaving when one speaks of the text, although the latter has etymological sanction. Lifting the lid, Marx discovers that the pot of the economic is forever on the boil. What cooks (in all senses of this enigmatic expression) is Value. It is our task also to suggest that, however avant-gardist it may sound, in this uncovering Value is seen to escape the onto-phenomenological question [What is it?]." Gayatri Chakravorty Spivak, "Scattered Speculations on the Question of Value," in *In Other Worlds: Essays in Cultural Politics* (New York: Methuen, 1987), 155.

16. Marx, *Capital*, vol. 1, 962 (emphasis mine).

17. Ibid., 156.

18. Spivak, "Scattered Speculations," 155.

19. Marx, *Capital*, vol. 1, 125.

20. Ralph Nicholson Wornum, "The Exhibition as a Lesson in Taste," in *The Crystal Palace Exhibition: Illustrated Catalogue, London 1851*, special issue, *The Art Journal* (repr., New York: Dover Publications, 1970), I. On a similar note, see Christopher Dresser, "If an object is to be beautiful it should also be useful, to cause us to consider it as a primary principle of design that all objects which we create must be useful. To this as a first law we shall constantly have to refer." Dresser, *Truth, Beauty, Power*, 22.

21. "It is also quite true that, in the history of the arts of design, the discovery of right methods of execution is, in order of time, posterior to the effort of imitation to which the methods are subservient; and that they have arisen in a great degree out of the necessities of the means of imitation employed: but it does not follow, that in teaching the art of design this order can be pursued with advantage." DSA, *Introduction to the Drawing Book*, 42.

22. Ibid., vii.

23. Ibid., ix. For a contemporary appraisal of architecture as ornament in the modern movement, see Mark Wigley, *White Walls, Designer Dresses: The Fashioning of Modern Architecture* (Cambridge, MA: MIT Press, 1995).

24. See Christine Woods et al., "Proliferation: Late 19th Century Papers, Markets and Manufacturers," in *The Papered Wall: History, Pattern, Technique*, ed. Lesley Hoskins (New York: Harry N. Abrams, 1994).

25. Marx, *Capital*, vol. 1, 128, 148.

26. See M.D. Stephens and G.W. Roderick, *Education and Industry in the Nineteenth Century: The English Disease?* (London: Longman, 1978).

27. See Anne Puetz, "Design Instruction for Artisans in Eighteenth-Century Britain," in *Journal of Design History* 12, no. 3 (1999).

28. Ibid. Puetz lists the following books as examples of the didactic intentions of individual artisan-designers: Matthias Lock's *A New Drawing Book of Ornaments, Shields... &c.* (1746), and *Principles of Ornament, or the Youth's Guide to Drawing of Foliage* (c. 1740s); *A New Book of Ornaments for the Instruction of Those Unacquainted with That Useful Part of Drawing: By Copland and Others* (c. 1758); P. Baretti's *New Book of Ornaments for the Year 1766 ... Particularly Calculated to Initiate Youth in the First Principles of Drawing Ornament*; Matthias Darly's *The Ornamental Architect, or Young Artist's Instructor* (1770); Thomas Pether's *A Book of Ornaments Suitable for Beginners* (1773); and Thomas Sheraton's *The Cabinet-Maker's and Upholsterer's Drawing Book* (1793–94).

29. Barbara Maria Stafford, *Artful Science: Enlightenment Entertainment and the Eclipse of Visual Education* (Cambridge, MA: MIT Press, 1994).

30. Ibid., 163.

31. See Puetz, "Design Instruction for Artisans."

32. Rafael Cardoso Denis, "The Educated Eye and the Industrial Hand: Art and Design Education for the Working Classes in Mid-Victorian Britain" (PhD diss., the Courtauld Institute, University of London, 1995). See chapter 1, "Drawing and Vision."

33. Earl Granville, "Extract from a Speech Delivered by Earl Granville, K.G., Lord President of the Council, at the Distribution of National Medals at Manchester, on the 10th of October 1857," in DSA, *The Advantages of Teaching Elementary Drawing Concurrently with Writing as a Branch of National Education (DSA Addresses)* (London: Eyre and Spottiswoode, 1857).

34. This scenario offers a contrast with the diminishing power of guilds, which could behave only as interest groups for the particular members within the guild. However, in many cases, the decline of trade guilds was squared off by the emergence of unionism, the genesis of which often lay in the history of the guilds themselves. For an early treatment on this mixed history in the case of the building trades, for example, see R.W. Postgate, *The Builders' History* (1923) (New York: Garland, 1984). For a more recent account of the continuing importance of "tradition" in labor relations in the building industry, see Richard Price, *Masters, Unions and Men: Work Control in Building and the Rise of Labour, 1830–1914* (Cambridge: Cambridge University Press, 1980).

35. See William Dyce, *Report Made to the Right Hon. C. Poulett Thomson, M.P., President of the Board of Trade, on Foreign Schools of Design for Manufacture* (March 3, 1840), 1.

36. Although several writers have noted, correctly, that Dyce finally favored the German *Gewerbeschule* over the French schools, he devotes almost thirteen pages of his forty-one-page report to the relationship between the school and silk industry in Lyons.

37. Dyce, *Report ... on Foreign Schools of Design,* 11. Recent commentary on German Romanticism has borne out the observation that its influence was heavily undergirded by the institutionalizing impetus of the bureaucracy. See Steven Moyano, "Quality vs. History: Schinkel's Altes Museum and Prussian Arts Policy," *The Art Bulletin* 72, no. 4 (December 1990); also see Theodore Zialkowski, "The Museum: Temple of Art," in *German Romanticism and Its Institutions* (Princeton, NJ: Princeton University Press, 1990).

38. See Friedrich A. Kittler, "The Mother's Mouth: Motherliness and Civil Service," in *Discourse Networks: 1800/1900,* trans. Michael Metteer with Chris Cullens (Stanford, CA: Stanford University Press, 1990).

39. Pestalozzi offers a critique of the Socratic method when used on young children by a future collaborator of his, Kruesi: "The children catechised by Kruesi were held up by the minister as examples to his elder catechumens. Afterwards it was required of Kruesi, that he should, after the fashion of those times, combine this narrow analysis of words, called catechising, with the Socratic manner, which takes up the subject in a higher sense. But an uncultivated and superficial mind does not dive into those depths from which Socrates derived spirit and truth; and it was, therefore, quite natural that, in his new system of questioning, Kruesi should not succeed. He had no internal basis for his questions, nor had the child any for their answers. They had no language for things which they knew not, and no books which furnished them with a well-framed answer to every question, whether they understood it or not." George Eduard Biber, *Henry [sic] Pestalozzi and His Plan of Education* (London: Thoemmes Press, 1831, 1994), 188. Also see Johann Heinrich Pestalozzi, *How Gertrude Teaches Her Children: An Attempt to Help Mothers to Teach Their Own Children and an Account of the Method,* trans. Lucy E. Holland and Francis C. Turner (New York: Gordon Press, 1973).

40. See Uday Singh Mehta, "Molding Individuality: Direction and Compromise," in *The Anxiety of Freedom: Imagination and Individuality in Locke's Political Thought* (Ithaca, NY: Cornell, 1992).

41. DSA, *Introduction to the Drawing Book,* 44–45.

42. Madras DPI Reports, 1856–1857, 70, 72.

43. Owen Jones, *The Grammar of Ornament* (London: Day and Son, 1856), 9.

44. The predicament thus posed is somewhat like a Ruskinian formation in reverse. Ruskin's dislike for the DSA drew what he considered their embrace and "promotion of mechanical,

and therefore vile, manufacture." Of Jones's beloved Alhambra, in contrast, he considered it somewhat symptomatically of his views of the Orient in general, "detestable ... it is a late building, a work of the Spanish dynasty in its last decline, and its ornamentation is fit for nothing but to be transferred to patterns of carpets or bindings of books. ... Alhambras and common Moorish ornament [are only fit to be classified] ... under the head of Doggerel ornamentation." First quote, q. Robert Hewison, *Ruskin and Oxford: The Art of Education* (Oxford: Clarendon, 1996), 21; second quote, q. Tony Herbert and Kathryn Huggins, *The Decorative Tile in Architecture and Interiors* (London: Phaidon Press, 1995), 145.

45. Alexander Hunter, *Correspondence on the Subject of the Extension of Art Education in Different Parts of India* (Madras: Gantz Brothers [Adelphi Press], 1867), 12.

46. Baden Henry Baden-Powell, "On Some of the Difficulties of Art Manufactures," *Journal of Indian Art* 1, no. 5 (1886): 38.

47. Amin Jaffer, "Furniture in British India, 1750–1830" (PhD diss., V&A/RCA joint course in the history of design, June 19, 1995). Also see his *Furniture from British India and Ceylon: A Catalogue of the Collections in the Victoria and Albert Museum and the Peabody Essex Museum* (Salem, MA: Peabody Essex Museum, 2001).

48. Baden-Powell, "On Some of the Difficulties," 38.

49. See Gauri Viswanathan, *Masks of Conquest: Literary Study and British Rule in India* (New Delhi: Oxford University, 1998), 156. "The poor man's son by painstaking will for the most part be learned, when the gentleman's son will not take the pains to get it. Wherefore if the gentleman's son be apt to learning, let him be admitted; if not apt, let the poor man's child that is apt enter the room." Henry Cole, *The Functions of the Science and Art Department* (London: Chapman and Hall, 1857), 6–8.

50. *Report on Industrial Education. Part II: Proceedings of Conferences* (1903) [IOL: V/27/865/4, 8].

51. See Norma Evenson, "The Long Debate," in *The Indian Metropolis: A View from the West* (New Haven, CT: Yale University Press, 1989).

52. Baden-Powell, "On Some of the Difficulties of Art Manufactures," 38. In an 1894 conference on art education in India, similar sentiments were expressed: "It is the Indian craftsman himself who is hastening his own ruin; he accepts the suggestions and orders of all patrons, however crude they may be, and because he has evidence that European knowledge means *power* and *profit*, he thinks everything *European* must be good, or at all events will bring in money. You all have daily practical illustration of the truth of my statement. You know how difficult it is to get the artist to keep in the straight path of Oriental design; how, if your backs are turned for a moment, some objectionable European feature, good enough in its proper place, but wholly unsuitable and barbarous when applied to Oriental art, is introduced. It requires your constant vigilance to defeat this tendency. You know, moreover, how even the best men deteriorate, and scamp their work when left to their own devices. ... The Indian workman is peculiarly susceptible to such influences." *Proceedings of the Art Conference Held in the Technical Institute at Lahore on the 1st, 2nd, 3rd and 4th January 1894* (Calcutta: Govt. Central Printing Office, 1894) [IOL: DPI files], 12. All pagination to this document refers to IOL pagination.

53. H. Goodwyn (Bengal engineers), *A Lecture on the Union of Science, Industry and Art, with a View to the Formation of a School of Industrial-Art and Design, Delivered to the Bethune Society, 2 March 1854* (Calcutta: Thacker Spink, 1854), 21–22.

54. q. Mahrukh Tarapor, "John Lockwood Kipling and the Arts and Crafts Movement in India," *AA Files* 3 (January 1983), 20.

55. Frederic Salmon Growse, "The Art of '*Tár-Kashi*,' or Wire-Inlay, as Practised by the Carpenters of Mainpuri in the North-West Provinces," *Journal of Indian Art* 2, no. 22 (April 1888): 52–53.

56. Ibid., 53–54.

57. B.A. Gupte, honorary member of the Bombay Art Society, offered the following in 1902 as part of the proceedings of the Industrial Education Conference held in Nagpur: "The Native system of apprenticeship is immensely superior to the average Industrial School, which admits anybody and everybody without the hereditary aptitude of the Indian artisan, and it can be extended in practice under the supervision of a qualified European Director of Art whose expert suggestions would be invaluable. He will, of course, not interfere with the time honoured designs beyond advising when and where to apply them" [IOL: V/27/865/4, 139].

58. "Government School of Art, Report from June 1887 to January 1894," in *Proceedings of the Art Conference Held ... at Lahore.*

59. See Appendix F, "Mr. [John] Griffiths's Report on the Reay Art Workshops in the Jamsetji Jijibhoy School of Art," in Bombay DPI Annual Report, Maharasthra State Archives, N-3956/2.

60. Bhai Ram Singh, Kipling's trusted aide, had been deputed by the latter to build a room in Victoria's new palace at Osbourne. This fact of an Indian's running matters quite efficiently was the subject of some discomfort in the context of theories of "European supervision." An internal circular that discussed the question of replacing Kipling brings this up explicitly: "While holding ... that the Mayo School of Art is conceived on a grander scale than is called for by the requirements of the Province, the Lieutenant-Governor would not go so far as to say that it should be deprived of all European superintendence. It may be that a man like Bhai Ram Singh could be counted on to carry on the work if the School was made a branch of some institution embracing other objects as well, as contemplated by the Secretary of State; but we can scarcely reckon on getting Natives of this stamp; and for this and other reasons ... whether a school of this sort is to remain an independent institution or to become a branch of some larger institution, there ought to be one European teacher to preside over it." *Proceedings of the Art Conference Held ... at Lahore,* 703.

61. The conference thereby resolved to put pressure on the provincial education departments. *Proceedings of the Art Conference Held ... at Lahore,* 19.

62. John Griffiths, "Report Called in for Government Resolution in the Educational Department, No. 1957, 13th September 1892, on the Question of the Restoration and Maintenance of a Higher Standard in the Art Industries of the Country," reprinted in *Proceedings of the Art Conference Held ... at Lahore,* 29–30.

63. Ibid., 28–29.

64. Richard Redgrave, "Address," in *The Advantage of Teaching Elementary Drawing Concurrently with Writing as a Branch of National Education,* ed. DSA (London: Eyre and Spottiswoode, 1857), 9–10.

65. Hendley was a crucial colleague of Kipling in authoring the *Journal of Indian Art* and the designer, with Swinton Jacob, of the Albert Hall museum in Jaipur. The following is his presidential address to the Lahore conference: "If we wish to have new ideas and new manufactures, I would suggest that we should go further in search of them, and on the whole would prefer to seek fresh models from Byzantine or Moorish art—the parents of our Indo-Saracenic Schools—or from Hungary where are still to be found many ancient Oriental designs. The museum at Buda-Pesth, for example, will, I believe afford much that would be of value to us in India." *Proceedings of the Art Conference Held ... at Lahore,* 19.

66. Edmund Husserl, "The Origin of Geometry," in *Edmund Husserl's Origin of Geometry: An Introduction,* ed. Jacques Derrida (Lincoln: University of Nebraska Press, 1978), 172.

67. Immanuel Kant, *Critique of Pure Reason,* trans. and ed. Paul Guyer and Allen W. Wood (Cambridge: Cambridge University Press, 1997), 108.

68. Husserl, "The Origin of Geometry," 169.

69. Derrida, *Edmund Husserl's Origin of Geometry: An Introduction,* 148.

70. For Hegel, "shape" is the *external* form that receives the aesthetic projection onto the object: "But beauty can devolve only on the *shape* [e.a.], because this alone is the external appearance in which the objective idealism of life becomes for us an object of our perception and sensuous consideration. *Thinking* apprehends this idealism in its *Concept* and makes this Concept explicit in its universality, but the consideration of *beauty* concentrates on the reality in which the concept *appears.* And this reality is the external shape of the articulated organism." Georg Wilhelm Friedrich Hegel, *Aesthetics: Lectures on Fine Art,* vol. I, trans. T.M. Knox (Oxford: Oxford University Press, 1998), 124–25.

71. Husserl, "The Origin of Geometry," p.178.

72. DSA, *Introduction to the Drawing Book,* 37–38.

Chapter 4

1. Rohit Parihar, "Fettered Creativity; Convicts Bring Colour into Their Dour Lives by Weaving Exquisite Carpets," *India Today,* April 6, 1998.

2. "We know which places produced carpets, the circumstances under which they were made and in many instances the exact amounts produced and their values on the international market. Nevertheless, we have been given only the slightest clues as to the different designs woven in these many jails … and, given [any] group of such carpets … almost no way of distinguishing one centre of manufacturing from another." Ian Bennett, "Introduction," in *Jail Birds, An Exhibition of 19th Century Indian Carpets Held at the Mall Galleries. The Mall, London, SW1. From 24th to 28th March, 1987,* comp. Kennedy Carpets (London: Springbourne Press, 1987), 7.

3. Caspar Purdon Clarke, in *Proceedings of the Department of Revenue and Agriculture* (March 1901): 23–24 [IOL:P 6138].

4. Malcolm Baker, "A Glory to the Museum: The Casting of the Pórtico de la Gloria," in *Victoria and Albert Museum Album* I (London: V&A, 1982). I am grateful to Diane Bilbey at the Sculpture Department, V&A, for both this reference and others detailing out the history of the casts section.

5. HCM XIV.

6. One of the interesting segues from this notion can be seen in the DSA's quintessentially Utilitarian strategy toward preservation. In distinct contrast to the depredations of the Napoleonic Empire across the cultural landscape of Europe and Egypt, the DSA's (at least) avowed impetus toward decentralization also laid the cultural provenance of the art object in its national setting. In the DSA's 1869 *Inventory* of reproductional desiderata, Cole writes, "In like manner most of the art museums of the continents contain similar works. … Such objects must always remain, permanently, as national treasures of the respective countries." DSA, *Inventory of the Electrotype Reproductions of Objects of Art, Selected from the SKM, Continental Museums, and Various Other Public and Private Collections. Produced for the Use of Schools of Art, for Prizes, and Generally for Public Instruction* (London: Eyre and Spottiswoode for HMSO, 1869), 23. Even if this strategy is spelled out primarily out of economic considerations, one of its indirect effects was to be felt (or not felt), as we shall see, in India, whose monuments were mostly preserved in place, spared the normal archaeological practice of removal to Europe. "In the matter of Provincial or Colonial Museums, the limited pecuniary resources of such Institutions, and the difficulties in their way in regard to the proper selection and acquisition of original specimens, point conclusively in the direction of copies and reproductions, and indicate that the staple of these Collections must in future mainly consist of such matter." VAA: File Ed. 84, p. 166.

7. The DSA acquired its artistic copies from electrotyping companies far and wide on the Continent: Brucciani and Franchi in London, Brunn in Munich, Von Lutzon in Vienna, Martinelli in Athens, and Dielitz in Berlin. See VAA: File Ed. 84, p. 169. In addition to this, it was the DSA aficionado, designer, and friend of Cole, Herbert Minton, whose interest in a technology capable of reproducing colored tile patterns (thus saving his agents the physical effort of lugging actual tile samples across the country) fostered significant improvements in chromolithography.

8. See Mark Haworth-Booth, *Photography; An Independent Art: Photographs from the Victoria and Albert Museum 1839–1996* (Princeton, NJ: Princeton University Press, 1997), for a comprehensive account of the V&A's substantial photography collection.

9. Ray Desmond, *Victorian India in Focus* (London: HMSO, 1982).

10. HCM XIV.

11. Cole writes, in a letter marked "private," dated June 19, 1868, "If we had wanted architectural casts from Spain, Turkey or Norway, we should simply have sent a competent person to the country [with] proper workmen and should have got what we wanted by this time: but with antique Casts in the Queen's dominions in India we write & write and get no further than words and even those with difficulty and delay … no head or authority is appointed to see what is done, the Governor General [of Bombay] at best cares nothing for the arts and as he said would prefer to spend the money in a canal than recording 'tumble-down' old buildings. Really the incidents are good enough for a farce. … We have just written again to the India Office to repeat the suggestion about a joint Committee to settle some plan of action. If this be impossible, it will be best to say that so and to tell us we must get casts from India ourselves as we can & at our own cost just as we should do in any foreign country." HCC I.

12. Mitra's work was to become the subject of his well-known book on Indian antiquity. See Rajendra Lala Mitra, *The Antiquities of Orissa* (1875) (2nd repr., Calcutta: Indian Studies, 1962).

13. Henry Cole, "On the International Results of the Exhibition of 1851," in *Lectures on the Results of the Great Exhibition of 1851, Delivered before the Society of Arts, Manufactures and Commerce,* vol. I (London: David Bogue, 1853), 432.

14. PP-1881 3-VIII: 301.

15. Appendix to the *Report of the Proceedings of the Designs Office from the 1st July 1829 to the 31st December 1852, Furnished in Conformity with the Directions of the Lords of the Committee of Privy Council for Trade.*

16. Thomas Webster, *On the Amendment of the Law and Practice of Letters Patent for Inventions* (London: Chapman and Hall, 1851), 29.

17. "Industry of All Nations; Be Just Before You Are Generous," handbill in the personal collection of Charles Wentworth Dilke; NAL.

18. Kenneth Frampton, "Industrialization and the Crisis in Architecture," *Oppositions* 1 (September 1973): 67.

19. "Circumstances now connected with the Exhibition of the Works of Industry of all Nations, to take place in 1851, render the discussion inevitable. And it is to prepare for this discussion that the Committee consider that the present attempt to define the principles of jurisprudence relative to invention may have some practical use." Society of Arts, *First Report from the Committee on Legislative Recognition of the Rights of Inventors* (London: Chapman and Hall, 1850), 17.

20. HCD 1850.

21. John Stuart Mill, "On Liberty," in *On Liberty and Utilitarianism* (New York: Bantam Books, 1994), 70–71.

22. For more qualified histories of IPR in this period, I point the reader toward H.I. Dutton's work on patenting activity before 1851, and Maureen Coulter's book on the period after 1851. Note that both these authors take 1851 as their cutoff date. H.I. Dutton, *The Patent System and Inventive Activity during the Industrial Revolution, 1750–1852* (Manchester, UK: Manchester University Press, 1984); and Maureen Coulter, *Property in Ideas: The Patent Question in Mid-Victorian Britain* (Kirkville, MI: Thomas Jefferson University Press, 1991).

23. Society of Arts, *First Report from the Committee on Legislative Recognition of the Rights of Inventors,* 15, 23.

24. Society of Arts, *Rights of Inventors: Second Report from the Committee on Legislative Recognition of the Rights of Inventors* (London: Chapman and Hall, 1851), 10.

25. See Henry Cole, *Fifty Years of Public Works of Sir Henry Cole, Accounted for in His Deeds, Speeches and Writings,* vol. I (London: George Bell and Sons, 1884), 37.

26. See John Easton, *Postage Stamps in the Making* (London: Faber and Faber, 1949), 23 (first draft by F.J. Melville).

27. q. Ibid., 23.

28. See the *London and Westminster Journal,* no. 65 (1840).

29. Henry Cole, *The Passion of Our Lord Jesus Christ, Portrayed by Albert [sic] Dürer* (London: Joseph Cundall, July 1844).

30. See Alexander Welsh, *From Copyright to Copperfield: The Identity of Dickens* (Cambridge, MA: Harvard University Press, 1987), 32.

31. Charles Dickens, "A Poor Man's Tale of a Patent," *Household Words,* October 19, 1850.

32. PP-1864 XII: 134.

33. PP-1864 XII: 138.

34. Henry Cole, testimony in PP-1864 XII: 138.

35. William Hawes [chairman, Council of the Society for Arts], *On the Economical Effects of the Patent Laws: A Paper Read before the National Association for the Promotion of Social Science at Edinburgh, on Friday, the 9th October, 1863* (London: Victoria Press, 1863).

36. F. Marcus Arman, "Anti-Fraud Devices of 1840," in *Stamp Collecting,* February 10, 1967.

37. Society of Arts, *Rights of Inventors: Second Report,* 11.

38. John Stuart Mill, "Utilitarianism," in *On Liberty and Utilitarianism,* 208.

39. James Emerson Tennent, *A Treatise on the Copyright of Designs for Printed Fabrics; with Considerations on the Necessity of Its Extension: and Copious Notices of the State of Calico*

Printing in Belgium, Germany, and the States of the Prussian Commercial League (London: Smith, Elder, 1841), 112.

40. The relevant quote was used earlier; Mill, "On Liberty," 71.
41. Karl Marx, "Wage Labor and Capital," (1849) in *Selected Writings,* ed. David McLellan (New York: Oxford University Press, 1977).
42. Karl Marx, "The Eighteenth Brumaire of Louis Bonaparte," in *Surveys from Exile: Political Writings,* vol. 2 (New York: Penguin Classics, 1992), 239.
43. Gayatri Chakravorty Spivak, "Can the Subaltern Speak?" in *Marxism and the Interpretation of Culture,* ed. Cary Nelson and Lawrence Grossberg (Urbana: University of Illinois Press, 1988), 276.
44. Hillel Schwartz, *The Culture of the Copy: Striking Likenesses, Unreasonable Facsimiles* (New Haven, CT: Yale University Press, 1996).
45. Kipling used this pseudonym in his articles written in the *Civil and Military Gazette,* published from Lahore.
46. Jacques Derrida, *Limited Inc.* (Evanston, IL: Northwestern University Press, 1988), 57.
47. Andrew Saint, "The Architect as Professional: Britain in the Nineteenth Century," in *The Image of the Architect* (New Haven, CT: Yale University Press, 1983).
48. John Summerson, *The London Building World of the Eighteen-Sixties* (London: Thames & Hudson, 1973),
49. Charles Dickens, *Martin Chuzzlewit* (New York: Alfred Knopf, 1994), 13. Dickens's eponymous hero Martin Chuzzlewit spends all of one week in being disillusioned of his ambition to be an architect and then runs off to the United States to seek a better fortune.
50. Angela Mace, *The Royal Institute of British Architects: A Guide to Its Archive and History* (London: Mansell, 1986), xvi.
51. James Fergusson, "A Lecture on Architecture to the Royal Engineers," in the *Builder,* February 7, 1863.
52. RIBA, *Early Committee Minutes* [26.1.1847–27.4.1869], 208–10. Also see *Special Committee Minutes* [7.2.1868–18.4.1877], 11–12, 388, 395–96. For subsequent events relating to copyright during the rest of the century, see *Special Committee Minutes* [12.3.1886–15.6.1889], 111–14, 140–41. RIBA archives, London.
53. PP-1862 I: 485.
54. PP-1878 XXIV: 234.
55. Copyrights were granted for related components of the building industry, for instance, designs for ceramic and terra-cotta tiles, furniture, and so on. In one case, an applicant was granted copyright for a new kind of building foundation, clearly more the province of technology than "nonuseful ornament."
56. James Fergusson, *Indian Architecture: Extract from … a Meeting Held at the Society of Arts, on Wednesday, 19th of December, 1866* (London: John Murray, 1867), 14.
57. "[If the Gothic style is to be emulated], it must be by free thought, not by servile copying." James Fergusson, *A History of Architecture in All Countries, from the Earliest Times to the Present Day,* vol. I (New York: Dodd, Mead, 1885), xv.
58. From the *Builder,* August 5, 1865. V&A archive file, "Press Cuttings" titled "Paris Exhibition, 1867" in 3 vols., July 1863–July 1867.
59. Theodore C. Hope, *The Architecture of Ahmedabad, Capital of Goozerat. Photographed by Col. Biggs, with an Historical and Descriptive Sketch by T.C. Hope, Bombay Civil Service, and Architectural Notes by James Fergusson* (London: John Murray, 1866).
60. The *Builder* XXV, no. 1261, April 6, 1867.
61. A Hindustani word, meaning artisan, corrupted from the English *maestro* (pl. *maestri*).
62. On the government's side, the deliberation centered precisely on its jurisdiction in terms of being able to determine the terms of novelty: "It has, however, been suggested to the Government of India that it is doubtful whether, in making such enquiries into the novelty of an alleged invention, the Executive Department is not in reality traveling beyond the province assigned to it in the patents act." IOL: Home, Revenue and Agricultural Department Proceedings, July 1883.
63. IOL: Home, Revenue and Agricultural Department Proceedings, July 1883. This case is not unique in the IPR annals of rural India. In the case of Rajaram Dass, iron founder, native of North Bantrah in the district of Howrah, another claimant for a sugar mill in 1882, a similar reason was given for rejection ("time immemorial" is here a well-used term in common

law): "Sugarcane rollers made of wood have been in use in India from time immemorial. ... The conclusion I arrive at is that sugarcane rollers, for which the petitioner seeks a patent, is not a patentable article in itself, it having been used in wood and iron for years in India, and that *it is public property.* Therefore [it] cannot be considered a novelty."

64. Walter Benjamin, "The Work of Art in the Age of Its Reproducibility," in *Selected Works* 3, 1935–38 (Cambridge, MA: Belknap Press, 2002), 102.

65. Siegfried Giedion, *Mechanization Takes Command: A Contribution to Anonymous History* (New York: Oxford University Press, 1948), 40–41.

66. Adrian Rifkin reaches a similar conclusion in his account of the early history of the Schools of Design: "The 'auratic' value of great art will find its recognition and effect precisely in the process of its mass reproduction—a process that itself will increase the productive forces." Adrian Rifkin, "Success Disavowed: The Schools of Design in Mid-Nineteenth-Century Britain (an Allegory)," in *Journal of Design History* 1, no. 2 (1988): 97.

67. A full treatment of Giedion's collection of U.S. Patent Office texts and their subsequent percolation into his *Mechanization Takes Command: A Contribution to Anonymous History* of 1948 is available in Sokratis Georgiadis, "Siegfried Giedion: Patents in Historical Investigation," *Rassegna,* no. 46 (June 1991), special issue on patents and design.

68. Emphasis added. Thomas Webster, *On the Amendment of the Law,* 4.

Chapter 5

1. H. Maxwell-Lefroy and E.C. Ansorge, *Report on an Inquiry into the Silk Industry in India,* vol. 1 of 3 (Calcutta: Superintendent Government Printing, 1917), 167.

2. Marx, "The Division of Labour and Manufacture," in *Capital* (New York: Penguin Classics, 1990), 459–60.

3. *Report of the Cottage Industries Sub-committee, United Provinces* (Allahabad: Superintendent, Printing and Stationery, United Provinces, 1950).

4. Vijay Krishna, "Living Weavers at Work," in *Banaras Brocades,* ed. Ajit Mookerjee (New Delhi: Crafts Museum, 1966), 76.

5. William J. Ashworth, "Memory, Efficiency, and Symbolic Analysis: Charles Babbage, John Herschel, and the Industrial Mind," *Isis* 87, no. 4 (1996): 637.

6. Charles Babbage, "On the Application of Machinery to the Purpose of Calculating and Printing Mathematical Tables: A Letter to Sir Humphry [*sic*] Davy," in *The Difference Engine and Table Making,* vol. 2, *The Works of Charles Babbage,* ed. Martin Campbell-Kelly (London: William Pickering, 1989).

7. These included the "Taylor's logarithms" computed according to the "calculus of finite differences," involving the well-known Taylor expansion, devised by the mathematician Brook Taylor in 1715.

8. Luigi Frederico Menabrea, "Sketch of the Analytical Engine Invented by Charles Babbage from the *Bibliothèque Universelle de Genève,* October, 1842, No. 82," in *Scientific Memoirs,* trans., with notes, Ada Augusta Lovelace, September 1843, republished on http://www.fourmilab.ch/babbage/sketch.html.

9. The passage ties Babbage's conception to antecedents as far back as Descartes's materialist separation of the "indivisible" mind from the "divisible" and mechanical body, and the views forwarded by Julien Offray de la Mettrie in his 1747 essay "Machine Man," which further elaborated the Cartesian image of the body as a wound-up clock. See René Descartes, "Sixth Meditation: The Existence of Material Things, and the Real Distinction between Mind and Body," in *Meditations on First Philosophy* (Cambridge: Cambridge University Press, 1996); and Julien Offray de la Mettrie, "Machine Man," in *Machine Man and Other Writings* (Cambridge: Cambridge University Press, 1996).

10. Babbage wrote a book on the topic of insurance rates after being invited by investors to organize a life insurance company, which eventually failed to take off. Charles Babbage, *A Comparative View of the Various Institutions for the Assurance of Lives,* vol. 6, *The Works of Charles Babbage.*

11. It must be remembered here that logarithmic tables simplify calculation by converting all numbers as powers of 10, rendering operations of multiplication and division into addition and subtraction, on the principles given here: $10^a \times 10^b = 10^{a+b} 10^a \div 10^b = 10^{a-b}$, and so on.

12. q. Margaret Bradley, *A Career Biography of Gaspard Clair François Marie Riche De Prony, Bridge Builder, Educator and Scientist* (Lewiston: Edwin Mellen Press, 1998), 17.

13. Charles Babbage, *The Economy of Machinery and Manufactures* (1832), vol. 8, *The Works of Charles Babbage*.

14. Andrew Ure, *Philosophy of Manufactures, or an Exposition of the Scientific, Moral, and Commercial Economy of the Factory System of Great Britain* (1835) (New York: Burt Frankling, 1969).

15. Marx's reading of Babbage and Ure is available in his notes for *Capital*—specifically, Part Four on "Relative Surplus Value" in Notebook XX—later published in the MECW as his *Economic Manuscripts of 1861–63*. See MECW, vols. 30 and 33. The passages here are taken from the Marx-Engels Internet Archive, http://www.marxists.org/archive/marx/works/1861/economic/index.htm.

16. The relevant paragraph, which reads differently in English in the MECW, because of its translation *back* from the German, is from chapter 5, "Laws of Variation," Charles Darwin, *The Origin of Species, by Means of Natural Selection, or the Preservation of Favoured Races in the Struggle for Life* (London: John Murray, 1859), 149.

17. Marx, "Relative Surplus Value."

18. Ibid.

19. William J. Ashworth, in addition to other historians of science, has questioned this progressivist narrative, suggesting that the superiority attributed to Babbage's faction—the "analytics" in nineteenth-century British intellectual history—draws from the triumphalism of industrial society rather than a supplantation based on intellectual merits alone. "Through a combination of Newtonian bigotry and French prejudice, so the traditional tale goes, Cambridge had sunk by the second half of the eighteenth century into what Joseph Priestley famously described as a 'stagnant pool.' The mathematics taught there was fashioned for an environment designed to produce clergymen for the church, which, in turn was intrinsically concerned with the preservation of the political alliance between the church and the state. [Babbage and Herschel's Analytical Society of 1812] has been the source for a wealth of secondary material that has considered, variously, the society's place in the reform of English mathematics and the Cambridge Tripos. ... [What has been neglected is] that the really important, and hitherto neglected, aspect of the analyticals' work is their link with industry and its accompanying values of efficiency and power." The argument in the following couple of passages is drawn substantially from Ashworth. William J. Ashworth, "Memory, Efficiency, and Symbolic Analysis: Charles Babbage, John Herschel, and the Industrial Mind," *Isis* 87, no. 4 (1996).

20. Karl Marx, *Mathematical Manuscripts of Karl Marx* (London: New Park Publications, 1983), 3.

21. Ashworth, "Memory, Efficiency, and Symbolic Analysis," 640.

22. For instance, see Charles Babbage, "Observations on the Analogy Which Subsists between the Calculus of Functions and Other Branches of Analysis," in *Philosophical Transactions of the Royal Society of London* (1817), vol. 107. In addition, see "On a Method of Expressing by Signs the Action of Machinery," "Laws of Mechanical Notation," *The Analytical Engine and Mechanical Notation*, in *The Works of Charles Babbage*.

23. The passage quoted is taken from Note A of Lovelace's many notes published, the contents of which exceed by far Menabrea's essay in length, explanatory strength, and polemic argument. Menabrea, "Sketch of the Analytical Engine."

24. This last aspect is spelled out not so much by Lovelace as by a much later presentation given by Babbage's son, Herschel P. Babbage: "This brings me to the second great distinguishing feature of the engine, the principle of 'Chain.' This enables us to deal mechanically with any single combination which may occur out of many possible, and thus to be ready for any or every contingency which may arise." Babbage, *The Analytical Engine and Mechanical Notation*.

25. Ada Augusta Lovelace, in Menabrea, "Sketch of the Analytical Engine."

26. Thomas R. Ashenhurst, *A Practical Treatise on Weaving and Design of Textile Fabrics, with Chapters on the Principles of Construction of the Loom, Calculations and Colour* (Huddersfield: J. Broadbent, 1879, 1893), 59.

27. Ibid., 159.

28. See Augustin Cournot, *Researches into the Mathematical Principles of the Theory of Wealth* (1838), Trans. Nathaniel T. Bacon (New York: Augustus M. Kelley, 1971).

29. Charles Babbage, *The Exposition of 1851*, vol. 10, *The Works of Charles Babbage*, 5–6.
30. I am grateful to Prof. Dipak Malik of Benares Hindu University and the late Dr. Som Majumdar for their generous assistance during two all-too-short research stints in Benares.
31. "The mounting surplus of labour was reinforced by poor efforts and private institutions towards enhancing human and non-human capital. The history of public investment in colonial India is a history of unrelentingly conservative fiscalism. Despite the sustained pressure of opinion and examples of other countries urging a more activist State, there are few instances in which the government made unorthodox long-term expenditure commitments, and carried them through by innovations in the budget. The result was, except in pockets, supplementary inputs to an industrialization process—chiefly formal credit and education—changed sluggishly. ... In British India, this role was marginal in contrast with Britain itself." Tirthankar Roy, *Traditional Industry in the Economy of Colonial India*, (Cambridge: Cambridge University Press, 1999), 59.
32 See Abdullah Yusuf Ali, *A Monograph on Silk Fabrics Produced in the North-Western Provinces and Oudh* (Allahabad: N.W. Provinces and Oudh Govt. Press, 1900), 50, 57.
33. Ibid., 65.
34. See A.C. Chatterjee, *Notes on the Industries of the United Provinces* (Allahabad: Superintendent Government Press, United Provinces, 1908); *Report of the Cottage Industries Sub-committee, United Provinces* (1950); Anand Krishna, "Historical Background," and "Living Weavers at Work," in *Banaras Brocades*, ed. Ajit Mookerjee (1966); Bijoy Chandra Mohanty, *Brocaded Fabrics of India* (Ahmedabad: Calico Museum of Textiles, 1984); Nita Kumar, *The Artisans of Banaras: Popular Culture and Identity, 1880–1986* (New Delhi: Orient Longman Limited, 1988, 1995). Abdul Bismillah's novel *Jhini Jhini Bini Chadariya* is significant in that it narrates significant anthropological observation as literature. Abdul Bismillah, *Jhini Jhini Bini Chadariya* (New Delhi: Rajkamal Paperbacks, 1987, 1998); translated into English as *The Song of the Loom*, trans. Rashmi Govind (Madras: Macmillan India, 1996). Most important, see "The Informal Sector Workers in Varanasi," special issue, *Labour File* (January–February 2003).
35. One informant, however, interjected strongly that this was not the case in *contractual* arrangements.
36. "[Department] I: *Means of production*: commodities that possess a form in which they either have to enter productive consumption, or at least can enter this. [Department] II. *Means of consumption*: commodities that possess a form in which they enter the individual consumption of the capitalist and working classes." Karl Marx, *Capital*, Vol. II (New York: Penguin, 1992), p. 471. For a further Marxist elaboration of this portion of *Capital*, see Rosa Luxembourg, *The Accumulation of Capital* (New York: Routledge and Kegan Paul, 1951).
37. Malcom McCullough, *Abstracting Craft: The Practised Digital Hand* (Cambridge, MA: MIT Press, 1998), 63, 83.
38. Samuel Butler, *Erewhon* (London: Penguin Books, 1985), 210–11.
39. See Anson Rabinbach, *The Human Motor: Energy, Fatigue and the Origins of Modernity* (Berkeley: University of California Press, 1992); Frederic L. Holmes and Kathryn M. Olesko, "The Images of Precision: Helmholtz and the Graphical Method in Physiology," in *The Values of Precision*, ed. M. Norton Wise (Princeton, NJ: Princeton University Press, 1995).
40. Michel Serres, "It Was before the (World-) Exhibition," in *The Bachelor Machines*, Exhibition Volume, ed. Jean Clair and Harald Szeemann (Venice: Fantonigrafica, 1975), 67.
41. Donna Haraway, "A Cyborg Manifesto: Science, Technology, and Socialist-Feminism in the Late Twentieth Century," in *Simians, Cyborgs, and Women: The Reinvention of Nature* (New York: Routledge, 1991).
42. Ibid., 170.
43. Sadie Plant, *Zeros + Ones: Digital Women + The New Technoculture* (New York: Doubleday, 1997).
44. Letter to Anne Millbanke, Lovelace's mother, 1845, cited from Betty Alexandra Toole, ed., *Ada, the Enchantress of Numbers: A Selection from the Letters of Lord Byron's Daughter and Her Description of the First Computer* (Mill Valley, CA: Strawberry Press, 1992), 319.
45. Sadie Plant, *Zeros + Ones*.

46. Charles Shepherdson, *Vital Signs: Nature, Culture, Psychoanalysis* (New York: Routledge, 2000), 5.

47. Ibid., 2.

48. Sigmund Freud, "Femininity," in *New Introductory Lectures on Psycho-Analysis* (New York: W.W. Norton, 1989), 164.

49. "If weaving was to count as an achievement, it was not even one of women's own. Their work is not original or creative: both the women and their cloths are simply copying the matted tangles of pubic hair. ... Weaving is an automatic imitation of some bodily function already beyond the weaver's control. She is bound to weave a costume for the masquerade: she is an actress, a mimic, an impersonator, with no authenticity underneath it all." Sadie Plant, *Zeros + Ones*, 24.

50. See Jacques Donzelot, *The Policing of Families,* trans. Robert Hurley (Baltimore: Johns Hopkins University Press, 1979); Gilles Deleuze and Felix Guattari, *The Anti-Oedipus: Capitalism and Schizophrenia,* trans. Robert Hurley et al. (Minneapolis: University of Minnesota Press, 1983).

51. "Freud, like Keynes, we said. Perhaps there is something more than a simile in this juxtaposition. Keynes theorized about the characteristic ways in which Western societies combined the social and the economic. He indicated the means by which they could be functionally adjusted, showing how the distribution of social subsidies could be organized in a way that renewed consumption would ensue, production would be stimulated, and economic crises as well as the social ills they engendered would be averted. He managed to broaden the economic sphere precisely where its laws seemed to be swept aside by chance, giving way to insouciance, suffering, and revolt." Donzelot, *The Policing of Families,* 231.

52. Friedrich Engels, *The Origin of the Family, Private Property and the State* (New York: Penguin, 1986).

53. Gayatri Chakravorty Spivak, *Death of a Discipline* (Cambridge, MA: Harvard University Press, 2003), 14.

54. "The next round of East–West tension will be fought over this question: whether democracy promotes or erodes social stability; whether free speech is worth the cultural trash it also produces; whether the health of a collective matters more than the unfettered freedom of the individual. To the West this authoritarianism seems a temporary aberration, a deviation from the norm; but it is more likely that a new norm is being synthesized in Singapore: a hard-core Confucian shamelessness, a kind of ultimate power of efficiency that will fuel Asian modernization." See Rem Koolhaas, "Singapore Songlines," in *S, M, L, XL* (New York: Monacelli Press, 1995), 1017.

55. See Swasti Mitter, *Women Encounter Technology* (London: Routledge, 1995).

56. Kenneth Frampton, *Modern Architecture: A Critical History* (New York: Thames and Hudons, 1987), 126.

57. Thomas Holbein Hendley, "Address of the President of the Art Conference Held at Lahore, January 1, 1894," in *Proceedings of the Art Conference Held in the Technical Institute at Lahore on the 1st, 2nd, 3rd, and 4th of January 1894* (Calcutta: Govt. Central Printing Office, 1894), 19.

58. "I am prepared to undertake, as a portion of my official duties in connection with the Indian Section of the Victoria and Albert Museum, to select, from our large store of Persian and Indian designs, patterns of the best periods and to send them to India with the necessary technical directions for their proper reproduction. Care will be taken to strictly keep within commercial bounds, and although a high standard of design and colouring will be tried for, no unnecessary fineness in the weaving counts will be used to increase the expense." Caspar Purdon Clarke, in *Proceedings of the Department of Revenue and Agriculture* (March 1901) [IOL: P/6138], 23–24.

59. Baden-Powell, "On Some of the Difficulties of Art Manufactures," p.37.

60. See Wise, *The Values of Precision.*

61. For a significant study of the manner in which the architectural interior of the factory affected work practices in different cultural contexts, see Richard Biernacki. *The Fabrication of Labour; Germany and Britain, 1604-1914* (Berkeley: University of California Press, 1995).

62. Baden Henry Baden-Powell, "On Some of the Difficulties of Art Manufactures," *Journal of Indian Art* 1, no. 5 (1886): 37.

63. " 'This material [mosaic] is found to have many advantages over the ordinary tile pavement, and is being extensively used in the South Kensington Museum, where the name *Opus Criminale* has been applied to it. It is composed of fragments of refuse marble, such as is thrown aside in marble work. The mode of manufacture is as follows: The Pattern which it is intended to produce, is traced on a board, or on paper placed on a table, and enclosed within a frame. It is found that, after a little instruction, a woman can perform each of these stages of the manufacture at the following rates: Setting: .99 ft. per diem / Cementing: 9.44 ft. per diem / Facing: 1.80 ft. per diem. The preparation of the patterns is of course the work of a foreman or instructor, and the designs may be furnished by an artist.' No doubt Henry Cole found the lady felons much cheaper than Minton or Powell." Henry Cole, quoted in John Physick, *The Victoria and Albert Museum: The History of Its Building* (London: V&A, 1975), 69.

64. The Jabalpur School of Industry was established in 1837 by Captain Charles Brown under the direction of Colonel Sleeman. Sleeman set out the guiding aims of the school in a letter dated March 7, 1837: "With regard to [the] proposal for establishing the approvers in villages and in agricultural pursuits, I am of opinion that they should never be relieved from the strict surveillance or confinement in which they are now employed, and that the only way in which they can ever be safely employed is where such surveillance can be provided, such as manufactures requiring the application of manual labour in concentrated numbers. Employed in villages … , they would assuredly either follow their old trade of murder themselves, or teach others to follow it. … If we could establish a kind of Manufactory for them, or find any one willing to receive them, it would be the best mode of providing for them." See "Papers Regarding the Jubbulpore School of Industry," in *Selections from the Records of the Government of India (Foreign Dept.)* (Calcutta: Thomas Jones, Calcutta Gazette Office, 1856), 2.

65. Kidderminster carpets were a multipurpose, reversible, flat weave carpet popular from the eighteenth century to the twentieth century. The carpets had no pile, and the pattern was shown in opposing colors on both faces, making it possible to turn the carpet over when one side was worn or soiled.

66. "Papers Regarding the Jubbulpore School of Industry," 17–18.

67. [Alex Hunter], *Reports and Proceedings of the Committee of the Madras School of Industrial Arts, Established May 1860* (Madras: Messrs. Pharaoh [Atheneum Press], 1853), 29–30.

68. J.A. Crawford and J.M. Downleans, *[Report of the] Bengal Agricultural Exhibition* [IOL: India Public] (July 1864), 659.

69. IOL: India: Judicial files. P/206/65, 657–58 (emphasis mine). By 1860 convicts in Moulmein jails were occupied in the following trades, all of which substituted government spending in that sector: writers, cooks, sweepers, barbers, dhobies (launderers), hospital servants, cleaners of arms, painters, blacksmiths, carpenters, rattaners, basket makers, rope makers, soorkey pounders, gunny makers, chucklers, weavers, tailors, brick makers, jute collectors, masons, coolies, stone breakers, road makers, peons, cart drivers, marine storekeepers, and woodcutters.

70. Ian Bennett, *Jail Birds, An Exhibition of 19th Century Indian Carpets Held at the Mall Galleries. The Mall, London, SW1. From 24th to 28th March, 1987,* comp. Kennedy Carpets (London: Springbourne Press, 1987), 7.

71. L.H. Marshall Upshon, *Manual of Jail Industries, Compiled for Use in the Madras Jail Department* (Madras: Superintendent, Government Press, 1931), 7–9.

72. For a concise treatment of this debate, see Padmini Swaminathan, "Prison as Factory: A Study of Jail Manufactures in the Madras Presidency," *Studies in History* 11, no. 1 (1995).

73. For instance, the Madras School of Art and Industry was the primary institution which, under the mantle of its metal-working department, introduced the manufacture and use of aluminium articles into the Indian market. By 1902, the school was supplying not only military needs but catering to the increased domestic use of aluminium articles as well. However, private industries entering the market such as the Indian Aluminium Company (Limited) immediately saw the substantial position of the school in the incipient market as a "injurious" to their interests, even though the school was instrumental in introducing the technology. Letters written between government and private concerns directly refer to the legislative history regarding prison manufactures as the economic precedent for their case. See *Proceedings, Deptt. of Revenue and Agriculture*, October, 1901, IOL: P/6138 and January, 1902, IOL: P/6368.

Chapter 6

1. Henceforth Congress, or INC.
2. A. Moin Zaidi and Shaheda Zaidi, *The Encyclopaedia of Indian National Congress*, vol. 4 (1901–1905) (New Delhi: S. Chand, 1976), 92–109.
3. INC, *Detailed Report of the Proceedings of the Seventeenth Indian National Congress, Held at Calcutta, on the 26th, 27th, & 28th December, 1901* (Bombay: Commercial Press, 1902), 22.
4. Omkar Goswami, "*Sahibs, Babus,* and *Banias:* Changes in Industrial Control in Eastern India, 1918–50," in *Entrepreneurship and Industry in India, 1800–1947*, ed. Rajat Kanta Ray (Delhi: Oxford University Press, 1992).
5. Aditya Mukherjee, "The Freedom Struggle and Indian Business," in *Footprints of Enterprise: Indian Business through the Ages*, ed. Federation of Indian Chambers of Commerce and Industry (New Delhi: Oxford University Press, 1999), 138.
6. Omkar Goswami, "*Sahibs, Babus,* and *Banias,*" 228.
7. See David Hardiman, "The Indian 'Faction': A Political Theory Examined," in *Subaltern Studies*, vol. 1 (New Delhi: Oxford University Press, 1982).
8. Mohandas Karamchand Gandhi, *An Autobiography, or the Story of My Experiments with Truth* (Ahmedabad: Navjivan Publishing House, 1927, 1997), 191.
9. See Joseph Alter, "Gandhi's Body, Gandhi's Truth: Nonviolence and the Biomoral Imperative of Public Health," *Journal of Asian Studies* 55, no. 2 (1996): 301–22.
10. See Benjamin Zachariah, "The Debate on Gandhian Ideas", in *Developing India: An Intellectual and Social History* (New Delhi: Oxford University Press, 2005).
11. Chimen Abramsky and Henry Collins, *Karl Marx and the British Labour Movement* (New York: St. Martin's Press, 1965).
12. See George Watt, *A Dictionary of the Economic Products of India*, vols. 1–6 (Calcutta: Superintendent, Government Printing, 1889).
13. Peter Stallybrass and Allon White, "The Fair, the Pig, Authorship," in *The Politics and Poetics of Transgression* (London: Methuen, 1986), 34.
14. C. Planck, *Sanitary Arrangements at the Gurhmooktessur Fair of 1868*, in *Selections from the Records of the Government of the North-Western Provinces*, 2nd series, 2–3.
15. *Reports on Trade Routes and Fairs on the Northern Frontiers of India; Presented to Both Houses of Parliament by Command of Her Majesty* (London: Eyre and Spottiswoode, 1874).
16. See Henry Cole, *A Special Report on the Annual International Exhibition of the Years 1871, 1872, 1873, & 1874 … Presented by the Commissioners for the Exhibition of 1851* (London: Eyre and Spottiswoode, 1876).
17. "Memorial from the Secretary for the Society for the Encouragement of Arts, Manufactures, and Commerce, to the Secretary of State for India," in *Reports on Trade Routes.*
18. Ibid., 38.
19. Clarke is referring here to the extent of official intervention rather than actual duration of the fair, which continued for a few days.
20. Theodore C. Hope, *Report on the Broach Exhibition, 1868–1869* (Bombay: Education Society's Press, 1869), 52.
21. *Lahore Chronicle,* January 13, 1864, 28.
22. q. Caldwell Lipsett, *Lord Curzon in India, 1898–1903* (London: R.A. Everett, 1903), 127.
23. The artisan could be expected to undergo a corresponding self-transformation, "the iron smiths of Nagpore and the surrounding Districts could examine the massive iron Machinery, the iron fountains, the iron gates manufactured by European workmen. These cutlers could observe the make and finish of the English cutlery and carpentry tools. … Workers in brass could compare their things with the best brass articles from other districts. Stone carvers of Chandah and Nagpore could see how their handiwork, good as it might be, was excelled by the Agra stone cutting [… and so on]." *Report of the Nagpore Exhibition of Arts, Manufacture and Produce* (Nagpore: [Central Provinces Printing Press], 1865), 24–25.
24. Notes by Kipling's daughter, Mrs. Fleming. Box 3/19. Kipling Archives, University of Sussex Library.
25. Gandhi, *An Autobiography,* 192–93.

26. W.S. Caine, *Picturesque India: A Handbook for European Travellers* (1898) (New Delhi: Neeraj Publishing House, 1982), xliii, xliv.

27. Paul Greenhalgh, "Education, Entertainment and Politics: Lessons from the Great International Exhibitions," in *The New Museology*, ed. Peter Vergo (London: Reaktion Books, 1989).

28. Gandhi, *An Autobiography,* 250.

29. "The handloom weaving [sic] is in a dying condition. Everyone admits that whatever may be the future of the mill industry, the handlooms ought not to be allowed to perish. ... The object of the Ashram, therefore is for every inmate to learn hand-weaving and thus study at first hand the secrets and defects of the art and then find out the means of saving the industry. ... The enterprise is expected in 10 years' time to resuscitate hundreds of weavers who have for the moment abandoned their trade in hopeless despair." M.K. Gandhi, "Circular Letter for Funds for Ashram," in *The Collected Works of Mahatma Gandhi,* vol. 15, *Mahatma Gandhi* [interactive CD-ROM] (New Delhi: Publications Division, 1999), 459–60.

30. Gandhi, *An Autobiography,* 408.

31. See Romesh Chandra Dutt, *The Economic History of India,* vol. 2 (1902–1904) (Delhi: Low Price Publications, 1995), 408–409.

32. See Louis Dumont, 'The 'Village Community' from Munro to Maine,' *Contributions to Indian Sociology,* 9 (1966), 67-89. Also see Henry Sumner Maine, *Village-Communities in the East and West* (New York: Arno Press, 1974), 119.

33. Hope, *Report on the Broach Exhibition,* p.32.

34. INC, *Report on the Eighteenth Indian National Congress, Held at Ahmedabad on the 23rd, 24th and 26th December* (Bombay: Commercial Press, 1903), 161–62.

35. Ibid., 79–80.

36. Ernest Binfield Havell, *Essays in Indian Art, Industry and Education* (Madras: G.A. Natesan, 1910), 158, 162.

37. See Aditya Mukherjee, *Imperialism, Nationalism and the Making of the Indian Capitalist Class, 1920–1947* (New Delhi: Sage, 2002), 20.

38. More hands were hired per unit than its Western counterparts owing to cheapness of labor; work habits tended to be less chaperoned, allowing for frequent breaks in keeping with the rural habits of workers. See Kenneth L. Gillion, *Ahmedabad: A Study in Indian Urban History* (Sydney: Australian National University Press, 1968), 100–101.

39. "The merchants take more part in public affairs now-a-days than before. ... This being so, I have to say with regret that it is the merchant class which has brought ruin to the Swadeshi practice and the Swadeshi movement in this country. ... No one wants you not to earn money, but it must be earned righteously and not be ill-gotten. ... Trade is the cause of war, and the merchant class has the key of war in their hands. Merchants raise the money and the army is raised on the strength of it. The power of England and Germany rests on their trading class." *Speech at Reception by Merchants, Broach,* October 19, 1917. See Gandhi, *Collected Works,* vol. 16, 69.

40. See B.R. Nanda, *In Gandhi's Footsteps: The Life and Times of Jamnalal Bajaj* (New Delhi: Oxford University Press, 1990); Ghanshyamdas Birla, *In the Shadow of the Mahatma* (Bombay: Vakils, Feffers and Simons, 1968); and Medha Kudaisya, *The Life and Times of G.D. Birla* (New Delhi: Oxford University Press, 2003).

41. "Why, after all, should the abandonment of a trade that harms India be a matter of life and death to many of you? Surely you are resourceful enough to find some other trade beneficial alike to you and the country? The stopping of imports means a saving of sixty crores per year. But it means operation on a much larger capital. It means that all the processes on cotton will be gone through in India. That means business for you. It means a healthy circulation of money as today it is [sic] a progressively exhausting drain of money from our dear country. I ask you to disengage your great talents from an unhealthy channel and direct them into the healthy channels that open out to you. You must organize hand-spinning and hand-weaving." Gandhi, "Open Letter to Cloth Merchants," July 7, 1921, in *Collected Works,* vol. 23, 394.

42. Gandhi, "Discussion with Charles F. Andrews," October 15, 1924, in *Collected Works,* vol. 29, 246.

43. Gandhi, *Village Swaraj* (Ahmedabad: Navjivan Publishing House, 1962), 78, 84, 87–89.

44. For a fascinating theorization of Gandhi's social commentary as a mode of experimentalism with his own body as the guinea pig for the Indian future, see Joseph Alter, "Gandhi's Body, Gandhi's Truth: Nonviolence and the Biomoral Imperative of Public Health," *Journal of Asian Studies* 55, no. 2 (1996).

45. Gandhi, *Village Industries* (Ahmedabad: Navjivan Publishing House, 1960).

46. Ibid., 37–39.

47. The Industrial Policy Resolution of 1948 was critical in formulating policy approaches toward artisans. The Karve Committee recommendations of 1955 led to the formation of Khadi and Village Industries Commission (KVIC) in 1957. The Central Silk Board was set up in 1949, the Coir Board in 1953, the Small Industries Development Organization in 1954, the District Industries Centers in 1978, and the District Rural Development Agencies in conjunction with the Lead Bank concept in 1970. Numerous credit, R&D, training, and other development organizations cater to the artisanal sector as an integrated element of rural development agencies. India has a network of 31,000 co-operatives and 1,138 registered institutions catering to the program of Khadi. The KVIC has set up 13,000 sales outlets throughout India. For a short historical account and critical discussion, see Society for Rural, Urban and Tribal Initiative, *India's Artisans: A Status Report* (New Delhi: Sruti, 1995).

48. See Zachariah, *Developing India*. Also see Vivek Chibber, *Locked in Place: State Building and Late Industrialization in India* (Princeton: Princeton University Press, 2003).

49. First quote, S. K. Mishra, director-general of the Festivals of India. Second quote, Niranjan Desai, Washington-based Indian cultural consul, both quoted in *India Today* (15 June, 1985), 47.

50. See Amiya Kumar Bagchi, ed., *Economy and Organization: Indian Institutions under the Neoliberal Regime* (London: Sage, 1999).

51. See Sukumar Muralidharan, "Democracy: The Legacy of the Emergency," *Frontline* 17, no. 14 (July 8–21, 2000).

52. See Jolle Demmers (ed.), *Miraculous Metamorphoses: The Neoliberalization of Latin American Populism* (London: Zed Books, 2001).

53. As it happened, in June 1985, Janata activists organized five hundred marble quarry workers and occupied the lobby of New Delhi's posh Taj Mahal hotel, protesting against the government's expenditure on "expensive" festivals abroad while the broad mass of artisans in India continued to live in dire economic conditions. *Philadelphia Inquirer*, June 14, 1985.

54. This example of the village-based student is more or less apocryphal, or at least tokenist, given the actual demography of the National Institute of Design's students.

55. Mary C. Combs, "India's National Institute of Design: Linking Past, Present and Future," *Smithsonian News Service*, July 1985; Record Unit (henceforth RU) 531, Box 30 of 32.

56. In a U.S. Department of State communiqué, it becomes clear that the funding effort was very much one-sided, at least in the case of the American Festival: "Mr. [S. Dillon] Ripley [secretary of the Smithsonian], a renowned India-phile, [said that] … the Indian Government … 'is wonderfully enthusiastic about the project and has spent more money so far in proportion than we have been able to raise from our government in this country.'" Smithsonian Institution (henceforth SI) Archives, Accession Number 01-114, Box 11 of 24, Office of Foreign Relations, Country Files (India) 1960–94.

57. IOL: *MSS Eur/F215/2*. Confidential/Fm Delhi 170059Z Nov 81/To Priority FCO/Telegram Number 853 (November 16, 1981).

58. "James Becker, formerly of IBM, grad of USNA & Harvard, hard-nosed type, says multinationals are our best bet—get the Indian offices to transmit the requests back to US headquarters, because the money would have to come from the US. Talk about the SI's ties w/ India, & ask each corp for $5000. He also thought Anderson & Union Carbide might especially welcome an opportunity to improve their image (you've probably had the same idea yourself)." Letter dated December 19, 1984 (SI Archives, RU 497, Box 3, Festival of India: Fund Raising 1). The Smithsonian later internally axed this opportunistic idea of benefiting from the genocide.

59. SI Archives, RU 497, Box 3, Festival of India: Fund Raising 1. Dillon was later reprimanded by the Smithsonian for seeking funding outside of the normal cycle of fund-raising, the implication being that smaller grants from corporations for individual projects would

compromise larger grants for the institution as a whole. The entire incident can be read as a peculiar manifestation of the asymptotic relationship between cultural and economic capital.

60. "[We] believe that one of the best ways of giving a fair wind to this financing operation would be to get together a group of 40 or so leading industrialists, including those all those with significant investments in India and major Indian contracts in the offing. Part of the purpose of such a gathering would be to get over the point that the Festival of India is not simply a question of cultural charity but, to a degree, of enlightened commercial self-interest. The Indians, from Mrs. Gandhi downwards, are keenly interested in the Festival and will take notice of the firms who are willing to contribute to its success." Letter from Michael Walker, chairman, Festival of India, to Margaret Thatcher. IOL archives, MSS Eur/F215/80—correspondence with prime minister.

61. IOL: MSS Euro/F215/108: Meeting at Ministry of Education and Social Welfare [minutes], September 1, 1979 (11 a.m. to 1 p.m.).

62. Rajeev Sethi, "Preface to Catalogue," *Aditi: The Living Arts of India* (Washington, DC: Smithsonian Institution Press, 1985), 18.

63. I will leave aside a discussion on the overtly *Hindu* sources of this ulterior ethos—in the roiling context of Indira's own dalliance with Hindu right-wingers in Jammu and Kashmir and elsewhere during this period—and its effect on the hitherto-ignored Indian diaspora of the United States and the United Kingdom, and their subsequent radicalization and financing of the rise of the Hindu right in India in the late 1980s. See my forthcoming *Sahmat 1989–2004: Liberal Arts in the Liberalized Public Sphere.*

64. Rajeev Sethi, "Introduction—Golden Eye" (undated manuscript, SI Archives, RU 531, Box 29 of 32).

65. Manuscript for "A Brief Guide to the Exhibition" (undated, *The Golden Eye: An International Tribute to the Artists of India,* SI Archives, RU 531, Box 30 of 32).

66. "One day Liza Taylor called me from New York to ask if I wanted to make drawings for the Indian craftsmen, drawings of objects to be exhibited at a Cooper Hewitt show. I was very happy and said I would have been glad to do those drawings. Then, on a Sunday afternoon, someone phoned and said that at the Diana hotel there was Mister Rajeev Sethi, an Indian gentleman who wanted to see me. So I went and entered a room at the Diana Hotel, where there was a very tall Indian gentleman, with the look of a true intellectual, wearing a wonderful sherwani woven of very thin Kashmiri wool of the natural colours of the sheep; he was very elegant and was speaking in a low, very soft voice. Then he opened a lot of suitcases to show me the samples of every possible technique used by the Indian craftsmen since ever [*sic*]. That was a very strange Sunday afternoon." Note by Ettore Sottsass for *Golden Eye* captions (SI Archives, RU 531, Box 29 of 32).

67. Philip Johnson, Yves St. Laurent, Tadao Ando, and Cedric Price were also approached but eventually didn't participate because of either disinclination or logistical reasons.

68. See "Designer's Agreement" (SI Archives, RU 531, Box 30 of 32).

69. See Rudofsky correspondence (SI Archives, RU 531, Box 29 of 32).

70. Ibid.

71. Geeta Kapur, Sovereign subject: Ray's Apu, in *When Was Modernism: Essays on Contemporary Cultural Practice in India* (New Delhi: Tulika Press, 2000).

Chapter 7

1. See Gulammohammed Sheikh, "An Unfinished Canvas," *Tehelka,* July 25, 2001, http://www.tehelka.com/channels/ane/2001/july/25/printable/ane072501jangarhpr.htm; Jyotindra Jain, "Trapped in Crossing," *Art India,* July 2001, http://www.artindia.co.in/specialreport.php; and S. Kalidas, "The Death Visit," *India Today,* July 23, 2001, 71.

2. Friedrich Schiller, "Sixteenth Letter," in *On the Aesthetic Education of Man in a Series of Letters* (Oxford: Oxford University Press, 1982).

3. I refer here particularly Part Two of Kant's *Anthropology,* where he considers questions of sexual, national, and racial character from the context of his three critiques. Immanuel Kant, *Anthropology from a Pragmatic Point of View* (Carbondale: Southern Illinois University Press, 1978).

4. Guha-Thakurta's work has been foundation in making colonial and nationalist aesthetic debates at the turn of the twentieth century into a full-fledged research agenda. Her work has shed substantial light on the emergence of the "Bengal" school of art, a correlate of the cultural phenomena that Sundaram frames within his installation. Tapati Guha-Thakurta, *The Making of a New "Indian" Art: Artists, Aesthetics and Nationalism in Bengal, c. 1850–1920* (Cambridge: Cambridge University Press, 1992); also see her *Visual Worlds of Modern Bengal: An Introduction to the Pictorial and Photographic Material in the Documentation Archive of the CSSSC* (Calcutta: Seagull Books, 2002).

5. Nandalal Bose, "Śilpakathā," *Vision and Creation* (1944), trans. Kalpati Ganapati Subrahmanyam (Calcutta: Visva-Bharati Publishing Department, 1999), 22.

6. Raymond Williams, "When Was Modernism?" in *The Politics of Modernism: Against the New Conformists* (London: Verso, 1989).

7. "After Modernism is canonized, however, by the post-war settlement and its accompanying, complicit academic endorsements, there is then the presumption that since Modernism is *here* in this specific phase or period, there is nothing beyond it. The marginal or rejected artists become classics of organized teaching and of traveling exhibitions in the great galleries of the metropolitan cities. 'Modernism is confined to this highly selective field and denied to everything else in an act of pure ideology, whose first, unconscious history is that, absurdly, it stops history dead. Modernism being the terminus, everything afterwards is counted out of development. It is *after*; stuck in the post." Williams, *The Politics of Modernism*, 35.

8. See "Introduction" in Georg Wilhelm Friedrich Hegel, *Aesthetics: Lectures on Fine Art*, vol. 1, trans. T.M. Knox (Oxford: Clarendon, 1975).

9. For a penetrating study of Hegel's aesthetic schema, see Jean-Marie Schaeffer, "The System of Art (Hegel)," in *Art of the Modern Age: Philosophy of Art from Kant to Heidegger*, trans. Steven Rendall (Princeton, NJ: Princeton University Press, 2000).

10. The word is a neologism coined by Philippe Lacoue-Labarthe and Jean-Luc Nancy when referring to the Jena school's reworking of the Platonic deliberations on eidetics in the aftermath of Kant. See Philippe Lacoue-Labarthe and Jean-Luc Nancy, *The Literary Absolute: The Theory of Literature in German Romanticism*, trans. Philip Barnard and Cheryl Lester (Albany: State University of New York Press, 1988), 37.

11. Kant, *Critique of the Power of Judgment*, trans. Paul Guyer and Eric Matthews (Cambridge: Cambridge University Press, 2000). For "lawfulness without law," see p. 125. For "purposiveness" see the entire Third Moment in the "Analytic of the Beautiful," 105–20.

12. Jacques Derrida, "The Parergon," in *The Truth in Painting*, trans. Geoffrey Benton and Ian McLeod (Chicago: University of Chicago Press, 1987).

13. For a recent example, see Elaine Scarry, *On Beauty and Being Just* (Princeton, NJ: Princeton University Press, 2000).

14. Lyotard, *Lessons on the Analytic of the Sublime*, 164.

15. "Out of a text like Schiller's *Letters on Aesthetic Education*, or the other texts of Schiller that relate directly to Kant, a whole tradition in Germany—in Germany and elsewhere—has been born: a way of emphasizing, of revalorizing the aesthetic, a way of setting up the aesthetic as exemplary, as an exemplary category, as a unifying category, as a model of education, as a model even for the state." See Paul de Man, "Kant and Schiller," in *Aesthetic Ideology* (Minneapolis: University of Minnesota, 1996), 130.

16. For a curriculum vitae of Sundaram's work, see http://www.indianartcircle.com/vivansundaram/vs_profile.shtml.

17. Two recent accounts might be said to fondly reinvoke this past. See the chapter on "*Adda*: A History of Sociality*," in Dipesh Chakrabarty, *Provincializing Europe: Postcolonial Thought and Historical Difference* (Princeton, NJ: Princeton University Press, 2000). Also see the section on "Culture and Communication" in Amartya Sen, *The Argumentative Indian: Writings on Indian History, Culture and Identity* (New York: Farrar, Straus and Giroux, 2005).

18. For an account of the trade, the political context of the play and its banning, and a translation of the play, see Amiya Rao and B.G. Rao, *The Blue Devil: Indigo and Colonial Bengal* (New Delhi: Oxford University Press, 1992).

19. For a specifically historical understanding of the emergence of Ramakrishna as a bourgeois phenomenon, see Sumit Sarkar, "Kaliyuga, Chakri and Bhakti: Ramakrishna and His Times," in *Writing Social History* (Delhi: Oxford University Press, 1997).

20. "When Bengali historians began to conceive of their culture as a coherent, organic entity possessing both temporal duration and spatial location, it was partially by means of [the] contradictory notions of the aesthetic that such definitions became possible." Henry Schwarz, *Writing Cultural History in Colonial and Postcolonial India* (Philadelphia: University of Pennsylvania Press, 1997), 21.

21. See Chaudhuri, Rosinka, *Gentlemen Poets in Colonial Bengal: Emergent Nationalism and the Orientalist Project* (Calcutta: Seagull Books, 2002).

22. "In Schiller's view, it is education which has the important role of developing both roles within their proper spheres. Our sensuous being needs to be developed, and protected from domination from the form-drive. Our rational being needs to be developed, and protected from domination from the sense-drive. Schiller sees the development of a drive as being itself the provision of protection for it *vis-à-vis* the other drive. Thus the educative process involves fully developing our capacities to feel and to reason." Patrick T. Murray, *The Development of German Aesthetic Theory from Kant to Schiller: A Philosophical Commentary on Schiller's Aesthetic Education of Man* (Lampeter, Wales: Edwin Mellen Press, 1994), 121.

23. James Fergusson, *Archaeology in India with Special Reference to the Works of Babu Rajendralala Mitra* (1884) (repr., New Delhi: Asian Educational Services, 1999).

24. Romesh Chandra Dutt, *The Economic History of India*, vol. 2 (1902–1904) (Delhi: Low Price Publications, 1995).

25. The reception of two books by American-style cultural studies as offering formulaic templates for Third World nationalism are a case in point. These are Partha Chatterjee's *The Nation and Its Fragments: Colonial and Postcolonial Histories* (Princeton, NJ: Princeton University Press, 1993) and more recently Chakrabarty, *Provincializing Europe*. Both use archival work largely based on Bengal to make a case for reevaluating Eurocentric historiography.

26. "The history of this revolution in the way of thinking [of mathematics as an autonomous science]—which was far more important than the discovery of the way around the famous Cape—and of the lucky one who brought it about, has not been preserved for us." Immanuel Kant, *Critique of Pure Reason*, trans. Paul Guyer and Allen W. Wood (Cambridge: Cambridge University Press, 1997), 108.

27. Jean-François Lyotard, *Lessons on the Analytic of the Sublime* (Stanford, CA: Stanford University Press, 1994), 133.

28. In its narrowest compass, the informal collective composed of the art critic Geeta Kapur, film historian and critic Ashish Rajadhyaksha, feminist and theorist Kumkum Sangari, the musician and scholar Madan Gopal Singh, the architect and writer Romi Khosla, the literary critic Malini Bhattacharya, and others. It would not be entirely reductive to state here that this section derives its ethical impetus from the tremendous energy and aesthetic experimentation initiated by the communist-affiliated Indian People's Theatre Association in the immediate prelude and aftermath of Indian independence. In its wider compass, the work of this collective has often sought affinity with other Indian scholars such as Tejaswini Niranjana, Madhava Prasad, Vivek Dhareshwar, S.V. Srinivas (these four were key members of the Bangalore-based Centre for the Study of Culture and Society), and the already mentioned art historian Tapati Guha-Thakurta.

29. Kapur, "Sovereign Subject: Ray's Apu."

30. Utpal Dutt, the Marxist theater-artiste and film actor, star of Ray's many films, had this to say about Ray's relationship to his audience: "Ray seeks to place [his middle-class] characters not in their daily routine of drudgery, but in an exceptional moment of their lives. He takes them out on a weekend to the forest ... or on a vacation to the hills. ... [The characters] have broken out of sentimental sympathy for their class through the power of their art, and can analyze their characters dialectically, bringing to the fore the pettiness of their protagonists, without shedding a single tear for the death of a useless class. But all three, by the very manner of their forcible transference of the action away from daily city-routine, are confessing the worthlessness of their material." Utpal Dutt, "On Satyajit Ray," in *People's Art in the Twentieth Century: Theory and Practice*, special issue, *Nukkad Janam Samvaad* 2/3, no. 4–8 (July–September 2000): 319.

31. See Norma Evenson, "The Long Debate," in *The Indian Metropolis: A View toward the West* (New Haven, CT: Yale University Press, 1989).

32. Thomas Raleigh, *Lord Curzon in India: Being a Selection from His Speeches as Viceroy and Governor General of India, 1898–1905* (London: Macmillan, 1906), 544–45.

33. Jacques Derrida, "Force of Law," in *Acts of Religion*, trans. Mary Quaintance, ed. Gil Anidjar (New York: Routledge, 2002).

34. There, once again, the stormers of the Bastille offer the archetype in their subsequent battles over the Louvre. See Françoise Choay, "The French Revolution," in *The Invention of the Historic Monument* (Cambridge: Cambridge University Press, 2001); and Andrew McClellan, *Inventing the Louvre: Art, Politics, and the Origins of the Modern Museum in Eighteenth-Century Paris* (Berkeley: University of California Press, 1994).

35. Gauri Viswanathan's work might serve as an adequate contemporary introduction; see her *Masks of Conquest*. For a more general introduction to the imperial scope of this debate, see J.A. Mangan, *The Imperial Curriculum: Racial Images and Education in the British Colonial Experience* (London: Routledge, 1993). The following publications offer critical windows into the official correspondence on the matter: Alfred Croft, *Review of Education in India in 1886, with Special Reference to the Report of the Education Commission* (Calcutta: Superintendent. of Government Printing, 1888), and *Report of the Indian Education Commission: February 3, 1882* (Calcutta: Superintendent of Government Printing, 1883). For an account of principal educational institutions, see Mushirul Hasan, ed., *Knowledge, Power and Politics: Educational Institutions in India* (New Delhi: Roli Books, 1998).

36. The seven-point tabulation laid out by Sabyasachi Bhattacharya in his analysis of hegemonic education and the disprivileged in colonial and postindependence India will do here as starting point. "The system of asymmetry in access to education, distinguishing the privileged from the disprivileged in terms of caste/tribe/class/gender, and securing certain forms of hegemony, was located within a broader framework of hegemony in the colonial social formation. ... Being located within the above-said asymmetricals metropolitan-colonial relationship, the inequalities inherent in indigenous society in terms of privileges/disprivileges in access to education, are liable to be exacerbated. Old privileges tend to get reinforced in the colonial educational system due of the greater access of the privileged (from pre-colonial times) to 'English' education, 'modern' knowledge, and consequent access to careers in the new professions." See Sabyasachi Bhattacharya, "Introduction: An Approach to Education and Inequality," in *Education and the Disprivileged: Nineteenth and Twentieth Century India* (New Delhi: Orient Longman, 2002), 3, 7.

37. S.F. Markham and H. Hargreaves, *The Museums of India* (London: Museums Association, 1936), 19, 60–61.

38. One can make the necessary connections in the Bengali context to Friedrich Kittler's description of the mother function in German foundational pedagogy, circa 1800. Kittler, Friedrich, "The Mother's Mouth," in *Discourse Networks 1800/1900* (Stanford, CA: Stanford University Press, 1990), 35.

39. Cited in George Eduard Biber, *Henry [sic] Pestalozzi, and His Plan of Education* (1831) (Bristol: Thoemmes Press, 1994), 242–43.

40. "[Through drawing] ... we hereby obtain, so to speak, another language, another intelligible mode of communicating thoughts and explaining things; having, moreover, this advantage over other languages, spoken or written, that it is universal, that it is almost alike intelligible to all the diverse races of mankind, needing no translation, but at once 'known and read of all men.'" Richard Redgrave, "Address." In DSA, *The Advantage of Teaching Elementary Drawing Concurrently with Writing as a Branch of National Education* (London: Eyre and Spottiswoode, 1857), 9–10.

41. John McIlroy and Sallie Westwood, eds., *Border Country: Raymond Williams in Adult Education* (London: National Institute of Continuing Education, 1993), 228.

42. Curzon, "Public Meeting in Calcutta," in Raleigh, *Lord Curzon in India*, 521. Also discussed in Giles H.R. Tillotson, "A Visible Monument: Architectural Policies and the Victoria Memorial Hall," in *The Victoria Memorial Hall, Calcutta: Conception, Collections, Conservation*, ed. Phillippa Vaughan (Mumbai: Marg Publications, 1997).

43. Curzon, "Address to the Asiatic Society of Bengal," in Raleigh, *Lord Curzon in India*, 547.

44. In the context of the postindependence history of the memorial, see Narayani Gupta's excellent "India and the European Cultural Inheritance: the Victoria Memorial Hall," in Vaughan, *The Victoria Memorial Hall*.

45. See Arindam Dutta, "Designing the Present: The Cole Circle and the Architecture of (an) Imperial Bureaucracy" (PhD diss., Princeton University, April 2001).
46. See Tapati Guha-Thakurta, "The Museumised Relic: Archaeology and the First Museum of Colonial India," in *The Indian Economic and Social History Review* 34, no. 1 (1997).
47. Kapur, "Sovereign Subject: Ray's Apu," 202.
48. Kapur, "Cultural Creativity in the First Decade," 18.
49. Walter J. Ong, *Orality and Literacy: The Technologizing of the Word* (London: Routledge, 1982), 46.

Postscript

1. Jean-François Lyotard, *The Différend: Phrases in Dispute* (Minneapolis: University of Minnesota Press, 1988), xi.
2. Mukulika Banerjee, *The Pathan Unarmed: Opposition and Memory in the North West Frontier* (New Delhi: Oxford University Press, 2001), 45.
3. William Wilson Hunter, *Rulers of India: The Earl of Mayo* (London: Oxford Clarendon Press, 1891), 180.
4. Ibid., 198.
5. See John Stuart Mill's comments on the subject in John Stuart Mill, *Writings on India*, vol. XXX, *Collected Works* (Toronto: University of Toronto Press, 1990), 116.
6. See chapter 6.
7. Rudyard Kipling, *Kim* (New York: Penguin Books, 1997).
8. Tapati Guha-Thakurta, "The Museumised Relic: Archaeology and the First Museum of Colonial India," in *The Indian Economic and Social History Review* 34, no. 1 (1997). Much of my account of the politics of the Archaeological Survey of India derives from her analysis.
9. This is not restricted to the First World. At the height of the first wave of secular nationalisms in the Third World, to the astonishment of many, "religion" was introduced as one of the two fundamental principles to be discussed at the famed Bandung conference in 1955. Albert Memmi noted this with not little consternation in the aftermath of the Algerian revolution. And ironically, in a classic instance of derivative postcoloniality, Third World leaders pledged to build solidarity in the shared fight against underdevelopment and European colonialism on the principles of Buddhism. Albert Memmi, *The Colonizer and the Colonized* (Boston: Beacon Press, 1965), 133. Also see Mike Mason, *Development and Disorder: A History of the Third World since 1945* (Hanover: University Press of New England, 1997), 31.
10. That starvation-based genocide across the world under British imperialism was an unintended effect of its economic policies made it no less a *planned* event. See Mike Davis, *Late Victorian Holocausts: El Niño Famines and the Making of the Third World* (London: Verso, 2001).
11. S.F. Markham and H. Hargreaves, *The Museums of India* (London: Museums Association, 1936), 10 (emphasis mine).
12. See Charles Allen, *The Search for the Buddha: The Men Who Discovered India's Lost Religion* (New York: Carroll and Graf, 2002).
13. Peter Hopkirk, *The Great Game: On Secret Service in High Asia* (Oxford: Oxford University Press, 1991); *Foreign Devils on the Silk Road: The Search for the Lost Treasures of Central Asia* (Oxford: Oxford University Press, 1980); *Trespassers on the Roof of the World: The Race for Lhasa* (Oxford: Oxford University Press, 1982); *Setting the East Ablaze: On Secret Service in Bolshevik Asia* (Oxford: Oxford University Press, 1984); *Quest for Kim: In Search of Kipling's Great Game* (Ann Arbor: University of Michigan Press, 1996); *Like Hidden Fire: The Plot to Bring Down the British Empire* (New York: Kodansha International, 1997).
14. Louis Althusser, "Contradiction and Overdetermination," in *For Marx,* trans. Ben Brewster (London: Verso, 1969).
15. Ibid., 97–98.
16. *New York Times,* October 6, 1996. Cited in Gayatri Chakravorty Spivak, "Foucault and Najibullah," in *Other Asias* (Oxford: Blackwell, forthcoming).

17. See Peter Hopkirk, "The Great Game Revisited?" http://www.rsaa.org.uk/thegreatgamerevisited.pdf.

18. Noah A. Chick, *In Memoriam: A Complete Record in a Permanent Form of All the Mournful Circumstances, Public Ceremonies, and General Expression of Sorrow and Sympathy in Connection with the Assassination of the Late Earl of Mayo, Viceroy and Governor General of India, to Which Is Prefixed a Biographical Sketch of His Excellency, Expressly Written for This Work* (Calcutta: Thomas S. Smith, 1872), 46.

19. George Pottinger, *Mayo: Disraeli's Viceroy* (Salisbury: Michael Russell, 1990), 188.

20. W.W. Hunter, *A Life of the Earl of Mayo*, vol. II (London: Smith, Elder, 1876), 366.

21. See Ranajit Guha, "The Prose of Counter-Insurgency," in *Subaltern Studies II: Writings on South Asian History and Society* (New Delhi: Oxford University Press, 1983, 1992).

22. Walter Benjamin, "Critique of Violence," in *Reflections: Essays, Aphorisms, Autobiographical Writings*, ed. Peter Demetz (New York: Schocken Books, 1978).

Bibliographic Note

Space constraints for this publication do not allow me to list the substantial bibliography for this work. The full bibliography for this volume can be found on my department website: http://architecture.mit.edu/people/profiles/prdutta.html

Index